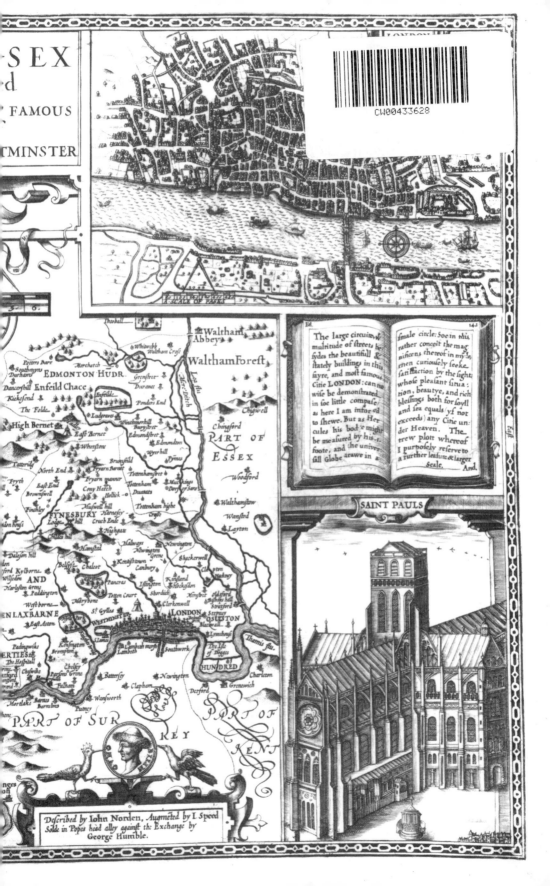

A Cup of Kindness

… for whosoever shall but consult his own experience as to the ebbings and flowings of Temporal Goods, and the many Revolutions of Providence, though Prosperity, at present, may seem with a smile to invite his Soul to take its rest, shall have reason without a blush or shame, to think it not altogether impossible, but to if not himself, yet some of his Relations who are dear to him, to at some time or other be obliged to that wherewith at present his Charity is pleased to oblige others.

An Answer to Several Letters Written by Scotish Gentlemen In His Majesties Dominions beyond the Seas, to the Master & Governors of the Scotish Corporation and Hospital in London, London 1677

A Cup of Kindness

The History of the Royal Scottish Corporation,
a London Charity, 1603–2003

JUSTINE TAYLOR

TUCKWELL PRESS

First published in Great Britain in 2003 by
Tuckwell Press Ltd
The Mill House
Phantassie
East Linton
East Lothian, Scotland

Copyright © The Royal Scottish Corporation 2003

ISBN 1 86232 292 9

British Library Cataloguing-in-Publication Data

A catalogue record of this book is available
on request from the British Library

Typeset in New Caledonia and Meta Display
by Koinonia, Manchester
Printed and bound by
Cromwell Press, Trowbridge, Wiltshire

Contents

List of Illustrations

ILLUSTRATIONS

Foreword by the President of
the Royal Scottish Corporation

The Royal Scottish Corporation has been a well-kept Scottish secret since around the time of James I's accession to the English throne in 1603. Now in 2003 the charity has decided to step out from the shadows and celebrate its 400th anniversary. This new history is the first definitive account of the Corporation's origins and growth, and reveals how over one million immigrant Scots were relieved by the establishment of the Scots Box and the later foundation of the Scottish Hospital of King Charles II.

I hope that the publication of this fascinating book will be a timely reminder of how philanthropic Scots and others in London, Scotland and abroad came to the aid of their poorer compatriots in the city. It will surely also serve to promote the implementation of a new three-year strategy which aims to sharpen the ancient charity's focus, tighten its management and update its assessment procedures. I especially hope that the book will encourage many others to give a helping hand to Scots living in London on low incomes today.

The charity has begun its fifth century with a refurbished King Street headquarters and a new president. I am honoured to have been asked to take up the post in May this year on the retirement of the sixth Earl of Rosebery. His father, the fifth earl, was also a worthy president of the charity, and I would like to repeat the words that he wrote at the opening of the Corporation's refurbished Fetter Lane building in 1927. Above all, Rosebery then hoped, and I too now hope – 'May it grow and prosper.'

Sir Thomas Macpherson of Biallid

Preface

When James VI of Scotland became monarch of England in succession to Elizabeth Tudor in 1603, he was intent on creating the Stuarts as a British dynasty. Although his plans for a full and complete union of Scotland and England came to grief in four years through implacable opposition in the House of Commons, his imperial ambitions for the Stuart monarchy led him to adopt a British approach to foreign, frontier and colonial policies. Integral to this imperial project was the development of London as not just the English capital, but the British metropolis, the entrepreneurial hub of global commerce and imperial expansion.

As well as the inevitable and much criticised bands of courtiers and vagrants who followed in the train of James at the regal union, there were also entrepreneurs and adventurers. These less-heralded migrants were as much intent on profiting from the development of London into Europe's largest city as from the commercial opportunities opened up by an expansive British Empire. The Scottish émigré community in the city exhibited two distinctive features – their clannish networking to maintain Scottish landed and commercial standing, and their philanthropic concern for their less well-placed countrymen. A further factor promoting mutual support was the ineligibility of migrant Scots for parochial relief during their initial years of settlement in the city.

The Royal Scottish Corporation, though formally established in 1665, had effectively operated as a philanthropic association since the regal union, with a poor box in existence from 1613 to help impoverished Scots. The second royal charter of 1676 confirmed the Corporation as the premier ethnic anchor for Scots in the city and as an example for philanthropic agencies throughout the Empire. Social welfare was subsequently augmented by educational provision for disadvantaged children, who would otherwise have been left to their own devices in a city becoming notorious for plague, fire and crime as well as commerce.

By the time of the award of a third royal charter in 1775, Scotland and England were united by parliamentary union and the Stuarts were no longer the ruling dynasty. Their pretensions had been permanently exiled with the failure of the last Jacobite rising in 1745–6 to complete its march from Scotland to London. However, the Royal Scottish Corporation had become the premier philanthropic outlet for a Scottish émigré network in and around London that was entrenched politically, militarily and commercially as a pillar of Empire. In turn, money poured in from the Empire, particularly from India, to facilitate the welfare work of the charity in the nineteenth century. Enduring Scottish values of community support and charitable giving outlasted and transcended the British Empire in the twentieth century.

Notwithstanding the coming of the welfare state, the Royal Scottish Corporation remains a valuable agency for supplementary support. It has been able to refocus its efforts on those who remain inadequately provided for and on those whose benefit entitlements are limited but who are no less deserving of care. At the outset of the twenty-first century, the charity has undergone a productive but compassionate overhaul that prioritises shelter for the aged, relief for the temporarily incapacitated, education and training for those who need it, and aid for the homeless. Nevertheless, the flight and plight of the impoverished Scottish émigré in London remains a perennial challenge. This absorbing, informative and entertaining book marks four centuries of caring by Scots and for Scots in the city that still remains the British metropolis.

Professor Allan I. Macinnes
Burnett-Fletcher Chair of History
University of Aberdeen

Acknowledgements

A short period of research and writing has meant that I have had to call on a number of people and archive collections for help, but has also meant that I have not had time to visit many others who might have revealed more about the story of the Royal Scottish Corporation. All of those whom I did call on showed great interest in the project and were most generous with their time and expertise.

First of all, I would most like to thank the Corporation's committee of management, its chairman Wylie White, and its chief executive, Willie Docherty, for commissioning me to write the 400-year anniversary history of the charity. I would additionally like to thank trustee Tom Thomson for suggesting my name to them in the first place. I am particularly grateful to Douglas Robertson and John Brown for allowing me to interview them about their many years of support and hard work for the charity. Douglas Robertson gave me valuable insights into his chairmanship of the Corporation's committee of management from 1977 to 1989, especially when he led the way into further property and equities investments. John Brown shared his particular interest in the charity's welfare activities and was also helpful on all aspects of the charity's management and administration, providing me with copies of papers from his own archive. Thank you also to Hazel Brown for her hospitality and memories. My discussions with these great Corporation Scots were particularly illuminating on the later twentieth-century workings of the charity, as well as their own motivations to join such an institution. More memories of Scots in London and abroad, and their clubs and societies, were kindly recalled for me by trustee Jimmy Brown. I also enjoyed further conversations with the late Dr Archie MacDonald and Dr Gill Park (both honorary physicians), and with Lady Jean Macpherson and Pat Parsons. Another trustee, John Clemence, a former Regimental Colonel of the London Scottish Regiment, kindly read through my section on the regiment in Chapter 24, and gave me further military detail and information on the relationship between the regiment and the Corporation. I am grateful to the Reverends Sandy Cairns and Dr Sigrid Marten of Crown Court Church of Scotland, both honorary chaplains to the Corporation, for a copy of the guide to the church. Discussions with the Corporation's chief executive Willie Docherty, finance manager Pat Marshall and welfare manager Ruth Smith provided me with much information on the present-day management of the Corporation, the administration of its charitable services and its future plans. Marc Knox and Sharon Hennelly and former temporary employees Corinne Moore and Darren Rank gave me further support. Norman Macleod, a retired welfare visitor, also provided useful background information on the RSC archives and a note on his own past research into the history of the Corporation.

I am also grateful for discussions with Nigel Goldie and Keith Smith of the Compass Partnership, the charity's strategy consultants, and would like to thank Patrick King of Story Shop for providing me with the transcripts of interviews from the documentary video that his company made on the charity in 2000. Jimmy Brown introduced me to Ian Menzies, the chairman of the Caledonian Club, who showed me round this Scottish institution and told me of its history and traditions. John Horsfield of the Royal Caledonian Schools Trust provided information on the Royal Scottish Corporation's 'sister' charity and kindly offered access to its archives dating from 1815, a fruitful place of research if there had been more time, and more space in this book for additions to the story of the Caledonian schools.

Gavin Henderson of the British Records Association provided key early support in helping me to sort and briefly list the archives of the charity from 1877. Christine Mackenzie of the National Register of Archives (Scotland) kindly provided me with a copy of a 1973 survey of the records by her organisation and another, fuller listing from a survey carried out in 1995 by the Business Archives Council of Scotland. Dennis Savage was a great help with additional research at the National Archives, tracking down the 1676 and 1775 petitions, charters and more information on the Corporation amongst the public records. Gavin Henderson also found James Kynneir's will, a vital document, at the Family Record Centre. I would also like to thank the staff of a number of archives, libraries and museums in England and Scotland who searched their collections to answer my requests or who allowed me access: Sarah Millard of the Bank of England Archive (who confirmed that the charity's accounts had been destroyed); Tracey Earl, archivist of Coutts Bank (who found some); Michael Webb and other staff for making the Bodleian's Duke Humphry Library in Oxford a pleasure to visit; the staff of the British Library's Rare Books and Manuscripts reading room, and, in particular, that of the Oriental and India Office Collections – especially curators Margaret Makepeace and David Blake – for revealing Scots in India; staff of the Corporation of London Record Office; and the staff of the Corporation of London's Guildhall Library and its Department of Manuscripts for livery company records access and searches – especially Stacey Gee; Christine Starck of Leith Museum; the National Archives in London (both the Public Record Office and the Historical Manuscripts Commission);

Nottinghamshire Archives; Dr Joseph Marshall and staff of the National Library of Scotland for helpful and prompt email answers and packages fulfilling my various photocopy requests; Margaret Thompson of the United Reformed Church History Society for more than fully answering my questions on the records of the Scots churches in London; the Wellcome Institute for the History of Medicine for providing access to their 'Scottish Hospital' papers, and answering my question on their provenance; Hazel Forsyth of the Museum of London for giving me the benefit of her expertise when she came to examine a number of the charity's muniments; and Anne-Marie Conroy of the Office of National Statistics for answering my census 2001 enquiry on where to find present-day London Scots.

A trip to Boston, Massachusetts meant that, thanks to Bill Budde, I was able to visit the library and archives of the New England Historic Genealogical Society and to examine the records of the Scots' Charitable Society of Boston. Bill took me to see the Saugus Ironworks at Lynn in Massachusetts where the Scots prisoners of 1650 were sent, and many thanks are due to Curtis White, its curator, for giving us a fascinating tour of the museum it has now become. I would like to thank the Scots' Charitable Society of Boston and Tom Smith, its president, for inviting me to their quarterly meeting and dinner, and am also very grateful to Tom and his wife, Corinne, for their kind hospitality during my Boston visit. I am indebted to Bill Budde for offering to write the outline of the Boston charity in Appendix 5.

I am particularly grateful to Professor Allan Macinnes of Aberdeen University (who was also on a three-month sabbatical at the University of Chicago for some of the time) for kindly writing the preface to this book. As the historical adviser for the history, and as a specialist on seventeenth-century Scots, he started me out with a number of approaches and sources for my research and, along the way, has given me expert guidance on the history of the Scots diaspora. His supportive comments and edits on a final draft read-through, including some on a warm sunny day in a usually wintry Chicago, were invaluable.

A discussion with Professor Peter Clark of Helsinki University, an expert on early British clubs and societies, helped crystallise my early thought processes about what the charity had actually achieved, what kind of hospital it really was and what the final conclusions of the history might be. So too did emails with medical historian Dr Keir Waddington of Cardiff University – especially how the Scottish Hospital fitted into the context of its time and how unique it might have been. I would also like to thank a number of old historian friends and newer contacts who have provided additional support during the writing process, and who have answered simple and not so simple history questions. Robert Baldwin, a former curator at the Museum of London and the National Maritime Museum, gave me a history lesson about Scots in London since the earliest times and provided me with a starting point and other valuable learning, as well as the loan of some useful books from his library. Dr Keith Surridge of Queen Mary, University of London, read and commented on the first draft, put me right on a number of early dates and other facts, and generally gave me much encouragement. Dr Andrew Mackillop, of Aberdeen University, enhanced information I had about Scots and their activities in India and was a great help in confirming the identities and backgrounds of early Scots benefactors in London like James Foulis. I would also like to thank Dr Richard Bingle, a former head of the European Manuscripts of the Oriental and India Office Collections, for pointing me towards 'Bengal Wills' so 1 could find William Kinloch. Tillman Nechtman, visiting from the University of Southern California, gave me his views on eighteenth-century Scottish nabobs, and Mike Armstrong, a fellow-researcher in the India Office Records, provided further guidance on the complexity of this series.

Image libraries and photographers have been most helpful in my final selection of pictures for this book and are acknowledged in the captions to the cover and plates. I owe a particular debt to Jeremy Smith and other staff of the Corporation of London's Guildhall Library print room where I spent a number of happy hours. I would additionally like to thank Deborah Hunter and Susannah Kerr of the National Galleries of Scotland in Edinburgh; Clem Webb for taking the time to show me the photographic collection of the London Scottish Regiment; Paul Johnson of the National Archives, London; Dr Joseph Marshall and Irene Danks of the National Library of Scotland; Caroline Badenoch of the National Portrait Gallery reference library; Ruth Smith of the Royal Bank of Scotland Archives; Sian Cooksey and Lucy Whitaker of the Royal Collection in Windsor and St James's; Andrew McKie of the Corporation of London press office; Tina Craig of the Royal College of Surgeons of England; Martin Durrant of the Victoria & Albert Museum; and Willie Docherty of the Royal Scottish Corporation. Photographer Charlotte Krag has done a great job in capturing the charity at work, the faces of those people it is currently helping, its buildings and some of its historical artefacts. For the reproduction of key historical documents and photographs at the Royal Scottish Corporation, the London Scottish Regiment and the Guildhall Library Print Room I am indebted to the speedy and friendly cooperation of photographer Geremy Butler. I am grateful to Doug Cameron and the *New Statesman* for their kind permission to publish extracts from Cameron's article on contemporary Scots in London.

I am also grateful to John Tuckwell of Tuckwell Press for the copy-editing, indexing and the resulting printing and publication of this book. Stefan Kraus of Polimekanos kindly helped supply the digitised images used for a number of the plates. Thank you also to friends and family for additional support and writing space.

Finally and above all, I would very much like to thank the management, staff and pensioners of the charity for making the research for and the writing of this history such an interesting, enlightening and rewarding project. In its 400th anniversary, the Royal Scottish Corporation is well into the first year of its three-year journey towards modernisation. I hope that, by being able to bask in a warm glow from the charity's great past, the travelling forward will be even more full of hope and helpful to those Scots in London who are in need.

Justine Taylor
Greenwich,
26 August 2003

Introduction

The Royal Scottish Corporation is an 'ancient' Scottish charity that has operated in London for four centuries. Originally established soon after James I's accession in 1603 as a national mutual-aid society to benefit seventeenth-century Scots merchants and craftsmen in Westminster and the City of London, it was later incorporated by royal charter in 1665 as 'The Scottish Hospital of the Foundation of Charles II'.[1] Three more charters followed, and royal patrons, including Her Majesty Queen Elizabeth today, have continued to support the charity.

The history of such a charitable organisation is also especially a history of the Scots and their networks in London. It is a tale of those Scots who came to the English capital in 1603 with perhaps the greatest London Scot of all, James VI and I, of those who stayed and came afterwards, and also a story of those who passed through on their way to the wider shores of the British Empire. It is also a history of why people left their native land over four centuries. It is a description of poverty, private philanthropy and official aid in the British capital, as well as an account of the church, education and the conditions in Scotland itself that gave her people the drive to leave their country. It is above all a history of national charity for those 'sober and industrious' Scots who suddenly had little or nothing 'through no fault of their own' and who needed to survive in, and make sense of, a mainly welcoming but also strange and bewildering city. Successful Scots used their London networks to get on or go abroad but other Scots found themselves growing ill or old without the support of friends, family and parish relief, while many in the post-war twentieth century began to fall through gaps in the new welfare state.

This book provides the first comprehensive account of the Royal Scottish Corporation and its supporters from its earliest beginnings up to 2003. A short

---

[1] This is still the official name of the Royal Scottish Corporation and the name under which it is registered with the Charity Commission. Since incorporation of the Scottish box club, the charity has been variously called 'the Scottish Hospital', 'the Scots Corporation', 'the Scottish Corporation' and 'the Scots Hall'. The 'Royal Scottish Corporation' became the common term from the early twentieth century. This book will also refer to it as 'the Corporation' or 'the charity'.

period of research and writing has meant that this cannot be the full story. Further research and analysis will no doubt especially shed more light on the earlier periods of the charity's history and those Scots connected with it. The Corporation's own archives were lost in a devastating fire in 1877, and a lack of archive material before that date has naturally provided a concentration of examples from the late Victorian period onwards. A number of useful contemporary accounts, printed by the Corporation since 1677, have also been found in English and Scottish libraries.[2] Sometimes with some detail, these show how and why the charity was established, organised and administered; where it carried out its business; who were its masters and presidents, governors and patronesses; and what were its activities.

The Corporation is all about helping people, and this book also provides examples of deserving (and undeserving) cases to show how people were referred or how they applied; and how they were examined, accepted or refused. It will also periodically instance, through four centuries, the numbers of cases where the charity was able to help, at what cost and with what income. As introductory background the book provides at intervals a brief overview of Scots in London generally from 1603 – who they were, why they came and what they did – particularly concentrating on figures connected with the Royal Scottish Corporation, and those thought to be connected with the early Scottish box club. It also provides a summary examination of Anglo-Scottish relations in London throughout this 400-year period. The book shows, in particular, how the Corporation became a focal point for Scots in London, not just for the Scots poor but as a rallying point for the Scottish nobility and merchants, ministers, lawyers, doctors and other Scots professionals who wanted to help their poorer compatriots. Some did so through reasons of personal insurance, a sense of religious piety, or to promote a business or empire network; others helped as a result of feelings of real compassion.

The development of London's poor laws, hospitals, its charities, voluntary organisations, clubs and societies in Stuart, Georgian and Victorian periods is also discussed, and an overview of twentieth-century welfare development, concerns and solutions is given as it is reflected in the charity's more recent history. The book aims to show how the charity has survived for so long and how important its royal charters and patronage were in that survival. It also shows that the charity – with its box-club origins, its first charter in 1665 and its first Blackfriars buildings in 1673 – became the first hospital established in London for an immigrant group as well as being one of the earliest hospitals of a workhouse type set up by individual voluntary contribution in London. It confirms that the Royal Scottish Corporation is the oldest Scottish charity outside

---

[2] See the Select Bibliography for more information about these early printed accounts of the 'Scots Corporation'.

Scotland and one of the oldest charitable institutions in London and the UK. Finally, it considers the twenty-first century needs of Scots in London and the charity's new strategy for 2003.

In 1603 King James VI of Scotland became King James I of 'Great Britain & Ireland'[3] following the death of his mother's cousin, Queen Elizabeth. A Scots community had already settled in London long before James became king, but it was small. The accession of Elizabeth I had enforced Protestantism in London and she had kept a close watch on her capital's immigrants. Their numbers in the English capital had been recorded in surveys of 'aliens' from time to time. Only around 40-60 Scotsmen compared to 3,300 Flemish immigrants were officially recorded as resident in London in the late 1560s. Many of these Scots had been in the city for over twenty years and had stayed mainly for religious reasons or because they were married to Englishwomen. Some were weavers, some worked for goldsmiths and others called themselves domestic servants; (short-stay Scottish sailors would have gone unrecorded). From James's accession the number of Scots living in London began to swell significantly as courtiers, poets, musicians, goldsmiths, clockmakers, wool merchants, weavers, tailors and others followed their king south. The English crown was not as rich as the Scottish king had imagined and, to raise cash, James quickly granted trade monopolies to city companies, creating fresh activity, a new class of merchants in the City of London and a real vision of potential wealth. Enterprising Scots came to seek their fortunes as opportunities gradually arose for making money at the English court, in England's capital city and by means of the country's early colonial expansion.

Westminster appears to have been a magnet for the first Scots making the trip to the English capital. The Whitehall Palace apartments where the kings of Scotland had traditionally stayed when on royal visits were located around Old Scotland Yard, giving the Scottish nobility and other visitors a useful starting point for their court networking after James's accession.[4] Scottish merchants and craftsmen would have gravitated more towards the City of London, meeting up with Scottish sailors who already knew the river well. Many of the early seventeenth-century Scots merchants who came were Presbyterians and they were generally welcomed in a City of London that had a strong core of people with similar Puritan beliefs. They also found it relatively easy to join the more like-minded of its livery companies. Scots like William Alexander, Earl of Stirling and Robert Carr, Earl of Somerset, flourished at court in the early years of James's reign. A number of lesser court servants, merchants and craftsmen had also come south with James I and some had made fortunes, but a number

---

[3] James's own preferred title.

[4] Roy Porter in his social history of London writes that after passing Charing Cross, 'the traveller to Westminster passed virgin soil stretching down to the river, called "Scotland" – hence Scotland Yard – after one Adam Scott who had owned it in Edward I's day'.

had also needed charitable help in times of sickness and commercial depression. Later, during the English Civil War (1642–46), leading Scots nobles and politicians like Robert Baillie were prominent in London owing to their alliance with Parliament, although by 1650, under Oliver Cromwell's Commonwealth, Scots had to have a licence to stay in England and its capital. More and poorer Scots did not make their appearance in significant numbers until after the Restoration in 1660, fleeing plague and fire for a short time from 1665–67.

The English poor laws and parish overseers, as we shall see, were not the only aggravations to Scots in London from the end of the sixteenth century. Many were often subjected to a certain depth of anti-Scottish feeling at periodic intervals. James I's Scottish favourites drew caustic comments from his first English parliaments, and some early traders no doubt felt the City's jealousy of the Scottish flair for business and administration. Presbyterianism in England was not tolerated after the Restoration, and until 1707 Anglo-Scottish relations were often fractious. They were further undermined by Jacobitism which was not finally crushed until 1746, while the subsequent prominence of Scots in Britain's politics, army and empire excited more envy, especially during the 1750s and 1760s. Nevertheless, these were certainly exciting times for Scots in or passing through the British capital. With an adventurous spirit, and fully liberated by the union treaty to join in English trading opportunities, Scots had begun to fill the East India Company and continued to take up positions of power in the Empire. Relations between the two peoples were finally strengthened by the end of the eighteenth century and grew apace in Victorian London.

Scottish links – between Westminster and the City of London, the river port and the railway, the East India Company and the British Empire – provided Scots with their London networks and gave the Royal Scottish Corporation its origins and also suitable locations from which to found, fund and carry out its charitable activities.

PART I
1603–1688

CHAPTER 1

London by 1603

L ondon had always been a place of great trade and immigration. Before
1603, and before the organisation of a Scottish box club led to the establishment of the Scottish Hospital and Corporation by royal charter, an existing
Scottish community would have provided a basic, though small, support network for any new arrivals from Scotland. Early entrepreneurial Scots in the
capital had long understood the importance of London and its river port at the
centre of a European trading community. Medieval Londoners had also taken a
considerable interest in Scotland and its trading potential, particularly as a
source of wool. That Scots came south to the city even in this era is attested by
the establishment in London of a cult of St Andrew, ensuring that the saint's
name was the second most common dedication of churches in the City of
London after St Peter.[1]

James IV of Scotland married Margaret Tudor, daughter of Henry VII of
England, in 1503 and the diplomatic retinue that James brought with him to
London included William Dunbar, the Scottish poet and graduate of St Andrews.
Dunbar wrote his 'Thistill and the Rois' especially for the royal wedding, and his
other famous poem, entitled 'In honour of the City of London', revealed the
English capital's ever-enduring appeal to Scots:

> London, thou art of Townes a per se.
> Sovereign of cities, seemliest in sight
> Of high Renown, Riches and Respite:
> Of Lords, Barons and many goodly knight;
> Of most delectable lustie ladies bright;
> Of famous prelates in habites clericall;
> Of merchants full of substance and might;
> London, thou art the flour of Cities all.

[1] This was a balance that remained unaltered until the Great Fire of 1666. Two surviving
medieval pilgrim badges found in London attest to the sea trips that sustained these links. Other
pilgrim badges found in London show that a similar cult had also grown up around St Margaret
of Scotland.

The Reformation in both England and Scotland saw the destruction of long-established abbeys, friaries and chantries and the redistribution of church lands to rising families. Many schools and such social services as the care of the long-term sick and the destitute were also destroyed in both countries. Social strain started to show in London from the 1540s and especially during times of plague in the 1560s. The lack of local support provided the impetus (religious or otherwise) that now drove the wealthier and more successful of the capital's citizens to replace the dissolved ecclesiastical institutions and their almonries, schools and hospitals with new charitable institutions.

These establishments, together with the royal re-endowment of London's medieval hospitals over the next century, formed part of the context in which pressure emerged to create other charities and merchant friendly societies, like the Scottish box club at the beginning of the seventeenth century. New voluntary hospitals and workhouses for the orphaned, sick and elderly poor, like the Scottish Hospital in 1665, were to be key charitable foundations of the period.

London by 1603 covered three areas – the City of London, Westminster and land south of the river over London Bridge, called Southwark. The Thames estuary was still recognised as the best means of carrying goods, and the city's contemporary chronicler John Stow called it 'the principal storehouse and staple of all commodities within this realm' where '3,000 poor men, at the least be set on work and maintained'. London was such a mass of trading ships that William Camden in 1586 could write that a 'man would say, that seeth the shipping there, that it is, as it were, a very wood of trees disbranched to make glades and let in light so shaded it is with masts and sails'. The east part of the city began to develop as a place for sailors and warehouse men to settle (many of them Scots), especially once the East India Company established its Blackwall Dockyard in 1614.

The capital was one of Europe's five biggest cities by 1603, both in trade (especially cloth) and numbers of people. Its population at the beginning of the century has been calculated at around 200,000; no other city in England had even one-tenth of that number or such a high growth rate. By 1625 it had increased another 120,000 and had reached around 700,000 before the end of the century. Despite this huge population boom, London's birth rate was low while its death rate was high; the city's population only continued to rise because of a constant flow of immigrants. Even James I could see it happening: 'all the country is gotten into London, so as with time England will only be London and the whole country left waste,' he wrote, as people continued to arrive 'from all parts of the island, from Flanders and from every other place'. The newcomers also brought trade advantages with them and Thomas Gresham's Royal Exchange, opened by Queen Elizabeth in 1570, now dominated Europe as a marketplace, having usurped Antwerp. At the time of James I's accession, three-quarters of

England's foreign trade was run by the London merchants and paid its tolls in the city's customs house.

On arrival, Scots would benefit from a form of 'community government' that was evolving at the beginning of the seventeenth century which made it easier for those living in London to cope with 'the stresses and strains of city living'. Such self-government was achieved not just by the city administration itself, but linked to it, and to the registration duties and moral, educational and financial administration of parish churches, were the 'guilds' or livery companies that had grown out of the City of London's medieval crafts. Among a number of other civic duties, these companies supervised and policed the manufacturing and trade of their craft in the city; they settled disputes, and monitored and administered apprenticeships. Most importantly, it was after serving a seven-year apprenticeship that the companies' freemen were granted the right to trade. These guild freemen were also able to become freemen of the City of London and, once elected 'Aldermen', were able to participate in the running of the city itself, holding the position for life. In fact, to be a freeman was so sought after that it has been estimated that about three-quarters of London's adult male population in the mid-sixteenth century were freemen.

The lord mayor and his court of aldermen executed city government around the Guildhall and there was much intermarriage between livery company families to hold on to power and status, but young men coming from the countryside (and Scotland) brought fresh blood. Twelve of the richer companies dominated the rest and provided most of the aldermen and thus the lord mayors. The richer freemen in these 'higher' guilds were mostly merchants rather than craftsmen and also were more likely to have been wholesalers than retailers. The top twelve companies were (and still are), namely, and in hierarchical order, the Mercers, Grocers, Drapers, Fishmongers, Goldsmiths, Skinners, Merchant Taylors, Haberdashers, Salters, Ironmongers, Vintners and Clothmakers. All companies built magnificent halls for carrying out their business, organised their own religious and other festivals and set up charitable funds, almshouses, hospitals and schools to provide for their pensioners as well as for their members' widows and orphans. They also disbursed poor relief on an *ad hoc* basis. Above all the livery companies were 'a powerful civic cement' and a key networking opportunity for Scots.

The Royal Scottish Corporation would later benefit from the many Scots who were to take advantage of such city administration, as they became freemen of the city, masters of livery companies and also lord mayors. The more prosperous Scots then found themselves in a City of London which was regulated and ordered. Their poorer fellows had to find homes, 'beyond the walls', with other migrants and immigrants in the city's 'Liberties'. Here life was starting to teem, unregulated and disordered – in a place seen by contemporaries as a breeding-ground for crime and epidemics.

CHAPTER 2

Scots in Early Stuart London

As a ruler of multiple kingdoms, James I wanted more than just a union of the English and Scottish crowns, and his early parliamentary sessions were to be dominated by the question of further union between the two countries. In a proclamation on his arrival in London, he asked both his Scottish and English subjects to think of 'the two realms as presently united, and as one realm and kingdom, and the subjects of both the realms as one people'. But the English were not always to agree with their new king's view of such a 'union of hearts and minds'. The Scots on the other hand more or less supported the union as a practical move, hoping to limit problems in Scotland caused by James's absence. In April 1604, James tried to unite the two kingdoms under the name 'Great Britain' but English MPs refused their support, fearing the loss of English laws and a union with people they called 'barbarians'. Even so, James continued to push ahead and called himself 'King of Great Britain' in a proclamation of 20 October. Fortunately, realising the serious opposition to his plans, he later scaled back his ambitions and, more symbolically, issued a new union currency with a 20-shilling piece which he named 'a unite', and in April 1606 proclaimed that all British ships should carry a new flag – the Union Jack.

On his arrival in 1603 James had made several proclamations which went some way to minimise the way in which Scots had hitherto been treated as 'aliens' by the English. On 8 April 1603 he fixed the value of the Scottish currency in England (one pound Scots was worth one twelfth of an English pound), and in July and August he promised equal justice to both English and Scots offenders against the law. In May 1607 the so-called 'hostile laws' which limited trade, aid and communication across the border were abolished, and in 1608 Calvin's Case, named after an infant Scottish heir to English lands called Robert Calvin,[1] gave English legal, especially property, rights to the *post nati*: those Scots born after James's accession. A number of Scots at court were also granted 'denization' (naturalisation granted under the royal seal) by James. Despite the reduction of the alien status of Scots, the English Parliament's anti-

---

[1] Sometimes referred to as 'Colvin' and 'Colvin's Case'.

Scots stance would prevent further attempts at assimilation. Francis Bacon tried to show that 'England was not so overpopulated that the influx of a few Scots would make any real difference', but other English MPs were worried that hordes of Scots would overrun their English lands. They considered a commercial union and the naturalisation of Scots out of the question. Although Sir Edwin Sandys, a key opponent, conceded that the Scots were 'better than aliens', he certainly thought them 'not equal with natural subjects'. The peoples of England and Scotland might have lived under a 'double crown' but they still inhabited separate kingdoms.

The personality and political astuteness of the monarch were to be all-important in overcoming these difficulties. James made his royal person accessible at court and, as a result of his experience in keeping his Scottish nobles in check, was good at playing much of the politics within his new English court. Dispensation of royal patronage at court was essential to the smooth running of affairs, right down to the local gentry. The king's job was also to prevent any political and personal infighting within the court circle breaking out in, and disrupting parliament itself: something both James and, more so, Charles I, failed to do. Underlying the politics was the fact that court officials were not paid much and many lesser clerks even went unpaid; such dependency on fees and other gifts made it easy for corruption to creep in. This network of national patronage also made it easier for Scots to find their way into James's court and London society.

England was generally a welcoming place for Scottish immigrants, even if its members of parliament were not. In comparison with other European economies of the time, England's was not 'outstandingly backward' and, compared to the Scottish economy, it was considered 'rich and buoyant'. The Scots left behind what was for most a harsher life. Travel and trade between London and the provinces began to increase and records of the ships leaving the port of London in 1619 reveal their Scottish cargoes, merchant owners and captains.[2] Coastal routes and rivers were the chief means of getting such cargoes from place to place but roads were relatively good by the early seventeenth century following the introduction of the stagecoach in the late 1500s. People generally were used to moving around and the Scots, even more than the English, were well known

---

[2] In the *Jennet* of Kirkcaldy (bound for Kirkcaldy), Stephen Boyd had much cloth and millinery valued at over £200, including English serge and fustians, 'Turky grosgrans', 230 yards of 'tiffeny', satin and calico collars, leather gloves and hats for both adults and children. Andrew Mackoloch's Kirkcaldy cargo was valued at £36 and included bowstrings, stirrup leathers, stirrup irons and snaffle bits. His boat was also carrying searing candles, worsted lace, leather girdles, black thread, small looking glasses, small padlocks, horn cups and horn hooks, small beard brushes, scissors, tailors' shears, nails, iron tacks, hinges for windows, green drinking glasses, earthenware jugs and tobacco pipes. Alexander Seton's cargo (£147) was bound for Hamburg and included spectacles, Sheffield and London knives, worsted and leather stockings and taffeta nightcaps.

as a mobile people. Possibly because of the expense and distances involved, Scots were encouraged not just to visit, but to stay and settle. Wealthy and professional classes chose to come up to London for extended periods; the poor were forced to come to find work or to board a boat bound for the developing colonies. Young people also moved away from their parents and settled down in new places after marriage. It is likely that Scots nobles had political, legal (especially as they bought London or English property) or social reasons to be closer to the new court. Some may have wanted their daughters to marry wealthy Englishmen, a practice James I disliked, thinking that 'one of the greatest causes of all Gentlemens desire, that have no calling or errand, to dwell in London, is apparently the pride of women: For if they bee wives, then their fathers must bring them up to London'.

Although some Scots would have arrived with James during 1603, many more, because of the plague that year and the consequent lack of trade and jobs, would have found the city a healthier place in 1604. Those arriving by 15 March that year would have been among the crowds lining the streets to see James I ride 'in triumph' through the City of London. In fact, Stow reported that 'to behold the beauty thereof besides the Clergy, Nobility, and chief gentry, of every country, and great numbers of strangers from beyond the seas, there repaired thither such great multitudes of people from all places, as the like in London was never seen until that day'. The Scots came to London in 1603-04 especially because the city had long had a reputation for size and variety. London was additionally an unusual city in Europe, being a place where commerce and a capital city came together; a court of 1,500 people, politics, law, state administration and business were to be found in one place. Above all, the Scots arrived in a city where there was, as William Camden had written, 'a super-abundance of all things which belong to the furniture or necessity of man's life'.

CHAPTER 3

James I and Courtly Scots

James I was not the first London Scot but he was perhaps the greatest and one to whom the Royal Scottish Corporation owes its existence. The 36-year-old Scottish king took over the throne of England with a peaceful handover of power, and there was 'no tumult, no contradiction, no disorder'. His accession encouraged many of his fellow countrymen to join him in the English capital. Moreover, he was considered a good choice by the English – mainly because he was an intelligent, Protestant and experienced king, with two healthy sons as heirs. He also remained popular throughout his reign, and it is now thought by many historians that James was actually as successful a king of England as he was of Scotland. Much damage to his character had been done in his own lifetime by Sir Anthony Weldon, a disgraced courtier. Weldon had vilified him in a book entitled *The Court and Character of James I* after he had been removed from the royal household by James for publishing another book in 1617 about what Weldon considered the awfulness of Scotland. The exiled courtier's later book about James provided future generations with the well-known picture of the king as a weak and physically unattractive man, forever 'fiddling about his codpiece'.

James had set off for London in early April 1603 and no doubt carefully assessed people's reactions to their new king during his journey south. He was certainly pleased with the look in his new English subjects' eyes, which he thought he saw 'flaming nothing but sparkles of affection'. The Scottish court also came with him – more or less uprooted and brought wholesale to London. The king was the source of all patronage and public office, and members of James's royal household and other members of the nobility who followed him south felt they all had a claim on his person; even the lesser Scots who would have served this retinue were able to benefit from it. James, of course, also had his favourites. The most favoured Scot at court was Robert Carr, later Earl of Somerset (from 1613), although he was also the butt of much of the anti-Scottish feeling in the House of Commons. Carr became the first Scot to sit in the House of Lords, but he was to be mightily disgraced in 1615, an event which opened the way for George Villiers, Duke of Buckingham, to take his place at the king's side. In 1613 Somerset had married Lady Frances Devereux (née Howard), the Earl of Suffolk's daughter. James had personally supported her divorce from the Earl of Essex the same year, due to alleged impotence. Two years later the couple were implicated in one of the greater scandals of James's reign as they were arrested, tried and sentenced to death for the murder of Sir Thomas Overbury in 1613. Overbury had opposed Lady Frances' divorce and probably had some incriminating evidence useful to the prosecution. The couple's death sentence was later commuted to imprisonment. Their daughter, Anne, later married the Duke of Bedford and it was probably through her influence that the duke donated property in Covent Garden to the Royal Scottish Corporation in the late 1660s for use as its Westminster hospital.

Despite English complaints, James had also tried to balance his lesser favours equally amongst the English and Scots at court. Some Englishmen received Scottish peerages and the king himself felt he had been equally generous to both sides, writing to Robert Cecil in 1610 that 'the English have tasted as much, and more, of my liberality than the Scots have done'. But the king had certainly made gifts to many Scots up to 1610 and they had gained around an average of £40,000 a year in gifts or pensions, while the English received only around £10,000. These figures appear to show that the complaint of Sir John Holles – 'the Scottish monopolise his princely person, standing like mountains betwixt the beams of his grace and us' – may have been justified. The State Papers for the first few years of James's reign indeed abound with grants and pensions to Scottish names linked to the royal household.

Many Scots petitioned the king for jobs and other aid and favours. James was to be so inundated with such requests that by 1614 he appointed Sir William Alexander, later the first Earl of Stirling, as 'Master of Requests for Scotland' to sort the petitions. Alexander, the 'guidman of Menstrie', had been knighted by 1609 and had become more permanently attached to James's court, gradually taking on the secretarial role of the king's publicist and general fixer, as well as being his court poet and a colonial adventurer. He had been introduced to James in Scotland by the Earl of Argyll, and the king and Alexander then wrote poetry and translated the Psalms together, James calling him 'my philosopher poet'. Alexander dedicated his Darius epic to James in 1603 and was also tutor to Prince Henry. He was later granted the right to mine silver in Scotland and also had a monopoly on copper coinage in the country. He also 'had a living vision of a great Scotland overseas' when he founded Nova Scotia in 1624, finishing his *Encouragement to Colonies* (1624) with an appeal to the king:

> but I must trust to be supplied by some publick helps, such as hath beene had
> in other parts, for the like cause whereunto, as I doubt not, but many will be
> willing out of the noblenesse of their disposition, for the advancing of so
> worthy a Worke, So I hope will some others … as so meane an abilitie as mine

may reach, what (I conceive) may prove for the credit or benefit of my Nation, to whom I wish all happinesse.

Alexander became secretary of state for Scotland for 1626–27 and died in 1640.

Having men like Alexander around meant that James's cosmopolitan court was also a place of cultural entertainment. Shakespeare wrote his plays and poems, and Ben Jonson and Inigo Jones collaborated on masques during this time. Shakespeare's troop of actors were known as the 'King's Men' once James came to the throne, and scenes from *Henry V (Part I)*, written before James's accession and first performed in 1600, had to be cut after 1603 because of a few passages that did not flatter the Scots.[1] Scottish court entertainers – musicians, poets, painters and tutors – made friends with these English playwrights. Another famous poet of 'Scoto-Britaine' and a key courtier was Sir Robert Aiton, secretary to both James's queen, Anne, and Charles I's queen, Henrietta Maria. Aiton was also a friend of Ben Jonson and a 'well-loved figure of the Jacobean and Caroline court'. He had been educated at St Andrews and had spent some time in Paris before coming to London to write his songs. Like other 'Scoto-Britons' he took 'denization' in 1614–15 to protect his English property holdings, and used his poetry to collect patronage and position from fellow-Scots at court. William Murray, later the Earl of Dysart, was another Scottish court poet who was also the young Prince Charles's companion.

Alexander, Aiton and Dysart, like the Earl of Somerset, were to have future family connections with the Royal Scottish Corporation – Alexander through his grandson Henry, Earl of Stirling, who became master of the Corporation in 1687; Aiton was a probable kinsman to the childless Sir John Aiton, who was to be a donor of £190 to the charity in 1671, also giving it some property in Soho; Dysart's daughter, Lady Elizabeth, was to become the influential second wife to John Maitland, the Earl of Lauderdale and Charles II's secretary of state for Scotland, a man who was instrumental in gaining royal assent for the Royal Scottish Corporation's first two charters. It is also probable that the three poets of James I's court, especially William Alexander, had some involvement with the Scottish box club established in the aftermath of regal union.

---

[1] *Henry V (Part I)*, Act III, Sc.III, 'JAMY: By the mess [mass], ere these eyes of mine take themselves to slumber, ay'll de gud service, or I'll lig i' th' grund for it. Ay owe Got a death, and I'll pay't as valorously as I may, that shall I suirely do, that is the brief and the long.' Earlier in the same play (Act I, Sc. II), Anglo-Scots and Anglo-French relations are the theme and the Scot is unflatteringly described as a 'giddy neighbour' and a 'weasel'. Scotsmen had been ridiculed in English comedies since at least 1579 and then frequently enough for James himself to complain about it by 1598. The next play after *Henry V* to depict a Scots character was *Eastward Ho* in 1605, and this so offended James that two of its authors, one of them Sir Robert Aiton's friend Ben Jonson, were imprisoned. A more favourable play, Shakespeare's *Macbeth*, was probably written and performed in 1606.

CHAPTER 4

Merchants and Trade

When James I acceded to the English throne, England was at war with Spain and supporting the Dutch in a similar Spanish war. James was soon to be known as the 'peacemaker king' as he brought immediate benefits and prosperity to his new kingdom. He achieved peace with Spain in 1605, maintained the Dutch alliance and signed a new trade treaty with France. Early seventeenth-century London reflected the economic advantages brought about by such stability, and the city 'was outstanding in the channels of profit open to merchants'. These were mainly overseas and domestic trades in which over 70 of the 140 Jacobean aldermen made their fortunes; other profits were made from 'government loans and customs administration'.

One of the more famous and prosperous Scots was the goldsmith George Heriot who came south later in 1603 to follow 'his patron, King James'. He had a terrible journey (his two sons died on the way) and he went back to Scotland in 1608 after the death of his first wife. He returned to London in 1609 with his second wife (an aunt of the Earl of Rosebery) and, by advancing money to the royal family and buying up London and Edinburgh property, 'he prospered here as he had prospered in the North'. Heriot was also known as 'Jinglin' Geordie' by contemporaries after his supposedly jangling pockets, and Sir Walter Scott later revived Heriot's early years for a new generation of Scots when he used Heriot's story as the basis for his character Nigel Oliphaunt in *The Fortunes of Nigel*. Heriot was one of the earliest of Scottish philanthropists, leaving around £23,000 in trust to the city of Edinburgh for a 'hospital' to nurse, bring up and educate 'poor orphans and fatherless children of decayed burgesses and freemen of the said burgh, destitute and without means'. As Heriot's school, the foundation still exists today. Heriot had no doubt visited the City of London's Christ's Hospital for freemen's orphans and had seen how the city's livery companies also set up schools for their own children. It is also tempting to think that he may have known about, and even had a hand in, the Scots merchants' mutual-aid society. David Ramsay, clockmaker to James VI in Scotland, also came to London with the king in 1603. By Charles I's reign he was inscribing his beautifully-made clocks of 1625 and 1630 'David Ramsay Scotus me fecit'.

Many clockmakers had initially enrolled in the City of London's Blacksmiths' Company until they successfully petitioned for their own company in 1631. David Ramsay was elected the first master of the Clockmakers' Company that year.

Various European trade crises were to be a characteristic of James I's reign as he searched for much-needed cash. Sixteenth-century inflation had been the cause of the king's great need for money as he came to the throne, and further inflation created more financial burdens. The income from crown estates during Elizabeth's reign had fallen about 40 per cent in real terms and James took on a debt of over £400,000. His 'eating canker of want' grew to £735,000 at its height with an annual deficit of around £180,000. Royal attempts at business to bring in more cash for the court were also to produce a certain lack of stability for City of London merchants. Further depressions occurred in the 1620s and James established committees of merchants and politicians to help end the crisis. Trade trouble recurred in 1640-42 just before the outbreak of civil war; financial crises of 1647-50 followed in the wake of harvest failures.

Further away from London, the overseas trade beyond the Baltic and the Mediterranean had been expanding and there was money to be made and reputations to be gained from new joint-stock companies, both to the east and to the west. Foundations of an empire were being laid in which the Scots were later to gather, network and flourish – to the great benefit of the Royal Scottish Corporation. The East India Company had been granted its royal charter by Queen Elizabeth I in 1600 and it quickly set about establishing trading posts in Indonesia and India. West across the Atlantic, the first British colony was set down in America at Jamestown in Virginia in 1607. The American schemes, in particular, attracted some of Britain's growing population and provided much-wanted religious independence for colonists in New England from the 1620s. William Alexander's scheme for colonial expansion to Nova Scotia in the Canadian Maritimes also helped offload surplus and 'idle' Scots from London's streets.

CHAPTER 5

Civil War and Commonwealth Scots

James I died in 1625 and was succeeded by his son, Charles I, but by 1640 the new king had lost the support of the 'the vast majority of his powerful subjects'; Charles's personality and political ability were markedly different from those of his father, and he further proved 'inflexible and uncompromising to the point of ineptness'. Charles had also not understood Scottish opinion even though he had Scottish advisers in London, and his lack of adequate counselling in Scottish affairs contributed to the rise of the Covenanting Movement which was intent on limiting his powers in both kirk and state. When Charles refused to accept Presbyterianism in the kirk and parliamentary accountability in the state, the Covenanters instigated the Bishops' Wars in 1639. In May 1640, the City of London refused to lend £100,000 to the king to resist the Scots army which then crossed the Tweed unopposed in August as the royal soldiers ran away. London celebrated the defeat, embracing the Scots propaganda of 'We must stand or fall together … We are brethren', encouraged by the Scots promise not to interfere with the sea-coal coastal trade now that they occupied Newcastle. The calling of what was to become the Long Parliament had owed its existence to the 18,000 Scottish troops, and Robert Baillie, a Scot arriving in London in 1640, wrote that he 'found that all men professed that, under God, they owed their religion, liberties, and parliament to the Scottish army'. Baillie and a number of other influential Presbyterian Scots in London had probably helped to draft one of the petitions received by this Parliament in December 1640 – their Root and Branch Petition against episcopacy was signed by 15,000 Londoners. Its debate in the House of Commons highlighted Parliament's already marked divisions which were later to split into the Parliamentarians (for) and the Royalists (against).

In 1643 the Covenanters negotiated with Parliament for the Solemn League and Covenant, and an assembly was formed in Westminster to undertake the reform of the English church which included eight Scots observers. In 1644 a 'Committee of Both Kingdoms' was appointed to oversee the treaty's application. Political disagreements over Presbyterianism, the trustworthiness of Charles I and the arrears of 'brotherly assistance' owed to the Scots gradually fractured this alliance. The unilateral execution of Charles I by the English regicides in January 1649 led to an open breach with the Scottish Covenanters, who promptly recognised Charles II as king of Great Britain. This recognition of the Stuart heir led to Oliver Cromwell's military occupation of Scotland in 1650–51.

The freedom of Scots in London was limited while Oliver Cromwell was at war with Scotland. By 1650 Scots were only permitted to stay in 'the Commonwealth of England' if they had a licence from the Council of State to do so, or if they had been naturalised by Act of Parliament, made denizens under the Great Seal of England, or if they were in prison. If they had no licence, they had to depart from English cities by 10 August and the Commonwealth itself before 1 September, otherwise they 'shall be adjudged, deemed and taken as Traytors and Enemies'. The Scots made their petitions for residence in the capital to the Commonwealth's Council of State. On 6 August the council met and decided to set up a 'Committee for Scots' to supervise 'the better ordering of the business of the staying in town of such Scotts as are here, and they are to consider of such petitions as are alredie offred to the Council by Scotts men for their stay in the same'.

Anti-Scots pamphlets were also distributed. On 12 September 1651 licensed London Scots would have come out to watch the defeated Scots army which was marched through the City of London after the battle of Worcester, a battle that forced Charles II into exile. They would have witnessed the way in which the Scottish soldiers were generously supported and given alms and other charity by the people of London as they passed:

> The last night the Scots, Highlands, or Redshanks, about 4,000 in number lay on Hampstead heath … and this day they were with a guard brought by Highgate on the back-side of Islington to Kingsland, and from thence to Milingreen, they were suffered to receive such charity as people would give them, and had a cart load or two of bisket carrying after them, which is better food than heretofore they carried in their Oatmeal bag. The next day being Saturday they were brought into Aldgate, and so marched through Cheapside, Fleet-street and the Strand, and likewise through Westminster. For the most part they were very sturdy surley knaves, … yet were many of our Scorified Citizens so pitiful unto them, that as they passed through the City they made them (though prisoners of Mercy) masters of more money and good whitebread than some of them ever see in their lives …

About 150 of the Scottish prisoners taken at Worcester, and at the earlier battle of Dunbar in 1650, were sold as indentured servants to the London Company of Undertakers and shipped across the Atlantic to New England. The company had invested in America's first successful ironworks at Lynn (Saugus) in Massachusetts and a number of the Scots soldiers were set to work there for a term of seven years. These indentures began to expire by 1657, when the

Scots' Charitable Society of Boston, the oldest charity in the United States, first came into existence. It later credited its organisation to the London charity of Scots.[1]

---

[1] For an overview of the Scots' Charitable Society of Boston by its historian Bill Budde, see Appendix 5.

CHAPTER 6

London Hospitals, Poor Relief
and Sturdy Beggars

The English poor law in London and the city's hospitals made little or no provision for the incoming Scots if they became sick. Self-help was going to be crucial to their survival. The early medieval hospitals – St Bartholomew's, St Thomas's, Christ's and Bethlem – were voluntary institutions that had been founded during the twelfth and thirteenth centuries as part of monasteries. By 1538 the City of London and its leaders, distressed by the 'sick, lame and impotent poor' who now lived on the city's streets as a result of Henry VIII's dissolution of the monasteries, successfully petitioned the king to take over the old hospitals. The four medieval hospitals were joined in 1555 by Bridewell when Edward VI gave his house in Blackfriars as a workhouse for the poor 'and idle persons of the city'.

The king further gave the city 500 marks for 'the upkeep, comfort and lodging' of the poor. Enough room was also made at St Bartholomew's for 100 men and women and for one matron and twelve other women 'to make beds and wash and attend, provide food, drink and clothing, bedding, wood and coals'. A priest was also appointed to visit and administer to the poor. There was also one physician and one surgeon. Eight people were appointed 'beadles'. Their duty was to walk the streets of London and bring in 'such poor, such aged and impotent people' but to 'expulse and avoid such valiant and sturdy vagabonds and beggars as they should find daily'. The City of London companies also paid 500 marks for the upkeep of these hospitals and vetted their condition from time to time. The citizens and companies of the City of London were later to base the seventeenth-century charitable giving of their own guilds on such institutions.

In addition to the hospitals and workhouses, a further compulsory poor rate in every parish had been established in 1572. Two more acts in 1598 were to provide the main basis for poor relief until 1834. Constant migration and immigration meant that not all those who came found work and some genuinely fell through the city's 'relief nets', but others discovered that they could obtain more money by begging and taking occasional handouts. The first of the two acts dealt with these 'sturdy beggars' or the 'idle poor' over the age of seven who were seen as a problem, whipped and forced to return to the place 'where they had last lived for over a year'. In 1610 a further act forced every parish to establish a house of correction for the employment or punishment of such beggars. The 'deserving poor' in the second of the 1598 acts, on the other hand, were given poor relief or pensions, or put in workhouses. These early English poor relief acts and those following in 1601 and 1603 effectively handed the responsibility for relieving the poor to the local parishes. Overseers were appointed to administer the relief and collect the poor rate from parishioners. In practice, many parishes did not wish to establish workhouses; they wanted to keep down the costs of poor relief and were none too keen to help stranger paupers.

From 1603, though, the contrast in different levels of society became more obvious for the first time in London. As the rich got richer, the poor got poorer and London also just kept on expanding. The growth in population at the beginning of the seventeenth century also brought business booms as well as slumps for the first time and London's citizens soon saw a clearly visible increase in poverty on a wider social scale. People had become used to the harshness and shortness of life and were also used to church preaching that blamed their sinful lives as the reason for the bad harvests and their poverty. Even so, some started to raise questions about its extent. In 1609 one contemporary English commentator, Robert Gray, had written of the poverty he saw around him: 'Our multitudes like too much blood in the body, do infect our country with plague and poverty. Our land hath brought forth but it hath not milk sufficient in the breast thereof to nourish all those children which it hath brought forth'. It was a problem desperately needing a solution, and officials and private individuals both tried to help.

This gap in poverty relief in London before the Restoration in 1660 was filled by private contributions, especially those from city merchants. Whether this form of charity was growing in value or more important than the parish relief is debatable, and it is probable that the private foundations were no better organised than the parochial poor law institutions. The 'nests of communities', provided by the livery companies, also offered much security in times of trouble and recipients were expected to be eternally grateful for such poor relief and other charity. Most city companies had a poor box and were also regular recipients of charitable bequests and donations from individuals. Parish, company or private poor relief did relieve but did not usually cure the accepted lot of poverty. Certainly, as a system of support in times of crisis it was particularly helpful to the vulnerable – the elderly, widowed and orphaned poor. It is probable that such relief may also have had its part to play in maintaining order in the harshest of times. Poverty was also acute at certain periods when charity beyond parish relief was much in demand. London food prices went up seven times between 1500 and 1640, whereas wages increased only three times, and food crises in the early 1600s meant certain hunger for some. Less money was also available for buying manufactured goods, and fewer people could be paid to make them. Harvest failures in the 1620s, 1630s and 1640s brought more cases of extreme poverty, and from 1647 to 1650 there was a serious lack of parish help. These social crises explain some of the disbursements from the Scottish box club during these years. Plague and other epidemics, exacerbated by London's poor and growing immigrant population, were also common, and became a major strain on charity.

A national mutual-aid society could have been of immediate aid to any Scots who followed James VI and I to the capital in 1603. There was no parish poor relief or burial funds for strangers. This year had seen the most serious outbreak to date of the bubonic plague and had left around 25–30,000 Londoners dead. It also delayed James's processional entry into the City of London until 15 March 1604. On 10 September 1603 there was 'plague feared in the Tower' and 'Disorders in London and the suburbs occasioned by the plague'. By 17 September a proclamation was issued 'for the execution of the statute against rogues, vagabonds, etc.' Believing it to be the hand of God, the city authorities at the time never fully understood the cause of the bubonic plague and its different variations. Nor did they suspect and contain the black rats brought in by the trading ships and the particular type of rat flea that carried the bacillus as it jumped to new human hosts. In fact, all the city's dogs and cats that could have controlled the rats were themselves killed by the authorities in vast numbers. The insanitary conditions in which many people lived in the city were a major contribution to the spread of the infection and, during serious outbreaks, orders were issued to help control the epidemic. Houses with any sick had to be shut up with the families inside for a month, and only one person could be nominated to go for provisions. Washing was not to be hung in the streets and these had to be cleaned and washed down twice a day by all householders who had wells or pumps. Further orders regulated the treatment of the poor, the vagrant and those without legal settlement:

1. That all such as be diseased be sent to St. Thomas or St. Bartylmewes hospital, there to be first cured and made cleane, and afterwards those which be not of the Cyttye to be sent awaie ... for the avoiding of all such vagrant persons as well as children male and female, soldiers lame and maimed, as other idle and loitering persons that swarme in the streets and wander up and downe begging to the great daunger and infecting of the Cyttye for th'increase of the plague and annoyance of the same.
2. That all maisterless men who live idlie in the Cyttye without any lawfull calling, frequenting places of common assemblies, as Interludes, gaming houses, cockpits, bowling allies, and such other places, may be banished the Cyttye ...

During the 1603 outbreak many Londoners escaped to what they thought was the relative safety of the countryside but, without help, a great number 'died in high-ways, fields and barns, near unto good towns, and villages, where too many of them were let remain too long unburied'. However, few courtiers and merchants would have stayed in the city, since all trade and other work had been halted.

CHAPTER 7

A Scottish Box Club

Some idle Scots may have been apprehended as a result of the plague vagrancy proclamation of 1603 but they would not have been accepted by the parish houses of correction established by statute in 1610. Such Scots were certainly enough of a problem by 1615 for James to issue a warrant ordering Sir Thomas Vavasour, his Marshal of the Household, and all England's justices of the peace to come to the aid of Sir William Alexander and John Phillip 'who are appointed to apprehend and send into the kingdome of Scotland all idle persons of that kingdome'. Alexander, as well as being controller of Scots petitions for jobs and other grants, was also helping to rid London's streets of a peculiarly Scottish burden. Alexander in fact had royal orders by April to keep 'idle and vagrant' Scots out of England, lest they 'discredit their countrey', allowing in only 'gentlemen of good qualitie, merchands for trafique, or such as shall have a speicall licence' to cross the border. Some Scots had been sent back by London parishes but had returned 'privniely bak agane'. The provost and bailiffs of Edinburgh were asked to help contain them, and masters of Leith ships were ordered not to transport south any such persons under threat of punishment.

The majority of Scots who were allowed through did well in their new city and made sure they kept out of the poverty trap, having already seen or even experienced such hardship in their own country. Setting up in business would not have been a big cost to these early entrepreneurs. Respected artisans could earn a reasonable living if they were prepared to work hard and could even make a substantial amount of money from their trade when times were good. Joining a guild as a foreign master, journeyman or apprentice was essential in a city where holding some kind of local office was key to getting on or finding a helping hand. But there was still a class of merchant and artisan Scots who may have lost money in the bad times of the 1603 plague or the depressions of the 1620s. Once adversity had been overcome and riches had been achieved, a mark of a higher status would be to make an obvious donation of some kind, and the growing wealth of many London merchants began to sustain the ambitions of those who wanted to help the poorer elements of their own social circle, companies and parishes. It is likely that this philanthropic example was followed by a number of

Scottish merchants and craftsmen, some who wanted a national body to look after their interests if sickness or poverty struck. The many Scots merchants in Westminster and the City of London could have helped establish or could have contributed to the early collections of Scottish box money. Scots at court like William Alexander, and even James I himself, may have encouraged its establishment soon after 1603.

The box club was certainly in operation by 1613 and was said to have been the first means of such support for an immigrant community. A 1677 account of the history of the 'Scotish Corporation' recalls how the directors of a box-money club for Scots were consulted before the charity's royal charter was applied for. A later commentator, William Maitland, wrote about the charity's foundation in his *History of London* in 1739. Maitland's account provides key information about this early Scottish mutual-aid society. He describes the box club as having been 'set up in James the First's Time', and, he writes, ''tis suppos'd to have been the First of its Kind in this City'. He also confirms that the relief was for the contributors themselves 'during Sickness, or other Contingence, whereby they might be render'd incapable of getting their bread'. He further adds that the contributors were actually 'Journeymen Taylors of the Scottish Nation' and that the box club was 'very considerable' by 1665.

Some of the Scots who collected the artisans' mutual aid may have known of the mariners' insurance society established in London at Chatham during the Armada period (or had even seen its huge chest). Scottish sea-box societies were also common along Scotland's east-coast ports – the mariners' poor box in Aberdeen by 1598, the United General Sea Box of Bo'ness by 1634, and also the sea-box societies of Pittenweem and St Andrews, operating in 1633 and around 1643 respectively. Trinity House in Edinburgh was attracting donations from Batavia in 1625, and a wooden box for casting votes or a smaller one for collecting donations for the poor was also common in the seventeenth century in most city livery companies. The East India Company had a wooden ballot box from 1658, borrowed from the Skinners' Company, and the Weavers' Company had a 'Poores Box' by 1666. The Scots' Charitable Society of Boston in New England also followed the box-club tradition a few years earlier.

The early history of the London box club's establishment is hazy because all the records of the Royal Scottish Corporation then existing were burnt in a fire in November 1877. Fortunately some information about the extent of the archive is revealed in an account of the charity published in 1874. This shows that the lost archives had dated from 1620 (a time of economic crisis), but that a reference in them was made to a 1613 date. The lost archives revealed that all members 'contributed equally 6*d*. per quarter, with an entrance fee of 5*s*., soon raised to 1*s*. and 10*s*.' and that 'small sums were lent on bond to the poorer members without interest, aid afforded in sickness, and burial expenses paid'.

The chronology then jumps to 1638 when the lost archives had recorded that during a later plague outbreak, twenty Scottish box-club benefactors did find time to meet in Lamb's Conduit to decide how to spend their burial fund; and out of the money then in the box, they allowed '20s. for those dying of the Plague, 30s. for others'. During 1656–57 the box club was recorded as meeting at the King's Head in Covent Garden, and on 5 October 1658 the society could report 'Money in the box counted in presence of the Members, £61 3s. 6d.', while in 1661 'Quarterly disbursements amounted to £9 4s.' In 1665–66, as the newly incorporated Scottish Hospital, these men were to continue to meet in Covent Garden taverns, and did so until their hall was opened in Blackfriars in 1673.

A date of 1611 is inscribed in the brass decoration of an oak box, called in the inscription the 'Ancient Scots Box'. This was 'found' in 1923 and is now on display at the charity's offices. A verse from Psalm 133 (in the metrical version of the First Scottish Psalter) is also inscribed on its lid:

Behold How Good a Thing It Is
And How Becoming Well
Together Such As Brethren Are
In Unitie To Dwell

It is debatable whether it is the original Scots Box of the early seventeenth century, but however it is regarded, the box is certainly symbolic of an original and lasting intention.[1]

---

[1] This brass inscription and accompanying decoration were said to have been added around 1713, a date which is picked out in large brass studs on the back of the box. The box itself suddenly reappeared in 1923, supposedly discovered by a governor of the Royal Scottish Corporation in the house of an architect, who, forty years earlier, had bought the box from a marine dealer. This governor wished to remain anonymous except to the treasurer, and the box was presented to the charity by its secretary, Thomas Montcrieff, on the unknown governor's behalf. The box carries another brass inscription inside, this time from 1923, which dedicates it to Moncrieff himself as grateful thanks for his many years' hard work. No mention of a missing box is made by any Corporation governors either before or immediately after the fire when surely the loss of such a precious relic would have been noted, especially since the charity's minutes do record in some detail the paintings that were destroyed and also tell of the efforts expended to redesign and remake the lost seal. On the other hand, there is no mention either of the silver cup of James Kynneir, the Corporation's first master and bequeathed by his estate in 1683–84; and this did survive the Victorian fire.

CHAPTER 8

The Scots Artificers' Petition
and the First Charter

Charles II's restoration had been a time of celebration, although it was a smoke-filled, stinking and populous London that greeted the new king. John Evelyn, in his *Fumifugium* of 1661, named the culprits those 'few particular tunnels and issues, belonging only to brewers, dyers, lime-burners, salt, and soap-boilers, and some private trades'. He deplored that 'this glorious and ancient city ... which commands the proud ocean to the Indies, and reaches the farthest Antipodes, should wrap her stately head in clouds of smoke and sulphur, so full of stink and darkness'. That the buildings and alleys

> should be composed of such congestion of misshapen and extravagant houses; that the streets should be so narrow and incommodius in the very centre, and busiest places of intercourse; that there should be so ill and uneasy a form of paving underfoot, so troublesome and malicious a disposure of the spouts and gutters overhead, are particulars worthy of reproof and reformation; because it is hereby rendered a labyrinth in its principal passages, and a continual wet day after the storm is over.

Despite the discomfort, Charles diplomatically made a point of entering the City of London before riding on to his palace at Whitehall. The urbanity and patronage of the 'merrie monarch' was to be a welcome relief to many of his new subjects, especially in the times of crisis ahead. The city developed further as a financial centre and a greater number of Scots started to arrive, keen to come to the capital. But at the same time, a London Scot could still experience some anti-Scottish feelings. Scottish merchants may also have felt the effects of the Corporation Act and the Clarendon Code which limited the public life and influence of Presbyterians for a while from 1661 unless they joined the Church of England. Samuel Pepys notes St Andrew's Day in his diary of 1663 and again in 1666 when, because of the Pentland Rising in Scotland, some anti-Scottish feeling was directed at those celebrating the day as he made his way to Whitehall: 'and pretty to see it ... how some few did wear St Andrew's crosse; but most did make a mockery at it, and the House of Parliament, contrary to practice, did sit also: people having no mind to observe the Scotch saint's days till they hear better news from Scotland'.

The demand for charity towards London's poor, and any poorer Scots, had additionally grown by the second half of the seventeenth century as the population of London after 1660 increased, food prices rose and jobs became scarce. The Acts of Settlement passed in 1662 had institutionalised public poor relief, limiting it to those accepted by the workhouses, and it had also made life much harsher for poorer Scots. These new laws even more effectively forced paupers to return to the parishes where they had been born if they wanted to claim relief. The box club of Scots had also grown into something greater and the members of this original Scottish charity realised that a more formal organisation was needed for their donations.

An individual Scottish act of philanthropy gave the Scots Box its greatest boost. In 1664 a wealthy Scotsman in London, who 'being visited with a long Fit of Sickness and in doubt of Life', on his recovery 'resolved to communicate to the Poor of his Countrey (whom he found to be numerous and under great Streights), part of the Fruits of those his Labours, which the Lord had been pleased to bless with Success'. Thanking God for his lucky escape, he wanted to establish something substantial, something that would perhaps last for all time, if organised properly:

> his Charity having a farther Prospect than a present Supply to the Indigent at that time, and being willing to mortifie a Gift, that might be the standing Stock for the Relief of the Poor not only of the present but future Ages; and to secure the same to Posterity, as far as worldly Contingencies could permit, and beyond the uncertainties of private trustees, whose malversation or decay, often disappoint the pious Intentions of Donors.

The Scotsman's lawyers advised him that the best way to set up such a formal society for sustained poor relief was by obtaining a royal charter 'for the erecting of an Incorporation of Scots in London which having the Privileges of a permanent and authorized Society, would be by Law impowred to act and oblige themselves and Successors, in such a manner as no private Consociation could pretend to'. The benefactor then approached the 'most sober and discreet Men of our Countrey' in London, who had 'the direction of box money', with his resolution. These men 'maturely weighed the matter first privately among themselves', and then discussed it

> in a general Meeting of our Countreymen, who all foreseeing the advantages of the Design, and applauding the Councel, notwithstanding their doubts of procuring the Patent, bestirred themselves so zealously in that Affair, that having made application to the Earl of Lauderdale, and made appear to him the profitableness of that Project, they obtained of His Gracious Majesty ... after a Reference and satisfactory Report made to His Majesty on that Subject, a Patent in ample Form.

A petition had been sent to Charles II via Lauderdale on 11 April 1665, in the name of 'sundry Artificers of the Scottish Nation Inhabiting within the Citties of London and Westminster and the Liberties thereof'. They asked for a patent to enable a number of them to erect a workhouse for 'divers Indigent impotent sickly persons or orphans of the said Artificers' who are 'oftentimes reduced to great extremities & like to perish for want of reliefe becoming burdensome to the parishes & places wherein they live to the great dishonestie of their Nation'. Such a 'convenient Workhouse' would relieve the craftsmen and train them and their families for 'manual occupations'. Morevoer, the petition claimed, this work-house would be to 'the credit of their Nation and the advancement of trade'.

The document was signed in two columns by nineteen Scots: John Allayn, David Jolley, Alexander Blair, Piter Coknigham (sic), John Tail(is), Andrew Caldwell, Robert Patersone, James Love, James Smith, James Kynneire, Alexander Gordon, William Johnson, A. Littlejohn, Andrew Macdougall, Thomas Hendersone, Robert Nisbet, Andrew Hodges, William Bruce and George Loromer. Allayn, Jolly and McDougall were gentlemen, Kynneir was a weaver merchant, and the other men were probably also weavers, merchant taylors or other artisans. The king referred the petition to his attorney general, who inves-tigated the matter and gave his nod of approval. He cited certain precedents which could be 'pertinently offered … to encline his Majesty to grant his Royall favours in this intended so pious Christian and Charitable a worke'. Leaving aside monasteries, colleges, schools, and 'houses for education & reliefe of English Scottish and Irish Monks, Nunns, Students, Schollars, orphans,' he wrote, the parallel post-Reformation precedents that could be cited were:

- All Hospitals, almshouses, and Workhouses, erected for the Poor, in London, Westminster, & other places
- the Dutch Corporations in Canterbury, Norwich and Colechester, and other places
- the foundation of Jesus Colledge in Oxford for Welsh Schollars and Students and Queenes Colledge for Northerne

On 31 May the king ordered a warrant for 'erecting an Hospital within the City of Westminster or the libertys thereof to be called the Scottish Hospital of the Foundation of King Charles the 2nd'. The warrant also ordered that 41 Scotsmen be governors and one of their number the annual master. The new corporation should have 'a Common Seale with the power to sue and be sued', and 'also the power to make laws and constitutions of the Government of the said Hospitall and … Revennues thereof, and also power to administrate Oaths to the members … and to purchase lands in Mortmaine not exceeding five hundred pounds per annum'. The warrant was concerned that there should be a special clause which ensured that all 'members & officers take the oaths of Allegiance &

Supremacy'. This last point was important. Such oaths specifically kept out any practising Catholics and Covenanters and ensured that the Corporation's new officeholders were of the Episcopalian faith. Benefactors and recipients were not so curtailed and could have included both Presbyterians and Catholics.

The workhouse for poor Scots artificers had become a 'hospital'. The Letters Patent were duly enrolled according to this warrant a month later on 30 June. These changed the terminology again, stating that it was now to be a 'hospital or workhouse' in Westminster for 'the divers indigent impotent sickly Persons and Orphans of the said Artificers' but not for 'anie lazie or desolute people'. Eight 'able honest and discreet men' of the Scottish nation were appointed 'Governors' and the 'first and present Governors' were named as: 'James Kinneir, merchant; John Allan, Gentleman; John Ewing, merchant; James Donaldson, merchant; David Jolly, Gentleman; Alexander Gordon, Gentleman; Alexander Blaire, Gentleman; and James Blaitchie the Elder, Gentleman'. James Kynneir was chosen as the first Master. The new charter mistakenly omitted the royal warrant's terms which covered the City of London as a place for building, the assistant governors and a £500 property clause. Perhaps the fear of encroaching plague caused the writer of the patent to forget these points or mislay the original warrant.

John Maitland's help, as the second Earl (later first Duke) of Lauderdale, secretary of state for Scotland from 1661 and a gentleman of the king's bedchamber, had been instrumental in getting the Scotsmen's petition quickly brought to royal notice. The Letters Patent were granted in what looks like record time, especially in a month of increasing plague. Fees were usually paid for the granting of charters and these may have been waived in 1665 as they were to be in 1676 when the Corporation's second charter was granted, also with Lauderdale's assistance. Lauderdale was a powerful man and a member of the 'cabal' around Charles II. In August 1643 he had been one of the Scots commissioners who carried the Solemn League and Covenant to the Parliamentarians at Westminster. By 1647 he had persuaded Charles I to sign the Engagement whereby the Covenanters re-entered England to fight for the restoration of royal authority. He supported the Scottish patriotic accommodation with Charles II, but was taken prisoner at the battle of Worcester in 1651 and kept in the Tower of London and elsewhere until the Restoration in 1660. After this time, despite scarce personal resources, he regained his royal position. His character had been hardened by his experience and adversity, and he had 'a strong will, coolness and courage, extreme selfishness, readiness to strike at the right moment, keen discernment in choosing his tools, and utter unscrupulousness'. He also knew how to play politics at court and in Scotland, understanding, as he said, 'how to make use of a knave as well as another'. He was supposed to have been a great liar but hated others who lied, was extremely well read in religious teachings and languages but 'soon proved himself as well the rival in debauchery, so far as embarrassed means would allow, of the most licentious of Charles's courtiers'. He was physically an unattractive figure but robust in health, and 'by dexterity and industry he soon made himself indispensable to Charles'.

He was also a builder, and Ham House, his house in Richmond, was a place of court business and intrigue. Samuel Pepys met Lauderdale several times over a lunchtime dinner or a late supper in the 1660s, and on 1 July 1666 he found the Scots a strange bunch as he dined with Lauderdale at Ham. He wondered at his host's taste, thinking the Scots 'Pretty odd company; though my Lord Brouncker tells me, my Lord Lauderdale is a man of mighty good reason and judgement'. Lauderdale also encouraged a tradition of British nobles associating themselves with the Royal Scottish Corporation; these were to include William, fifth Earl and first Duke of Bedford, another great builder and property owner. Through his 'early and magnificent Bounty' the Corporation on the duke's death in 1694 remembered that the 'noble Patriot' had given the Corporation 'a Piece of Ground in White-hart-yard, near Covent-Garden, whereon to build their then intended Hospital'.

Covent Garden taverns were still used for the charity's meetings, and with the granting of the 'Scottish Hospital's' first charter in 1665, management and fiscal matters were now in the hands of the new masters and treasurers elected annually.[1] Some time after 30 June that year, the first meeting of the newly incorporated society was held at the Cross Keys tavern in Covent Garden and monies were counted: 'First regular account approved by the First Quarterly Court … receipts £116 8s 5d.' More money could also be raised that day or evening from the company's drinking: 'For every Oath or curse at Courts 2s 6d; being drunk at Courts, 10d; striking, or giving abusive language, to be fined as the Court shall determine'. Another meeting in 1666 is again recorded as taking place in the west part of Covent Garden, this time at the 'Cock & Pie Tavern', in or near what was once called Cock Lane, now Upper St Martin's Lane.

The earliest accounts of the Scots Corporation indicate that the dangerously ill Scotsman, who made the original donation that led to the grant of letters patent, was James Kynneir, also the Corporation's earliest and largest benefactor. William Maitland, in his *History of London*, published in 1739, asserts: 'The Origin of this Corporation is owing to James Kinnier, a Scotsman, and Merchant of this City; who, after a long and dangerous Sickness, determin'd to give Part of his Estate toward the Relief of the aged and necessitous Poor of his Country, within the Cities of London and Westminster'. Kynneir was also the first annual master of the Royal Scottish Corporation, an initial appointment usually accorded to individual founders of similar societies.

---

[1] For a list of their names, see Appendix 2.

CHAPTER 9

James Kynneir and the Weavers' Company

James Kynnier's name is the one most associated with the early history of the Royal Scottish Corporation. His signature, neatly squashed between two others (as if he were the last man to sign), is preserved in the original petition of 1665, and the name of 'James Kinneir, merchant' is also the first listed of the new governors named in the Letters Patent of 1665 when he also became the first of the Hospital's annually elected masters. He took up the post of master again in 1676, the year of the second royal charter. Kynneir was also one of the Corporation's earliest benefactors and gave the charity around £487 in total. He probably donated around £200 to the Scottish Hospital on its establishment in 1665 and left the charity another £200 in his 1681 will; £100 was for seacoles and a dinner for the poor on St Andrew's Day and another £100 was to be held 'forever in trust only' for the 'reliefe of poore distressed Scotch Merchants that by stresse of weather are come into England and are in a waiting condition and by reason of their poverty are Objects of Charity'. Kynneir's Welsh widow, Eleanor, also bequeathed another £30 to the Corporation when she died.[1]

Kynneir's experience of the city's Weavers' Company would have influenced the organisation of his own charity and the preservation of his initial substantial donation. The Weavers' Company was the oldest of the city's guilds, having been granted a royal charter by Henry II in 1155, the first granted to any London craft. By 1603 it was still 'vigorous and vigilant'. The regulations of the Weavers' guild allowed for a management by a 'Court' of sixteen men made up of two annually-elected bailiffs and two wardens (known as the 'Officers'), and twelve assistants. One of the two bailiffs was voted the Upper Bailiff or Master by the others and another forty or fifty liverymen assembled in a 'Common Hall'. The court performed the usual livery company administrative, judicial, and financial functions. Its jurisdiction extended over two miles from the city gates and covered the city's liberties and suburbs, places where, like other craftsmen, the weavers (and many Scots) mainly lived and carried out their work.

As in other livery companies, a freeman was the highest rank to which a

---

[1] A later account says Kynneir's widow left £517, but this is probably just the £487 and £30 amounts added together.

weaver could aspire. The freeman would have served usually seven years as an apprentice to a master weaver, followed by two to three years as a journeyman, or he could also be admitted by 'patrimony or redemption'. Weaver freemen also became freemen of the City and were then entitled to call themselves 'Citizen and Weaver of London'. The number of looms, journeymen and apprentices defined the status and seniority of a master weaver, and usually depended on whether he was a liveryman, a 'denizen or foreigner' or 'a stranger (alien)', and whether he was also one of the four Weavers' Company officials. Despite these restrictions on numbers, they were not always kept to in good times when trade was brisk. Those weavers, including Scots, who had not been apprenticed to a freeman of the City of London could set up as 'foreign' masters, and some also set up as foreign journeymen if they had served an apprenticeship but had not yet been admitted to a foreign master.

James Kynneir was probably a native of Edinburgh, but how he came to London and when is not known. That he was a weaver is confirmed by both this will and records of the Weavers' Company itself. These show Kynneir taking an apprenticeship – perhaps a formality for entry as a foreign master – between 1665 and 1670. He was himself also noted as being a master weaver when Thomas Denton's apprenticeship to him was recorded.[2] Kynneir does not appear to have held any high office at the Weavers' Company and is not listed as having subscribed to the rebuilding of their Hall during 1667-69 after the Great Fire. He could, though, afford to leave a bequest and start a Scots tradition among the poorer Scottish members of the company. According to an indenture dated 24 November 1679, 'James Kennier' gave the Weavers' Company £50 on condition that it would 'lay out yearly for ever £2. 8s. 0d. in Seacoles and so distribute them among the Almes People and lay out 12s. for Meat and drink for them on St. Andrews's Day for ever under the forfeiture of 50li.' A later accounting note points out that the almshouses were in Shoreditch and that James Kynneir's gift should be handed out to the poor in June, July or August. The almshouses were actually in Hoxton and had been built in 1669–70. Coal was expensive for the poor to buy, probably still having at this time a duty on it that went towards the rebuilding fund of St Paul's Cathedral. The summer months would also have been a good time to buy when the coal was at its cheapest. Kynneir's gift was paid in two instalments, the first of £35 being paid up immediately alongside gifts of similar amounts made by other Weavers' Company benefactors. In his will, Kynneir left any debts to be settled by his executors and the Weavers' balance was paid at the end of 1684.

---

[2] Guildhall Weavers' MS 4660 lists 'James Kenier' but the reference to 'fol. 38' beside his name refers to records since lost; the date of 14 February 1686/7 recorded here was probably Denton's apprenticeship end date, since Kynneir died in 1684. Although there appear to be a number of other Scottish names, the extant weaver freemen records for 1600–1646 do not list Kynneir as having been granted admission during this period.

The Weavers' Company connection continued when it was required by Kynneir in his will of 1681 to ensure that the 'Scots Corporation' carried out its duties also to give out 'Seacoles' in June, July or August to its own poor and to host a dinner for them on St Andrew's Day. The Weavers' Company had a silver cup by 1662, and the Royal Scottish Corporation still has in its possession a similar silver cup bequeathed to it by Kynneir, on either side of which he also specified that his and his wife's coat of arms and the 'Emblem of Charity' from the Corporation seal be engraved. This was duly done when he died.[3] Robert Kirk also remembered that the Corporation had a tradition of drinking to James Kynneir and his Welsh wife annually on St James's Day.[4]

Kynneir was said in Maitland's *History* to have been a merchant also. As a weaver by training and trade, it is likely that Kynneir had a merchant's export interest in wool or 'the new draperies', the lighter more colourful cloth and silk. *A Collection of the Names of the Merchants Living in and about The City of London* was published in 1677 as 'very Usefull and Necessary'. The directory describes the merchants' names as having been 'Carefully Collected for the Benefit of all Dealers that shall have occasion with any of them; Directing them at the first sight of their name, to the place of their abode'. The list contains the names of a number of Scots associated with the Scottish Hospital and Corporation, including one 'James Kinier'. He was listed as being contactable in 'Michael Lane', probably another name for Miles Lane or St Michael Crooked Lane in Cornhill near Lombard Street in the City of London (both streets were removed in the 1820s to make way for King William Street). This was also a useful area for networking in the many long-established coffee houses in the area, especially in St Michael's Alley.

---

[3] The Weavers' cup had the company's coat of arms on one side. The later cover for Kynneir's Corporation cup is also inscribed, showing that it was presented to the charity by A. Drummond and George Campbell in 1749.

[4] The tradition of weaver Scots was certainly strong and so much so that there were still Scottish weavers in London's East End over a hundred years later in December 1793 when the Scots Corporation chaplain, Henry Hunter, preached a sermon at the Scots Church at London Wall, entitled *The Day of Judgement*, as an appeal for relieving the weavers of Spitalfield.

CHAPTER 10

Plague and Fire

The Scottish Hospital had an immediate test of its philanthropic resources when plague struck the same year as the society's 1665 patent. A year later, a great fire swept through the city burning Scottish homes and further destroying the livelihoods of Scots. The newly incorporated Scottish charity survived – but only just:

> So good a Work was almost stifled in the Birth; for the Contagious Plague, which then almost dispeopled *London*, and those fatal Flames (which the Year following by the deplorable ruine of the City purified it from Infection to the very foundation;) if not wholly crushed, yet suspended for some time the Execution of our good Intentions.

Fortunately 'The Scottish Hospital of the Foundation of Charles II' already had its royal charter and had found its first master and benefactor before these two disasters struck. Outbreaks of plague had been relatively common in London, but the 1665 visitation was by far the most severe when possibly nearly 100,000 people died. Scares of bubonic plague and other epidemics were to follow in later centuries, but an outbreak as terrible as that of 1665 has never visited London since.[1]

Particularly vivid pictures of the epidemic were given by the Reverend T. Vincent. In his account, called *God's Terrible Voice in the City*, he described how 'many houses are shut up where plague comes, and the inhabitants shut in, lest coming abroad they should spread infection. It was very dismal to behold the red crosses, and read in great letters, LORD HAVE MERCY UPON US, on the doors …'[2] Many Londoners escaped to the country as they had done in previous outbreaks: 'fear puts many thousands on the wing, and those think

---

[1] Smallpox and typhus were common in the seventeenth century. Later epidemics were to include cholera in 1832 and influenza in 1918. An Al' Qaeda biological or chemical attack on London as a result of the current threat of international terrorism, possibly using weapons of mass destruction, is the key risk today. The British Government has preparations in hand to cope with a smallpox epidemic from such a source. An essential team of doctors, nurses and other healthcare workers are to be inoculated against the disease.

[2] The lettering on the doors was, in some cases, as much as six feet high.

themselves most safe, that can fly furthest off from the city'. By late July the situation, Vincent recounts, was much worse and the increase in deaths much greater: 'from 2010, the number amounts to 2817 in one week; and thence to 3880 the next; thence to 4237 the next; thence to 6102 the next …' All shops were shut, the streets were quiet, and those left alive walked solemnly and silently, hearing 'no rattling coaches, no prancing horses, no calling customers, no offering wares, no London Cries sounding in the ears …', only the groans of the sick and the tolling of bells for the dead. Vincent continued:

> Now in some places where the people did generally stay, not one house in a hundred but is infected; and in many houses half the family is swept away; in some the whole, from the eldest to the youngest; few escape with the death of but one or two; never did so many husbands and wives die together; never did so many parents carry their children with them to the grave, and go together into the same house under earth, who had lived together in the same house upon it. Now the nights are too short to bury the dead; the long summer days are spent from morning unto the twilight in conveying the vast number of dead bodies into the bed of their graves.[3]

Graveyards overflowed and large pits were dug to bury the dead. Vincent's days were spent visiting his dying friends:

> I had been abroad [from Aldgate] to see a friend in the city whose husband was newly dead of the Plague, and herself visited with it. I came back to see another, whose wife was dead of the Plague, and he himself under apprehensions that he should die within a few hours: I came home, and the maid was on her death-bed; and another crying for help, being left alone in a sweating fainting fit.

He experienced the 'fears there are amongst us that within a while there will not be enough alive to bury the dead'.[4]

Poorer Scots craftsmen and their families who fell ill or who died with no one left to pay funeral expenses were taken care of by the Scottish Hospital. Scots born in Scotland were among those classed as being outside the 'legal settlement' of the parish poor relief system and would have been desperate for help.

---

[3] Interestingly, one of the first victims of the 1665 plague is said to be buried at St Paul's Church in Covent Garden, directly opposite the present headquarters of the Royal Scottish Corporation.

[4] Daniel Defoe in his novel, A Journal of the Plague Year, similarly relives the horror for his readers. Writing in 1722 at a time of another plague scare, he relied on contemporary tales and official records from 1665 for his fictional account, although the text reads like that of a journalistic eye-witness. In fact it is an idealistic healthcare tract for an impending crisis. Trade and employment stopped, Defoe wrote, and the poor lost means of getting their bread and many were 'without any one to give it them, for many of them were without what we call legal Settlements, and so could not claim of the Parishes, and all the Support they had, was by Application to the Magistrates for relief, which Relief was, (to give the Magistrates their Due) carefully and chearfully administred, as they found it necessary'.

The charity was forced to use up much of its first donations for hospital building money on such an immediate and worthy cause:

> These dismal Times, however, put not a stop to the main Wheel of Charity; for during the Sickness Year, when our Beginnings were but small, there were Three Hundred *Scots*, and of *Scottish* Extraction, who dyed of the Plague in and about *London*, buried at the Charge of the Company, with as much Decency as the Calamity of the Time would permit; and many who were Infected maintained, and taken care of, until they recovered, and by God's Blessing the Contagion ceased, without putting the several Parrishes where they had lived to one Farthing of Expenses.

Even at this early date, the Scots were very conscious of not burdening the English with their national needs. Doctors' and apothecaries' bills of the plague victims would have been paid and funeral expenses met in full or part by the Scottish Hospital governors. How much this charity cost was not recorded. Nor was the place where these three-hundred Scots were buried, but probably no cross would have marked the spot. Most plague victims during the height of the epidemic were buried in deep pits with little ceremony as most parish churchyards in London were full to overflowing. Many of the Scots who died, no doubt James Kynneir's fellowweavers, would have lived around Spitalfields, Hoxton and other places in Shoreditch and may have been buried near these areas.[5] Others may have lived closer to Westminster and the court. Alexander Davies, a 'scrivener' and an early plague victim, is buried in St Margaret's Church-yard. His widow gave £10 to the church in his memory. St Margaret's Church in Westminster recorded bills of around 10 shillings each given to poorer members of the parish to help with the cost of burial. If transferred to the Scottish charity, this puts the outlay of the Scottish Hospital's burial and sickness fund at around £150-£200 – all (or nearly all) of James Kynneir's initial donation.

Scots merchants and artificers returning to the English capital would have refilled the Scots box, and Samuel Pepys noted how people flocked back to London after the Great Plague, even by the first days of 1666, exclaiming how busy the city was. He further noted, 'such begging of beggars!', showing that the need for charity to remove Scots from the streets was probably acute after such devastation. Unfortunately the Royal Scottish Corporation's plans to build their workhouse for such people were put off for another four years as the whole of the City of London, except a narrow circle around its boundary, was destroyed in the Great Fire of 1666. James I had made a proud boast that '… we had found our Cities and suburbs of London of sticks, and left them of bricke, being a

---

[5] The walls and gates of the nearby Bunhill Fields in Finsbury had actually been built in 1665–66 for plague burials but is thought never to have been used for the purpose, though later Presbyterian Scots may have been buried there as it became much used by Puritans and other non-conformists like John Bunyan, Susannah Wesley, Daniel Defoe and William Blake.

material farre more durable, safe from fire and beautiful and magnificent'. He may have patronised a number of substantial buildings through his support especially of the architect Inigo Jones (who clad a wooden St Paul's in stone), but the City of London itself was very vulnerable to fire, being mainly of wooden housing, very close-packed and with overhanging gables – and especially so after a long, hot summer and with a strong wind blowing.

According to Samuel Pepys, hearing it from the Lieutenant of the Tower, the fire started on 2 September 'in the King's baker's house in Pudding Lane'. He saw the Lord Mayor in a panic, 'with a handkerchief about his neck', crying 'like a fainting woman'. Later the same day Pepys watched the city burning while he was at Bankside, on the south side of the river:

> ... we saw the fire as only one entire arch of fire from this to the other side of the bridge, and in a bow up the hill for an arch of above a mile long; it made me weep to see it. The church, houses, and all on fire and flaming at once; and a horrid noise the flames made, and the cracking of houses at their ruine. So home with a sad heart, and there find everybody discursing and lamenting.

The final scene was one of near devastation and the Scots merchants were no doubt glad that they had not yet started building their hospital. About four-fifths of the medieval city had been burnt down in three days, around 87 parish churches, 44 livery-company halls, 13,200 houses, and the Royal Exchange; extensive damage was done to St Paul's, Bridewell and the Fleet prison. Around 373 acres were destroyed inside the city and 63 acres outside the city walls. Money and rebuilding schemes were top priorities for several years to come. Christopher Wren, John Evelyn and Robert Hooke designed broad new street plans but the city needed a much speedier solution than the architects could provide, and a cheaper form of rebuilding quickly began on top of the charred ruins. The old Saxon and medieval street plan was mainly kept but some public improvements were made – especially along the waterfront – and an open quayside was decreed from Blackfriars to the Tower, with warehouses all along its edge.

New regulations and safety stipulations called for new buildings of brick and stone and allowed for buildings four storeys high in the main streets, three storeys in secondary streets and two storeys for houses in side streets. Sewage and paving were improved and wooden door and window frames had to be set back at least four inches, while wooden eaves and cornices were prohibited. The Scottish timber industry was to benefit from the use of such wood in the city's rebuilding schemes. A few weeks after the fire, Pepys records that Sir William Pen had an idea that he and Pepys should join up and work on a design 'of fetching timber and deals from Scotland ... which, while London is building, will yield good money. I approve it'. The Great Fire of 1666 had also resulted in the establishment of fire insurance and fire brigades. Nicholas Barbon, one of the rebuilders and speculators of London after the fire, founded the first of the fire insurance companies. As well as insuring properties and goods against fire, these companies also set up fire brigades to put out fires and, clothed in 'resplendent uniforms', they competed against one another using wall plaques to mark their clients' buildings. Nearly two hundred years later, such fire insurance and fire engines were to be well used by the Royal Scottish Corporation.

CHAPTER 11

Building in Blackfriars and the Second Charter

Once the new building regulations had been issued, money was raised and market buildings and livery-company halls were quickly rebuilt. Most private houses had also been completed and were occupied by the early 1670s; trade and immigration also revived. Scots had also started returning in numbers to take up their past activities in the capital as well as to take time out to rebuild their charity:

> Whilst the City lay buried under its own Rubbish, though many of our Members who had been scattered by these two heavy Visitations, were again returned, and as earnest in their desires as formerly to promote that Work of Charity; yet the Lowness of their Stock, which was hardly sufficient to supply the Necessities of the Poor that then lay upon us, made us almost despair of bringing our designs to any accomplishment. We wanted a Hall for our Meetings, Ground to build upon, and Money to purchase and effectuate both.

After several tavern meetings 'to consult about the Measures we were to take', Kynneir and his fellow-Scots in 1670 'had Notice given us of a piece of Waste Ground in Black-Fryers, where formerly had stood a large Dwelling-house belonging to a Pious Widow-Lady'. The governors went to view it but the widow was unwilling at first to entertain the Scotsmen's plan but, 'being informed of the Pious and Charitable use that it was designed for, she frankly granted us a Lease of it for a Thousand Years'. The land, in St Ann's Parish in Water Lane, Black-friars and facing the Fleet Ditch, was leased for £40 a year from the widow, a Mrs Katherine Austen, who owned several parcels of land north and south of Fleet Street.[1] This area of London had been popular earlier in the century but

---

[1] Katharine Austen's diary had recorded her agreement with the charity. On her death she willed that the £40 rent from the Corporation should be paid direct to Christ's Hospital. An older neighbour of the Scottish Hospital in Blackfriars Lane throughout the second half of the seventeenth and most of the eighteenth centuries was the 'Trinity House on Deptford Strond'. Its establishment in 1514 had been a response to the petition drafted by Thomas Spert who claimed that many foreigners, notably Scots and Flemings, had already learned the secrets of navigating the Thames. He wanted to put an end to this foreign knowledge and to organise more effective pilotage of the river. It was also clear that Spert would have had to absorb these exiled Scots as members of the new organisation. Later in the 1530s, Spert created a school for

by the 1660s, and especially after the fire, it was not one of the most sought-after places to live and was relatively cheap. It would also have been squalid, being so close to the Fleet River, then not much more than an open sewer with the City of London's dungheap at its mouth. The Bridewell workhouse faced the Scots from the opposite bank of the tributary and Alsatia, that part of London 'no-one owned and everybody feared', was close by. A little further north and west stretched Fleet Street with its smelly printworks but also many lively, literary taverns.

Houses could only be built after the fire in piecemeal fashion and as the owners could afford it. Three surveyors for private buildings were appointed to 'measure and mark out' each plot. Having acquired their lease, the Corporation would then have had to pay a survey fee of 6s. 8d. for each foundation surveyed to the 'Chamber of London' who would give the surveyor the go-ahead to lay out the foundations. The three surveyors were Robert Hooke, Peter Mills and John Oliver, and they catalogued much of the city's rebuilding work in their survey. The Chamber officers noted in their receipt book that three foundations were to be surveyed in 'Blackfryers Lane' for the 'Wardens of the Scotch Corporation' on July 30 1669. Mills was given the job of laying out the Corporation's foundations for its 1668–69 master, city merchant John Ewan.[2] In his survey of 'Ground Staked out after the Fire of London', Mills made the following entry for 30 July (calling Ewan, 'Newen'):

> Four foundations set out the day abovesaid Situate in Blackfriars belonging to the said Mr. Newen containing upon the front North and South 72 foot 4 inches from the middle of each party and in breadth at the West and North and South 72 foot from the middle of the party wall South to the out of their own wall North and in depth East and West 38 foot from out to out Mr Williams on the South and Mr Cousens on the North.

Although the foundations were laid, the Corporation's governors met several times to consider how to raise more money to complete the building work. Luckily they 'found so great readiness not only in the Members of our own Society, but also in several persons of worth and quality of our Nation, who liberally and bountifully both gave and lent us money, upon no other Security but the Bond of the Corporation'. This included donations of money and property. Two baronies in Nova Scotia were also supposed to have been sold by Charles II in 1668 to raise money for the building fund. Sir John Aiton,

----

the orphaned children of those pilots, some of whom were Scottish. (It is even possible, though unlikely, that the Scottish box club's wooden box, as a prized possession, could have been stored at Trinity House for safe keeping and may account for a marine dealer having possession of it in the late 1880s).

[2] He was called 'Ewing' when nominated as one of the original eight governors in 1665 and in the 1677 merchant directory.

'Gentleman Usher of the Black Rod', was especially generous, donating £195 in 1671 and 'gave also to the Corporation certain Houses in Soho'.

The charity was then enabled to build its hospital in stages and built 'first four Dwelling Houses fronting the Street in Black-Fryers that leads to the River, with an Inscription on the Frontispiece, declaring them to be for the Use of the Poor of our Countrey'. These were finished in 1671. Under the name of Andrew Caldwell, master 1672–73, two new sets of foundations were surveyed for the Corporation, again in Blackfriars Lane, on 10 January 1672. 'Next' was built 'our Hall, and a House contiguous to it, the Hall having its entry from the Street in Black-Fryers, and lying open to Bridewell Ditch, with an Emblem of Charity cut in Free Stone, and fastened in the Wall, finished in the Year 1672'. John Oliver's survey notes additionally show the Corporation bordering a plot on the south side belonging to a Mr Thomas Fitch 'at Bridewell Stairs on Blackfryers Side' in October 1672. Further foundations in 'Bridewell Docke or Precinct' were set out for the 'Scotch Corporation' on 26 February 1673 and, again in the name of Andrew Caldwell, on 8 April 1673.[3]

Finally, 'another House' was built 'which stands upon a parcel of disputed Ground that lay long undetermined, with a Kitchin and two Rooms over it for a Dwelling-house for our Beadle'. These last buildings were completed in 1675 and 1676 'at the sole Charge of the Members of the Company'. The building expenses for the completion of the 'Seven Dwelling-Houses, the Hall with two small rooms adjoining to it, the Kitchin and two Rooms over it for the Beadle', eventually, 'by a true Computation', amounted to about £4,450 *'English'*. This, the Corporation considered in 1677, was 'no inconsiderable Sum to have been raised and disbursed in so short a time', but it also acknowledged that it had 'by such a vast Expence contracted debts'. But the charity was full of hope of raising more physical and spiritual donations to free it of its 'Incumbrances' when it considered 'the cheerful and free Contributions of those who already concurred with so much Unanimity in that charitable Work, and the former experiences we have had of the Goodness and Blessing of Almighty God, in raising us up many times unexpected Supports to our languishing Hopes'. Donors were reminded of the fact that

> God almighty, who charges as a Debt on Providence what is chearfully given to the Poor, having many times imperceptible wayes to repay what that way is lent to himself: And that moreover all such whose hands have been open in their Charity, besides the inward satisfaction of Conscience, the inseparable Companion of Virtue, and the hopes of future Bliss, the promised Reward of Well-doing, have also their Names and Benevolences recorded to Posterity in

---

[3] Caldwell was actually master for the year from November 1672; no foundations appeared to have been set out under the names of the intervening masters from November 1669 to November 1672, namely James Donaldson, Alexander Blair and James Blacklaw.

a large Sheet of Parchment hung up in the Hall, for their present satisfaction, and an encouragement to others hereafter to imitate their laudable Example.

Under James Kynneir's second term as master in 1676, the Royal Scottish Corporation's charter was examined and renewed. The 1665 charter needed to be 'altered and enlarged' and several omissions had to be added. The Earl of Lauderdale (now the duke) was again approached for help. Lauderdale's second marriage to Elizabeth, later Countess of Dysart, in 1672 caused him to lose close friends at court but he had maintained his influence over the king. Another petition was sent in October 1676 and, 'at the earnest desire of the duke', a warrant was issued by Charles II on 3 November ordering the new Letters Patent; these were then issued on 18 November. The usual fees were waived 'with a Generous and Charitable Liberality' by 'the Lord Chancellor of England, and other Officers of State through whose hands it past' and 'whose Noble Munificence we do acknowledge our selves Eternally obliged'. The governors were also grateful to 'the Magistrates and Governors of this famous City of London, who have not been wanting to encourage us by many Favors'. They were grateful too (thinking especially of the Duke of Bedford's beneficence) to the 'many other Charitable Persons of the English Nation, who professing themselves much taken with so laudable a work of Charity, have freely and bountifully assisted us with their Benevolence, and which we hope will not be frustrated of Reward'.

The ability to own, buy, lease and sell property was an important tenet of the first Royal Charter. In the 1676 version the Scottish Hospital's powers were widened and its reach was extended to include the City of London, where the Blackfriars building now stood, as well as keeping the original Westminster-location clause. Thirty-three 'Assistants' were now added to help the original eight appointed governors, this time meeting annually on St Andrew's Day or the day after. At this meeting, the assistants were to nominate two of the governors (who had not been master), or two 'of the ancientest of their own number, who have served in the principal offices of the said corporation, or two names of another of the principal persons of the Scottish nation for birth or estate'. The governors would then choose one name and make him master for the year. This time the governors, while praised for their charitable intentions, were also warned to be discriminating in their charity, being required to

take speciall care not to encourage or receive any vagrant beggars or other idle and dissolute persons of the said Scottish nation who are able to worke and not fitt to receive the charity erected and established by these our Letters Patent, but that they doe cause such vagrant, loose and dissolute persons to be apprehended and brought before a Justice of the Peace or other Magistrate that soe they may be sent to the house of correction or other place of punishment as the case shall require.

A number of other Scots mentioned in the 1677 merchants' directory besides Kynneir were also members of the Corporation. These included men like John Campbell and James Fowles or Foulis. The introduction to the directory's 1863 reprint notes that the Fowles family 'appear to have been long settled in London in connection with their countrymen' and were said to have helped William Paterson on his arrival. East India Company director John Drummond also stayed in James Foulis's house and had written that 'Foulis was a very useful friend to me when I settled here first'. More importantly, James Fowles, or Foulis as he is also called in Corporation and other records, was probably James Kynneir's 'loveing nephew Mr James Ffowles' and executor to whom he bequeathed the residue of his estate. Kynneir also left money to his nephew's wife Anne and their children. A 'James Foulis' was treasurer of the Corporation in 1674 and followed that (as was often the tradition) by becoming master in 1679. Two other members of the Foulis family, possibly a brother and his wife, were 'Mr John and Mrs Janet Foulis, Edin.' who were listed as Corporation donors of £20 between 1665 and 1714. James Foulis, James Donaldson, John Alexander and Archibald Wilson were Kynneir's executors. Foulis and Alexander were both merchant taylors as well as Scots Corporation governors. Kynneir's nephew Fowles/Foulis, his 'good friends' James Cunningham, James Donaldson and John Lorimere, as members of the 'Scotch Corporation', were also charged with seeing that the money left to the Corporation for the benefit of poor merchants was rightly distributed as specified. Kynneir also left money for these men to have 'rings to rotate in remembrance of me'.

By 1677 the Corporation also had 'Subservient Officers' to the master who were appointed by the assistants as 'Register, Treasurer, Stewards and Beadle'. There were also 'entered Members'; these were said to have numbered 338 by 1680. Some time after the second charter and possibly before 1681, the charity's hospital, as a place where Scots could actually stay, closed its doors. Later tradition explained that the popular hospital had subsequently become overcrowded and difficult to manage and that the Scotsmen and Scotswomen wanted to regain their independence. It was said that the charity's management had decided to help them in their own homes as 'out-patients' and 'out-pensioners'. James Kynneir's possible failing health (he made his will in 1681 and died in 1683) may also have meant a lack of strong leadership and vision at the top. Possibly also the Scots box donations had continued to be paid in as usual, even after 1665, as insurance against an uncertain future. Whatever had happened and whenever it had closed down, the workhouse activity had certainly failed by the beginning of the eighteenth century as advertisements asked people to subscribe if they wanted future assistance and relief in their own homes.

As the Scots Box club had been an innovation in the city, so too was the foundation of 'The Scottish Hospital of the Foundation of Charles II'. The

Scottish charity could claim to be one of the first hospitals and workhouses in London, outside the medieval hospitals and livery company charities, to run under an individual voluntary contribution scheme. With its stated interest in keeping poor Scots off the streets and preventing them from becoming 'burdensome' to their English neighbours and parishes, the Scottish Hospital was certainly the first hospital of a national character to help sick and poor immigrants – French, Italian and German hospitals were not founded until later in the early eighteenth and nineteenth centuries. The French Protestant hospital, founded in 1709, was closest in character to the Scottish Hospital. Other seventeenth-century charitable bodies and the early eighteenth-century London hospitals for the 'sick poor' had organised their management along the lines of the medieval hospitals. The Scottish Hospital had been similarly set up when it was granted its royal charter in 1665, and by 1673 it had established its tradition for acquiring property and building its own premises. Like the later hospitals, the Scottish Hospital had 'a hierarchy of subscribers who supervised the running of the hospital, appointed the staff, admitted the patients and shaped how the institution was financed'. Like them, it was small in size and required only 'a few hundred supporters' limiting its management 'to a group of active but wealthy men'. The Scottish Hospital was the forerunner of other hospitals founded later by 'wealthy or naturalised immigrants for the benefit of London's alien communities', and in a similar way to these later national institutions, it too provided relief and medicine to an immigrant community.

Other box clubs had been organised and other hospitals had been founded in London in the seventeenth century but they did not last long. The Scottish experience was therefore probably not unique, but it was innovative in an age and a city where survival was difficult. But the fact that it survived at all was testimony to its first royal charters, to James Kynneir and to its other merchant supporters, not to mention a few noble Scots benefactors and a charitable English duke. The first governors of the Royal Scottish Corporation crucially risked changing and rearranging its activities, probably some time before the beginning of the eighteenth century when the original workhouse idea proved unsuccessful. Like the many specialist hospitals which were to follow, and which were also to be founded by similarly small groups of men, the Scottish charity found management of their native poor difficult at times. Above all, the Scots discovered, as many of the smaller eighteenth-century London hospitals were also to discover, that its 'evolution was haphazard and erratic', and that it shared with these hospitals similar 'concerns over the high mortality and low morality of the poor'. The merchant Scots soon realised that founding the institution had been the easy part; responding to the needs of the orphaned, sick and elderly poor in an overflowing workhouse setting had proved more difficult than they had imagined, despite two royal charters.

PART II
1688–1815

CHAPTER 12

Scotland and London I

By the beginning of the eighteenth century Scotland's population numbered over a million and was mostly concentrated in the more fertile lowlands – the towns of Edinburgh and Glasgow and the communities around them, with a smattering of settlement in the Highlands and Islands. Out of this number, Edinburgh claimed around 30,000 inhabitants and Glasgow's population, though less, was increasing as eager migrants exploited its western focus towards Ireland and across the Atlantic. Many Highlanders were also starting to leave for the Lowlands.

But Scotland had to deal with an economic headache on an international scale as the country struggled with new trade tariffs imposed by its key export markets – the Scots having little influence to thwart them. In particular, the English Parliament had levied customs duties on the top Scottish exports of linen, cattle, salt and coal, exceedingly unwelcome when England was becoming Scotland's principal customer. William III began to see that James I's original idea for a proper union of the two countries needed reviving again, and it was not to be an easy task. The English were not happy at the prospect of Scots getting their hands on colonial trade, and the Scots Presbyterians shuddered at the thought of coming under an Anglican church ruled by bishops. William III's war with France and coastal harassment by England's Royal Navy further prevented Scottish exports to the English American colonies. Pressure was ripe in 1695 for the Darien adventure to take off, led by William Paterson, fresh from his pioneering work in founding the Bank of England.

The daring voyage aimed to establish a Scottish colony on the Isthmus of Panama with which Scots could legally trade. The scheme also needed the more adventurous Scots nobles and merchants to take enormous risks with their money. But by 1700 the project had dismally failed, partly due to the company's own mismanagement and the Scottish colonists' susceptibility to tropical disease; and partly because English and continental Europeans investors refused to lend their financial support after receiving petitions against the scheme from the London merchant community. Primary responsibility for failure in fact rested with William III himself who, unwilling to antagonise Spain with a colonial venture that would upset that country's imperial interests in the Americas, had been especially concerned not to risk the Spanish succession coming under the control of his arch-rival Louis XIV of France. Under instructions from William, English colonial governors in the Caribbean had even refused to send much-needed provisions, and about 2,000 Scots men, women and children lost their lives as a result of the venture. Such huge personal investment by the Scots was wiped out at a generally awful time in Scotland of bad harvests and poor rents. Perhaps between one-quarter (or one-sixth) of Scotland's liquid capital had been lost – around £153,000 sterling.

The entrepreneurial Scots were desperate to get their money back and the disaster finally gave William the push he needed for a union of parliaments. His successor, Queen Anne, was to see this happen in 1707, but it was far from a done deal at her accession in 1703. The Alien Act of 1705, which aimed to make aliens of all Scots not living in England and promised to halt major Scottish exports to England, eventually brought the Scots to negotiating point. In both Scotland and London there was much disagreement and discussion, but the Articles of Union were eventually signed and sealed by all commissioners on 22 July 1706 and the Union formally declared nearly a year later on 1 May 1707.

Beyond the union of parliaments and a preservation of their religion, laws and education, the Scots had won compensation for their Darien losses and, importantly, the right to trade with the English colonies in America and the East Indies. Once the 1715 Jacobite rising was calmed, most Scots from the 1720s onwards enjoyed a more peaceful existence and an expansion of trade, especially after the final defeat of the Jacobites at Culloden in 1746. Scotland sold nearly 70 percent of the country's linen exports to England and her colonies by the 1760s. The rise in the urban population that fuelled emigration to Ireland and across the Atlantic meant there was also a greater move south to London and, for the more ambitious, even further away – to Britain's growing army, navy and Eastern empire. Statistics show individual emigration to have reached between 78,000 and 127,000 by the later seventeenth century, and the following century saw it increasing further as opportunities arose to make a Scottish mark outside Great Britain itself, and away from English control – some Scots making fortunes in the linen export trade and, especially in Glasgow, in American tobacco.

Many Scots also became enthusiastic and patriotic British subjects, supportive of 'Great Britain' in general as the Scotsman James Thomson wrote 'Rule, Britannia', in 1740. Anglophile Scots increasingly educated their children in England and some changed their Scottish accents to a more understandable English.[1] Some Scots went even further and began to reject the Gaelic-Irish heritage of Scotland and show closer links with the south; Sir John Clerk of

---

[1] Samuel Johnson, writing up an account of his trip to the Western Isles in 1773, found that 'in splendid companies Scotch is not much heard, except now and then from an old lady'.

Penicuik even went so far as to argue that the early Scots had spoken 'Saxon'. The majority of the poorer Scottish people, on the other hand, especially in the lowland areas, still held on to their heroes like William Wallace and Robert the Bruce and the ideals of the Covenanters. The poor in Scotland had suffered badly and many had died during the famines of the 1690s; the eighteenth century was to see slow developments for a people who still worked hard for low wages compared to their English cousins. Agriculture was gradually changing as ways were sought to supply the growing cities; roads and canals were constructed to make it easier to distribute both goods and people. Such 'Improvement' was also social. Many agricultural workers, especially cottars, had also been persuaded to move off the land by the beguiling attractions of Scotland's cities, colonial emigration or London.

Before 1707, London was the place to be for eighteenth-century Scots who wanted to seek their fortunes if they did not head west to America (only a handful had joined the East India Company's ranks before the union). These Scots would have seen how easily the city's quays handled around 80 percent of England's imports, 69 percent of its exports and 86 percent of re-exported goods. Patrick Colquhoun (a Scot and an economist) showed that by the end of the century, in 1796, everything came to London – from the East Indies, the West Indies and the Baltic. The development of this world trade meant that the capital needed 'Agents, Factors, Brokers, Insurers, Bankers, Negotiators, Discounters, Subscribers, Contractors, Remitters, Ticket-Mongers, Stock-Jobbers and a great Variety of Dealers in Money'. These last helped to develop London into a financial centre, initially meeting in coffee houses around the old Royal Exchange until the establishment of the Bank of England in 1694. In 1672 Charles II had stopped the Exchequer from recovering his royal debts and had ruined many goldsmiths and bankers in the process. To stop such a thing happening again, an entrepreneurial Scot, William Paterson, had put forward a grand design in 1691 for the proper establishment of a national debt in the form of a national bank; his scheme was accepted and the first subscribers became members of the company of the Bank of England in 1694. Paterson became one of its first directors (but a falling out with others left him free to pursue his Darien ambitions a year later).

Towns in Scotland by 1707 contained about nine percent of the country's total inhabitants; on the other hand, London alone contained about ten percent of England's population, continuing to bring politics and economics together as the court and port continued to grow. By the time of Queen Anne's accession, the City of London's administration was again also emerging as a powerful administrative force. Under the Georges, although it became more independent, the city's financial relations with parliament were severely tested as the South Sea Company collapsed in 1720, and its citizens petitioned angrily over the ministers and directors who had cashed in on the flotation, not to mention the bribery and corruption that had taken place on such a fantastic scale. They had witnessed an unbelievable time – 'The mad spirit of speculation which seized all classes alike, the foolish unreasoning belief in the possibility of realising fabulous wealth, the floating of innumerable companies, many of which were of a most absurd character, the panic which followed inevitably on the inflation of prices'.

Coffee houses remained as essential to business as socialising. John Macky, who had also written of the Scottish Hospital in Blackfriars in 1723, wrote about the nearby coffee houses that he also visited:

> If you would know our manner of Living, it is thus … About Twelve the *Beau-Monde* assembles in several Chocolate and Coffee Houses: the best of which are the *Cocoa-Tree* and *White's* Chocolate-Houses, *St James's*, the *Smyrna* and the *British* Coffee-Houses; and all these so near one another, that in less than an hour you see the company of them all. We are carried to these Places in Chairs (or Sedans) which are here very cheap, a Guinea a Week, or a Shilling *per* Hour, and your Chairmen serve you for Porters to run on errands as your *Gondoliers* do at *Venice*.
>
> If it be fine Weather, we take a Turn in the Park till two, when we go to dinner; and if it be dirty, you are entertain'd at *Picket* or *Basset* at *White's*, or you may talk Politicks at the *Smyrna* or *St James's*.

By 1714 there were about 500 such places in London. Some took on distinctive characters. Merchants used those near the Royal Exchange; the Cocoa Tree was frequented by Tories; St James's was for Whigs; clergymen went to Child's in St Paul's Churchyard; and marine insurers were to be found at Lloyds in Lombard Street. Most coffee houses, though frequented by men, were usually run and owned by women, and coffee was also a richer man's drink, costing about £1 a 'dish'. Scots had developed their own national coffee and chocolate houses in the city, where they could also get 'an ordinary or a fixed price meal' of Scottish cuisine. Not necessarily clean and certainly very smoky, coffee houses also later became famous clubs and Brook's in St James's after it opened in 1764 'became the greatest gambling den of all' – the then Earl of Lauderdale remembering £70,000 being lost in a single night. The earlier merchants and later governors of the Corporation would have found that these club and society gatherings 'consolidated friendships, supported professional ambitions, and became important patronage sources'. The Scots also had their own London taverns and dining circles, no doubt carrying on the tradition we have already seen at an earlier Lord Lauderdale's seventeenth-century dinners. But emulating the tradition of the Scot who wanted to fit in, James Boswell was keen to avoid most of the capital's Scots at dinner, declaring that the 'Scotch who come up to London are like galley-slaves chained together. They only coast it and never get into the main ocean ...; when a Scotsman asks you to dine with him here, instead of letting you see English company, he asks at the same time a number of the very people whom you see at home'.

New bridges were built over the Thames at Westminster in 1750 and Blackfriars in 1769, giving easy access to Southwark and the south bank of the river. As was happening only to a certain extent in Scotland, London's masses vastly increased the demand for foodstuffs from the countryside, and the spread of Georgian fashion during the century increased city sales of provincial manu-facturers. New plate-glass windows encouraged shopping and allowed people to browse with pleasure before they bought. One Scottish novelist resident in the eighteenth-century capital was Tobias Smollett. His character, Matt Bramble, up from the country for the first time, described London's bustle:

> All is tumult and hurry ... The foot passengers run along as if they were pursued by bailiffs. The porters and chairmen trot with the burthens. People, who keep their own equipages, drive through the streets at full speed. Even citizens, physicians, and apothecaries, glide in the chariots like lightning. The hackney-coachmen make their horses smoke, and the pavement shakes under them; and I have actually seen a waggon pass through Piccadilly at the hand-gallop. In a word, the whole nation seems to be running out of their wits.

The mail service set up by James I between London and Scotland had also been improved and expanded by the end of the seventeenth century. Letters and packets by the 1680s were being despatched to Scotland on Tuesdays, Thursdays and Saturdays and were returned to London from there every Monday, Wednesday and Friday (in comparison, the Welsh mail went out only on a Tuesday and came back on a Monday and Friday). The mail coaches themselves covered 120 miles every twenty-four hours and the cost of a letter was threepence a sheet.[2] Delivery of goods and people to and from places further away had already got easier with coastal shipping and scheduled stage coaches that could make almost fifty miles in a day. Alternatively, one could always ride post and it could also be tried both ways. It had taken Sir John Clerk of Penicuik two weeks to travel painfully back from Edinburgh to London in 1708 by coach, a few days after having broken his collar bone on the way up when his post-horse fell with him in the ice and snow as he neared Alnwick in Northumberland. By 1750 it took three days to get from London to Manchester by stage coach with about another three on to Edinburgh.

The eighteenth-century houses of London's gentry were now numbered rather than signed, the West End's Quality Street was developing and fashion-able addresses were now an important asset. Scientists and surgeons – including

---

[2] By the end of 1830 it may have become more expensive, as the Reverend Dr William Manuel of Morningside asked if there was a way to avoid paying postage on his communications with London concerning the setting up of the Edinburgh branch of the Scottish Hospital.

the Scottish anatomist John Hunter – moved into addresses around Soho and Leicester Square. Artists and writers like Sir Joshua Reynolds and William Hogarth also lived in the area, and in the 1760s Boswell lived in Downing Street and later chose to lodge in Bond Street. He thought a 'genteel lodging in a good part of the town is absolutely necessary ...' and that 'seeking a lodging was like seeking a wife. Sometimes I aimed at one or two guineas a week, like a rich lady of quality. Sometimes at one guinea, like a knight's daughter, and at last fixed on £22 a year, like the daughter of a good gentleman of moderate fortune'. The city area around Holborn, Hoxton and Hackney was inhabited by a couple of hundred thousand 'solid' citizens, and around 1707 a successful master crafts-man might own property worth several thousand pounds and wealthier manu-facturers might be worth a few thousand more. The professions – lawyers, doctors and tutors – were to grow ever richer during the eighteenth century and, with them, the Scottish professionals in London.

The labouring masses were now many and varied – being street sellers of goods and services, porters, carmen, sedan chairmen, grooms, coalmen, scaven-gers, drovers, builders, not to mention the river watermen and lightermen. Domestic services became the great employer of female labour. Away from the good addresses, the East End was growing ever more populous and over-crowded, housing over 90,000 people at the beginning of the eighteenth century. Craftsmen, especially Huguenot, Scots and other (mainly silk) weavers, occupied Spitalfields, Shoreditch, Hackney and Bethnal Green into the 1760s before they lost out to the takeover of their industry by the English Midlands. Many Scots found work as sailors or boatyard workers as these occupations came to dominate the eastern riverfront areas, especially at the East India Company's Blackwall Yard and the Royal Navy's new docks. A community of Scottish shipwrights had settled on the Isle of Dogs working for the Napiers' iron shipbuilding yard and there building their own Presbyterian church.[3]

Young people especially came to seek employment and around 8,000 a year probably came to seek their fortune in the first years of the 1700s. Shops and offices liked boys from the North of England and Scotland because of their better education. Servants from outside London were also especially valued, being thought more naïve and therefore more trustworthy. Mortality rates had grown as the migrant population had increased, fuelling further epidemics, especially after 1670, and the increased death rates in turn boosted the need for more immigrant workers. It was thought in 1757 that probably 'two-thirds of the grown persons at any time in London come from distant parts'; in fact, many who did well were thought not to originally have come from London. 'London will not feel any want of recruits,' a customs commissioner could say in 1751 and, with its higher wages, the city certainly became a 'magnet for Scots'. But it is

---

[3] Now an arts centre.

hard to find many of the Scots themselves. There was no serious record of the numbers and nationalities of these immigrant workers, though a Dr Bland kept a record of cases at the Westminster Dispensary from 1774 to 1781. Out of a total 3,236 married people he saw during these years, he calculated that 209 or one in fifteen were born in Scotland. He further broke this Scottish number down into 135 men and 74 women.

CHAPTER 13

Anglo-Scottish Attitudes

S ocial advancement and commercial opportunities had awaited Scots coming south to London since 1707. Scottish peers increasingly left their estates and disappeared south of the border, especially during the winter; so much so that Erskine of Grange complained in 1733 that 'The country now, and for some years, has lookt on it self as deserted, not only by courtiers but by the principall of its nobility and gentry'. Many Scots had actually settled in London and other parts of England by the middle of the eighteenth century. Archibald Campbell, later the third Duke of Argyll and the leading political manager in a post-union Scotland, was in fact born in Surrey and went to Eton. For other Scots, it was harder to get on in London's politics and administration until after the 1760s, unless you were a city merchant with family trade connections. The attractions of empire then beckoned and those of the East India Company in particular. But first, and for getting much-needed patronage and references, as Dr Johnson said, 'The noblest prospect which a Scotchman ever sees, is the high road that leads him to England!'

Some form of anti-Scottish feeling in London amongst the English politicians and merchants had always been in the background from 1603 to 1707 and was to resurface in the later eighteenth century. Queen Anne's English ministry and the Scottish Court Party were able to bring about what other kings and their supporters had unsuccessfully tried to do, and relations, though difficult during the prolonged negotiations on both sides of the border, reached new heights of friendliness once they achieved their 1707 goal. Sir John Clerk of Penicuik thought 'it wou'd be next to madness to imagine that the Scots cou'd set up a seperat King, or force any King on England but the persone already chosen by the nation'. The Scots had realised that there was money as well as influence to be gained in London as compensation. They were also well received by the city. When the Duke of Queensberry arrived in London, Sir John Clerk of Penicuik, riding with him, recalled that at Barnet the duke 'was met by the Ministry of England and most of the nobility then attending the two Houses of Parliament. Their retinue consisted of 46 coaches and above 1,000 Horsemen'. About six of the new Scots Commons members were then in London and sat with Clerk at the ceremony of celebration in St Paul's Cathedral. Three or four hundred coaches had processed through Westminster and the City of London to the cathedral and back:

> On this occasion I observed a real joy and satisfaction in the Citizens of London, for they were terribly apprehensive of confusions from Scotland in case the Union had not taken place. That whole day was spent in feastings, ringing of Bells, and illuminations, and I have reasone to believe that at no time Scotsmen were more acceptable to the English than on that day.

The Jacobite threat soon returned as English attempts to tax the Scots proved increasingly unpopular. Taxes on the crucial commodities of salt and malt were introduced periodically from 1711 and, as a result, nearly all Scots north and south of the border wanted to revoke the treaty of union. Besides the Duke of Hamilton, another wavering Scots noble and Corporation supporter, who also led the Jacobite cause (and to support the Scots Corporation with £20), was the Earl of Mar, also known as 'bobbing John'. Once he had fallen out of favour with George I, Mar raised 10,000 troops in 1715 to lead the next challenge. His generalship was inept and he was unable to defeat the 4,000 soldiers in the opposing army, as a result of what has been described as a 'fatal combination of caution, timidity and ambiguity' in his character. It was to take another unsuccessful Jacobite rebellion in 1719 before Scotland came under the peaceful leadership of the Earl of Islay, later the third Duke of Argyll. Steady relations with Sir Robert Walpole brought some stability to Scotland from the 1720s until Argyll's death in 1761, despite the final Jacobite rising of 1745–6. The years following 1746 saw a major clampdown on Jacobitism by the English, by contrast with their leniency towards the rebels of the previous risings, and there was probably little support for the cause among the mainly Protestant London Scots and their Presbyterian ministers. In fact, it is likely that the Stuart defeat at Culloden would have been celebrated among Scots in the City of London much as it was in Presbyterian Scotland. There, the *Glasgow Journal* recorded that the city rang out with 'the greatest rejoicings that have been known'.

Once more, the London Scots of the 1760s began to experience increasingly anti-Scottish sentiments from fellow Londoners who were fervent English nationalists. The Scottish Hospital's inmates and management would have been eye witnesses to the riots of the 1760s as some of the violent action took place around their buildings in Blackfriars. There was also increasing London envy of recent Scots public positions and prosperity in the capital as well as in the empire. Eight Scottish MPs had held offices of state in the British adminis-tration between 1745 and 1753, but twenty-eight had reached the top spots in the short period between 1761 and 1767.

Dr Johnson's future biographer, James Boswell, had also heard of the famously anti-Scottish feelings of the great man himself, and was much aware of them in 1763 on first meeting him with Thomas Davies, an actor and bookseller:

> Mr Davies mentioned my name, and respectfully introduced me to him. I was much agitated; and recollecting his prejudice against the Scotch, of which I had heard much, I said to Davies, 'Don't tell where I come from.' – 'From Scotland,' cried Davies roguishly. 'Mr. Johnson,' said I, 'I do indeed come from Scotland, but I cannot help it.' I am willing to flatter myself that I meant this as light pleasantry to soothe and conciliate him, and not as a humiliating abasement at the expense of my country … But … with … quickness of wit … he seized the expression … and retorted, 'That, Sir, I find, is what a very great many of your countrymen cannot help.'

Boswell later wrote that, 'If he [Dr Johnson] was particularly prejudiced against the Scots, it was because they were more in his way; because he thought their success in England rather exceeded the due proportion of their real merit; and because he could not but see in them that nationality, which I believe, no liberal minded Scotchman will deny'. Nevertheless, Johnson much enjoyed a later trip with Boswell to the Hebrides, and as his companion said, 'returned from it in great humour, his prejudices much lessened'. Putting him on the coach back to England, Boswell remembered how Johnson had often said that 'the time he spent in this tour was the pleasantest part of his life …'

English prejudice against the Scots meant that both the Scottish churches in London and the Royal Scottish Corporation saw it as their duty 'to promote a better understanding on both sides'. The 'Rage against the Scots' in the 1760s may have caused the London-Scottish community to become more aware of the Scots in London and had perhaps encouraged a sense of Scottishness.[1] This is no doubt what led many of them to begin and then to continue subscribing to the cause of the Royal Scottish Corporation in the capital. On another level, other movements like the Enlightenment and key Scottish writers, like Adam Smith and David Hume, encouraged them to donate and otherwise to act in the national charity's interest.

---

[1] Sometimes the boot could be on the other foot, and some Scots in 1796–97 were certainly, like the English, fervently anti-French when invasion threatened. A Scot and London alderman George Macaulay recorded in his London 'war' diary for 1797 that 'there is nothing so atrocious and diabolical of which a Frenchman in my opinion, is not capable, and therefore, though many unfortunate and worthy people may suffer, yet if I had the rule of the Roost, not one single French person should be permitted to remain in this Country'.

CHAPTER 14

Poverty and Charity, Workhouses
and Hospitals

The livery companies, which had begun to decay with the decline of specific trades, slowly started to turn into 'the chummy dining-clubs with charitable functions familiar today'. They had found it increasingly hard to keep up with the capitalist progress of individual merchants and professional men around them. Finding themselves often unsupported by legal process, many abandoned the quality-control enforcement that had previously occupied them and also found that they now had to give up enforcing the right to search, fearing prosecution for trespass; instead they focused on 'property management, charity and junketings'. Even so, company membership still remained a popular means for townsmen to affirm their social identities and exploit networking opportunities.

The Scots in London still entered the livery companies but also found that they had new places to go as the guilds declined. Freemasonry had begun to grow in popularity once the Grand Lodge of England was established in 1717, and formalised after 1722. Many London meetings gave professional London Scots additional trade contacts and access to insurance credit in hard times. Friendly societies proliferated for the lower classes. Colquhoun estimated in 1797 that there were around 1,600 friendly societies in or near London, of which 800 had registered themselves under the 1793 Friendly Society Act. These were mostly for 'mechanics and labouring people' who distributed sick and burial grants to around 80,000 people paying on average 20 shillings a year. Many other clubs and societies sprang up catering for all kinds of hobbies, sports and interests: music, arts, debating or just general self improvement. Other important social and charitable networking in London occurred in church or chapel settings. Even some Presbyterians were prepared to go to the established church as a means to get on if the parish was in a popular location for attracting like-minded people. London's parishes had grown stronger as the traditional wards had weakened and had increasingly picked up the responsibility for law and order, as well as for the care of the orphaned, aged, sick and unemployed.

Despite such seeming support, doctors diagnosed London as a hotbed of disease. In his influential *The English Malady* of 1733, the Scottish physician George Cheyne, and Scots Corporation donor of five guineas by 1730, credited the capital with being 'the greatest, most capacious, most close, and populous city of the *Globe*'; and for those very reasons, considered it quite the most difficult place in which to survive:

> The infinite Number of *Fires, Sulphurous and Bituminous*, the vast expense of Tallow and foetid Oil in Candles and Lamps, under and above the Ground, the clouds of Stinking Breathes and Perspirations, not to mention the ordure of so many diseas'd, both intelligent and unintelligent animals, the crouded *Churches, Church Yards* and *Burying Places*, with the putrifying *Bodies*, the *Sinks, Butchers Houses, Stables, Dunghills* etc. and the necessary Stagnation, Fermentation, and mixture of Variety of all Kinds of Atoms, and more than sufficient to putrefy, poison and infect the Air for Twenty Miles around it, and which in Time must alter, weaken and destroy the healthiest of Constitutions.

To such critics London was 'iniquity itself' and a place that nourished vice, crime and riot. Samuel Johnson's poem *London* depicted it in words:

> For who would leave, unbrib'd *Hibernia*'s Land,
> Or change the Rocks of *Scotland* for the *Strand*? …
> Here Malice, Rapine, Accident, conspire,
> And now a Rabble rages, now a Fire;
> Their Ambush here relentless Ruffians lay …

Wealthier Londoners made sure they were 'well-armed' to go out to dine. In May 1798 Scottish alderman, George Macaulay, was robbed by footpads at the bottom of Barnet Hill. Of the three thieves who accosted him, he wrote:

> One held the Horses and one came to the door on each side of the chaise. Took £46 Bank [notes] and money, and Mrs M's dressing Box worth £50. It is a very awkward situation for a man to be in, placed in a confined situation, with pistols at your Breast in the trembling hands of such Rascals. Mrs M was a good deal alarmed when the danger was over, but behaved very well at the moment.

The city's paupers were often blamed for the increase in the capital's crime rate. In the 1730s and 1740s gin houses were cheap places in which to get drunk. And much was drunk; on average it has been estimated that two pints a week were drunk for every man, woman and child in London in the 1740s. Gin, reported the Westminster justices, 'is the principle cause of the increase of the poor and of all the vice and debauchery among the inferior sort of people, as of the felonies and other disorders committed in this town.' Gin was actually sold in workhouses, prisons, brothels and barbers' shops; and only legislation and price rises arrested the vice by the middle of the century. There was no metropolitan policing to control crime but only parish constables and beadles to keep watch. Magistrates Henry and John Fielding soon realised that most of those coming before them were 'guilty of no crime but poverty'.

As the eighteenth-century poor became a growing problem, parishes were allowed to set up workhouses by an act of 1722. Before Queen Anne's reign there had been little attempt to sort and separate the sick poor from those who were healthy. It had not been done because it was not thought easy to do, and 'the unemployed, the unemployable and the vagrants were ignorant and often verminous, usually undernourished and sometimes genuinely sick. Disease must often have been overlooked in the overall wretchedness of poverty'. The theory was that these new workhouses would be used to put the able-bodied to work or to train them for a trade as earlier seventeenth-century treatises had long proposed. Although the Scottish Hospital had closed around twenty years earlier, one of its aims had also been to train the able-bodied poor and their children in useful skills. In practice, as the Scots had already found, the new workhouses became 'doss houses' for the old, the sick and single-parent families. They were frequently found to be a disgrace and workhouse mortality, especially infant mortality, was a terrible scandal. A parliamentary inquiry of 1767 showed that only seven in a hundred children under a year, survived to reach their third or fourth birthday in such places.

The city also saw the development of five new London hospitals founded through private philanthropy; their foundations, like that of the Scottish Hospital, stemmed from motives both religious and humanitarian, as well as to assuage a sense of guilt. The Westminster General Infirmary in James Street was established in 1719 for the relief of the sick and needy. Guy's Hospital in Southwark was established a few years later in 1725 with accommodation for 400 patients by Thomas Guy. He was a Lombard Street bookseller who had made his fortune from printing Bibles and from astute investment in South Sea Company stock, and had founded the hospital to offset feelings of guilt. St George's Hospital at Hyde Park Corner was opened in 1733; the London Hospital, Whitechapel in 1752; and the Middlesex, for the sick and lame of Soho, in 1745. More hospitals were set up for the orphaned, sick, needy and otherwise incapacitated. Other charitable institutions also wanted to do more than just provide alms or a place to stay; churches set up charity schools and the Marine Society, established in 1756 in Bishopsgate, trained poor boys to be sailors. In Scotland doctors had been pressing for the establishment of hospitals by the 1720s, especially John Monro and his son Alexander. The Royal College of Physicians in Edinburgh had arranged that two of their number should visit the sick poor in 1682. An appeal for a city infirmary got under way from 1725 and the Little Hospital was established in 1729. Glasgow's infirmary hospital opened in 1733 and one was opened at Aberdeen in 1742. Many Scots doctors went to London, although until as late as 1858 Scots physicians were not legally allowed to practise in England and were regarded as 'illegitimate importees from the Scottish schools'.

Samuel Johnson in 1758 was especially worried about the future of the voluntary Hospitals 'because they subsisted not on funded capital but on gifts bestowed at pleasure'. To add to their investments many charities started to hold festivals, balls and bazaars to raise money. The Scottish Hospital held a concert in 1753 and 'produced £16'. Fundraising Corporation balls were held every year from 1754 until 1762, raising a total of £438 for the period. Like the Scottish Hospital's list of benefactors from 1714, voluntary hospitals and other London charities gave the rich the possibility of a privileged position that was published for all to see. Poverty was still regarded as a sin rather than a misfortune and disease was still seen as God's punishment for past misdeeds; man was ordained to be rich or poor and the idle poor, as always, received no pity. The sturdy beggar was also a continuing problem, but by this time was classed as the 'incorrigible rogue'.[1] By 1788 London had all kinds of charitable organisations but the plight of poorer Londoners was not necessarily any easier. These charities were mainly uncontrolled, and it was up to the sick to work out for themselves where best they might be treated. A governor with a reputation for sympathy had to be found, called on and his servants trusted not to turn away whoever called at his door.

---

[1] The Royal Scottish Corporation's secretaries later called such people 'imposters' in 1911 and 'scroungers' in 1938.

CHAPTER 15

Masters and Presidents

A variety of social crises and developments since the beginning of the seventeenth century had brought a number of changes in the types of people coming forward to claim relief from the Royal Scottish Corporation. The Corporation's most pressing concerns had always been the elderly and the sick, as well as the burial of those who had died. An apothecary named John Allan was on the Scottish Hospital's earliest list of benefactors (1665–1714) and he may have helped out with some cases. But an order of the 'Scots Corporation' in 1688 suggests that the charity did not have the right kind of doctor at this time since it asked that 'the Treasurer and Mr Bain take J. Garland to a Physician, and "agree" for curing his eyes, but no cure no money to be "payed"'. Even at this early date the Scots charity was also eager to protect its contributions.

By 1689 the charity included 'almost all Scotishmen that frequent London', according to the Reverend Robert Kirk, the minister of Aberfoyle and printer of the Gaelic Bible, who wrote a diary during his visit to London that year. Kirk also adds that 'in the city there are about 30 hospital corporations acquired by the bounty of pious persons for the use of poor scholars and sick persons … Amongst others in Blackfryers is the Scotish Hall … for maintaineing any poor Scotishmen recommended by the minister or churchwardens of the parish he lives in …', and he records that 250 members paid a penny a week. Kirk had also been fed the current publicity, and he adds that there was a serious purpose behind the charity which aimed to lift the poor Scotsmen out of the gutter: 'that he be troublesome to no Englishman in disparagement of his own nation'. On the closure of the workhouse and hospital building at the end of the seventeenth century the charity had concentrated on providing aid for the Scots in their own homes – if they subscribed again monthly – and some were also given passages home. In 1696, the year of the Darien expedition, the Corporation was able to organise the signing of the 'Association Oath', an oath of allegiance to King William III after an attempt had been made on his life. Over three hundred members of the Royal Scottish Corporation signed the document. The surviving parchment roll is sewn together in two parts – the officials of the Corporation (the master, eight governors and 33 assistants) have signed the top half of the list, and the names of the subscribing members occupy the rest of the roll. A few of the artificers were unable to sign and they marked their position in the list with a cross and had their names written alongside. Those of the charity's management who signed included Walter Stewart, the master; the lords Monro and Robertson; James Cunningham, Alexander Lorimer, David Nairne, William Murray, Evan Mackpherson, James Chiesly, Frances Grierson, Thomas and Horatio Coutts, and James Trumble. Some of these Scots merchants, like Chiesly and Nairne, were also closely involved in the organisation of William Paterson's Darien scheme, visiting his house in London's Denmark Street. David Nairne was a London banker for Scottish nobles and James Chiesly, another banker, had carried the scheme's papers to Edinburgh in 1695, seeking Scottish support.

The 1707 union brought more Scots to the English capital, and those sub-scribing to the charity as a means of mutual aid and future insurance were classed by the 'Scottish Hospital' as 'seamen, artificers, mechanics, and labourers ... who, as soon as they are qualified for any occupation, daily resort hither in great numbers to seek employment'. The Scots usually came

> soon after learning their respective Callings; and, as they fix here for their Lives, many of them marry, and honestly bring up a numerous Offspring to be Useful members of the Community. Some few of them, 'tis true, become reputable and substantial Masters and Housekeepers; but the Bulk of them will, in the Course of Things, ever remain Servants and Inmates all their Lives.

They had, it said, worked hard and 'necessarily continuing journeymen and inmates for life, although by their labour and industry, and early and prolific marriages, they contribute to the general stock, they are, for want of legal settlements here, considered as aliens, and excluded from the benefit of any parochial relief'. They had no means to find their way home either. The Scots were again being encouraged to think of their future, and to ensure their personal security and their own independence away from a life of abject poverty.

The Royal Scottish Corporation had kept records (as the box club) since 1620, but by 1712 'A Committee reported that they had seen all the books of the Corporation, and found them so intricate and perplext, that they judged them extremely hard if at all possible to be understood'. In 1723 the Corporation's income included quarterly collections and what was called 'Entry Money'; together these amounted to over £45, while expenses this year were 'Funerals, 30s; Coffins, 20s.' The workhouse and tenement almshouses closed at the end of the seventeenth century and had been already let out by 1723 when John Macky, who had journeyed through North and South Britain, wrote up the notes of his travels. Macky mentions 'the Scottish Nation having a Hall in Blackfryars, for relieving their indigent Countrymen, and providing them with necessary sums for Carrying them into their own country'. Eighteenth-century promotional accounts of the Corporation reminded their readers of this early change and recalled how the charity had found the management of the first workhouse difficult as more and more of the poorer sort of Scots had arrived in London and their buildings had become overcrowded. Many of these poor Scots had also 'preferred' being helped in their own homes and parishes, feeling the need to be closer to families and friends or just more independent: 'experience soon proved that confinement to a charity workhouse was altogether uncongenial to the instincts and habits of the Scottish poor'. An account of the Corporation of 1738 records that although 'the original Purpose of the worthy Promoters of this Corporation [was] to lodge their Poor (both old and young) all together, after the usual manner of Hospitals, or Alms-Houses', it had been shown 'long-since' by 'Experience'

> that they have been much better advised in following the present Method; For besides the various Difficulties of executing that complicated Design, in the very Nature of it, an Hospital is by no means proper for the Reception of Men with their Wives and Children, of which the Scots Poor chiefly consist ... On the contrary, by the excellent Plan, from the Beginning, pursued by this Corporation, all the useful and charitable Ends of an Hospital are more frugally attained, and with infinitely greater Benefit to the Publick. For by supporting their Poor and Sick at their own Habitations, they are not only enabled to extend their Charity to a larger numbers and Variety of Objects, but, which is of the greatest Consequence to the Publick, hereby many of them are restored to Health and Ability, to be again useful in their respective Callings, and such alone are supported in Idleness as are totally disabled from any kind of Labour, at the same Time that they are destitute.

The Corporation had made substantial changes and reached a new point of departure, not to mention another national innovation: 'The whole Oeconomy then of the Corporation, at their Hall, may not improperly be termed, An Hospital of Out-Patients and Out-Pensioners'. The poor, no longer kept in the hospital 'for life' and destined to 'become so many useless drones', were now also separated into categories of aid:

I.   Of such Poor, as either through Age, or incurable Distempers are quite disabled from earning any Part of their Livings; to whom, for that Reason, the Corporation allows a weekly Support till Death.

II. The Casual Poor, or such as, by Sickness, or other casual Misfortune, are, for a time, rendered incapable of helping themselves and Families; and These likewise have a weekly Allowance, till restored to Health and Ability ...

III. A third Sort are such who, though still able (as well as willing) to earn somewhat for their Livings, are nevertheless (by their growing into Years, large Families, and accidental Losses) frequently compelled to petition for occasional Relief: of which they have numerous Instances every Court Day at their Hall.

IV. The Corporation also frequently assists such of their Poor with Money for their Journey, as have Relations in their own Country, who may be willing to keep them.

Furthermore, the English parishes were still being saved from paying for Scots pauper burials as well as Scottish street beggars: 'Lastly they decently bury all the Poor at the Expence of the Charity; which is a considerable Saving to many Parishes in London and Westminster, and is, so far, a Demonstration of the publick Utility of this Corporation'. Medical men were in attendance too: 'the Sick are carefully attended by the Corporation's Physician, Surgeon and Apothecary, and duly supplied with Medicines at the publick Expence'.

The tradition of visiting the poor Scots in their own homes had also begun. This activity was even then considered onerous, and two of the 33 assistants under 'the troublesome Office of Visitors' took it 'charitably' in turns 'from Time to Time' to 'be duly acquainted with the true Condition of their Sick and Poor'. The visitor function was to be increasingly necessary in order 'To Prevent the Idle and Extravagant from reaping any Benefit from an Institution intended solely for the Sober and Industrious ...' These visitors promoted the charity and collected subscriptions as the Corporation began 'to engage Men, by the strong Motive of Interest, to contribute somewhat to the Necessities of others ...' and as insurance for themselves. By 1738 it was described as 'a standing Rule, that no Person can be entitled to this Charity, who did not whilst in youth and Ability, enter himself a Member of this Corporation', and

> subject also to the following Qualifications and Conditions, viz. 1. That he be known to some of the Governors or Assistants to be a sober and industrious Person. 2. That he have some lawful and regular Trade or Occupation. And 3. That he pay down a small Sum for Entrance-Money, and contribute One Shilling Quarterly during Life, or Ability.

The original Scots Box meetings had most probably also been a drinking club hosted by publicans of Covent Garden taverns, and in those days 'the members dined together quarterly, paying 5s. each, any overplus to go to the Charity'. Robert Kirk, while on his visit to London in 1689, may have witnessed James Kynneir's silver cup being used in celebration, when he recorded in his diary that 'This Mr Kennyer appointed that still on St James Day the whole congregation should take a bowl of wine and drink in remembrance of the Scotish man and Welch woman who was Mr K Wife, which they yearly and cheerfully perform'.

St Andrew rather than St James had been the saint most honoured by Scots in London since medieval times. By the end of the seventeenth century the most important festivity for the Royal Scottish Corporation was its annual St Andrew's Day dinner. The meeting of the 33 assistants had been assigned to St Andrew's Day in the 1676 charter, possibly as a result of a traditional meeting. In 1692 'the Master paid 40s., Governors 31s., Assistants 31s., towards the Feast on St Andrews Day to the Scottish Nobility'. Like the Scottish box club members, these early governors and assistants obviously paid their way at the annual festivals when they were held at the 'Scottish Hospital' in Blackfriars to raise money from richer Scots in London. By 1738 'the Governors and Assistants (many of whom are Gentlemen of Distinction and all of them Persons of Fortune and Character) do cheerfully contribute more quarterly than other Members', and were also described as being 'at the sole Charge of an annual publick Dinner at the Hall, on St Andrew's Day, for the Entertainment and Encouragement of Benefactors, &c.' The hall was also used for general (annual), quarterly and other special courts. In 1686, governors and assistants had been fined a shilling 'for non-attendance at Courts', and by 1735 these fines had risen to 'Governors 2s. 6d., Assistants 1s. 6d.' and the money collected was for a good time rather than for charity, being 'applied in aid of Festivals'.[1] Money was also gladly given by the Corporation's officers on appointment or otherwise: 'All is put to no Expence on account of any of the Committees, or other Meetings, for the Service of the Corporation. Moreover, every Assistant makes a handsome Donation at his Admission, and every Master a much larger one at the Conclusion of his office'. Nevertheless, the Corporation found itself heavily dependent on all kinds of benefactors to make up the 'Great Deficiency of their Funds':

> it is truly melancholy to be obliged to add, That the whole Revenue of the Corporation, as well as from the Rents of their Houses &c. as from their quarterly Contributions, does hardly, one Year with another, exceed two fifth Parts of the annual Charge for the urgent Necessities of their Poor. Nevertheless, by the good Providence of God they have hitherto been enabled, when under the greatest Difficulties, to supply the other three fifths, merely by casual Benefactions from well disposed Persons ...

By the late 1760s, nearly a hundred years since the first royal charter, the Corporation was beginning a decline that was to last for nearly twenty years. With the benefit of being able to look at the 1775 accounts, the writer of the 1874 account reflected that the 'whole receipts from the contributing members, as well as donations from many liberal benefactors, appear to have been for a long period annually distributed; for at the end of the century from the first Act of Incorporation, the funds were of little more in amount than at the commencement, the annual receipts less, and the Institution fast dwindling away'. The Corporation did have a bank account at Coutts in 1755–56 but the

---

[1] Fines were abolished in 1789.

only cash paid in and out was £21 – the credit was a donation from John Gray Esq. and the expenditure was cash paid to William Strachan, the charity's printer.

By 1761 the Corporation could claim a large number of London merchants and current and future East India Company men amongst its senior governors who had also been past masters – Andrew Drummond, Robert Ferguson, Henry Douglas, Alexander Hamilton, Sir Alexander Grant, Sir James Cockburn, William Bowden, and Robert Oliphant. Cockburn, a few years later, became a director of the East India Company, but at this time worked for Douglas, a West India merchant, and later married his daughter. After this time there is a gap in the accounts of the charity until the presidential reorganisation of 1775. Corporation organisation and support had been carried out on a relatively small scale but it was now felt that greater numbers were needed if the charity was to survive. The management of the Corporation was then 'fortunately undertaken by a few public-spirited and active individuals who saw the necessity of a change in its constitution in order to enhance its efficiency, and to enable it to extend relief to many objects not previously entitled to claim its charity'. As the population of London Scots rose, so too did their destitution, and 'disappointed in obtaining employment, and without having acquired any parochial settlement', they had become 'utterly destitute'. The necessity of contributing to the Corporation by way of insurance was done away with and the institution truly 'became a Charitable Institution, for the relief of poor natives of Scotland who might be reduced to poverty and want'. A 'Humble Petition' from the master, governors and assistants of the Scottish Hospital was signed by their agent, John Spottiswoode, and sent by him to King George III, signalling the increase in 'useful bodies of Scots' since the union. Spottiswoode wrote

> That it would greatly Tend to the Better Execution of the purposes of the said Charity, and Hospital of the Foundation of King Charles the Second, and the more Regular Government of the same, that the present Mode and Management should Cease and Determine, and that in all Time coming the said Corporation and Charity should be Managed and Governed by a President and such a Number of Vice Presidents, and Governors as to Your Majesty shall seem proper, or as under a Bye Law, or Regulation of the Corporation hereafter to be made, shall be Qualified and Appointed to these Offices.

With such a change Spottiswoode hoped that the effectiveness of the charity would be increased and extended. The king gave his consent and a new charter was proclaimed. The whole process had been expensive and had cost the Corporation £645, unlike the fees for the earlier charters of 1665 and 1676 which had been waived by the Earl of Lauderdale. The management was now to consist of a 'President', six 'Vice Presidents', one 'Treasurer' and 'such a number of Governors as to Us shall seem proper'. The annual festival of 1776 was the first since the newly re-invigorated charter, and from 1778 to 1781 there were sermons as well as collections on St Andrew's Day and the dinner cost each of the vice-presidents and governors 7s. 6d. The price of dinner tickets went up in 1784 to 10s. 6d. and 'if necessary' was even to be put up to 21s.

The Scottish nobility, sporadic supporters since at least the 1665 charter, and perhaps earlier directors of the Scots Box, had been persuaded to take more control. The senior figures were no longer merchant London Scots but Scottish earls and baronets. The first in a long line of elevated presidents was the Duke of Queensberry and Dover; his six vice-presidents were the Duke of Buccleuch, the Duke of Argyll, the Earl of Findlater and Seafield, Sir James Cockburn, Sir Laurence Dundas, and Archibald Dundas; and Duncan Campbell, a London merchant, was made Treasurer. The charter also set out days for annual business in the 'General Courts', starting with St Andrew's Day 'or the day immediately after'.

The Corporation still advertised in 1777 for 'such as are natives of Scotland or of Scotch extraction, who are not entitled to Parochial Relief, to become subscribing members, whereby they would be entitled to weekly pensions when sick or disabled', but despite its new charter the 'Scots Corporation' still seemed to be in a terrible state in 1779, and the noble management was lax. In that year a letter of appeal was addressed to the Corporation's president, Henry, third Duke of Buccleuch, by the Corporation's honorary chaplain, Henry Hunter. From his home in Hackney, Hunter asked for the duke's special attention 'to an object, of indeed very inferior importance, [compared to national defence] but yet of importance':

> The Scots Corporation is greatly on the decline; and a spirit of languor and despondency is unhappily gone forth, which threatens its dissolution. It is easily in your GRACE's power to prevent this; you have but to avow yourself its patron: a multitude will soon appear to support that cause which the Duke of Buccleugh [sic] is known to favour. It is the cause of good will among fellow citizens for promoting one of the best of purposes, the relief of the aged, the poor and the miserable. Your countenance, my LORD, will put success beyond a doubt; and you will have your reward, in the satisfaction which a good mind feels in contemplating the happiness which it has communicated to others.

From November 1781 to November 1799 the Corporation was rejuvenated by another Scottish duke and enjoyed an increase in its funds, property and charity which had been sadly lacking in previous years. A 'Progressive State of the Funds of this Charity' records that on 30 November 1781, when the Duke of Montrose was first elected president, the wealth, in terms of 'Estate and Capital Stock', of the Corporation 'was then a Freehold House in Crane Court wherein the business of the Charity is carried on, and Old South Sea Annuities'. The Old South Sea Annuities of this date amounted to £650. Annual donations and sub-scriptions amounted to £220. Montrose had probably also made the big decision to move out of the deteriorating buildings in Blackfriars and to buy for £1,000 the Crane Court house of the Royal Society, which had already moved to Somerset House.[2] The Royal Scottish Corporation had for many years previously also leased out the old tenements of the original workhouse, and in 1781 the land and buildings in Blackfriars were sold to the city's Corporation of London for £1,050 and the Corporation moved its offices to Crane Court in 1782.[3] After its move, the Corporation began to build up its property holdings in the surrounding Fetter Lane area. In 1783–84 it spent £165 on two more freehold properties in Fleur-de-lis Court, and in 1786–87 it bought a small freehold house, again in Crane Court, for £150.

After the South Sea Company's collapse in 1720 joint-stock companies could only be set up by royal charter. Consequently any investment had to be in government stock. Towards the end of the eighteenth and in the early nineteenth centuries, individuals and institutions started to dabble in these government funds and the stocks of the new infrastructure companies set up to build canals and docks or to provide water and gas supplies. By 1799 the Corporation had taken advantage of its investment powers, and the author of a short statement (probably James Dobie) reported that it 'appears from a progressive view that this Corporation has been gradually increasing in number and respectability – in its funds and utility'. The Corporation's assets now consisted of:

> a freehold house
> 'a large room behind built and finished at an expense of £1,200' (probably the chapel)
> 3 small freehold houses 'near adjoining'
> £5,000 Old South Sea Annuities
> £1,800 '3 percent Consol. Bank Annuities'
> donations & subscriptions of £780
> income total of £1,025 ('which is £307.13.6 short of 1798')

A year later the Corporation's Coutts bank account showed an increase of over £300 and pay-outs to its secretary Dobie of £717 in two instalments. The accounts for 1802–03 and 1803–04 show a decline, down to £891 in 1803 (£400 paid out to Dobie and £187 to a Mr [Lachlan?] Mackintosh) and £713 in 1804 (nothing to Dobie but £431 to Messrs Mackintosh and £282 to Alex Harper) respectively. In 1802 the Corporation had again invested in government funds, spending £449 on 3 percent consolidated stock worth £660 (it already had

---

[2] The Royal Society had held its anniversary meeting in Somerset House for the first time on 30 November 1780, according to a letter from Walter White of the Royal Society written to the Royal Scottish Corporation on 4 January 1878.

[3] Four of the Blackfriars tenements had been leased by at least 1773, probably earlier, and the City of London's own corporation had also taken over these leases, eager to buy up the property as an initial purchase and a basis for its plan to acquire a landholding in the Blackfriars area.

£3,200 of the stock and had invested in it since 1795 with an initial £200), an amount which also included the brokerage fee. By 1808 the Corporation still had £5,000 invested in the South Sea stock (there had been no change since 1798) and £9,000 in 3 percent annuities.

The careful administration of the Duke of Montrose and the Corporation secretary James Dobie from 1782 had encouraged a period of stability and growth by the early years of the nineteenth century. The decline since the 1760s had meant that in 1782 the number of 'poor objects relieved' had gone down to 62. The Corporation had little money with which to provide relief, but there was hope that year as the charity began a period of regeneration. In the year 1798–99, the number of relief cases had risen to a substantial 342, by which time the charity had been much rejuvenated and Montrose and Dobie had become increasingly active in attracting funds from noble benefactors. Even so, the members of the charity's committee who had organised the relief for that year declared that they 'often regretted they could do no more liberal things for the numerous poore desiring objects who monthly applied', but they 'were afraid of trenching on the Capital of the Corporation'. Numbers of known recorded cases from 1799 to 1815 are summarised in the following table:[4]

DATE	NUMBER OF CASES
1799	342
1803	1418
1804	1598
1805	1258
1806	1610
1807	1602
1809	1523
1810	1602
1811	1488
1812	1946
1813	2018
1814	2435
1815	2462

William, Duke of Clarence, agreed to take over and the charity continued to grow under his active guidance, aided by James Dobie's continuing secretary-ship, when the Duke of Montrose's presidency ended. Dobie was an active publicist and organised the St Andrew's Day meetings and dinners. He sent out

---

[4] Data were not recorded for 1808; figures for 1812 and 1815 include 275 and 335 passages to Scotland respectively.

a printed circular on 20 November 1807 calling all governors to the general court meeting on St Andrew's Day, held in the hall as usual at twelve o clock ('the chair to be taken at One O'clock PM precisely'), and afterwards the governors were to 'adjourn to the London Tavern for Dinner with the benefactors and friends of the institution. Dinner to be on the table at five O'clock precisely'; tickets for the event could be had at 15s. each from the festival stewards at the Corporation hall or the bar of the tavern on or before 28 November. A similar printed letter was circulated in November 1811 but the time of the dinner had moved to 6pm and those invited were requested to bring 'such Noblemen and Gentlemen as you may think ought to join in supporting the Institution.

CHAPTER 16

Governors and Patronesses

Initially the income of the Scots Box club had come from a merchant community willing to pay out money as insurance or mutual aid against an uncertain life, probably in the manner of a sociable drinking club.[1] The annual festival dinners on St Andrew's Day were great evenings for raising funds as well as for having a good time well into the later twentieth century, and many donations recorded in the benefactor lists would have been received at these events. Innovative ways of raising money were tried in addition to the dinners. More money had come in as a result of a petition for the sale of 'three Knights' Patent' in 1687 when the Scottish Hospital 'Ordered that the Knight Baronet's Patent for England, granted by his Majesty, be offered at 500 guineas, and the two Scots' Patents at 300 guineas each'. By 1688 the Corporation could report that 'Two appear to have been sold'. In 1695 it 'received a Tally on Births and Marriages for £400'. In 1713–14 the Scottish Hospital even gambled in London and abroad – 'A Lottery Ticket purchased by the Corporation having been drawn a blank, ordered to sell it at the current price, and purchase three tickets in the Dutch Lottery'.

The appeals to benefactors were largely successful and monetary support, in the form of donations, came not just from London Scots, but also from Scots in Scotland, especially when a 1686 petition had raised £200 from the 'Royal Burghs'. 'Many Citizens of the English Nation, observing the great Usefulness of such a Society, have contributed generously to it,' the charity could announce, remembering the Duke of Bedford's laudable seventeenth-century example and his great gift of property in Covent Garden. Irish peers like the Right Honourable Charles, Earl of Orrery (of the Boyle family), also subscribed by 1730. In addition a number of Scots abroad – merchants, ministers and military men in continental Europe, the West Indies, America and especially India – also sent sent back donations and left bequests to support the London Scottish cause. Those Scots contributing from 1665 to 1714 included famous Scots Presbyterians like William Carstares, William III's religious advisor at the time of the Glorious

[1] A future Royal Scottish Corporation secretary later even joked that the Caledonian Society had been set up in 1837 to revive this social tradition.

Revolution and his brother-in-law William Dunlop, principals of Edinburgh and Glasgow respectively; Anglicans like Gilbert Burnet, Bishop of Salisbury; and Jacobite nobles like the Earls of Perth and Panmure and Sir John MacLean of Mull.

Robert Kirk records in his diary of 1689 that a penny a week was given by the 250 members and that 'Almost all Scotishmen that frequent London are benefactors'. By 1723, quarterly collections amounted to £31 19s. with 'Entry Money' listed as £13 10s. In 1761, entry money was still one shilling quarterly and subscriptions were still being advertised in 1777. Robert Paterson, the last 'subscribing member', made his final payment at 'Midsummer' in 1786. The surviving printed lists documenting larger benefactors (taken from registers, and from 'tables hung up in their hall') were not comprehensive: 'For Brevity's Sake, no Donations under Five Pounds are here inserted'. Usefully, though, by this date, 'Those marked with 'Gov.' were or had been 'Governors after having served the annual office of Master of the Corporation'. Those marked 'Tr.' were 'those from the court of Assistants' who had been treasurer but not master, and those marked 'A. have been, or now are, of the Court of Assistants'.

Early eighteenth-century donors included Sir Richard Arnold Esquire, Deputy Secretary at War, who had for many years given £1.1s. a year. Donating craftsmen included a silkman, a dyer, a saddler, a pewterer, a laceman, a woollen draper, a hatter, and a watchmaker. Some donating physicians, surgeons and apothecaries were also the Corporation's assistants like William Lillie and David Middleton. Others were lawyers and politicians:

> Rt Hon. Adam Cockburn, Esquire, Lord Justice Clerk, £10
> Sir James Dick, Lord Provost of Edinburgh, £5
> Sir David Dalrymple, Lord Advocate, £10
> Hon. Robert Dundas, Lord Advocate, £20
> William Hamilton, Esquire, Counsellor at Law, Master Anno 1732. and Gov., £47
> Hon. James Johnston, Esquire, Secretary of State, £30
> Sir Edward Northey, Attorney General to Her Majesty Queen Anne, £5
> David Paton Esquire, High Bailiff of Westminster, £5.5

London financiers and merchants included William Paterson, 'James Chiesly, Merchant', 'Richard Barclay, Merchant', Andrew Drummond, goldsmith and master in 1722, 'William Law, Banker', and 'George Middleton, Banker, Master Anno 1725 and Gov.' Late lord mayors of London who had donated by 1738 included Sir William Stuart and Sir Francis Forbes, who gave £33 and £71 respectively. In Scotland, donors included John Brown and James Nicholson, Edinburgh merchants, and 'David Ross, Esquire, Commissioner of Excise in Scotland' who gave five guineas. Scots in continental Europe were also generous. These included the notorious 'John Law, Esquire, late Comptroller General of the Finances of France', who gave £15 and probably influenced the 'The Scots Young Men and Scots Box at Paris', who gave £40 by 1730. Three merchants in Stockholm, all named Lyell, had also donated by this time, as had Patrick Middleton 'at Cracow in Poland', and 'Sir James Kennedy, the Scots Conservator in Zealand [Netherlands]'. West Indies merchants and ministers were also included in the list, as were three governors or ex-governors of Jamaica and Barbados and 'Councillor' William Trent in Pennsylvania and John Borland, a New England merchant. Naval and army officers were generous, like 'Captain Alexander Hamilton, merchant, Master 1717 and Gov.', who gave £81, and especially the 'Officers of the Scots Foot-Guards' who gave £202.

Other significant supporters were 'Sir David Nairn, Knight, Master Anno 1690 and Gov.', 'Sir James Forbes, one of the Clerks Controllers of the Board of Green Cloth', and 'William Stuart, Esquire, Secretary to His Present Majesty, when Prince of Wales'.

In addition, there was also a non-partisan attitude to bringing in these donations, since the 'well-disposed Persons' appealed to were also 'of all Parties and Opinions; for 'tis impossible for this Charity to be of any Party'. Jacobite earls and Episcopalians rub shoulders with Presbyterians in these lists of benefactors. The Corporation appealed to all 'the charitably-disposed and publick-spirited Persons in general, as well English as Scots', especially those nearby:

> in particular, do they challenge the more immediate Regard of the Inhabitants of London and Westminster, for whose Service and Benefit they have spent their Youth, Time and Strength. And it is also humbly and especially hoped, That *those of their own Country*, who are Persons of QUALITY and DISTINCTION, and to whom Providence has been bountiful, will, agreeable to the Practice of their illustrious Ancestors to this Corporation, SET A LAUDABLE EXAMPLE TO ALL OTHERS.

Both men and women made donations, the men becoming governors and assistants and the women becoming 'Patronesses'. By 1714 four women, 'Madam Bromly', the Duchess of Lennox and Richmond, James Kynnier's widow as a bequest (here called Helen), and 'A Lady Unknown' via James Foulis, had together donated or bequeathed nearly £100. Separate lists of patronesses are attached to a number of early nineteenth-century accounts of the Corporation, and before this time the women were included in a general list of benefactors. These women, though their donations and bequests were gladly accepted, were not welcome in the running of the Corporation, a common theme in the predominantly masculine society and club life of the eighteenth and nineteenth centuries. Patronesses were perhaps actively encouraged to keep away from the Scottish charity when they were granted the privilege of voting by proxy at elections from 1798.

The quarterly contributions from subscribing members and property rental income had supplied two fifths of the money needed to pay for relief. Casual donations from 'well-disposed persons' just about covered the other three fifths. By the end of the late eighteenth century the Scottish nobility also began to take an interest in and to support the Corporation in much more substantial numbers, especially from 1782. Prior to this, some may not have been as effective as they might have been, as honorary chaplain Henry Hunter had reminded the Duke of Buccleuch in his sermon of November 1779. Noblemen and other men of senior rank, he said, might be exhorted to support such charity, 'for many are disposed to encourage and promote the cause which one eminent man is known to have espoused'. Hunter had also been keen to persuade those 'persons in the middle and lower spheres, who cannot even beg such a superiority to distress because they are so close to it', and because 'they themselves are accustomed to bear it: their own feelings [shall] instruct them in their duty'. He encouraged such people to subscribe in wealthier times as insurance against the future and as an example to society rather than as a necessary contribution: 'what men lay out upon works of charity, in the days of wealth and prosperity, is literally a stock put out at more than common interest, against the day of adversity'. Charity, as 'the tender mother', succours the infant and, as an 'affectionate Grecian daughter', supports the elderly. Donors, he said, should remember whence they came and give accordingly in preparation for a possibly poorer old age: 'many might be adduced, of the pupils of benevolent institutions, living to be advanced in life, the principal supporters of that which instructed and cherished their childhood: and of the decline of life cheated, and the pressure of want alleviated, by the munificence of youthful days, and affluent circumstances'.

From November 1781, the Corporation had a great fillip after James Graham, third Duke of Montrose, took over as president. He gave the charity something of a kick-start this year with its largest donation to date of £1,767. Philanthropy had been developing during the late eighteenth century, and the Corporation under Montrose and its new secretary, James Dobie, focused the charitable giving of Scots and increased the number of its nobleman governors (including baronets) from just two in 1782 to as many as 85 by 1808 (out of a total of 82 and 1,280 governors for the same years). The charity's income, as 'donations, subscriptions, interests and rents', had increased from £220 in 1782 to £1,782 by 1808. Montrose was later well known amongst Scots for helping the Highlanders recover their right to wear the kilt, but was also the saviour of the Scottish charity. Educated at Trinity College, Cambridge, he was also a financially astute lord of the treasury in the younger William Pitt's government. By 1789 he was a joint paymaster-general to the forces and also a vice-president of the board of trade and a member of the privy council. From 1791 to 1803 Montrose was commissioner for the affairs of India – a key period for the Royal

Scottish Corporation's connection with the army in India and East India Company directors – and from 1795 until his death was lord justice-general of Scotland. Under the patronage of Montrose the Corporation acquired other influential politicians and East India Company directors as benefactors. Corporation vice-president Sir David Scott MP wrote to the charity's secretary James Dobie in April 1796, assuring Montrose and the Corporation governors that he would have 'much pleasure in Complying with their Desire in Writing to India in favour of the Charity'. On the 'Solicitation and Favour' of Scott and General Norman McLeod (and others in 1785), special subscriptions lists were printed when money was received from Scots 'governors' in Bombay in 1801. The Madras Scots also had a list when they sent back money in 1811 for the school appeal.

The Corporation had been most grateful for its royal patronage ever since Charles II had first taken an interest in 1665. William III may have known about it through his Scottish religious advisors, Gilbert Burnet and William Carstares, but whether he agreed to become its patron is not known. George III signed its re-incorporation charter in 1775 but appears to have taken no active interest in the charity (although well known for his royal bounty). His sons had been active enough, though. George IV, as Prince of Wales, had donated £707 in 1790 and William, the Duke of Clarence and St Andrew's, donated £1,123 the same year. As president for twenty-two years from 1808, the Duke of Clarence also presided over many of the charity's Spring (started in 1790) and St Andrew's Day festivals.

Legacies and one-off gifts from this period were later printed up for all to see:

YEAR	BENEFACTORS OF OVER £200, 1688–1815	AMOUNT
1690	The Royal Burghs	£200
1698	The Scots' Foot Guards	£202
1782	James, third Duke of Montrose	£1,750
1790	King George IV	£707
1790	Duke of Clarence, later King William IV	£1,123
1792	General the Duke of Gordon	£482 15s.
1802	William, Fourth Duke of Queensberry	£264 14s.
1809	Thomas, Earl of Haddington	£210
1810	George, Second Duke of Sutherland	£1767
1811	Anna Maria, Duchess of Newcastle	£231
1812	Opera benefit, organised by William Taylor	£1,310
1812	General Lord Saltoun	£220
1813	Alexander Gordon	£231

Other lesser contributors of over £100 included the dukes of Sussex and Cambridge; the Duchess of Gordon; the Duke of Hamilton and Brandon; the earls of Dysart, Dalhousie, Haddington, Rosebery, Eglinton and Winton; the Marquis of Hastings (married to a Scot, he gave £101 in 1806) and Viscount Melville; Dr Howley, Archbishop of Canterbury, gave £178 in 1813 and B.A. Goldschmidt £110 the same year. Contributors of over £50 during these years included the dukes of Albany and York, Argyll, Atholl, and Bedford; the Duke and Duchess of Sutherland; the Marquis of Breadalbane; the earls of Oxford, Morton, Moray, Cathcart (General), Bathurst, Fife and Aberdeen; barons Thomas Dundas, Reay, Panmure, and Glenlyon; and the Hon. Jonathan Duncan, Governor of Bombay in 1801, and William Fullerton Elphinstone, a director of the East India Company, in 1803.

Figure 1 A double crown was combined in James VI and I at his accession to the English throne in 1603; a miniature of James by Nicholas Hillard, c. 1605, detail *(The Royal Collection © 2003, Her Majesty Queen Elizabeth II)*

Figure 2 The scourge of idle London Scots: Sir William Alexander, Earl of Stirling, c. 1614–15? *(Scottish National Portrait Gallery)*

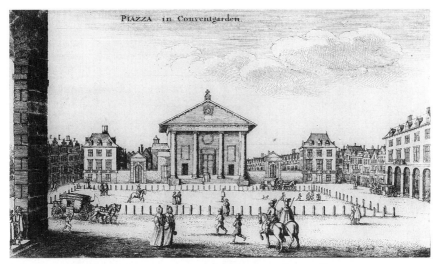

Figure 3 Covent Garden Piazza, c. 1650, etching by Wenceslaus Hollar; a Westminster meeting place for the Scots Box *(Guildhall Library, Corporation of London)*

Figure 4 Charles II, later the granter of the charity's first and second royal charters, enters the City of London at his Restoration in 1660, detail *(Guildhall Library, Corporation of London)*

Figure 5 John Maitland, Earl of Lauderdale, by Sir Peter Lely; a similar painting by Lely of Lauderdale (a great promoter of the Scots charity to Charles II) was owned by the Royal Scottish Corporation but lost in the fire of 1877 (*Scottish National Portrait Galley*)

Figure 6 A giver of Covent Garden property during the late 1660s: William Russell, 1st Duke of Bedford, by Sir Godfrey Kneller, c. 1692 *(National Portrait Gallery, London)*

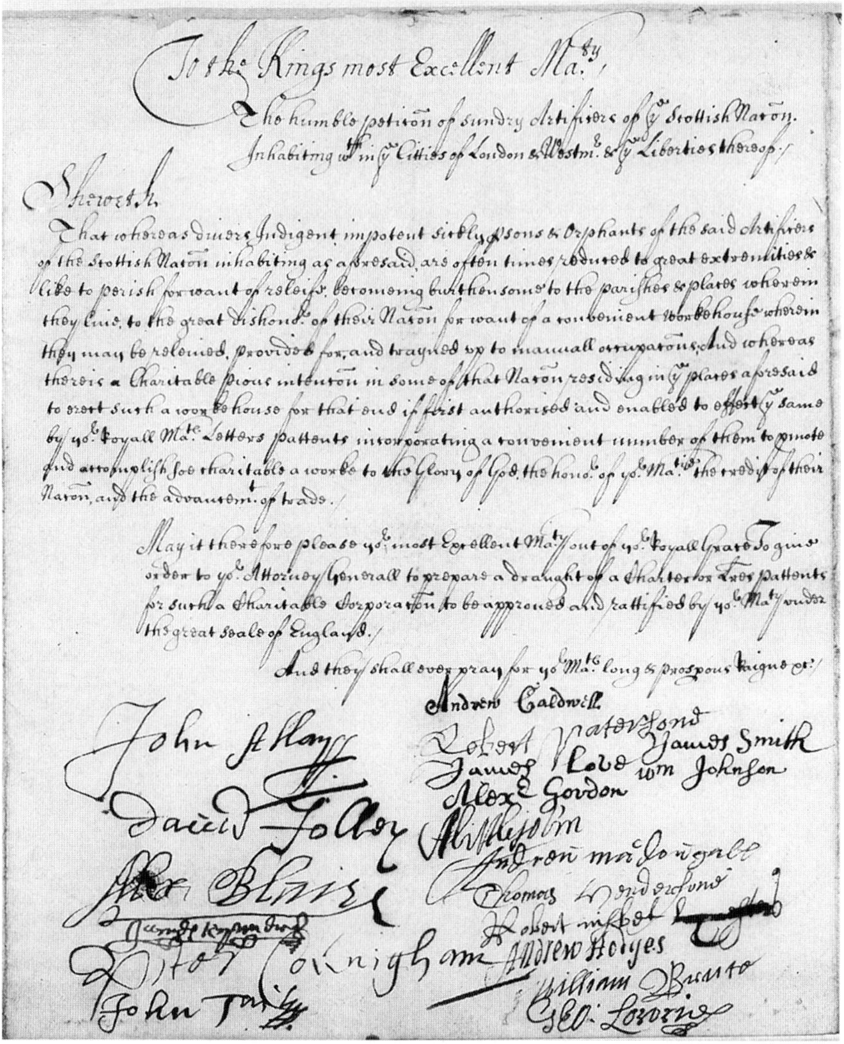

To the Kings most Excellent Maty.

The humble petition of sundry Artificers of ye Scottish Nacon. Inhabiting wth in ye Citties of London & Westmr. & ye Liberties thereof.

Sheweth

That whereas divers Indigent impotent sickly psons & Orphants of the said Artificers of the Scottish Nacon inhabiting as aforesaid, are often times reduced to great extremities & like to perish for want of releife, becoming burthensome to the parishes & places wherein they live, to the great dishonor of their Nacon for want of a convenient Workehouse wherein they may be releived, provided for, and trayned up to manuall occupacons; And whereas there is a Charitable pious intencon in some of that Nacon resideing in ye places aforesaid to erect such a worke house for that end if first authorised and enabled to effect ye same by yor Royall Mate Letters pattents incorporating a convenient number of them to promote and accomplish soe charitable a worke to the Glory of God, the honor of yor Matie the credit of their Nacon, and the advancemt of trade.

May it therefore please yor most Excellent Maty out of yor Royall Grace to give order to yor Attorney Generall to prepare a draught of a Charter or Lres pattents for such a Charitable Corporacon to be approved and ratified by yor Maty under the great seale of England.

And they shall ever pray for yor Mate long & prosperous Reigne &c.

Andrew Caldwell
James Smith
James Love
Wm Johnson
Alexr Gordon

Figure 7 Petition sent to Charles II asking permission to establish a workhouse for poor 'Scots Artificers', 11 April 1665 *(The National Archives, London)*

Figure 8 Detail from a Bill of Mortality for London's Great Plague of 1665 when the charity paid for the nursing and burials of over 300 Scots *(Guildhall Library, Corporation of London)*

Figure 9 Icy weather: the Frost Fair on the River Thames in 1683/4; note the weavers' tent at bottom right *(Guildhall Library, Corporation of London)*

Figure 10 Silver cup bequeathed to the Corporation by its first master, weaver merchant James Kynneir, 1683/4; the charity's original seal is engraved on the side shown while Kynneir's coat of arms is engraved on the other (*Royal Scottish Corporation/Charlotte Krag*)

PART III

Church, Education and Scots Abroad, 1665–2002

CHAPTER 17

The Church in Scotland and London

The Church of Scotland itself was vehemently against the early stages of the 1707 parliamentary union and preached against it, greatly influencing the Scottish people thereby. The pulpits eventually quietened when the Act of Security of the Church of Scotland was passed in November 1706, brokered principally by William Carstares, principal of Edinburgh University, and guaranteeing the preservation of the Presbyterian system of the Kirk as a basic provision of the new union treaty. The church also took care of civil and judicial matters in the Scottish parishes. A kirk session, made up of a group of lay elders, would appoint the minister and also closely supervised the morality of its parishioners and dealt with the less serious offenders. This form of discipline was gradually to be discouraged by the early 1800s and disappeared by the middle of the nineteenth century. Other duties that lasted were the session's responsibility for the relief of the poor and for the supervision of parish schools, where it often provided the schoolmaster. In 1843 a massive 'Disruption' occurred in the Church of Scotland as 450 out of a total of 1,200 ministers withdrew from it when the issue of lay patronage came to a head. By 1847 the breakaway Free Church of Scotland had established 700 of its own churches. This religious event paved the way for far-reaching reforms in the provision of relief for the poor.

Despite the spread of the Enlightenment among the literate classes, Scottish parishes had been severe places where progress and levity on the Sabbath had been frowned upon, even by younger parishioners. Stories of such severity were told to a Caledonian Society gathering in the 1840s by Sir Daniel Macnee, 'a constant visitor' to the London society, and a painter and president of the Royal Scottish Academy in Edinburgh. One concerned a friend of his (of the more severe sort) called Saunders who with some fellow 'God-fearin'' young friends, coming out of church on the Sabbath, had nearly 'brained' a young Highlander whistling for his dog.

Religion in London was more relaxed, and even in the early eighteenth century religious observance had already begun to wane when churches had found it hard to keep pace with the growth in population, especially outside the city walls. Taverns, street corners and clubs became more popular meeting places than the parish pews and pulpits mainly patronised by the rich. The poorer elements of society found the non-conformist chapels more welcoming, and the Scots found the Scots Churches no less interested in them. Scots philanthropists in London were able to show 'practical piety' in their giving to the Royal Scottish Corporation, which in turn gave to and worked with the Scots as well as with the English parishes. Poor Scots in need of relief were mostly recommended to the Corporation by the minister and churchwardens of the poor person's parish, since they had the responsibility of enforcing the poor law acts. Church ministers would also provide background and vetting information for applications for occasional relief and pensions. The Kinloch Bequest, a fund for disabled soldiers and sailors set up in 1818 and separately managed by the Royal Scottish Corporation, was also dependent on Scots ministers' help in Scottish parishes. Its chairman wrote in March 1830 that 'without the very kind assistance of the Clergy of Scotland, and the Secretary's discreet, assiduous and unremitting endeavours to induce them to lend their gratuitous and invaluable aid, the objects of the charity could not have been accomplished in the very satisfactory manner in which it has been done'.

Arguments over the poor laws had gone on, and while many agreed that work for the able-bodied poor was important, others, like the Scottish Hospital, had begun to envisage an early form of care in the community. A prominent member of the Anglican church and a Scot, Gilbert Burnet, was Bishop of Salisbury. He was also a valuable donor to the 'Scots Corporation'. He was listed by 1714 as having given a £30 one-off gift and a further £5 yearly; in 1682, as plain Dr Gilbert Burnet, he had started with a £1 donation twice a year. He was said to have given all the money he received from tutoring the Duke of Gloucester to private charity (about £1,500), and some of this money may have gone to the Corporation. He had also initiated support for poor clergy through what was known as 'Queen Anne's Bounty'. Burnet was described as a man 'perfectly healthy and robust in body and in mind; a meddler, and yet no intriguer; a lover of secrets, which he was incapable of keeping; a vigorous polemicist, but without either spite or guile; whatever the heart conceived the tongue seemed compelled to utter or the pen to write'. In 1708 he suggested (even while he thought he was dying) that the Poor Relief Act should be reviewed or removed as it encouraged the idle and the lazy. Such legislation had been unnecessary in Scotland or Holland, so why, he asked, had it been needed in England?

CHAPTER 18

The Scots Churches in London and Corporation Chaplains

The Scottish churches that had developed in Westminster and the City of London as a result of the movement of Scots to London were not much subject to serious prejudice and gradually became more involved with the Royal Scottish Corporation during the later eighteenth century. Their ministers, especially those of Crown Court, soon formed a close partnership as chaplains to the Corporation which still exists today.

Scots divines had been attracted to London before and after the Reformation. A Scots Catholic chapel had existed at the court of James I's queen, Anne of Demark, when she moved to the Savoy Palace on the Strand. Presbyterian ministers had come south to preach in Scottish churches in Westminster and the City of London before the union of the crowns, especially during 1584–88 when many leaders of the church left Scotland temporarily. Forbidden to preach in London after the Restoration of Charles II in 1660 by the Act of Uniformity and the Conventicle and Five Mile Acts, Scots Presbyterian ministers went underground or took to using the halls of the more puritan livery companies in the City of London. A slight relaxation in 1672 brought about by the Declaration of Indulgence meant that many ministers came out of hiding or out of prison and began to preach openly in places like the Embroiderers' Hall and Founders' Hall. The latter was itself situated in Threadneedle Street, Lothbury and a later minister of the Scots Church explained in 1838 that the Founders' Hall congregation had long existed, 'ever since there were a sufficient number of people from Scotland to form a public religious society'. He added that 'it is certain that the Scots congregation at Founders' Hall ... was in being before Charles II created by his royal charter the Scottish Hospital or charitable corporation'. This 'First Scotch Church' was established under the ministry of Alexander Carmichael, who, having been banished from Scotland in 1667, had arrived in London in time to be legally registered its minister as a result of the 1672 religious relaxation. Later in the seventeenth century a Scots Presbyterian congregation appears to have gathered near the Corporation's buildings in Black-friars. A 'List of conventicles and unlawful meetings' in *A Guide for Constables and Informers*, issued during another time of non-conformist persecution after the discovery of the Rye House Plot in 1683, noted that there was 'Another near the Scotch Hall, Scotch Presbyterian'.

Only with the Glorious Revolution in 1688 did the situation of the Scots Kirk in London improve. Scots and Scots ministers, who had been exiled or had been studying in Holland since 1663 or earlier, came over with the new king, William III. These men included the Earl of Argyll, Sir Patrick Hume, George Baillie and William Carstares. Robert Fleming, the minister of the Scots Kirk in Rotterdam, was asked by the Scots Church at Founders' Hall to take charge of their congregation in 1688. He accepted 'that he might have the better opportunity of uniting his endeavours with those of his excellent friend, William Carstares, for the prosperity of the Church of Scotland as well as for the general good'. William III was to call on Carstares and Fleming for advice in handling his delicate relationship with the Kirk in Scotland and the Jacobite Episco-palians. William Carstares and Thomas Coutts, a London merchant, master of the Scots Corporation and an uncle of the later banker of the same name, are recorded in 1702 as having given a £15 clock and £25 in money respectively for the rebuilding of Founders' Hall. Both men had also donated money to the Corporation by 1714. Carstares, said to have 'a Scotchman's attachment to his kindred', made a donation of £6 and his brother-in-law, the Reverend William Dunlop, 'Principal of Glasgow', donated £5. Thomas Coutts initially gave £5 as one of the thirty-three assistants and, as was the custom on finishing a year as master, donated £21. 10s. in 1702.

Robert Fleming was followed as minister at the Founders' Hall church by Dr John Cumming who in turn was followed by three others until the appointment of Robert Lawson who moved the church to a new London Wall location. Henry Hunter followed Lawson as minister in 1771 at the age of 30, having earlier declined the Swallow Street ministry on his arrival in London in 1769. He was 'soon marked out as one of the most distinguished writers and ablest preachers in London' and stayed for the next thirty years. He lived in Hackney and Hoxton, and died in Bristol in 1802, having survived four of his seven children and having begun, in 1796, a history of London, his new home.

Further west from London Wall, and by at least 1711, what became the Crown Court Church congregation had been meeting in an archway room above St Peter's Court in St Martin's Lane. This congregation had possibly evolved out of an earlier one in Covent Garden that may have included Scots as well as English wor-shippers. Money was raised by 1718 to build on a site in Covent Garden acquired from the Duke of Bedford at a cost of nearly £612, and the church opened the following year; by 1727 it was being referred to as 'the Church in Crown Court'.[1]

---

[1] The old meeting house at St Peter's Court became an artist's studio – first of Louis Roubiliac, the Huguenot sculptor of Newton and Handel, and then was used by William Hogarth's drawing school and his St Martin's Lane Academy, later to be called the Royal Academy of Arts.

The church had raised the money for its new building in London as well as in Scotland. Its benefactors were similar to those of the Scots Corporation and included eleven of 'the most noble the peers of North Britain'. Members of the House of Commons also donated among many others, including a number of citizens of Edinburgh. One of these was Sir Patrick Johnstone who had been Lord Provost of Edinburgh in 1706 and who was also a £10 benefactor of the Corporation by 1714. In 1736 he bequeathed another £10 to the church in Crown Court 'for the poor Scots in London'.

Another benefactor of both institutions was George Baillie (or 'Bailey') of Jerviswood, and he too had given the Corporation £10 by 1714. His father had been Robert Baillie, implicated while in London in the Rye House Plot, charged with high treason, and then tried and executed in Edinburgh. George Baillie had witnessed his father's execution, which experience (the body was quartered) 'ever after gave that grave, silent thoughtful turn to his temper which before was not natural to him'. Baillie the younger then escaped to Holland with Sir Patrick Hume, his father's friend, and returned to London with William of Orange in 1688; the king then made him Receiver General for Scotland. He was MP for Berwick in the Scottish Parliament and became a subscriber to William Paterson's Darien Scheme in 1696, and in 1708 he was one of the first Scottish members to sit in the new British parliament. His famous compassion is supposed to have extended even to the Jacobites who had ravaged his estate in 1715. He asked for 'mercy for the poor sufferers', because 'he had been bred in the school of affliction, which had instructed him in both the reasonableness and necessity of showing mercy to others in like circumstance'. He had married Sir Patrick Hume's daughter, Grisell, and it is her *Household Book* that still survives and provides many insights into their life in London and travel to and from Scotland.

Six ministers and several periods of vacancy followed the departure of Patrick Russell from the Crown Court ministry in 1746. This sequence of events culminated in John Cumming's appointment in 1832, and his ministry until 1879 'really set Crown Court alight'. He was a pioneer in social work and 'a man for change', as well as a well-remembered Corporation chaplain. He introduced gas lighting into the church and was 'the first to reverse the practice of sitting for singing and standing for prayers'. In 1845 he had opened the day and Sunday schools for the local Covent Garden parishioners, and his 'ragged' school taught 500 'needy children' in a building attached to the church. By 1879, when Cumming left, around 16,250 children had passed through his classes. Cumming was succeeded a few years later in 1881 by Donald Macleod. Macleod also became one of the Corporation's honorary chaplains in November 1882 and then left Crown Court in 1883 to make a move further west with nearly all his congregation and church elders, founding St Columba's church in Pont Street,

Knightsbridge. Some members of the church wanted to stay at Crown Court and the church was kept open, supported by St Columba's. The two London Scots churches became part of the re-unified Church of Scotland in 1929, and are the only Presbyterian churches in central London today.

Henry Hunter, minister of the church in London Wall and Corporation chaplain, had preached a sermon to the charity's governors at their annual St Andrew's Day gathering in 1779 on the 'Duty and Compassion towards Poor Brethren'. He asked his listeners to picture the 'happy' poor, having nothing, wanting little, but devoting all their efforts to serving others, whom 'princes may look up to … with envy'. He continues, however:

> there is in the world, poverty pining under sickness, poverty racked with pain, poverty distracted with anxiety and fear, poverty groaning under oppression, poverty sinking in despair … industry, frugality and an honest disposition have not been able to prevent the worst of human ills – he is fallen into debt.

Hunter warns his audience that their wealth and independence may not last: 'Who dare affirm it? … and had you not better secure a friend, though a humble one, by a little condescension and generosity, than create an enemy, by indolence or unkindness?' He concludes his sermon with a brief overview of the usefulness and importance of 'voluntary associations' for the relief of 'the poor, the aged and the infirm'. And finally he pleads with the Corporation's audience of governors and other members, 'you … men and brethren', to be generous:

> … with you I leave the cause of the infirm, the declining, and the unfortunate. As you value the honour of that land where you first drew breath; as you prize the character of humanity; as you regard your own interest; as you wish to promote your real happiness; as you respect the will of your Creator, and venerate the character of the Redeemer of mankind, let your hearts devise liberal things; open your hand wide unto your poor brother. And may God return a thousand-fold into your bosom.

Hunter also made a particular plea for the elderly who could not take up the offer of a passage home: 'by outliving most, if not all, their relations, and acquaintance, in a long course of absence, they become in a manner strangers to their native country; and so, besides the difficulty of supporting the expence of a return, have but little encouragement to attempt it'. The sermon was published the following year and anyone who had missed it, or wanted to read it at home, could buy it later from the Corporation in Blackfriars for a shilling. Hunter also maintained a long interest in the Society for the Propagation of Christian Knowledge (SPCK) and was elected to its Highlands and Islands London board in 1790. In this position, he promoted other ministers' sermons on behalf of the SPCK which were also available from the 'Scot's Hall' in 1800.

Similar annual sermons for the Corporation were held on the Sunday before

St Andrew's Day during 1778–81, probably under Henry Hunter's influence. They were also being preached again by 1811. In 1816 the honorary chaplain, the Reverend Dr William Manuel, organised a sermon at the Scots church in London Wall on behalf of the Corporation and collected over £64.[2] Even after he left London for Edinburgh, Manuel was actively supporting the Corporation and was instrumental in helping to set up and manage the 'Edinburgh branch of the Scottish Hospital' in that city from 1830. 'The Committee' of the Edinburgh branch were urged by London governors to procure the patronage and support of the Clergy, since 'we have reason gratefully to acknowledge the assistance derived, as well from the personal labours as from the public appeals of this very humane and meritorious body'. Manuel, because of his connections with the SPCK, could, he was told, also be particularly useful to the branch in suggesting how links between the Edinburgh and the London organisations should be established. The SPCK had set up a London branch and it was possible that the Corporation and its Edinburgh branch could look to the SPCK as an administrative model.

Later Corporation honorary chaplains continued to be appointed to share the spiritual burden of ministering to the Corporation – usually three or four in number and sometimes as many as seven (in 1911 and 1987). This clerical strength meant that the Corporation could include some more senior churchmen for the influence their names would bring rather than for their active support. The most senior Anglicans appointed were two Archbishops of Canterbury. Archibald Campbell Tait, probably because of his friendship with the Corporation's treasurer, Sir John Heron Maxwell, became an honorary chaplain when he was bishop of London in the early 1860s, continuing until his death in 1882. Another supportive archbishop was Cosmo Gordon Lang, later Lord Lang of Lambeth, who became a vice-president from 1932 and a senior vice-president in 1941.

The Reverend Alexander Macrae, chaplain to the Forces, formerly minister of Crown Court and the senior chaplain to the Corporation for over 35 years, had 'served the aged recipients with the utmost devotion' when he resigned in 1933. The Reverend Dr Alexander Fleming was vice-president and chairman of the committee of management during a crisis in 1935 which needed sensitive handling; financial affairs had gone awry and the secretary had to be removed from his post. The Reverend Joseph Moffett, minister at Crown Court from 1917, was one of the Corporation's honorary chaplains for 45 years. Moffett had also been the minister responsible for monthly services at the Corporation in 1925 which the charity reported as attracting 'a large assembly' and which were 'greatly appreciated', especially during a period of growing unemployment and high prices. Moffett increased the Crown Court congregation over threefold in

---

[2] This tradition continued after 1816, with sermons being preached regularly until 1911.

his time to 900 members. He was appointed a vice-president of the Corporation in 1947 and devoted himself with 'unfailing interest' to the Corporation's activities and 'wholeheartedly' to the promotion of the charity until his death in 1962. Crown Court Church's latest guide includes a child's impression of him as 'an Old Testament prophet' and 'as a seemingly forbidding person'. Even so, he appears to have had a great reputation as a preacher and described his 'ever-changing' congregational task as 'like preaching to a procession' of London Scots passing in front of him. He was concerned with homelessness in London through the Caledonian Christian Club and its hostel for young Scots new to London. This club was renamed the Church of Scotland Advisory Service (COSLAS) in 1982, and in the same year it used money raised from the sale of its hostel to set up an accommodation advisory service for homeless Scots.

Moffett was followed by John Miller Scott who started his ministry and became an honorary chaplain of the Royal Scottish Corporation in 1963. Having been an active member of the Corporation's committee of management for 22 years, Miller Scott became the minister at the Scots Memorial Kirk in Jerusalem in 1986 and continued his honorary Corporation responsibilities at a distance. The Reverend Stanley Hood, honorary chaplain from 1991 to 2000, recognised two classes of Scots in London, those he called 'nomads' who stay in London for a period of time but who will go back to Scotland periodically or eventually, and those he called 'natives' who assimilated and stayed in the capital. He and his wife had come in their fifties 'and we came too late to be anything but nomads. And for us Scotland will always be home'; but Hood liked London, as long as he was able to 'get fairly frequent trips to Scotland'. He had a 'delightful congregation to minister to' in Crown Court church and, 'like so many Scottish exiles,' he said he and his wife had become 'more Scottish than the Scots themselves' and 'had more Burns suppers in my first January here than I'd had in the previous thirty years'. Under Hood's ministry a Christmas carol service for the Corporation's pensioners, their friends and supporters was introduced for the first time on 14 December 1994, attended since 1995 by the deputy lord mayor of Westminster. Dr Sigrid Marten herself broke new ground in 2000 when she became the first woman minister of Crown Court and the first woman to be honorary chaplain of the Royal Scottish Corporation.

The Corporation had included a chapel in its buildings since its move to Crane Court in 1782. Its pensioners and petitioners worshipped there once a month before receiving their pensions and relief. The old chapel was damaged in the fire of 1877 and a new chapel was included in the rebuilding of Crane Court. In 1908–09, when Crown Court Church itself was being demolished and rebuilt, the charity allowed the church's congregation to meet in the 'Pensioners Hall' at Fetter Lane. The Corporation's move to King Street in 1973–74 meant that there was no longer a chapel but services were now held in the 'Court

Room'. Later the church allowed the Corporation to use its basement church hall for the pensioners' monthly lunches from 1980, 'the numbers attending having outgrown the facilities at King Street'. The charity refurbished this hall, and the church's kitchen and the Corporation's pensioners continue to meet here once a month for church services, now more conveniently held at their lunch tables.

CHAPTER 19

Schools and Skills

S cottish parishes had already run schools partly funded by local taxes by the 1660s and education was seen as a given. Always close to Scotsmen's hearts, this was also one of the main objects of the Caledonian Society of London. When established in 1837, the original intention of the society had been to encourage education in Scotland 'by sending prizes to parochial schools for competition at the annual examinations'. But this charitable idea was not put into effect, as the author of the *Chronicles* of the society records, quoting from his source:

> The Disruption in the 'Church of Scotland, however, sent its baneful effects to London,' disagreement was evident among members, the rule was abandoned, and 'one substituted in its place, which gave great satisfaction at the time, and which I believe does so still, viz., the furtherance of the Scottish Charitable Institutions in London, and other objects of charity connected with Scotland.'

The lucky charities which were to benefit from the society's patronage from now on were to be the Royal Scottish Corporation and both the Highland and Caledonian Schools.

In the 1840s Charles Mackie, the secretary of the Royal Highland School Society (RHSS) in London, gave a speech to the Caledonian Society concerning the history of education in Scotland and recounted how the accession of William and Mary had led to the establishment of the Society in Scotland for the Suppression of Vice (the Scots having been shocked by much Restoration romping), and that this society had received its royal charter from Queen Anne in 1709. The society was also called the Society in Scotland for Propagating Christian Knowledge (SSPCK). Already supported by Corporation chaplains like Henry Hunter, the RHSS, said Mackie, was now the London base of the Scottish SPCK, which by this time had been established for 150 years. Mackie told his audience that the society now managed 228 schools in 137 parishes, educating 12,000 children at an average expense for each child of 4s. 11d. a year.

The Scottish Hospital's own charter of 1665 had also covered the manual training of children and the able-bodied poor of the workhouse, if not their literate education. The aim was to ensure that the poorer Scots had skills to help them make a success of life in London or abroad – and, as the Scots artificers' petition had stated, for 'the benefit of trade'. When Robert Kirk visited London in 1689 to print his Gaelic bible, he described and probably visited the Scots Corporation in Blackfriars. At the same time he also noted that there was a small group of Scots Presbyterian schoolmasters who met as a club in London every Saturday, 'and any Scotish scholar that resorts to town and makes address to them, they contribute money to his charge till they find out a fit place for him and then he restores the money to their public box reserved for the like uses'.

In 1794 the Scots Corporation could write in its annual statement that 'the Scottish Commonalty are amongst the best educated in the world ... trained up in infancy in habits of order, temperance and industry'. Edward Drummond, preaching in 1800 to the Highlands and Islands board of the SPCK at the Church of St Botolph in London's Bishopsgate, agreed:

> Blessed be that goodness which, by removing the cloud of ignorance from the minds of the poor and unenlightened, opens to them "the means of Grace, and the hope of Glory!" ... Blessed be the pious intentions of those who cause this knowledge to be imparted to them; and may the blessing of God make these instructions effectual on their hearts and minds.[1]

John Knox and his fellow reformers had since 1560 emphasised the need for education to spread from the clergy to the laity and for it to follow the Calvinist ideal of 'a school in every parish'. This took time and by 1696 needed to be legally reinforced by the Scottish Parliament when it passed an 'Act for Settling Schools'. Fees were paid by parents, or in the case of poor children, by the kirk session. The SPCK in the Highlands and Islands of Scotland opened its first school in St Kilda in 1711 and had established another 24 schools by 1715. Many Scots knew how to take advantage of education and were well aware that knowledge not only meant an escape from Scotland but also from poverty.

In 1801 the Corporation was keen to set up a school to train the Scottish poor in London and to fulfil the educational provisions of its charter. It aimed to bring 'moral and religious improvement' to those who 'might finally become a burden or a bane to society'. This initial establishment did not immediately materialise but by 1810 the Corporation had decided to appeal again. On 3 April the Corporation (rather reluctantly) asked for money for its existing charity work and for the creation of a new school fund, declaring:

> The benefits resulting from the Establishment are extensively felt, both by the Poor and the Community at large; and it is anxiously to be wished that its

---

[1] The Reverend Drummond's sermon 'On the religious education of the poor' was afterwards 'to be had at Scots-Hall, Crane Court' or from the SPCK secretary at his house in Hoxton (this was Henry Hunter, honorary chaplain to the 'Scots Corporation').

funds were sufficiently ample to enable the society, not only to extend the sphere of their beneficence on their present system, still farther but also to combine with its other advantages Moral and Religious education to the Children of the industrious Scotish poor resident in the Metropolis. We therefore recommend the Interests of this excellent Institution to your Patronage and Support.

Fifty great and good London Scots and Corporation governors signed the piece of paper along with the Corporation's president, the Duke of Montrose, and James Dobie, the secretary. The Duke of Queensberry's hand was very frail, and the fourteen other Scottish nobles who signed were Buccleuch, Milford, Atholl, Huntly, Smeaton, Kinnoull, Selkirk, Breadalbane, Moira, Glasgow, Dalkeith, Melville (Henry Dundas), Dundas (Thomas) and Keith. Other notable Scots included Henry Dundas's son Robert, William Fullerton Elphinstone (brother of Lord Keith), Hugh Inglis (described by Sir David Scott in 1796 as 'able, industrious, perfectly correct and of a most accommodating disposition'), David Scott (junior) and Thomas Reid. These and the other East India Company directors on the list ensured subscriptions from India, especially from Bombay and Madras. The last two signatures on the appeal were those of William Fairlie and his business partner A. Gilmore. Fairlie was the former employer and one of the executors of William Kinloch, the Calcutta merchant who was to leave money to the Corporation for the establishment of the Kinloch Bequest two years later.

Regimental and other Scots in Madras generously responded to the appeal with donations for 'two charity schools'. They would also have seen other Madras charities promoting education and aid in the Indian city. The Madras Almanac of 1812 was itself published for the benefit of the Military Metropolitan Asylum and printed by the boys of the charity. The initial subscription was increased by other donations from India and England, including one for £100 from Sir Charles Forbes, who had already donated £108 to the Corporation in 1801 under its first school appeal. The Corporation's 1810 movement into schooling happened around the same time as the Highland Society of London began to think about establishing its Caledonian Asylum, founded in 1815; and the corporation's appeal may also have rivalled it for the asylum.[2]

The school money was invested and interest paid. In 1868 the Corporation's by-laws recount how interest from the school fund was awarded in 1840 to seven Scottish churches in London on condition that they gave free education to a number of children of Scottish parentage. The school fund accounts at the end

---

[2] Similar monies were also coming in at the same time from Scots in the West Indies who wanted to support the academy movement in Scotland. This movement standardised schools and curricula for the commercial, mercantile and colonial classes, acting as a vocational alternative to university.

of 1877 had been destroyed in the fire but had noted that £3,800 was invested in 'Reduced Annuities'. In November 1878 the various schools were reported as being very satisfactory and the School Fund showed a cash balance of £106. Some of the interest that year also went towards paying for one scholar at the Caledonian Asylum. A year later the annual court on 1 December 1879 was told by the committee of the school fund that the children taught at the expense of the Corporation had 'highly satisfactory' reports, 'both as to regularity of attendance and progress'. The school fund had paid out £26 in fees to the schools run by Crown Court Church and £141 to 'sundry parents and guardians'.

By 1882–3 the Corporation was paying part or the whole of the school fees for children under thirteen of poor Scottish parents recommended by the Corporation's visitor; all children were described as satisfactory, with 'one or two exceptions'. The church schools now had to pass the school board of London, which they did. John Bowers, the schoolmaster who ran the Crown Court Schools, told the Corporation that the school fee was likely to be fixed at 3*d*. a week, and since the new school board provided the books and paper, the 5*s*. that was usually provided by the Corporation 'for each Scholar' was 'more than requisite'. Bowers told the Corporation: 'If therefore you desire to spend as much as before, you will be able to educate 50 children instead of 30'. Fees had to be paid weekly and Bowers was happy to pay this weekly fee to the board schools and claim it back from the Corporation on a quarterly basis, 'for such children as you agree to educate'. He thought it better for him 'to pay the fees to the School rather than to the Parents, as a more regular attendance is secured'. This was considered most important. He added: 'I am glad to report that the children so generously paid for by your Society are the most regular attenders in the School'. He went on to ask: 'If your Corporation have a *surplus* of Education Funds – I may be allowed to suggest that you should offer a bursary to be competed for by all the children whose fees you pay, and who have reached the age of 13, the successful competitor being required to continue his education at one of the more advanced Schools or Colleges'.

At the April governors' meeting in 1883 the Corporation's visitor made his statement on the school money fund, stating that the Corporation gave relief to 97 children, 'of school age' (then between the ages of six and thirteen). 'These do *not* receive an allowance from the School Fund,' he declared, 'the reason of this being either the ignorance of the parents respecting the existence of such a fund, or their not knowing how to make application.' The names of the children were attached to his report (but not recorded in the minutes), the 'most deserving and necessitous' marked with a cross, and the visitor 'instructed' to enquire into their cases. Bowers also presented a report on children who had formerly had their school fees paid out of the grant made to the Crown Court Schools, and it was agreed to pay Bower the fees outlined. A printed form, approved the following month, was also sent to parents 'shewing the particulars required to be vouched for by the teachers'. Bowers pressed his case further. The church schools had handed over their pupils to the new school board and now found that they were 'considerably in debt' and, he said, 'as this is the last of the schools in connection with the church of Scotland in London that has continued to carry on the scheme of your committee, the education of poor Scottish Children', could the committee see its way to helping the Crown Court Schools clear their debt? He knew there was likely now to be a surplus of funds, and reminded the committee that the church schools had always educated a number of extra children at their own expense. Unfortunately for Bowers, the Corporation was loath to pay off the debt but considered how it might help more children with school fees. It calculated that there were 55 children and 33 'Scholars' in the board schools whose fees (£6 4s) were paid to the schoolmaster. The amount expended was £19 19s. in total. 'We could spend £29 10s per quarter, being a sum equal to 1/4th of £118; or about 38 scholars additional might be added to our present number.' The committee agreed that these children could easily be selected from the 97 whose parents, as previously reported by the visitor, were already receiving relief from the Corporation.

The 'Teachers' Certificates' were usually good. In April 1886 the visitor submitted his list of new cases and seven were approved:

> Mrs Niven, 6 Bells Buildings, Fleet Street for 1 child
> Mrs Burness, 41 Rowland Grove, Upper Sydenham for 2 children
> Mrs Halcrow, 6 Willoughby Grove Park, Tottenham for 2 children
> Mrs Ronaldson, 16 Upper Charles St, Fitzroy Square for 1 child
> Mrs Gow, 16 Lydford Road, St Peters Park for 2 children
> Mrs Johnstone, 3 William St, Marylebone Lane for 1 child
> Mrs Mckerracher, 55 Oakley Street, Lambeth for 1 child

On 6 October 1886 the school money (£3,800 in capital stock of reduced three percent annuities) was reinvested in Metropolitan Consolidated Three per cent stock, showing that the Corporation was beginning to spread its investments. By 1886 the school committee could report, as usual, that the 'attendance, conduct and progress of the children taught at the expense of the Corporation, as shewn by the teachers' certificates, continue to be satisfactory'. Elementary education was made free by 1893 and the Corporation transferred the school fund investments to its 'General Fund', but the interest was still earmarked for children. From this date the charity's annual relief costs were separated out into adults and children, probably as a result of this funding change and also as a new priority for relieving widows and orphans. The committee of the school fund was also disbanded but left 'with confidence the future disposal of the Fund in the hands of the Committee of Management of the Scottish Hospital'.

Children continued to be a focus for the Corporation, some also being supported, together with their families, in a new life in Canada in the early twentieth century, when a new suit of second-hand clothes and Atlantic passages were provided. Before and during the First World War help for widows and children had been a priority for the charity besides its elderly pensioners. A hundred widows and 300 children were being cared for by the Corporation in 1910–11 and skills training was being given to the children for whom

> every care is taken by the committee to ensure that the training ... shall be such as will enable them to fight their battles without coming on charity. They will be able to take their place as skilled workmen and, if there is no work for them in the United Kingdom, they will be sent to one of our Colonies where they will get every opportunity to make a successful start.

In 1916 the Corporation raised the maximum age of children who could receive charity, and also still ensured that 'provision was made to cover the early years of training in recognised trades'. The charity also encouraged the widows to help their children: 'The future benefit to their children, as well as to the state, in being enabled to enter the ranks of skilled rather than casual workers, will be steadily kept before the mothers'.

A good education, and the Scottish experience of it, perhaps enforced by church attendance, has always been important in ensuring an understanding of how to make London work to one's advantage, monetary or otherwise. Sir Donald Currie was the key player pushing forward the progress of nineteenth-century steamships and was also a vice-president of the Royal Scottish Corporation until he died in 1908, bequeathing the charity a substantial donation of £1,492. Currie also came from a strong Presbyterian background which had stressed the growing importance to the Victorians of the development of character and a sense of public duty combined with a responsibility for others. He recalled in 1896, during a speech in aid of the Presbyterian church in Liverpool (a city where, with other Scots, he had spent much of his early working life before coming to London), how his religious activity had kept him and others 'from mischief'. It had, he thought, helped to provide him with a 'consistency of character' essential for success if one were to reach 'something which should be worthy of the Church in which we were – of ourselves and of the town in which we lived, and of our history as Scotchmen'.

The Reverend Stanley Hood, one of the Corporation's honorary chaplains at Crown Court Church, interviewed just over a hundred years later in the year 2000, thought that there had always been this idea

> that if you had the will, you could get places, what we call in Scots, "the lad of parts." Now Robert Burns and David Livingstone are perfect examples ... Two men who came from very humble backgrounds, but made it because of

this determination. And … although both were rebels against Scottish Calvinism, they were influenced by it … the place of Presbyterianism is meaningful even to those who are not believers.

Don Cruickshank, having risen to the dizzy heights of a late twentieth-century captain of industry (and also similarly interviewed in 2000), believes that this too lay behind his own sense of public duty – 'there's the Protestant ethic, in my case … It's all about, if you're going to do a job, you do it well, do things for others, all of that drummed into you in primary school, in my time anyway. It lives with you'. Cruickshank, past chief executive of the Scottish NHS, Times Newspapers and the Virgin Group, has recently stepped down as chairman of the London Stock Exchange. He took an interesting view on immigration and the education of Scots and their London success. 'Immigrants,' he thought, 'are usually relatively less well educated than the country they end up in … Scots, however – immigrant Scots – have a better education than those in the country, or in this case, the capital city of London, that they end up in.' In the case of Scots coming to London, it was, he thought, a strange case of 'this peculiar group of immigrants who have to leave, and therefore have the energy of immigrants, but are coming with a better education, certainly historically …'

Educational activity has been a worthy activity pursued by the Royal Scottish Corporation. As the author of a study on London homelessness in 1971 wrote, 'Those with the most extensive overview, the greatest *savoir-faire*, the widest experience – in sum, the greatest knowledge – will cope best with London and gain most from it'. 'We help children of the Caledonian Schools with bursaries' and 'young students with student loans', reported the Corporation's secretary, Alan Robertson, in 1989. But Scottish education was not the prize it once had been, according to an article in the *Aberdeen Press and Journal* in September 2000, and the young Scots who found themselves living on the London streets perhaps needed to learn at school or college in Scotland, and certainly before they got on the bus heading south, that there was 'no pot of gold in London', and that even those who went 'laden with qualifications' found life hard. 'Those who have nothing to their names are doomed before they start,' the writer concluded.

Established almost in competition with the Royal Scottish Corporation's school activity in 1810–12, the Caledonian Asylum had been founded in 1815 by the Highland Society of London with the original aim of looking after the sons of Scotsmen killed in the Napoleonic wars which had come to an end that year. The school opened in 1819 in Hatton Garden under the presidency of Queen Victoria's father, Edward, the Duke of Kent and Strathearn (also a Scottish Corporation benefactor of £120 in 1808). The Scottish businessman-writer and Canadian entrepreneur, John Galt, became one of its first secretaries. The Caledonian Asylum's inaugural dinner was said to have had 70 musicians and 270 servants in livery; £5,000 was collected in subscriptions. The institution then moved around 1828 to Chalk Road, later renamed the Caledonian Road after the asylum which was by this time housed in a large brick orphanage. The asylum later provided a school for the children of Scottish soldiers on active service in general, taking in girls from 1846.

One of its sons in the 1840s eventually became famous for his poetry but died a poor drunk. James Thomson did not live to enjoy his fame as author of that famous dark portrait of Victorian London, *The City of Dreadful Night*:

> The City is of Night; perchance of Death,
> But certainly of Night ...

He had been born in Glasgow but had lived in London since he was very young, and after his mother died, when Thomson was eight, his father, a fervently religious merchant seaman, sent him to be educated at the Caledonian Asylum. On leaving the school, Thomson trained as an army schoolmaster and went to Ireland in the 1850s. He was 'discharged with disgrace' from the army in 1862 – probably for drunkenness, and then took up a position in the City of London, once travelling to Colorado to buy silver mines. He wrote for journals, contributed poems and literary translations, and became, briefly, a war correspondent in Spain. As a young man he fell in love with a girl who died soon afterwards, and his lonely life thereafter was a painful one. In this period he wrote his great poem, described by Herman Melville as 'massive and mighty'. It made Thomson famous, and he was admired by Meredith, Rossetti and Swinburne amongst others. But the poem's publication and that of other works could not save Thomson from his descent into poverty and the alcoholism which finally killed him.

Many other less poetic and tragic Caledonian children followed in Thomson's footsteps. In October 1878 the Royal Scottish Corporation began to take an interest in the school and made a change to its by-laws regarding its own school fund, voting to pay the interest from it direct to the Caledonian Asylum 'conditionally on the Committee having the Privilege of Electing one child annually'. In 1903 the old asylum building was demolished and the school moved to Bushey in Hertfordshire. In the 1970s the Royal Scottish Corporation donated £5,000 to the school and another £20,000 in 1985, towards its new sixth-form block. When the Berlin Wall came down four years later, the British Army had reduced its ranks and also the number of its Scottish soldiers; numbers of children at the soldiers' school therefore also fell greatly. What remained of the school was also being badly managed and its buildings, expensive to run, were no longer suitable for a modern school. With one pupil left, it was finally closed down in 1996. The building was leased out and the Royal Caledonian Schools Trust was established. The late Princess Margaret continued to attend the Caledonian Ball to raise money for the Trust in May 1996 and again in 1997. The Trust now provides funds for educating the children of Scots servicemen and women and also launched a scholarship scheme in 1999. Since then it has funded scholarships for young Scots to work on community projects in places as far apart as the USA, South Africa, Zimbabwe and Nepal. In January 2001 it provided £1,000 to a pupil from Elgin Academy to help fund a trip to India to teach English.

Bursaries are today awarded by the Royal Scottish Corporation to children of the Royal Caledonian Schools Educational Trust and as training grants to other deserving young Scots. By October 2002 the Corporation could also count 85 people who had received or were receiving training grants, one being a medical student awarded £1,500 in his third year of training. This is similar to the Scots educational tradition also pursued in the USA by the Scots' Charitable Society of Boston, a New England institution that looked to the Scottish charity of London in the late seventeenth century for its revival. Although the Boston charity today does provide a few payouts for general relief, it spends most of its money in providing educational scholarships for deserving American Scots.[3]

---

[3] See Budde, Appendix 5.

CHAPTER 20

Scots Abroad

Colonialism and the commercial revolution of the seventeenth century had meant more overseas trade, travel and rich pickings for merchants, many of whose names show up on the early lists of subscribers to the Royal Scottish Corporation. These merchants gradually took control of their own business destinies and built economic and social networks that put pressure on the English Parliament during the last years of the seventeenth and the early years of the eighteenth century. As early as 1677, in *An Answer to Letters written by Scottish Gentlemen in His Majesties Dominions beyond the Seas, to the Master and Governors of the Scotish Corporation and Hospital in London*, the Corporation was advertising itself as a place for potential overseas bequests from these wealthy merchants abroad, being 'likewise by our Patent enabled to be serviceable to our Country-men beyond the Sea, in performing the Wills of the Dead as Executors, and distributing their Legacies amongst our Friends as we shall appoint'.

Throughout the seventeenth century these adventurous Scots returned to homes in Scotland or London with many a traveller's tale. Some did not come back but emigrated for good to Scandinavia (especially Sweden), Poland, the Baltic States, France and Holland as ministers, merchants and mercenaries. The early subscriber lists of the Corporation from 1665 bear out this continental emigration, showing three contributors from Stockholm, and one each from Riga, St Petersburg and 'Dantzick'. The Scots community in Paris had in fact increased during Charles II's court exile in the city. The 'Scottish Hospital' received a single donation of £30 from J. Mowat, a tailor in Paris, during its first years, and more significant donations were given between 1714 and 1730 from societies of Parisian Scots who styled themselves 'the Scots Young Men and the Scots Box at Paris'. Together they donated £40. By the later years of the seventeenth century, America and the West Indies, especially Barbados and Jamaica, were also popular places to which to go and from which to send back money.

The British army was also an attraction for eighteenth-century Scots if they wanted to further their careers outside Scotland, and many Scots nobles had already left and enrolled, joining the army's general staff after 1707. Some 25 percent of them had reached this level between 1707 and 1745, compared to 17 percent for the previous fifty years. The Highland chieftains and their clansmen liked to channel their former Jacobite energy into the British army and became veritable empire warriors, raising regiments to create a 'tough, loyal and mobile light infantry' for the Seven Years War, the War of American Independence and the Peninsular Wars. Indeed the Jacobites themselves had benefited from the Highlanders' lightness of foot and ability to endure hardship, their mobility and clanship making them a formidable foe.

The Scottish educational system of Presbyterian parish schools and four universities had much to do with focusing the ambitions of younger Scots who with few opportunities at home, would have been familiar with tales of fortunes won (and sometimes lost) abroad. Colonial expansion and its attraction for Scots grew by the end of the Seven Years War with France in 1763, when the British were able to add more territory to their empire in Africa, India, the Caribbean and North America. The Scots who went away at this time also found less competition with the English and experienced less of the mid-century 'Scotophobia' which was then occupying the hearts and minds of a number of envious English Londoners supporting John Wilkes. Those Scots who emigrated and those who went into the British army and navy were to provide added impetus and much-needed subscriptions and bequests which boosted the Royal Scottish Corporation's funds and activities during the eighteenth and nineteenth centuries.

Emigration and colonial connections go far back with the western colonies, especially Canada. These derive from a time when Nova Scotia had been first founded in 1624 by the royal Scots poet and adventurer, William Alexander, Earl of Stirling. He was keen on encouraging colonialism and also needed a place to accommodate surplus Scots. The Scottish Hospital building fund was later to benefit from this Scottish colonial connection in 1668 when Charles II was said to have sold two baronies in Nova Scotia to help pay for the building of the new Scottish Hospital. The Corporation also aided emigration to Canada with a special project to give grants and clothes to those individuals and families preparing for their new life there in 1910–11. The Corporation also had a Scottish network in Canada that reported back to the London charity on the welfare of Canada's Scottish immigrants for the benefit of governors who wanted to support them; the charity's secretary said that he would 'be glad to give subscribers desiring to assist families to Canada the benefit of a large number of Scottish correspondents there'. He added that 'The families already helped by the Corporation to emigrate are turning out well'. Investments in stocks belonging to the Dominion of Canada and Bowaters Pulp and Paper Mills in Newfoundland provided another form of continuing Canadian interest for the Royal Scottish Corporation in the early twentieth century.

The Darien adventure of 1696 had not frightened future Scots emigrants, and an estimated 30,000, mainly lowland professional Scots, settled in North America after the union of 1707. By this year Philadelphia Scots were operating a successful tobacco trade (and some smuggling) to Scottish and English markets, including London. Around 150 doctors, numerous Scots ministers and teachers emigrated west. Scottish tobacco and other planters organised lucrative trading networks and George III's prime minister, Lord Bute, patronised many Scots in Florida in the 1760s. By 1783 over 15,000 Highlanders were living in Georgia and the Carolinas and over 60,000 Lowlanders had also settled in the Carolinas as well as the Chesapeake, New Jersey and Boston areas; Scots had been in Boston since at least the 1650s. Around five and a half (or some sources say twelve) million twenty-first century Americans can today claim Scottish ancestry, and it has been considered probable that no ethnic group contributed more to the formation and development of the United States than the Scots, although these later generations, readily absorbed into their new American home and unlike Irish Americans, no longer have a high profile or, perhaps, any true sense of their Scottish identity. Even so, Tartan Day is now a key Scottish celebration in America which perpetuates the romantic image of Scotland with a grand parade in New York of 10,000 pipers and drummers.

Scots had also begun to look after the less fortunate amongst themselves when they reached America. In 1684 those in Boston, influenced by London's Scottish charity, re-organised their own Scots' Charitable Society of Boston, founded in 1655–57.[1] One Scot in Pennsylvania was Councillor William Trent and, as the first known American donor, he gave the Corporation £5 before 1714. Trent was also a Scots' Charitable Society of Boston supporter, entering that society in 1697 and giving around the same amount. From 1714–1730, John Borland, a merchant in New England and also a Scots' Charitable Society of Boston supporter, is listed as having given £5 to the 'Scots Corporation'.

Scots living in the West Indies were also Corporation benefactors: William Gordon in Jamaica gave £10, so too did James Guthrey. The Honourable Brigadier (later General) Robert Hunter, the colony's governor and master of the Corporation in 1721, gave £30. In Barbados, merchant Thomas Stewart, minister William Walker and the Honourable Colonel Robert Stewart, the colony's governor, sent back donations of £50 between them. Also in Barbados, merchants William and Anthony MacKlean gave £5, while the Reverend Gilbert Ramsay gave over £35.

In the early twentieth century the Royal Scottish Corporation saw itself as the Scotsman's representative and ambassador in London, and a sense of worldwide

---

[1] The London charity was identified in a 1770 revision of rules and orders of the Boston society. I am grateful to Bill Budde, the Scots' Charitable Society of Boston and the New England Genealogical Society, for further information on this charity. See also Appendix 5 for a short history of this society by Bill Budde.

kinship was also felt by many in the Scottish diaspora. St Andrew's and Caledonian Societies existed and still exist today in many parts of the world to keep national traditions alive, and many of them have long supported the Royal Scottish Corporation.

An Australian amused his London Scots audience with a story that there were a 'good many' Scotsmen in Australia but that rabbits were the country's greatest pest. In Australia the top doctors, lawyers, bankers and shipping agents were all Scots, and those who had emigrated in the 1850s and 1890s were considered especially gritty. As one Caledonian Society of London and Corporation supporter of 1905 said, 'If new lands are to be annexed or new nations built up, the Scot is not usually the last man to dig in his spade or put on his apron'. In fact, he added, 'the finest road for any Scotsman worthy of the name is the one that leads to where he can be freest and most independent'. The Corporation helped a number of London Scots take this route to the southern hemisphere during the early 1900s, as a few years later it was to help those wanting to go to Canada.

Scots were certainly an asset to new colonial enterprises, and those Scots who went away were sometimes brave (or foolhardy) too: in India life expectancy was around three years by the mid-eighteenth century, and the hard-earned money sent back as bills of exchange to agents and families in London or Scotland, or that they brought back with them (if they survived), was worth the risk but perhaps not as important as a life (nearly) expended.

CHAPTER 21

Scots in India

A few, probably 'naturalised', Scots had been employed by the English East India Company during the early seventeenth century and, as a national group, Scots had also tried to get to India under the aegis of their own company. In 1618 Sir James Cunningham tried to found the Scottish East India Company, only to own a patent for a matter of months before it was taken away as a result of English opposition. The Indian ambitions of the later Company of Scotland Trading to Africa and the Indies were similarly thwarted once this, too, was excluded from achieving commercial success in the English colonies – even before the company collapsed as a result of its Darien venture in 1699.

One Scot who had made it to India by 1688 was Captain Alexander Hamilton, who told the Directors of the East India Company that he was 'a Scotchman that came out a supernumerary sailor in Your Worships' service on the *Shrewsbury* to Bombay'. His adventures and experiences over 35 years are told in his *New Account of the East Indies*. According to this (not always reliable) report he appears to have returned from India for good in 1723, spending much of 1724 in Holland settling business affairs. Interestingly, he had also brought back a charm from his travels 'that can keep out the meagre devil, poverty, from entering into my house'. Hamilton had been a merchant in Jamaica before 1688 and was possibly the same 'Captain Alexander Hamilton, Merchant, Master 1717 and Gov.' listed as having donated £81 to the 'Scottish Hospital'. As a merchant in the British colony of Montserrat in the Lesser Antilles, this man had also previously given £10. If it is the same man, this sheds new light on the life story of the adventurous Hamilton, previously only known from his *East Indies* narrative.[1]

Many Scots who came south to the capital after the union of 1707 followed Hamilton's example, using London as a leaping-off point for careers in the army, navy, civilian administration or in the East India Company, which they were now allowed to join and entered in increasing numbers – eager to 'shake the Pagoda

---

[1] There is also evidence for two men called 'Captain Alexander Hamilton' at this time. The death of one was reported in the *Gentleman's Magazine* of 1732; a letter from another appears in East India Company records a year later.

tree'[2] and return to Scotland as a 'nabob'. Once in, Scots, ambitious as ever, quickly established themselves, and the first Scottish director of the company was John Drummond, appointed in 1722. He is probably the same as the Corporation's 'John Drummond, of Quarrel, Esquire, Master 1724 and Gov.' who gave £60. By 1767 around 10 percent of the total senior civil servants (or 'writers') in Bengal and Madras were Scots, the Welsh and Irish together accounting merely for 5–6 percent. A number of Scots went out as 'free merchants' and then joined the London administration of the company when they returned from India. These men and others were behind the Royal Scottish Corporation when it received subscriptions from India, 'amounting to 4,648 Bombay Rupees' in 1785. A further donation from Bombay, 'through Governor Duncan', amounted to £700. Many young Scotsmen who joined the company did not survive and one, writing in 1784, described himself as the only survivor of nineteen young men who had arrived in India from England eighteen years previously.

Sir Hector Monro was a major in a new regiment of Highlanders when he found himself sailing for India in 1760. He was principally known for his fighting spirit in 1764 at Baksar, a crucial battle which enabled the East India Company to become one of the great powers of India. A later (unpublished) historian of Scots in India, Sir Francis Mudie, describes him as 'a daring dashing warrior, always on the alert, ready of any enterprise, however foolhardy it would appear'. Other notable Indian Scots included James Macrae, the first Scots governor of Madras from 1725 to 1730, and Sir John Macpherson (son of James Macpherson of Ossian fame), who took over from Warren Hastings in 1785. He was later accused of encouraging bribery and corruption, inventing a system 'of the dirtiest jobbery', although Mudie writes that in fact he really reduced the corruption. Lord Minto became governor-general of Bengal in 1807 and the same year sent the Royal Scottish Corporation £1,000 in Scottish subscriptions; out of the money, pensions were created for eighteen 'aged Recipients of the Charity'. Mountstuart Elphinstone, having spent some time with relations in London, reached India in 1796, rising to become governor of Bombay in 1819. He founded a society to promote the education of the native Indian population, and when he wasn't working, he spent much of his time reading:

> Rose at four. Read Antigone. Rode out. Ran a jackal but did not kill. Breakfasted. Read 36 pages of the Memorabilia. Ate sandwiches. Read Grotus. Went out in buggy … [a few days later] In bed with Locke in *Liberty and Necessity*.

His uncle, William Fullerton Elphinstone, had exercised considerable patronage during three chairmanships of the East India Company since 1790, gave to the Royal Scottish Corporation and supported its school fund appeal in 1810. As the

---

[2] A *pagoda* was an Indian gold coin.

youngest son in a Scottish family 'of declining fortunes' he had himself been helped into his first naval command by Sir Lawrence Dundas. Thomas Munro was a governor of Madras from 1820 to 1827 and was considered one of the finest of Indian administrators for his invention of the office of 'collector' in the Indian districts. It was said of him that 'Europe has never produced a more accomplished statesman, nor India so fertile in heroes, a more skilful soldier'. He was, says Mudie, 'in many ways a typical Scot – hardworking, reliable and independent.'[3]

Many of the Scots who went to India were said to have been Jacobites but the Munro clan, big in India, was known to be seriously anti-Stuart, as was Clan Campbell, the most powerful clan in Scotland with many kinsmen in India. There were so many Campbells in India that a book records their East India Company participation. The first Campbell officer soldier was recorded in 1704, and Sir Robert Campbell, a successful merchant in eighteenth-century Madras and later governor of the East India Company, encouraged his sons and many other Scotsmen to join the army. The Marchioness of Hastings, also a Campbell, had much to do with the promotion of Scots in early nineteenth-century India. As Lady Flora Campbell, the Countess of Loudoun, she was 'considerate to all her cousins, many of whom found partners for life in the East'. So successful was she in finding jobs for Scots that 'it was said that if one whistled or called outside Government House at Calcutta in her time (1813–1823), a red-headed Campbell or Mac would assuredly appear at the window'. Earlier, in 1806, the Marquis of Hastings, probably under the influence of his marchioness, had given the Royal Scottish Corporation £101.

Scottish infiltration of the East India Company had also meant advanced education for India, as Scottish ministers and missionaries had come to the sub-continent to minister to the members of the East India Company and from 1813 had been permitted to set up Presbyterian churches for their Scottish congregations. But with the help of the Reverend Alexander Duff, who arrived in Calcutta in 1830 and who thought that education in English was necessary for an understanding of religious teaching, Indians got a taste of their first modern system of schooling. Duff went on to found the University of Calcutta, also a leading teaching hospital in the city, encouraging a lasting Indian medical tradition. Commercial opportunities for other Scots were many and tea, jute, engineering, and the agencies that controlled them, continued to provide a commercial connection between India and Scotland well into the Victorian period. Many Scots also hunted for botanical specimens at this time and one

---

[3] A number of these East India Scots may also have been among Trinity House's influential 'Elder Brethren', controlling vessels hired by the government for war, supervising the supply and fitting out of fleets, and controlling Thames appointments such as those of pilots and lighthousemen.

took tea plants from China to India in 1848. A jute factory built by Scottish engineers in 1857 near Calcutta was still functioning in 1997, albeit in a reduced fashion.

Sir Walter Scott had written to Lord Montagu in 1821 that India was 'the corn chest for Scotland where we poor gentry must send our younger sons as we send our black cattle to the south'. Such Indian experience had benefited Scotland in the process, not to mention London Scots, and even a few Indian London Scots. The international and especially Scottish Indian network was particularly lasting when these men came home and spent their fortunes on Scottish estates, remembered their native parish poor or perhaps the Royal Scottish Corporation in London. William Kinloch was such a man and a wealthy Calcutta merchant, providing for both his parish and the charity in the will he made in March 1812 before he set off on the long voyage home. He was to miss the annual St Andrew's Day dinner of his fellow Caledonians and other Corporation supporters in Calcutta that 30 November (as will be seen in the following chapter):

> The hilarity and social spirit of the evening ... detained the numerous company at table, without the desertion of a single individual, till 3 o'clock in the following morning; at that time an interval was devoted to dancing, and a few Scotch Reels were executed with a high degree of vivacity. After the exercise of the dance, the company returned to the table; and at half past six on Tuesday morning about 18 or 20 jovial souls ... finished the festivities of St Andrew with 'God Save the King' in full chorus.

A much sadder Scottish military sight was experienced over 100 years later by Olive Douglas, writing of the enduring harshness experienced by Scots living in India in 1913:

> Yesterday I saw a pathetic sight. A couple in a *tikka-gharry*;[4] the man a soldier, a Gordon Highlander, and on the front seat a tiny coffin. The man's arm was around the woman's shoulder and she was crying bitterly. A bit of shabby crepe was tied round her hat and she carried a sad little wreath.

---

[4] 'The cheapest form of hired carriage.'

CHAPTER 22

William Kinloch and his Bequest

The Kinloch Bequest was one of the Royal Scottish Corporation's key Indian connections from 1812. William Kinloch also gave the Corporation a long-term connection with Scottish servicemen and women. Born in Arbuthnott in Kincardineshire, William Kinloch died in July 1812, leaving the residue of his estate for investment by the Corporation to the benefit of 'poor and disabled Scotchmen in distress, who may have lost their legs, or arms, eyesight, or otherwise wounded in the army or navy, in the service of their country'.

Like many Scotsmen before him, Kinloch had gone to seek his fortune in India. He is recorded as living in Bengal (based in Calcutta) by 1796 where he worked for a number of years as an assistant to Fairlie, Gilmore & Co before finally setting up on his own as an independent merchant in the city. He left India after 16 years' hard work and sailed for Europe in March 1812. The ship he took was the East India Company's 594–ton *Lady Lushington*, under the command of Captain John Hine and his mainly Scottish fellow-officers. The ship was bound for 'the Cape and eventually to Europe' via St Helena, and Kinloch's fellow-passengers included Lt General and Mrs Fuller, a Captain Fuller and four Fuller children; six prisoners-of-war were also on board. Sailing to the Cape of Good Hope took longer in the spring – about 70 days or more when the monsoons from the north-east would have affected the passage. It also took an extra twelve days to get from Calcutta itself to the coastal port of Saugor Roads, the real starting point for the long voyage of over 160 days in total. Whether William Kinloch had decided to make the long trip home for a break after years of working in Bengal or whether he had decided to leave India for good, due to illness or another reason, is not known – for he was to die in July on board ship. He made his will on 7 March, a week before he set out, a common enough practice for those leaving on such a long and potentially hazardous journey. 'Considering the Dangers of this Transitory life …,' he had prophetically written, 'First I recommend my Soul to God who gave it and my Body I commit to this Earth or Sea as it shall please God to order.'[1]

---

[1] If Kinloch had died in Calcutta, he would have been buried in the Scottish Cemetery in the city's Lothian Road, where many Scots still lie.

A week later, at noon on 14 March, his fellow-passenger General Fuller came on board the *Lady Lushington* to a 15–gun salute. By the afternoon all the other passengers, including Kinloch, had embarked and their luggage had been stowed. The next few days were calm, and the ship's log records that it was 'For the most part variable light wind and fair'; the crew were employed stowing the anchors and 'trimming the ship by the stern'. But by 24 May both the weather and the sea were no longer settled and a sailor was lost in the swirling waters. The weather continued foul, and on 30 May the log recorded: 'Throughout the day a Hard Gale with frequent Squals & a high Sea. Ship shipping much water & lurching heavy at times'. The weather eventually quietened and at the beginning of June the crew and passengers could see Cape Agulhas, the southernmost tip of Africa, about 7 to 8 leagues to the east; then, at 3 am on 2 July, the island of St Helena was spotted.

Once in port, the passengers had five days to relax on shore. On Tuesday 7 July, William Kinloch and the other passengers were back on board and the ship left St Helena in the company of a number of other East India Company vessels and 'several Whales'. A week later Ascension Island came into view, but the next day the surgeon from a nearby frigate was urgently called alongside at one o'clock in the afternoon. He had come aboard 'to see Mr Kinloch a passenger being very ill'. The ship's own surgeon must have needed extra help but the two doctors were unable to save him and on Sunday 19 July, the ship's log, giving no other details, simply records that 'At 8am departed this life Mr William Kinloch, passenger'. The weather was calm and the captain reported that in the morning a service of prayers was held, and the following day, 'At Sunset committed the Body of the Deceased to the Deep with the usual ceremony'. The ship finally reached England two months later.

Kinloch had no wife and no children. He left all his 'worldy goods' to his mother, other family, friends and the parish of Arbuthnott where he was born; the residue he bequeathed to the Royal Scottish Corporation in London (although not in so many words):

> Lastly the residue of my Estate both real and personal after the several bequeath before mentioned shall have been provided for and secured, I will and bequeath may be lodged in the British Funds at Interest under the Management of the Governor and Managers of the fund instituted in London for the relief of poor and indigent Scotchmen and that the Interest of this the residue of my Estate may be received annually … together with the Sum from the Principal annually equal to one fourth part of the Interest and that said Interest together with said part of the Principal be paid annually by the said Governors and Managers of the said fund or institution to poor and disabled Scotchmen in distress who may have lost their legs or arms, Eye-sight or otherwise wounded in the Army and Navy in the Service of their Country and

I request that the Governor and Managers for the time being of said fund or institution may continue to distribute the Interest of this residue of my estate together with a Sum from the principal annually equal to one fourth of the Interest ... only until such time as the residue of my said Estate is reduced to the sum of two thousand pounds sterling, and then the whole Two Thousand Pounds to be divided at once ...

He appointed John Ferguson, David Clark and James Dunlop of Calcutta and William Fairlie of the firm Fairlie Bonham & Co in London and Mr John Gourlay of Arbuthnott in the county of Kincardine, North Britain as his executors.

Why had Kinloch left money to the 'Scots Corporation' in London, and also what prompted him to want to set up such a fund for disabled servicemen? Around him in Calcutta he would have seen the local charities of the Military Widows Fund, the Calcutta Laudable Society and Lord Clive's Fund. Through his executor, William Fairlie, he had no doubt heard of the Corporation's good works since Fairlie, as well as 'A. Gilmore', were two of the signatories to an appeal put out by the Corporation for a school fund in 1810. Kinloch had perhaps also seen the appeal at the same time that soldiers in Bombay and Madras had seen it and had been prompted to donate. It is even possible that he had himself served in the British Army or that he had been influenced by the fighting against the French and the wounding of men he had seen around him as the Peninsular Wars became global and raged also in India. He did show another military connection in his will when he left £1,500 to a possible kinsman, Major William Kinloch, who was also in India, indicating that the bequest was 'a mark of respect'.

There are examples of Scotsmen looking after Scottish servicemen that Kinloch may have been familiar with. Many eighteenth-century Scots doctors honed their skills in military campaigns – Sir John Pringle set up regimental hospitals, Donald Monro specialised in military hospitals in Germany, and John Hunter's surgery probably became a science during military service in Portugal. A Scottish military hospital had also been established in Edinburgh in 1648 but proved too costly to run and was closed by the 1660s. By the time he made his will, Kinloch may not have heard of such a Scottish example, but he would have known of the two great charity hospitals for disabled soldiers and sailors which now existed in London, embodied in the Royal Hospitals of Chelsea (for soldiers) founded by Charles II in 1680 and Greenwich (for sailors) founded in 1694 by William and Mary. A number of physicians of Greenwich Hospital had additionally been Royal Scottish Corporation benefactors in the eighteenth and nineteenth centuries.

Whatever the reason, nearly a year after William Kinloch died, David Clark, one of his executors, obtained probate for Kinloch's will in Calcutta on 1 June 1813. After a lengthy court case in Chancery to ensure undisputed ownership of the bequest (Kinloch did not specifically name the Corporation in his will), the Royal Scottish Corporation was given the residue on 30 May 1818. A committee was set up to manage the fund and to administer its disbursements to the new Kinloch pensioners.

Figure 11 The illustrated frontispiece of the minute book of the Court of Directors of the Company of Scotland Trading to Africa and the Indies, 1696–98; Scots Corporation masters and benefactors also had their parts to play in the ill-fated Darien scheme (*Reproduced by kind permission from the archive collections of the Royal Bank of Scotland Group plc*)

Figure 12 Gilbert Burnet, Bishop of Salisbury and a generous charity benefactor by 1714; portrait after John Riley, c. 1689–91 *(National Portrait Gallery, London)*

Figure 13 'A Flight of Scotchmen' by Richard Newton, 1796 – the Scots charity benefited greatly from its Scots supporters both in London and abroad *(The British Museum)*

Figure 14 The seal of the Scots Corporation by 1738; this was probably a remake of the original 1665 version; another version was made in 1880 (*Trustees of the National Library of Scotland*)

Figure 15 'Entrance to the Fleet River', School of Samuel Scott, c. 1750; the Scottish Hospital's main buildings are in the centre of this idealised view of the Thames, just to the right of Bridewell Bridge, detail *(Guildhall Art Gallery, Corporation of London/The Bridgeman Art Library)*

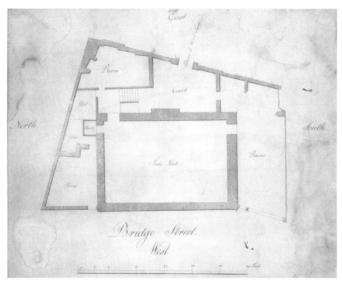

Figure 16 A plan of 'Scots Hall' in Blackfriars, c. 1782 – the year the Scottish Hospital sold its buildings and moved further north and west to Crane Court *(Corporation of London Record Office)*

Figure 17 'The entrance of George IV at Holyroodhouse', by Sir David Wilkie, painted
c. 1828; James Graham, 3rd Duke of Montrose, stands in the shadow behind the King as
Lord High Chamberlain, detail; the King was a royal benefactor and Montrose the Corporation's president and instrument of change from 1782 (*Scottish National Portrait Gallery*)

Figure 18 The launch of the East Indiaman, *The Edinburgh*, in 1825 at the East India
Company's dockyard, Blackwall; the East India Company was a great charity supporter and
employer of London Scots (*Guildhall Library, Corporation of London*)

Figure 19 An appeal for funds; Scottish nobles and East India Company directors support the Scots Corporation's charity schooling in 1810 (*Royal Scottish Corporation*)

Figure 20 An active president from 1811 when Duke of Clarence and patron when King: William IV by Sir Martin Archer Shee, c. 1800 (*National Portrait Gallery, London*)

Figure 21 An Edinburgh supporter by 1830 – Sir Walter Scott, by Sir William Allan
(*Scottish National Portrait Gallery*)

Figure 22 Patron of the charity for 63 years, the recently-crowned Queen Victoria arrives at
the City of London on 9 November 1837, detail (*Guildhall Library, Corporation of London*)

Figure 23 Lighthouse engineer, Robert Stevenson, by John Syme, c. 1833 – a director of the 'Edinburgh Branch of the Scottish Hospital'; from 1831 he arranged for the Leith lighthouse keeper to meet poor Scots returning home by steamer at the London charity's expense *(Scottish National Portrait Gallery)*

Figure 24 Robert Hepburn, c. 1860s, detail; a dental surgeon and Corporation supporter since 1832, chairman c. 1870s–1880s and a vice-president until he died in 1901; also a founder of the Caledonian Society of London and the London Scottish Regiment *(London Scottish Regiment)*

CHAPTER 23

Kinloch Management and Deserving Cases

The examination of Kinloch Bequest applicants and payment of its pensioners appears to have been quite an onerous task. This activity is detailed in a letter of 1830 from the Honourable William Fraser, chairman of the Kinloch committee of management and also the Corporation's treasurer, to Robert Dundas, Viscount Melville who was probably a Corporation vice-president. The charity was eager to reduce the salary of the Kinloch committee's secretary, but Fraser was equally keen to argue the case against such a reduction. In 1820 the Corporation had agreed to pay the Kinloch secretary £250 a year, but since the number of people claiming relief had gone down to 400, they thought that the salary could be reduced. The chairman disagreed.

Numbers had gone down, Fraser said, because of a temporary freeze on applications, and it was through the secretary that the committee had been able to accomplish 'the most scrutinizing enquiries, and to defeat all attempts at fraud without incurring any expense whatever, for agency in any quarter, which is a saving of vast importance'. He explained that, 'In the early stage of the proceedings this point was viewed with appalling anxiety'. Not to mention, Fraser added, the secretary's assiduous attentions in working with the Church of Scotland clergy to put forward and especially vet the applications. Besides which, the secretary had received the letters from individuals wanting to become pensioners, entered their names into a register of applications, sent back 'forms of various certificates', examined returned forms for correctness, and submitted them to the committee for 'classification' and for balloting. New certificates were then forwarded to all pensioners every six months and closely investigated on their return when the secretary 'has to fill up Bills for £1 each of which as many are sent to each pensioner as make up his half yearly payment'. These bills were next presented at the Corporation's offices by the pensioners themselves, their signatures were compared with those on original records, and the bills were paid. In total the Kinloch secretary had received 4,100 letters in seven years from 1823–29,[1] averaging 585 a year – and every letter was answered

---

[1] Early years were not included in the calculation.

and copies made that, in 1830, 'already occupy two folio volumes'. The register of cases in turn occupied 18 volumes and the secretary had also issued a total of 20,805 bills over a nine-year period from 1820–29, averaging 2,153 bills a year. He had also paid clerks for 'active and intelligent assistance' and had saved them money on stamps.[2]

Unfortunately there is no record of the decision on the Kinloch secretary's salary but it is an interesting and useful overview of the administration and care involved in receiving and accepting the many applications from the Scottish soldiers and sailors who had fought in the Peninsular Wars. Although there is no extant evidence to suggest it, the administrative activities of the Royal Scottish Corporation's secretary at the same time would probably have been similar and the person one and the same, Robert Auld. The Kinloch contact in Edinburgh at this time was Robert Johnston, a man who was also instrumental in helping to set up the Edinburgh branch of the Scottish Hospital in 1830–31, generously allowing his home in New Bridge Street to be used as a meeting place. Johnston had been described in October 1830 by Lachlan Mackintosh, one of the members of the Corporation's committee of management and the driving force behind the Edinburgh branch, as being one 'who has rendered valuable assistance to us in the management of the Kinloch Bequest'.

The amount of the original residue left to the Corporation by William Kinloch is unknown, though an inventory to his estate in 1814 appears to show an Indian currency account held by Fairlie & Co in London of over 300,000 'Sicca Rupees' that when converted into pounds sterling equalled around £38,000 – a huge amount. By the mid-nineteenth century the amount invested was recorded as being over £74,000, and after the fire at the end of 1877 the Bequest had dropped to £42,364, no doubt as a result of Crimean War and other grants. The Corporation was still taking out a quarter of the annual dividend as cash according to William Kinloch's will. This was a fairly lengthy process introduced as a result of new financial rules set up by a charity fraud committee that had sat in 1862. The procedure entailed the Kinloch committee of management writing a formal letter to themselves as the Corporation's court and then having to wait for the next court meeting to get the power of attorney sealed and yet another court to actually get the money out of the bank. In 1879 the Kinloch committee sold £321 in stock to raise £308 in cash. The Kinloch income and expenditure that year was £1,907. On 5 October 1881 the Corporation's auditor, James Fraser, was also appointed the Kinloch auditor. In April

2 The stamp-saving policy was probably because Kinloch letters from Edinburgh were free of postage if sent care of Sir Francis Freeling, at London's General Post Office, according to Robert Auld, the Corporation's London secretary. He explained the situation in a letter to the Reverend Dr Manuel on 15 January 1831; Manuel had hoped to be able to take advantage of the same privilege for his correspondence on the Edinburgh branch of the charity but was told by Auld that money was available to pay for his postage.

1882 the bequest spent £652 on pensions, sharing the Corporation's secretary at a cost of £75; a small allowance of £10 was paid to the Corporation's beadle, and rent for office space at Crane Court cost the bequest £60. That year a sale of stock was not made since, having paid the pensions, the committee realised it had 'a sufficient Balance' as a result of an income tax payout. On the other hand, its members were looking ahead and expecting 'a large increase of pensioners from the soldiers and sailors who were wounded in the late war in Egypt'. Over ten years later, on 5 October 1893, Kinloch stock amounted to £38,412, and at the beginning of 1895 Kinloch pensions were costing the bequest £1,235 a year.

Scottish soldiers who fought and were disabled in further wars of empire after 1815 kept the Kinloch committee busy – especially the Crimean War in 1854–56 and wars in Africa. By the end of June 1884 the bequest was awarding monthly pensions of £4 to 141 individuals elected since 1856 and a £6 pension to about 100 more. A number of men must have been aged 21 or younger when they were accepted into the bequest after the Crimea:

NAME	AGE IN 1884	WHEN ELECTED
David McDonald	57	Jan 1856
William Hastie	51	–
James Gilchrist	55	April 1857
George Machray	51	April 1857
Angus McKay	54	April 1857
George Ross	53	April 1858

Men from the 45th, 92nd, 26th, 79th and 30th regiments were among those admitted in 1879. In September 1885 the Kinloch committee decided to help the wife of James Stewart, a £4 pensioner, who had become an inmate of the Montrose Lunatic Asylum. Isabella Stewart prayed that the pension 'may be paid to her for the benefit of her children, who are dependent on her exertions'. By March 1886 she reported that the asylum's doctor had told her the news that her husband would soon be able to leave.

By 6 January 1886 the Kinloch Bequest was reporting 254 pensioners on its books. As always, applications were carefully examined and some were not accepted. The Kinloch (and Corporation) secretary and sometimes the Corporation's visitor undertook the task of inspecting each case in their own homes, usually around Glasgow and Edinburgh. The case of James C. Kerr, late of the Royal Artillery, who 'had sunstroke at Cawnpore and prayed that he might be put on the Pension list', was refused. Two other pensioners struck off the list appeared to have incomes of over £20 a year – one, Roderick Munro, was found by the committee to be a 'Sub Inspector of Police at Lanark & from that source must be in receipt of a decent income'. The other, Peter Ingram, was 'in a situation at 22/- per week, but from the statement of his Clergyman it appears he has a large family and had had a good deal of affliction to deal in it'. Another old soldier who was struck off had been the night watchman at the 'National Bank of Scotland' in Edinburgh for 12 years with a pay of not less than 25 shillings a week, according to a letter from the chief constable of the city.

Later wars of Empire in India, the North-West Frontier and the Boer War were to provide plenty of fighting experience for Scots. In the early 1900s £4 monthly pensions were paid to those deserving cases with army pensions of around 10*d*. a week on average and payments were being brought in line with the War Office's own improvements in 1904. Pensions for old soldiers in 1900s Glasgow were sometimes paid through the police, usually as a result of the 'intemperance' of the pensioner. One man's allowance was paid with a 'stern warning that if that method fails to ensure more regular habits' the pension would be withdrawn. One old soldier's pension was also paid in this way, not because he was a drunkard but because he was 'aged' and it was his much younger wife who was regarded by the Kinloch committee as 'very unsteady'. Another more moving case was that of a £6 pensioner who had died aged 74 in 1905 after two-and-a-half years on the fund. His wife had died at the same time and they had been buried together. The Kinloch committee paid for the funeral of both.

The Kinloch Bequest had been set up as a charitable scheme when the Royal Scottish Corporation had been granted the investment in 1818. A new scheme was applied for in June 1912 under the Charity Commissioners for England and Wales and was granted a year later. This scheme allowed the Corporation to appoint an agency (such as the British Legion) to help them in finding and managing beneficiaries. Regulations were allowed to be changed regarding payment after death, to a sailor's or soldier's widow or children, 'of moneys accrued due to him at his death on account of his allowance'. Candidates must be

> Scotsmen who had served in the Navy or Army, who have become disabled through no fault of their own, who are in need and deserving, who are not inmates of Greenwich Hospital or Chelsea Hospital, who are not possessed of or entitled to, an income from other sources amounting to or exceeding £311. 10s. per annum, and who have not during the last six calendar months received Poor-law relief other than medical relief, preference will be given to those who have been maimed or wounded in the service of their country.

Servicemen could be removed if their qualifications, on further investigation, did not fit the bequest's requirements and also if, 'in the opinion of the Committee', they were 'guilty of insobriety, breach of regulations, or immoral or improper conduct'. Candidates were to write formally to the secretary: 'Every applicant must state his name, address, age, and occupation; and the date of his entry into the Navy or Army, and the date and cause of his discharge therefrom, and must produce evidence of his qualification for the appointment'.

The 'Kinloch Bequest Applications for Allowance' forms dating from the 1950s and 1960s provide evidence of what happened to poor disabled Scots servicemen who fought for their country in the First and Second World Wars and show that applications continued to be carefully vetted by the Kinloch committee of management. At this time the applicants were brought to the notice of the Kinloch Bequest in London by the local Scottish branch of the British Legion, who also notified them of their deaths. Pensions were still only provided to those of upright and sober character. One man from Ayrshire was a Gordon Highlander who had been gassed in France in 1918. He was a widower with no other family. A personal reference was required to pass his application in May 1965: 'I would be obliged if you could tell me if, in fact, he is a man of sober habit and upright character', wrote the Kinloch committee. An Ayrshire Justice of the Peace replied, 'It is my pleasure to inform you that he is indeed a man of good character and sober habit, a well respected citizen who is now on bare subsistence level'. The JP continued that 'some help … would be useful in his case, and would be thankfully received by a man who is most humble and appreciative of anything that is done for him. His health is not too good, but he gets about: in other words, he puts a "stout heart to a steep hill" in his endeavours to meet life with a smile'. The old soldier's medical certification, like all others, had 'to be given if possible by a Medical Officer of the Navy or Army'. The information on the form was not disclosed to the applicant. Under the section marked 'For wage-earning capacity affected – partially or wholly', the doctor had written, '… he is under nourished and in poor physical condition, although there is no obvious particular disease. Underweight 7st. 4lbs. There is evidence of nervous debility'.

One Kinloch pensioner, who was not disabled by war but by generally poor health, came originally from Angus. He had been a naval petty officer in the Second World War. His pension had ceased on his death in 1969. He had received no injuries during his war service but had been 'suffering from an early disseminated sclerosis …', and had consequently had to give up work as a shipyard plater; he could have done light work but there was none available in the area. Another pensioner had served during the First World War in Salonika and France and died a widower, aged 90. In 1959 his total weekly income was £4.18s.6d., including 10s.6d from the Kinloch Bequest. He was '… known and respected in his community', and although 'His deafness does not allow one to become well acquainted with him', he was 'hardworking, sober and trustworthy'.

In 1979–80, J. Murray Napier, the Corporation's chairman and trustee John Brown visited the Charity Commissioners. The stipulation of William Kinloch's will and the chancery documentation of 1818 to use only 125 per cent of the bequest's annual income until it ran out was proving difficult to operate, and 'deaths did not conveniently fit the formula'. The Charity Commissioners agreed to issue an amendment to delete the restriction, and thereafter the bequest's administrators were allowed unrestricted use of the capital, thus enabling ultimate extinction. Registered with the Charity Commission of England and Wales as Charity No. 210067, the remit of the Kinloch Bequest was also expanded and the bequest began to provide pensions for disabled servicemen as well as servicewomen and also included those who had served in the Royal Marines and the Royal Air Force. Most Kinloch applications since 1912 have continued to come through local service support agencies, especially those in Scotland, such as the British Legion and the Soldiers, Sailors and Air Force Families' Association (SSAFA). The Corporation had 100 referrals from these and other agencies during the year 1994–95 but the number of referrals has declined over more recent years.

The Kinloch Bequest fund stood at £92,000 by the end of June 2002 and the income is now insufficient to warrant considering any new applications. The Royal Scottish Corporation, as the sole trustee, will be discussing with the Charity Commissioners the best way to wind up the fund, probably with small increases in pensions to the surviving eligible beneficiaries.

CHAPTER 24

Other Military Connections

S cots soldiers served with Marlborough at Blenheim and in Canada with Wolfe; in India, Egypt, Spain, at Waterloo, in the Crimea, the Indian Mutiny, the Chitral Campaign, at Dargai, Majuba, Omdurman and in the Boer War, not to mention two world wars and other campaigns since. One of the earliest, and at the time greatest, military contribution to the Royal Scottish Corporation was a large donation of £202 from the officers of the 'Scots Foot-Guards' in 1698. The officers of the smaller 'Scots Horse-Guards' contributed an additional £33, probably the same year. In 1817, after the conclusion of the Peninsular Wars, £300 was received from the Committee of Subscribers for British Prisoners of War. The later world wars and other British wars of empire meant that more help for Scottish servicemen was needed, and appeals for such topical causes were raised by the Corporation from time to time.

William Kinloch's charity could have been of later service to the poor but hardy and enterprising Highland piper that Henry Mayhew found busking on the London streets in the late 1850s:

> Although I had served ten years, and been in two battles, yet I was not entitled to a pension. You must serve twenty-one years to be entitled to 1s. $^{1}/_{2}$d ... I left the army just two years before war broke out, and I'd rather than twenty thousand pounds I'd been in my health to have gone to the Crimea, for I'd have had more glory after that war than ever any England was in ...

Sir Colin Campbell, later Lord Clyde, was remembered for his Crimean bravery and leadership by his old Highland soldier and also by Corporation members, socialising at the Caledonian Society. During the Battle of Alma, overhearing a lesser officer exclaiming that the Highland Brigade should fall back, Clyde firmly put him in his place with the words, 'It is better, sir, that every officer and man of Her Majesty's Guards should be dead on the field than that they should turn their backs upon the enemy!' The 93rd Regiment was the original 'thin red line', arranged in that fashion rather than in the usual square formation against the Russians at Balaklava: 'I did not think it worthwhile to form them even four deep,' Clyde was said to have later remembered. Another Corporation Crimean hero, and life member of the committee of management remembered at his death in June 1901 was Lord Wantage. Feeling 'privileged' in his charitable interest, the Corporation was also grateful for 'the splendid example of duty which his life afforded not only in his personal heroism at Alma and Inkerman, but in his devotion to the relief of suffering humanity as Chairman of the Red Cross Society'.

The St Andrew's Dinner of 1873 showed the Royal Scottish Corporation's concern for Scottish servicemen then fighting empire battles in Africa. The toast proposed to 'The Army, Navy, and Auxiliary Forces' was given by the lord mayor, then chairman of the festival. Britain, he said, 'was not a military nation', but it 'could fight battles and win them, which answered the same purpose', and he had no doubt that the Ashanti War would soon be brought to a successful conclusion. George Bouchier responded to the toast on behalf of the army, which was, he said, 'in a state of re-organisation', but 'whatever might be arranged respecting it', he was sure that 'so long as Englishmen, Irishmen and Scotchmen fought shoulder to shoulder, there would be satisfactory tidings received as to their doings'. In early 1874 the Corporation followed up this concern with a joint appeal for the soldiers wounded in the Ashanti Wars and their dependents, claiming, 'now that the war has ended in a triumphant success, we ought to think of the disabled, the widowed and orphaned'. On 23 March the Corporation's secretary, Macrae Moir, and governor Alexander Peebles wrote to a number of eminent Scotsmen to ask for their support for the '42nd' and other participating regiments at a fund-raising meeting to be held in the Corporation's hall 'to promote this most desirable object' and, 'as it seems to us – a national duty and a privilege'. This would be a meeting 'of Gentlemen', Moir wrote, when 'it is expected there will be representatives of the Caledonian Society, the Highland Society, the Royal Caledonian Asylum, the Royal Scottish Corporation and other Scottish Societies'. Later, the war in South Africa from 1899–1902 took away many more Scotsmen and increased demands on the Corporation from their widows and orphans. The charity also lost a noble supporter in 1900 when the Earl of Airlie, a colonel commanding the 12th Lancers, was killed in the Transvaal.

During the First World War, a group of Scottish Societies called the Federated Council of Scottish Associations was formed in London in October 1914 to care for Scottish fighting soldiers and prisoners-of-war. This association took over what had been started 'in a small way' at the Royal Scottish Corporation. The involvement of the charity included management help from its chairman John Douglas and its secretary Thomas Montcrieff who respectively became a member of the Federated Council's executive committee and its honorary treasurer. The Council was especially keen 'to prevent overlapping' and wasted charity; smaller Scottish regiments had recently received too much and the larger regiments had in turn got nothing. The new body was therefore asked to distribute socks, other woollen garments and 'comforts' to the soldiers of 38 battalions 'at the different fronts'. Donations and contributions, many hand-made by wives and lady friends of members, came from Scots in London, Scotland, and elsewhere in England as well as Scots abroad; 2,000 pairs of socks and money even came from the St Andrew's Society of the River Plate in Buenos Aires. The final war total of articles was over 75,000 pieces including 37,619 pairs of socks. Other articles included 'shirts, mufflers, mittens, gloves, hosetops, helmets, coats, towels, bandages, medical comforts, soup squares, pipes, tobacco, cigarettes, soap, games, sets of bagpipes, and other musical instruments', as well as books. Some more specialised articles, like 'football accessories', were procured by the association and paid for by the officers and soldiers themselves. By 1919 the Council still had 137 pairs of socks left which it distributed to the 'deserving' poor of the Royal Scottish Corporation.

The Federated Council started to send food parcels to Scottish prisoners-of-war in German camps and to 'friendless Scottish soldiers in Turkey, Bulgaria and elsewhere' in December 1915. This activity was stopped for a time when a central committee took over the organisation, but this soon proved inadequate and the Council's supplies to the prisoners were restarted. Bread was sent via the Bureau de Secours in Berne and the men thereafter received the best and freshest bread that could be found. The Council was also able to trace men when relatives had experienced little luck – one mother in Scotland had tried for six months to find her son; the Council found him in a matter of weeks in a German hospital. The efficiency of the operation run by Douglas and Montcrieff was such that the 48th Canadians (the Toronto Highlanders) also asked for the organisation to deliver supplies to their own 221 prisoners.

The Council, with the help of Montcrieff, working from the Royal Scottish Corporation, also arranged outings for badly wounded Scots soldiers in London hospitals and gave a little pleasure to a total of over 13,000 men. These soldiers were taken by bus and car to the grounds of the Caledonian Schools in Bushey and other private gardens and places of interest in and around London. Visits to wounded Scots soldiers in London hospitals also began, aided by the English County Folk Visitation Society which sent cards daily telling the Federated Council of new hospital arrivals. From 1914–18 around 100 visitors visited over 6,000 men in 100 hospitals in London, Middlesex, Surrey, Kent and Essex and also prompted many soldiers' reunions with their wives and mothers. Over 47,600 men had benefited from this form of aid by 1919.

Encouraged by the Council, St Columba's church members also met and entertained Scottish soldiers who were starting or finishing leave, and who were now 'coming from and returning to France on Saturdays and Sundays'. The army authorities would 'dump the men at Victoria Station at two o'clock on

Sunday mornings, and leave them to wander about the streets for 19 hours before their trains left for the North'. When the church authorities stepped in, 'the men were met at the trains in the bleak early morning' and taken to the church hall for a cup of hot cocoa and some biscuits. After a wash and shave, they went for a walk in Kensington Gardens and returned to a 'hot steaming breakfast'. The men then 'went to the baths for a plunge and a change of clothing', and returned to the hall to board buses which took them on a three-hour tour of London. Lunch and afternoon tea were provided in the hall, and after supper the soldiers 'were piped to the stations and given a hearty send off'. The total cost of all Federated Council activities from 1914–1919 had been just over £4,700, which had been covered by donations of £5,000. Goods received and sent abroad were estimated to have cost around £10,000.

Another servicemen's charity also managed like the Kinloch Bequest by the Royal Scottish Corporation's trustees today is the St Andrew's Scottish Soldiers' Club Fund, registered as Charity No. 233297. This fund was originally established to help serving soldiers of the Aldershot Garrison in Hampshire soon after the First World War. Initially called the Presbyterian Soldiers Fund, it had later changed its name and in 1972 the Corporation agreed to administer it, a number of its trustees being also trustees of the soldiers' charity. By the end of 1974 a new scheme for its administration had been agreed with the Charity Commission, at which time the Corporation expressed its 'pleasure' at the responsibility 'of helping the Scottish soldier'. A 1982 amendment to its bye-laws extended the charity's reach to allow income to be applied to any former Scots soldiers who had served in the British Army and to their families and dependants, in any part of the world – when they might be 'in need, hardship or distress'.

The London Scottish Regiment has had a similarly long connection with the Royal Scottish Corporation. The Highland Armed Association of London and The Loyal North Britons had been raised in 1793 and 1803 as part of the country's volunteer forces ready to repel Napoleon's threatened invasion of Britain. These militia formations were later disbanded, and it was not until after the Crimean War that the nation's security seemed again to be in danger. In 1859 the establishment of the London Scottish Rifle Volunteers was first discussed by members of the Caledonian Society at a meeting called by Robert Hepburn, a philanthropic Scottish dental surgeon (and a later chairman of the Corporation), and held in his house, then at 8 Davies Street. This group asked the Highland Society 'to join them in carrying out the scheme', which it gladly did. The regiment was raised under the command of Lt Colonel Lord Elcho, later the Earl of Wemyss and March.[1]

---

[1] Hepburn was enrolled as an original honorary member and much later attended a line-up of the regiment at Gosford in 1899 when he was aged 91. Many visitors that day were astonished to see him in uniform, his 'tall commanding figure, upwards of six feet, moving about the lawn'.

Members of the regiment later served in the Boer War, mostly with the Gordon Highlanders and the City Imperial Volunteers. As a result the regiment was awarded its first battle honour, 'South Africa 1900–02'. In 1908 the regiment became part of the Territorial Army (formed as a result of the Haldane Review), and was renamed the 14th County of London Battalion, the London Regiment. In August 1914 the 1st Battalion went to France and on 31 October became the first territorial unit to be committed to the line at Messines, near Ypres. This line was held at dreadful cost and the regiment has commemorated the event every Hallowe'en since. On 4 November 1915 a meeting at the Corporation was called by the Federated Council of Scottish Associations to help with recruitment. The meeting was chaired by the Secretary of State for Scotland, and as a result a second battalion was raised which saw service in Palestine and France; a third training battalion was also raised, and many members of the regiment were transferred to other units.

Over 10,000 men passed through the regiment during the war, more than 2,000 commissions were granted, and two VCs were awarded. The Corporation, with the active participation of its secretary and chairman, Thomas Montcrieff and George Paton, took on the role of 'almoner' for the London Scottish War Memorial, looking after the funds raised. A fine wooden memorial was erected to the 1,584 London Scots who died. This can now be seen in the regiment's London drill hall in Horseferry Road; another memorial was also erected on the Messines ridge in Belgium at the site of the 1914 action.

A brief mention must be made of a long and bitter dispute which upset relations between the Corporation and the regiment from 1967 until its settlement in 1986. The regimental headquarters is held in trust under a Trust Deed of 1886. This provides that in the event of the disbandment of the regiment, the proceeds of sale are to be divided three ways – between the Royal Scottish Corporation, the Royal Caledonian Schools and the Highland Society. In 1967 the Corporation, then under the chairmanship of J. Murray Napier, argued that the regiment had been disbanded when the Territorial Army was reorganised and that the London Scottish was no longer a major unit. Eventually, as part of the scheme to build a new drill hall, the dispute was finally settled with a Consent Order in the High Court in 1986 under which the regiment bore substantial legal costs and was ordered to pay each of the three charities a total of £21,000 over 19 years. When Douglas Robertson became chairman of the Corporation, he and other governors did not want to be seen taking money from the regiment and agreed to refund it £1,000, reimbursing most of the Corporation's share of the court award. Colonel John Clemence, Regimental Colonel of the London Scottish from 1989 to 1995 and an active Corporation trustee, has more recently succeeded in re-establishing good relations between the two institutions.

The London Scottish Regiment has been called the 'standing evidence of the patriotism of London Scots', and one volunteering Corporation Scot in 1906 was proud to boast of the fact that the regiment, as he said, then 'stood between this country and conscription'. The regiment has certainly been a great club for Scotsmen and a fine supplier of fighting and charitable Scots. Scots in the East India Company and the British Army have been strongly represented in the history of the Royal Scottish Corporation. These two institutions were also great Scottish networks that were largely organised, peopled and promoted by Scots in London.

PART IV
1815–2002

CHAPTER 25

Scotland and London II

Industrialisation through textiles and chemicals and the heavy industries of coal, iron, steel and shipbuilding ensured that the many nineteenth-century Scots who came to London possessed skills of their own in abundance. They also knew how to turn their relations with the English to their own advantage. By the early 1840s, the booms and slumps associated with capitalism meant that poverty was now geared more to the market cycles of commerce than to the seasonal cycles of agriculture. Thomas Chalmers told how many more people suffered 'calamities ... in the shape of beggared capitalists, and unemployed operatives', and how there was a 'dreary interval of bankruptcy and alarm'. By 1843, the great split in the Church of Scotland (led by Chalmers) and much social distress had prompted an investigation into the living conditions of the working classes across Scotland. This period of poverty was also compounded by the potato famine as it swept over the Highland areas in the later 1840s. Even so, some poor Scots in London by the late 1850s still thought of the cheaper and healthier life they could lead in Scotland if they went home:

> I can give the children a good breakfast of oatmeal-porridge every morning, and that will in seven weeks make them as fat as seven years of tea and coffee will do here. Besides, in Scotland I can buy a very pretty little stand-up bed-stead for 2s. which here would come to 4s.

Coming south was not an automatic ticket to success, however; emotional stress and continued poverty were often all these Scots had to look forward to, lightened only by the hope of one day striking the elusive gold. Henry Mayhew, a journalist and also London's great mid-nineteenth-century social commentator, found it difficult to see 'where the monster city began or ended'; to him it was this 'bricken mass of churches and hospitals, banks and prisons, palaces and workhouses, docks and refuges for the destitute, parks and squares, and courts and alleys'. London grew from having a population of around 700,000 by 1700 to around five million by 1900. In 1800 there were nearly a million people in London – and it was the first city in the world to have such a number of inhabitants. In the ten years between the 1841 census and that of 1851, London also became home to 330,000 immigrants and migrants – the vast majority coming from famine-stricken Ireland. More people came from agricultural areas after the 1860s, drawn to a busy and brightly lit city where they thought everything was possible. By 1891 Sydney Webb could say of London that 'if it were emptied tomorrow the whole of the inhabitants of Scotland and Wales could do no more than refill it'. By the 1900s, with 16 cities in Britain having a population of a million, people were starting to live much more urban lives than ever before.

People came to London especially to work in service jobs as well as manufacturing and construction, looking forward to the capital's higher wages and its industrial variety. Nonetheless, many thousands of London weavers had lost their jobs in the 1830s as the industry moved to the Midlands: a fact that could account for some of the increase in distress seen in London by the Royal Scottish Corporation's central administration (and its branch office in Edinburgh) at this time. The port and City were still importantly working together for the good of international trade and the British Empire. Businesses were small, but better-paid jobs could be found in shipping and banking, investment and insurance – all suitable for the professional sort of Scot. Seamen and 'riverside labour' saw huge capital investment being put into the building and revamping of London's dockyards, including West India Docks on the Isle of Dogs, London Docks at Wapping and the East India Docks at Blackwall. These had been designed for the tea trade by Scots engineer John Rennie in 1806. Rennie was also kept busy with London, Southwark and Waterloo bridges. Employing 400 men, his main engineering works were at Blackfriars, and the area's Albion Mills, also of his design, had been the first to use steam power and had met the great demand for bread from London's increasing population.

Carriages and hackney cabs had long been available, and the first omnibuses started to ply their routes in the 1830s; by 1900, the 3,000 horse-drawn buses and trams carried 500 million passengers a year. Suburban living was now within reach of clerks and tradesmen who could move away from traffic jams and find more security and space in 'outer London'. The London County Council (LCC), established in 1888, covered the area outside the City itself and London now had a centralised form of government for the first time under its first chairman, the Earl of Rosebery. By 1909, city life had become, according to one contemporary writer, 'a life of Security; a life of Sedentary occupation; a life of Respectability ... Its male population is engaged in all its working hours to small, crowded offices, under artificial light, doing immense sums, adding up other men's accounts, writing other men's letters'. London had grown in its markets, its population, its transport and its buildings. One of the key reasons why the capital actually worked at all during these centuries, and why so many found jobs, was that there was, above all, a never-ending supply of people who wanted to work.

The London County Council remained in control of the city until 1965 when it was replaced by the Greater London Council. By 1970 this 'Greater London' was indeed a huge ethnic mix – largely on account of Commonwealth immigration. According to a homeless study of 1971, it was also 'a vast sprawling urban conglomeration housing more than a sixth of the nation's people and providing more than a sixth of all the country's employment'. London's sprawl was so extensive and its 'variety of people, jobs, conditions, and opportunities' so remarkable, that the study's authors could write that it, nevertheless,

> still has extremes of conspicuous wealth and conspicuous poverty, displayed arrogantly at the top and suffered with abject passivity at the bottom. The grossness of each is offensive in a society with pretensions to humanitarian concern and social responsibility. But the excesses of wealth and poverty in London are linked by more than their offensiveness to the social conscience, for they are causally linked: each depends to some extent on the continuation of the other through the perpetuation of systems of taxation, fiscal and financial policies, and even social services, that sustain the regressive distribution of wealth and other resources in society.

CHAPTER 26

The Poor Law, Parish Workhouses and Private Charity

B efore the Victorian period, and especially in 1815, more money in London was being given to voluntary and charitable bodies than was being put into the 'Poor Law machinery'. In 1819 it was estimated that as much as £850,000 was paid out for charitable purposes. The Poor Law Amendment Act for England and Wales was subsequently passed in 1834 but helped little. The act set up a Poor Law Commission and ruled that people could no longer claim poor relief outside a workhouse situation. In practice outdoor relief still continued, especially in London, although it was much reduced. Average payments for a parish in Southwark, for example, dropped to 1s. 3d. a week per family in 1843 and those without proper settlement got even less. Things became worse by the 1870s as more Poor Law inspectors and guardians enforced the workhouse ethic; one considered it 'character building' and even saw it as an 'inducement to a struggle for independence'.

Some social commentators recommended that outdoor relief should not be given to able-bodied males and that all outdoor relief should be stopped after three months and applicants forced to go into the segregated workhouse, parted from their wives and children. Despite this harsh suggestion, many of the poor worked the system so that, punitive and a threat to the hard worker though it was, the new Poor Law could still be a valued 'social safety-net' for the parentless, the sick and the aged. In addition, the philanthropy of Victorian Londoners grew despite the thoughts of some that it might discourage self-improvement and encourage dependence. The livery companies in particular were now mainly concerned with their charitable giving, their almshouses and the running of schools for poorer members' children. These and other charities operating during this period relieved the problems brought about by industrialisation and urbanisation. The faults in society itself were rarely acknowledged and much faith was placed in 'self-help'; Charles Booth's surveys of London's social life in the 1890s, though, did 'hint' at them. Furthermore, philanthropy was also seen as an undeniable Christian duty, and subscribers to such charitable institutions enjoyed the fact that they now had rights to nominate patients and other cases for treatment or relief.

The great growth of cities and towns brought an increase in disease and epidemics and forced the Victorians to look at their lack of medical care, hospitals and sanitary conditions. Drinking water was undrinkable by 1834 and it was said that 'He who drinks a tumbler of London Water has literally in his stomach more animated beings than there are Men, Women and Children in the face of the Globe'. There had been a cholera epidemic in 1832 when 5,000 people had died, and another in 1848–9. Many of the poor also died of smallpox, whooping cough and scarlet fever. The able-bodied poor who claimed relief usually did so because they were sick, and one in three children died before their first birthday in poorer districts. On the other hand, the new Poor Law meant that the first public health officials were created by default when medical officers were appointed and some even visited the sick in their own homes. By 1890 the city had 21 general hospitals (eleven of them with medical schools), 67 specialist hospitals and 374 beds within a mile of Charing Cross. Despite this, the hospitals were not the only providers, or the even the main providers, of healthcare to Londoners. Many hospitals even actively avoided having to deal with the deaths of paupers, hoping that the state would look after the chronically sick, the incurable and the dying. To this end, the infirmaries of the London parish workhouses and other private charities, like the Royal Scottish Corporation and its medical officers and visitors, worked alongside the hospitals to care for these unwanted people. Additionally, ownership of city property rather than landed estates had helped some of the great hospitals, like St Bartholomew's, survive the agricultural depression of the 1870s better than others. On a smaller scale, such city property was something in which the London Scots' charity had also invested.

In 1848 the first Public Health Act was passed, creating the General Board of Health and making town councils responsible for sanitation, drainage, water supplies and rates; among other duties they could also appoint medical officers. The City of London was outside Metropolitan London's jurisdiction and later created its own sanitation and medical administration and practitioners. John Simon was appointed to the post of Medical Officer for Health in the City of London in 1848. He thought 'educated men' should visit the poorer areas and see for themselves how the other half lived:

> Let him fancy what it would be to himself to live there, in that beastly degradation of stink, fed with such bread, drinking such water ... Let him talk to the inmates, let him hear what is thought of the bone-boiler next door, or the slaughter-house behind; what of the sewer-grating before the door; ... what of the artisan's dead body, stretched on his widow's one bed, beside her living children.

Simon's efficient efforts at sanitary reform with cleaner drinking water, more frequently flushing privies and fewer cesspools meant that the City experienced fewer effects of the 1848–49 cholera epidemic and fewer again during another in 1854. It was up to the Metropolitan Board of Works, set up in 1855, to fix the 'great stink' coming from the Thames in June 1858; as a result Sir Joseph Bazalgette was given the go-ahead to construct his great sewerage scheme still cleaning up London today.

In 1861–62 Henry Mayhew divided the poor into three groups, 'according as they will work, they can't work and they won't work'. Although for the most part sympathetic, he also saw the poor as agents of their own misfortunes and accused them of 'a want of temperance, energy, cleanliness, morality, knowledge …' Mayhew also showed that treating the poor sick in 1848 had been more expensive than just giving them food. Once an order was applied the same year refusing relief to able-bodied and healthy men, the numbers of 'casual' vagrants needing to stay in the workhouses dropped considerably, and so too did the relief costs. Examination was effective and appeared to be working.[1]

Seventeenth- and eighteenth-century workhouses had been notorious for overcrowding but some nineteenth-century workhouses had sympathetic and friendly staff and the workhouse porter at Holborn showed Henry Mayhew around his institution in the 1850s. The porter described to Mayhew how in the mid-1840s he had experienced what he called 'a glut of Irish' who 'besieged the doors incessantly'; but he liked them. As an Englishman he found the English in the casual wards 'generally a bad cadging set, as saucy as could be … I've heard them, of a night, brag of their dodges – how they'd done through the day – and the best places to get money'. He had heard them talk of the best streets in London to get bread, ale or money and thought that 'there might be one deserving character to thirty cadgers … We haven't had one Scotch person … or two Welshmen in a month among the casuals'.

The only real place for the homeless in London was the Asylum for the Houseless Poor in Cripplegate. Here Mayhew saw 'men from every part of the United Kingdom' the night he was there, and they were for the most part all in rags. One of the inmates he spoke to was a Scottish soldier's wife, with a 'decent appearance' but whose pinched features had only 'the remains of prettiness'. She looked as though she had seen 'better days', and wore a 'very clean checked cotton shawl, and a straw bonnet tolerably entire'. She told Mayhew that she had been born near Inverness and had been a servant since she was eleven, always in good places, with good masters and mistresses and keeping her good character: 'In all my distress I've done nothing wrong, but I didn't know what distress was when in service.' She had worked until she had married and had looked after her

---

[1] The Wandsworth and Clapham workhouse paid out £24 10s. in 1849 to relieve 3,900 people and Mayhew wrote that a similar 'decrease throughout all London has been particularly striking'; in 1847–48 the total number had reached a high of 310,058 but by 1848–49 the number had gone down to 143,064.

widowed mother, her father having died when she was two years old. Her money didn't go far and she found it difficult to save: 'Wages are very low in Scotland to what they are in England'. She lived for two years in the barracks at Fort George with her husband, remembering: 'I was very comfortable. I didn't know what it was to want anything I ought to have. My husband was a kind, sober man'. He was then posted to Nova Scotia and only six soldiers' wives were allowed to go with each regimental company; lots for the seventeen men were drawn from the officer's cap. 'My husband drew a blank,' she said and described the scene as the regiment left from Woolwich. Some of the men were just as upset as their women and children, 'but I couldn't look much at them, and I don't like to see men cry. My husband was sadly distressed.'

She had thought it would be easy to get a passage and had not considered the expense of the £6 fare across the Atlantic. This money she had tried to collect by washing and sewing but had suffered two attacks of cholera, thus using up her meagre savings:

> I was then quite destitute … It's now a month since I was entirely out of halfpence. I can't beg; it would disgrace me and my husband and I'd die in the streets first. Last Saturday I hadn't a farthing. I hadn't a thing to part with. I had a bed by the night, at 3d. a night, not a regular lodging-house; but the mistress wouldn't trust me no longer, as I owed her 2s. 6d., and for that she holds clothes worth far more than that. I heard of this Asylum, and got admitted, or I must have spent the night in the street – there was nothing else for me; but thank God! I've been spared that … All my wish is to get out to my husband. I care for nothing else in this world.

She showed Mayhew a letter her husband had recently written from Nova Scotia which also held out the same sense of hope and patience. It was unfortunate that she did not apply to the Royal Scottish Corporation, which might well have helped with an assisted passage.

CHAPTER 27

City Scots

Taverns along the Strand and near Charing Cross played host to many of the arriving and departing Scots at the end of the eighteenth and during the early nineteenth centuries. The Edinburgh-London mail coach arrived in St Martin's Le Grand and the Blue Anchor in Little Britain was the place of arrival of the Edinburgh coach. A prominent Scottish journalist of the early nineteenth century, Robert Mudie, did not like this 'Babylon the Great' as he called London, seeing that all was gilded pleasure or villainy or 'desolation, where every street is a crowd ... and yet comfort from no lip, and pity from no eye'. Another Scottish writer in London was Thomas Carlyle who thought the city a form of hell and described it to his brother in 1824: 'I had much rather visit London from time to time than live in it'.

Writing in 1890, David Hepburn, a Scots Corporation chairman and the chronicler of the Caledonian Society of London, wrote that 'the "big city" now teems with Scotsmen, but in 1837, although scattered in considerable numbers, they were by no means so plentiful as they are today':

> Many, however, found their way to the great El Dorado in the hope of picking up something. Some picked up a good deal; others were not so fortunate, and were sent back by the Scottish Corporation to 'whaur they'd cam frae.' The clannish feeling which knits Scotsmen together in all parts of the world was rife in London at that time. No longer do the sons of the North journey to the great Metropolis in cramped smacks, or on stage coaches, because well-fitted steamers and 'The Flying Scotsman' supply the place of these primitive methods of locomotion. Maybe some still plod their way on foot, chawing speldrons, tougher than the soles of their worn-out boots, as they turn the scant bawbees in their pouches, and arrive to begin the great struggle, with little more than an empty oatmeal bag as their stock-in-trade. But in whatever way they come in ever-increasing numbers, they bring along with them at least one grand possession, that is their love and pride for the country which gave them birth, an inheritance common to all Scotsmen, and one which, if cherished, spurs them on to honourable achievements, and lends them a distinctive character in whatever quarter of the globe they may be located.

Some in the capital still had a harder life than others. Henry Mayhew made only a few references to Scots in his reports compared to the vast numbers of the Irish and English poor he describes. One poor English grocer tried his hand at hawking tea but it was no good, since 'the Scotchmen in that trade are the only men that can do any good in it'. Of women street-sellers, who usually sold goods with their men, Mayhew records that they were of all ages and classes but 'chiefly of two countries, England and Ireland. There are (comparatively) a few Jewesses, and a very few Scotchwomen and Welchwomen who are street traders; and they are so, as it were, accidentally, from their connection, by marriage or otherwise, with male street-sellers'. Nevertheless, Mayhew usefully includes profiles of two Scots Highland pipers earning their living on the streets of London. The first bagpiper he meets is a 'well-looking young man, dressed in full Highland costume, with modest manners and of slow speech, as if translating his words from the Gaelic before he uttered them'. The man tells him his story:

> I am a native of Inverness, and a Grant. My father was a soldier, and a player in the 42nd. In my youth I was a shepherd in the hills, until my father was unable to support me any longer. He had 9*d.* a day pension for seventeen years' service, and had been thrice wounded. He taught me and my brither the pipes; he was too poor to have us taught any trade; so we started on our own accounts. We travelled up to London, had only our pipes to depend upon. We came in full Highland dress. The tartan is cheap there, and we mak it up oursels. My dress as I sit here, without my pipes, would cost about 4l. in London. Our mothers spin the tartan in Inverness-shire, and the dress comes to maybe 30s., and it is better than in London. My pipes cost me three guineas new. It's between five and six years since I first came to London, and I was twenty-four last November ... I was rather a novelty at first, and did pretty well. I could make 1l. a week then, but now I can't make 2s. a day, not even in summer ... A Scotch family will sometimes give me a shilling or two when they find out I am a Scotchman[1] ... We have our own rooms. I pay 4s. week for an empty room, and have my ain furniture.

The second piper, McGregor, said that he had left the 93rd Regiment as a corporal in 1852. He now played his pipes as he wandered around England and Scotland:

> Whenever I go about the country I leave my wife and family in London, and go off with my girl. I send them up money every week, according to what I earn. Every farthing that I can spare I always send up ... I do pretty well in London, taking my 4s. a day, but out of that I must pay 1s. 9d. a week lodging-money, for I can't go into apartments, for if I did it would be but poorly furnished, for I've no beds, or furniture, or linen ... My old lady couldn't live when I travel if it wasn't for my boy, who goes out and gets about 1s. a day.

---

[1] And not an Irishman dressed as a Highland piper.

Lord Panmure is very good to him, and gives him something whenever he meets him.

Not all Englishmen or even this Scot of the mid-nineteenth-century would have agreed with J. M. Barrie's later (1908) sentiment that 'There are few more impressive sights in the world than a Scotsman on the make'. There was always the age-old Highland versus Lowland prejudice to make up for the otherwise friendly welcome. McGregor tells Mayhew about what he considered the meanness of Lowland Scots in both London and Scotland; and he liked the French:

> About my best friends in London are the French people – they are the best I can meet, they come next to the Highlanders. When I meet a Highlander, he will, if he's only just a labouring man, give me a few coppers. A Highlander will never close his eye upon me. It is the Lowlander that is the worse to me. They never takes no notice of me when I'm passing: they'll smile and cast an eye as I pass by. Many a time I'll say to them when they pass, 'Well, old chap, you don't like the half-naked men, I know you don't!' and many will say, 'No, I don't.' I never play the pipes when I go through the Lowlands – I'd soon as play poison to them. They never give anything. It's the Lowlanders that get the Scotch a bad name for being miserable, and keeping their money, and using small provision. They're a disgrace to their country.

More Scots had begun to arrive in London, especially by the end of the nineteenth century. Speaking in the late 1860s, the Caledonian Society of London's Honorary Secretary and Corporation governor, J. Seton Ritchie, counted 40,000 Scots 'in the Metropolis' while there were 'upwards of three million inhabitants of Scotland'. As a result, he considered that the Caledonian Society (and hence also the Corporation) 'might be fairly held to be representative of the zeal and energy' of the Scots population as a whole. By 1901 there were around 50,000 Scots in the County of London itself and around 100,000 in all of Greater London, especially after the First World War. According to census statistics there were also usually more women, except for 1901. The 1901 figure for Scots generally remained stable for the rest of the century, and by 1991 there were 113,000 being counted in that year's census, a national amount only second to that of the Irish (much higher at 256,000). It was the large and growing Irish Catholic community (especially after the 1840s famine), and then other immigrants from British Commonwealth countries and thereafter Eastern Europe who were to feel the English prejudice which the Scots had been subjected to periodically in the mid-seventeenth and mid-eighteenth centuries.

The Scots knew how to network and make the most of patronage in Scotland, London and abroad. They also knew how to use and improve the administration and institutions set up by the English, and on the whole they did well out of Great Britain and its empire. Scots also knew the right words to use in reply to those who annoyed them on the city's streets. One story from 1902, told by Dr

Daniel Forbes, one of the Corporation's honorary physicians, concerns an elderly Scottish woman,

> whose feelings were sadly shocked by the jeerings and attempted mimicry of some of the juniors of London with whom she came into contact, and who finally turned on her tormentors with the remark: 'Gang home, ye ill-mannered brats, and tell yer mothers to teach ye the story aboot Bannockburn.'

Mostly, though, 'Englishmen now show as great a desire to blend with us as we do to blend with them,' thought William Scott as early as 1869. He told the Caledonian Society members that year that really

> the current was setting in another direction, for the sporting and pleasure-seeking Englishman that no better field for enjoyment can anywhere be found than the mountains and glens, the rivers and lakes of Scotland. In fact, their enthusiasm not infrequently carried them the length of trying to pass themselves off as genuine Scottish natives; and a good story is told by Dean Ramsay of one of these Southerners accosting a Scotsman of the old school in that character. The old gentleman was at first staggered, but discovering the fictitious article:– 'Man,' said he, 'I'm just thinkin' ye're nae Scotsman after a'; but I'll tell ye what ye are, ye're just an impruived Englishman.'

The nineteenth century also brought more creative Scots to London who improved the lives of Londoners. The Adam brothers, Robert and John (and their father William) had made city living much more architecturally stylish in the previous century, and in 1800 the Scots architect James Burton had similarly taken on the redesign of Russell Square. By 1807 he had built Tavistock Square, Burton Street and Burton Crescent. Despite such Scottish builders, there was no Scots 'ghetto' in London apart perhaps from the earlier East End weavers' communities around Shoreditch and Spitalfields and a smaller number of the richer, ministerial or gardening Scots who lived not far from the Scots church in Pont Street, Knightsbridge. Twentieth-century London Scots lived all over London, and even in the depression of the 1930s the city was still a better place to be than Scotland. Nevertheless, members of the Caledonian Society (and Scots Corporation governors) became worried about the capacity of a new generation of migrant Scots to adapt to the changing conditions. On 11 December 1930 Sir John Reith, head of the BBC, gave a talk to the Caledonians on democracy, education, and mediocrity:[2]

> Is mediocrity a by-product of Democracy? Is it inevitable? Is courage gone from us? Have we lost the faculty for thinking and speaking and acting in the

---

[2] Reith himself was said to have used his Scottish networking skills when he applied for his BBC job, adding in a postscript on his application to a fellow-Scot, 'perhaps you know my people in Aberdeen ...'

first person singular? Is it unfashionable and undemocratic? Are we coming to the stage when a man with ability and intelligence beyond a point is as unpopular and unemployable as a man with ability and intelligence below a point?

If the Scot drifted with the current, he warned, it would be 'a bad day for the Empire and the world'. He finally asked, 'Is Scotland turning out the kind of men that she once did? Is there the old independence of character, the strong religious faith, the high principle, the stern determination, the diligence and the great achievement? I doubt it'. These concerns continued to carry political resonances notwithstanding the key role of Scots in successive British governments.

H. R. Boyne, political correspondent of London's *Daily Telegraph*, and chairman of the Parliamentary Press Gallery, spoke about Scotsmen in the UK government to a another gathering of Corporation Scots at the Caledonian Society in 1961. That year, he said, there had been seven ministerial posts under the Scottish Office; three always went to lawyers, and the minister of state was usually a peer, which left at least four government posts including a seat in the Cabinet open to Scotland's then 71 MPs. In practice, these posts were probably open to only half that number 'according to which party happens to be in power, so the ratio of hits to misses is no worse than about one in nine'. Furthermore, Boyne thought, 'Scots are as liable as Englishmen or Welshmen and a good deal more liable than Ulstermen to be chosen for other posts in the Government; for example, look at Viscount Kilmuir, Lord Home, Iain MacLeod, Lord John Hope, Lord Dundee, Lord Perth, Hugh Fraser, Niall Macpherson, John George; or, for that matter, the Prime Minister'. All things considered, Boyne thought that 'the young Scottish politician' had 'a pretty good "each way" chance of advancement'. He sincerely hoped that the Caledonian and Corporation Scots would promote politics to any young Scotsmen and Scotswomen with whom they had influence, because 'despite all the mud thrown at that despised calling through the ages', it was 'a noble pursuit well worthy of their serious attention'. He was convinced that there was 'no better or quicker way of advancing Scotland's interests than getting the best of her men and women, irrespective of party, to represent her in Parliament'.

As Scots invaded politics, financial institutions and the professions in London, many supported the Corporation and also succeeded as MPs, bankers, lawyers, doctors, politicians and policemen[3] – and many also became freemasons in an effort to fit in, perform their public duties and perfect their craft. Londoners could thank many Scots for nineteenth- and twentieth-century bank accounts, church ministry and medical advances. They could place their souls in their

---

[3] In 1930–31, Colonel Sir Hugh Turnbull had been Commissioner of Police for the City of London and a Caledonian Society member; he had actively looked out for young Scots 'anxious to come to London' as 'good material' to join his force.

Scots chaplain's hands and their lives in those of their Scottish physician or surgeon. The Scots reputation for banking and finance around the world was also based on a similar sense of safe keeping, as Scots looked up to many past and present economic Scots. In the year 2000 Don Cruickshank picturesquely described banking 'as a peculiar thing to do', especially when it meant you had 'to take your money along to another person and give it all to him, even if he is sitting in a marble hall with gates outside; ... you need to trust that person'. Jimmy Brown, a retired chartered accountant with a past career in the Middle East and currently a member of the Corporation's committee of management, remembers:

> When I came to London, the city was considered the capital of Empire ... And a lot of people came, for several years in London, either to join an overseas bank or go planting or whatever it was ... I joined the London Scottish Rugby Club ... [and] I joined the [London Scottish] Regiment because I'd served in a Scottish regiment, it's as simple as that ... We probably thought that ... though London was the capital of Empire, ... it was our Empire as much as anybody else's ... Most Scots thought of themselves as being British, I think, before being Scots. I think in later years, the nationalism has risen up and you've noticed it in hotel registers where people sign in as Scottish, but I don't think that happened ... just post-war 1945.

Many Scots liked to belong and joined existing communities wherever they went, relating well to their new surroundings and neighbours in London or abroad. 'They didn't,' as Jimmy Brown says, 'keep themselves completely aloft ... they merged in, they learned the languages ... if you take the planters in Assam, ... most of them learned to speak to the people ... they became very much part of the community.' A Presbyterian upbringing and a sense of public service might have also helped in some cases. This was possibly something that was uniquely Scottish, thinks Don Cruickshank, who in his late thirties surrendered to 'this public duty thing' and gave up working for Richard Branson's Virgin Group to 'search out ways of making a difference'. London gave him that opportunity because of its seat of power and (then) central role in public policy. He thinks that 'a lot of Scots feel that the relationship between the citizen and the state is such an important one, that working for the state in the interests of citizens is something that very many of them want to do and do well. There's a different relationship between the citizen and the state in Scotland, from that in England and London ... which is one of the reasons why there's a lot of tension between the two countries, particularly in areas of social policy'.

London still provides great opportunities for those who are canny enough to look for them, despite today's technology slump. Doug Cameron, a *Financial Times* journalist and a football-supporting London Scot of the younger type, wrote a memorable piece in the *New Statesman* in July 2002 which summed up why he thought the Scots had stayed in London and why they continued to keep coming. He particularly thought that 'London's role as an international gateway has never been lost on the Scots; it was a thrilling place in which to lose oneself and to make some money:

> As I grew up near Edinburgh in the early 1980s, London's allure stemmed, for me, from the Live pages of the *New Musical Express*. While the Scottish capital boasted a list of bands that I could swat with two ink-stained fingers, its English equivalent boasted two columns. Every week …
>
> Whatever our ambivalence towards London, the simple truth is that everybody goes there … The city's sheer scale allows us to enjoy our surprising yearning for anonymity. London's Scots by and large eschew the communities favoured by other imports, save gatherings in the William Wallace by Baker Street Station or the Caledonian Club near Hyde Park. No Irish-themed or Brazilian samba bars for us. We blend in nicely to the throng, so we think, while maintaining our snooty sense of Not Being English. Even in the heart of the capital, we could rephrase the Millwall chant: 'There's nae one like us, and we don't care …' For all the talk of Scottish mafias and Media Scots, our gatherings tend to be strictly informal …
>
> Commerce is the final binding attraction of the city for the Scots here, who cannot bring themselves to admit that they may love what few would dare to call their adopted home. We are here because we are paid to be here, many kid themselves, a southbound economic clearance from barren employment opportunities at home. This carefully ignores a housing boom in Edinburgh fuelled by bankers and fund managers returning home misty-eyed after a lucrative stint in the City. With more pounds in our pockets, the rise and rise of the discount airlines has only cemented the capital's affections in our hearts, with its convenient connections to Luton and Stansted. An open-ended return, please. And do you do discounts for senior citizens?[4]

---

[4] Reproduced with kind permission of the *New Statesman*.

CHAPTER 28

St Andrew's Day Celebrations

L ondon was home for many Scots because they grew to love the city as their English cousins did, both rich and poor. Lord Byron, who experienced the rigours of Aberdeen for ten years during his childhood from 1789, afterwards considered London 'a damned place to be sure, but the only one in the world (at least in the English world) for fun'. The Royal Scottish Corporation itself in Crane Court and Fetter Lane from 1782 had become a famous landmark for Scots and Scots gaiety. Its nineteenth-century St Andrew's Day dinners were well known and the Corporation's premises hosted many of the Scots societies in London that in turn supported the charity. The Caledonian Society of London, the Highland Society of London, the Caledonian Asylum, the London Scottish Regiment and Burns Nights at the Royal Albert Hall during this period also helped to promote the Scottish cause in the capital.

The London newspapers of the early 1800s published advance notices of the Corporation's courts and festival dinners, not to mention everything else that was going on in the capital – concerts, balls, and other society meetings. The festival dinner tickets provided an account of the charity's activities on the back. The ticket for Saturday 16 April 1831 reminded guests to be 'at the Freemason's Tavern, Great Queen Street, dinner on the table at 6, tickets 20 shillings. Duke of Gordon in the chair'. The tickets also gave the names of the stewards of the festivals who, as usual, organised the dinners and collected the monies. Many toasts were drunk at these events but one that had inappropriately toasted Queen Caroline in 1820 forced William, Duke of Clarence, the charity's president and regular festival chairman, to write in strong terms to the Corporation's management. In a letter from St James's on 8 December he wrote:

> I cannot approve of what passed on St Andrew's Day, tho' I may admit it could not have been prevented: at the Spring Festival I hope to be supported by the Noblemen in preventing any political or seditious toast being drunk where charity only should exist. I cannot admit of this Queen's health being drunk … I think the less notice that is now taken of this disgraceful business the better and I rejoice Sir Thomas Bell conducted himself with so much propriety.

The Corporation's London office twice asked its Edinburgh branch if it would keep up the St Andrew's Day tradition with a dinner, but it was never the right time. In 1830 it was far too early and by November 1831 James Nairne reported from Edinburgh that, firstly, there was no immediate need for funds; secondly, he had no time to organise it; thirdly, there was no report with which to interest the Edinburgh and Leith public sufficiently; and fourthly (and probably most importantly), several other institutions had dinners on that day – notably the College of Physicians, the Society of Antiquaries and the Freemasons. These were events, declared Nairne, that 'would materially operate against any efforts which the Directors might make to bring together a respectable Company on so short a notice'. But in 1832 the branch office did offer to insert a note advertising the Scots Corporation's St Andrew's Day festival in London in the Edinburgh *Courant* and *General Advertiser*.

The St Andrew's Day festival dinner of 1843 was presided over by the Duke of Sutherland and the subscriptions and donations amounted to £359. The anniversary dinner of 1863 attended by Lord Palmerston brought in a hefty £1,200. Scots lord mayors of London have given to the Corporation since the early eighteenth century and have attended the St Andrew's Day festival dinners as chairmen of the festival or as honoured guests. Lord Mayor Alderman Sir Andrew Lusk was in the chair for the anniversary festival dinner on 1 December 1873 and was given 'a very hearty reception' even though he was an 'English-man'. This dinner was quite a splendid occasion in a large hall. Five hundred gentlemen were present clothed in 'the garb of old Gaul', and the 'general effect' was described as 'decidedly pleasing', notwithstanding the social conven-tion that confined the ladies to a gallery at one end of the room, where 'their presence, lent an additional charm to the scene'.

The food too was 'by no means lacking in specialities, inasmuch as one of the courses was devoted entirely to Scottish dishes, and southerners were enabled to test for themselves the merits of haggis, white puddings, black puddings, collops, shepherds' pie, and sheep's heads'. In addition, the wines 'were of excellent quality and liberally served'. Alderman Lusk's fundraising speech pleased the Scots and some of the English present, 'who fully recognised the force of his ejaculatory "Scots whae hae" ' with which he began. The main toast of the evening was 'The Scottish Corporation', and glasses were raised to its long history and charitable tradition, supported by bountiful patrons. Only a limited number of the 200 applications for assistance could be fulfilled due to lack of funds, Lusk said, making 'a warm appeal' for 'those whom the institution was more especially intended to benefit, viz., aged and infirm natives of Scotland who were residents of the metropolis and neighbourhood'.

The list of contributions, counted by the Corporation's secretary Macrae Moir at the end of the dinner, reached £2,600. An answering telegram was composed at the table and delivered that same evening to the senders of congratulatory telegrams received from St Andrew's societies in Cleveland (Middlesbrough), Ipswich, Belfast, Dublin and Glasgow, reading: 'Scotsmen in London drink flowing bumpers shoulder to shoulder, unite to conquer adversity and sorrow, and to succour the afflicted'. A final toast to the press was also drunk. To this Tom Hood replied, reminding the dinner guests 'that, long after those present were at home and asleep, the gentlemen of the press would be preparing, for the public enjoyment, those speeches which had afforded so much gratifications that evening. (Cheers.)' The dinner proceedings then closed and guests were led by the pipers to the ballroom 'where dancing was kept up till an early hour on Tuesday morning'.

The 1874 dinner followed in much the same way. This time the lord mayor of London was among the guests and responded to a toast to himself and his sheriffs, saying that 'there was one piece of satisfaction afforded him that evening: he was able to console himself and the Corporation of London by the feeling that the Scotch people took care of themselves'. Again the stewards had been active in promoting and organising the event and were heartily thanked for their efforts. 'In what they had done,' said Erasmus Wilson, their leader, 'they were not unconscious that a good dinner had a tendency to swell a subscription list (A laugh). He felt that they had been well fed and well drunk. (Laughter.) This, and the good subscriptions, were the only reward the stewards had looked for,' he said. The health of the 'ladies' in the gallery was as usual toasted and the vocalists were thanked, 'the selection of music' being 'in harmony with the occasion'. Contributions for the evening had this time amounted to £2,000.

We hear more about festivals when the Corporation's records continue after the fire in November 1877, which was a couple of weeks before that year's annual festival, already organised to take place at the Freemasons' Tavern in Great Queen Street. This dinner could well have been a sad event but was obviously a joyful occasion. Sir Stafford Northcote, chancellor of the exchequer,[1] presided over the dinner and afterwards on 3 December thanked the Corporation's committee in a letter from Downing Street. Enclosing a donation by cheque, he declared: 'I have not enjoyed myself so much for a long time'. Prince Leopold, Duke of Albany, presided over the 1882 St Andrew's Day festival, which was also attended by the Duke of Edinburgh. After the dinner the Corporation was feeling generous and agreed to reimburse the stewards for their meeting expenses, and the beadle received £5 for his 'extra festival help'. In October this officer was given a new suit of clothes – a Highland uniform – which he would wear at future festivals and other similarly ceremonial occasions. This grand dress may well have impressed the guests at the next dinner,

---

[1] Later elected a vice-president of the Corporation in 1881.

for donations that year went up to £3,166, the largest amount ever collected (except for the 1880 rebuilding appeal). More likely it was the festival's chairman and keen Corporation supporter, the Marquis of Aberdeen, who encouraged a large donation of £800 from a Scot abroad, the Honourable Donald A. Smith of Montreal, Canada (a future vice-president as Lord Strathcona). The dinner itself had cost the Corporation £590.

Dinner invitations were sent out to the great and the good in London. At the beginning of November 1885 the Corporation secretary was instructed to send out invitations to 'Her Majesty's Ministers – The Foreign Ambassadors – The Lord Mayor & Sheriffs of London' and 'The friends whom the Chairman might request'. Also included on the list were 'The Maharajah of Johore and 3 of his suite' and 'The Envoy of Siam and attendant'. Complimentary tickets ensured a press presence at the dinners and usually meant that the amount raised from the festival appeal was subsequently widely reported. But by the beginning of 1889 coverage had not been as good when the Corporation's quarterly court met on 2 January and celebrated a large donation from the previous November festival. The Corporation's court was most upset that it had not been as well reported by the press as usual, and the cause was later explained. The reporters had complained 'that the seats allotted to them at the Banquet were not suited to the proper performance of their duties'. The Corporation's committee of management agreed that it was 'desirable that adequate accommodation should be made for the representatives of the Press at the Festival Dinners'.

By 1893 and 1894 appeals for funds were getting harder and much of the fund-raising was due to the networking and organisation of the festival stewards. George Grant was so good at it that he attained the privileges of a donor of 250 guineas in November 1896 and was thanked for 'his great success as a Steward at every Anniversary Festival during the past twenty years'. Lord Rosebery was thanked for his presidency of the 1893 festival and the Corporation revealed that it had managed 'in a most trying season, satisfactorily to meet every appeal from our destitute countrymen'. On 2 January 1895 it thanked T. F. Bayard, the United States ambassador in London, for presiding over the 1894 festival dinner, finishing its letter in almost eighteenth-century style: 'You have also what we are sure will be most valued by your Excellency the prayers of the hungry you have helped us to feed, the naked you have enabled us to clothe and the homeless you have enabled us to shelter'.

Twentieth-century festival dinner highlights included the 1909 festival chairmanship of the Archbishop of Canterbury and that of J. M. Barrie, who donated £82 and presided over the festival in November 1928. A sugar replica of the Peter Pan statue in Kensington Gardens was placed opposite him on the table. The *Glasgow Herald* reported the occasion on 1 December and described 'Sir James' as one who had 'long resisted the blandishments offered to persuade him to become a social lion', but who had been 'enticed out of his hermitage by this gathering of his countrymen'. Having tried to find fault with Scots in several amusing tales, he announced his support of the Corporation and of the Scottish nation, and declared that 'There never was a more hospitable people. And again, experience has taught us that one of the best ways of being hospitable is to throw life-belts into the seas we have scrambled out of'. Festival dinners were not held during the Second World War but started again in 1946 when greetings were sent from the Scots Charitable Society of Boston (USA), the St Andrew's Society of Ottawa, the Mombasa Caledonians, the Liverpool Caledonian Association, the St Andrew's Society of Aberdeen and the St Andrew's Society of Manchester. The Scottish Clans Association, a regular American supporter, gave £257 in 1952 and more in future years.

One late twentieth-century highlight was the presence of HM the Queen and the Duke of Edinburgh at a reception during the Corporation's St Andrew's Day festival dinner in 1981 held at the Savoy. Two more, perhaps no less grand, receptions in the 1990s were held at the Mansion House, the official residence of London's lord mayor. At one, on 17 July 1991, the lord mayor, Sir Alexander Graham, welcomed the Royal Scottish Corporation 'to his "Croft," as he called it'. Another Scot, Sir Francis McWilliams, followed Graham as lord mayor in a few months and was guest of honour at the Corporation's St Andrew's Day dinner that year. Ties were growing stronger with the City and, for the first time, the Royal Scottish Corporation had a float for the lord mayor's procession, designed and built by students of the South Thames College and sponsored by the Bank of Scotland. It showed 'Scottish pride (the piper's music)' being 'carried through the rainbow into the Scots box, providing direct help for those in need'. Staff, dressed in seventeenth-century costume supplied by the Royal Opera House (and looking a little like actors from a *Jack and the Beanstalk* pantomime), stood under the rainbow in front of the lion shield from the Corporation's 1979 coat of arms.

Other Royal Scottish Corporation fundraising events besides the St Andrew's Day dinner and these receptions included concerts and balls, especially with the help of the Caledonian Society from the 1840s. Two balls had been held on behalf of the Corporation in 1823 and 1828, both taking place 'at Willis's', which together raised £596 for the charity. From 1832–43 the Corporation received half the proceeds of the Caledonian Balls which averaged £370 for each of the eleven years. But from 1844 until 1847 the Corporation received only a third of the Ball's proceeds, amounting in total to just over £259. A 'Grand Highland Ball' was held at the Guildhall in 1851 – no doubt to mark the occasion of the Great Exhibition in true Scottish style. Ladies made their society debut at these balls, and 'some of them got their sweethearts and some of them their husbands there,' wrote David Hepburn, the later Caledonian Society chronicler and

Corporation committee chairman, who also vividly recalled a ball of 1869: 'my youthful mind was much impressed with the brilliancy of the scene … The strains of the music, the gay attire of the ladies, and the sparkling ornaments of the Highlanders in their varied tartans … the spirited dancing in the Highland reels. It was grand'.

A Corporation ball 'under distinguished patronage' was suggested as a suitable way to raise money for the Ashanti War disabled soldiers' and dependents' fund in March 1874, but by 1888 the charity money raised by ball appeals, as well as the funds of the Caledonian Society, were well down; the society's ball attendance was, in fact, described as 'falling off' and the ball was cancelled. Dancing was perhaps not such a popular pastime, and many other Scottish societies had sprung up with competing entertainments. It was also considered 'a wise decision', since 'the finances of the Society had been crippled, instead of being augmented; indeed the funds had reached a dangerously low ebb, and, as a consequence, the Scottish charities suffered'. Despite this lull, nearly a year later the Caledonian Society could report that 'Scottish feeling grows apace in the metropolis'. Concerts were held at St. James's Hall and at Kensington Gore: 'In the building first named, Scottish fervour had everything its own way, and presented an astonishing spectacle to the few English people present. The place was crowded in nearly every part'; at the Albert Hall, 'Mr William Carter held a "Scottish Festival" of a like kind and in similar fashion'.

There was no Caledonian Ball in 1901 following the death of Queen Victoria, and in January 1917 the Corporation felt a sadness at the death of the seventh Duke of Atholl, reporting that 'although they fully realise that his main interests lay among his own people in his County and throughout the Highlands, they very gratefully remember at this time that the aged, bereaved and distressed among his countryfolk in London found in him a warm friend and advocate. His sympathy with their trials and sorrows took practical form'. His establishment of the Royal Caledonian Ball in aid of the Royal Scottish Corporation and Caledonian Asylum, a chief support of the two charities, had raised £20,000 during the duke's management of the event. His son, the eighth duke and the Corporation's treasurer for thirteen years, carried on the ball tradition, producing at least another £28,000 for the two Scottish charities during this time. During later good ball years annual money raised for the Corporation could be quite substantial and regularly amounted to £800 a year under the management of Sir Simon Campbell Orde, the Ball Trust's secretary and a Corporation governor, who made such a 'regular and magnificent effort' until his death in 1968, when the amounts dropped to £5–600. The Corporation has not received any support from the ball in recent times.

Fundraising and publicity have not been seriously on the Corporation's agenda for many years or in the range of its expertise, and although the Mansion

House receptions and the later receptions at the House of Commons for Scots Parliamentarians may have raised the profile somewhat at the time, the Corporation was no doubt quickly forgotten by these busy city and government London Scots. In addition, the Corporation's festival dinner in 2003 and those of the last few previous years have been more networking and social events than money-raising occasions.

CHAPTER 29

Sharing with Societies

Societies and networking were going to be increasingly important for the arriving nineteenth- and twentieth-century Scots, and the Royal Scottish Corporation's 'Hall' was to be a focus for Scots in London for much of the period. The new building in Crane Court in 1880 deliberately made a point of providing a central home for the many other Scottish societies setting up in early Victorian London. Their members in turn also supported the mother charity and the Corporation was able to raise additional funds from room hire.

Over a number of years before the fire in 1877, the charity's chapel had been let out for a low rental on several evenings during the week, 'for religious and certain other purposes'. Once the new building was ready in 1880, the hire of the new 'Pensioners' Hall' was allowed, and usually for an amount of 10s.6d. to cover cleaning costs. By June 1882 the 'Pensioners Hall' was being rented out to a minister of Trinity Church for divine service over a number of summer Sundays. In November, John Bowers, the teacher of Crown Court Schools, asked to use the hall for a Moray House Club social evening he was hosting. This was granted but on condition 'that there be no dancing and the meeting be finished before Midnight'. Then the Society of 'Old Caledonians' asked if it might have 'a little dancing' in the hall. James Lawrie, a member of the Corporation's committee of management and president of this society, tried to sway his fellow governors. 'I am sure [the society's secretary] will guarantee that whatever is done will be in perfect order,' he promised. The meeting itself was eventually agreed to but not the dancing. Among other hirers in 1883 was the volunteer band of the London Scottish Regiment – granted as long as it refrained from disturbing the neighbours. Two churchmen were turned down in 1884 even though they offered to pay £40 for holding their 'simple Christian and Gospel meetings', and added that 'the Christians forming our little company are, with few exceptions, of the poorer class'. By the beginning of 1885 tea meetings as usual were permitted, as was a course of history lectures; a class of gymnastics was refused.

After 1927, when the Corporation's premises in Crane Court were remodelled and rebuilt to face Fetter Lane, the charity was able to provide a more spacious home for the Corporation as well as the many Scottish societies in London. Despite some fire damage during the Second World War, dancing became a popular and welcome wartime pastime. Sometimes after the war, 120 people at a time participated in the dancing classes at four shillings a go, including refreshments – even during the bitter winter of early 1947. Scars from the intensive bombing of the city still showed and were apparent around Fetter Lane, and, remembered one attendee, 'the RSC Hall was in a sad state, with patched walls, and a heating system of dubious efficiency … The dances were well attended and music was provided by an assortment of bands with differing abilities'. The Corporation continued regularly to host many of these Scottish Country Dance Society's reeling nights until the Fetter Lane sale in 1972.

Most of the Corporation's long-serving trustees were also members of other Scottish societies in London. Some societies covered Scottish localities, like the London Perthshire and the London Ayrshire Associations, others encompassed Scottish clans like the Clan Donnachaidh; some had more of a Greater London feel, like the Harrow Caledonian Society. In a higher league than all these local affiliations were (and still are) the Highland Society of London and the Caledonian Society of London. These more select male clubs and their local Scottish cousins provided the linkage in the city's national network.

As the oldest, the Highland Society was founded in May 1778 and registered as a charity in 1965. Its first president was Lt General the Honourable Simon Fraser of Lovat, and its membership was originally drawn from 'the most distinguished among those Highlanders who spent a significant part of their time in London'. Other presidents who followed Lovat included James Graham, later Duke of Montrose, in 1780 and Sir Henry Dundas in 1799 – Montrose was also a key Scots Corporation president for over twenty years from 1782, and Dundas was another notable charity supporter. Another Corporation supporter and 1796 Highland Society president was Sir John Sinclair. He was also the society's first historian and wrote that 'The true qualification' for membership was 'not so much the Distinction of *"Highland Birth"* (though that is certainly desirable …), but the possession of a *"Highland Spirit,"* which is necessarily accompanied by all those manly virtues, those generous traits, and those noble qualities which distinguish the Hero in War and the Citizen in Peace'. Once the kilt could be worn again after Montrose's bill in 1782, the society's membership was strongly influenced by the army as the Highland nobility began to raise Highland regiments for service in North America. These included the London Scottish. Key criteria for Society membership at its foundation were to have owned land in the Highlands, to have been of Highland descent, to have served in a Highland regiment, to have given significant service to that part of Scotland, or to have been 'the Husband of a Highland lady'. The society still occupies itself with a few charitable acts and continues to support the widows of fifteen

Highland soldiers who were Far East prisoners-of-war and to whom it pays £204 a year and gives a Christmas box. The society mainly exists today to maintain interest in the Highland way of life; its membership is by invitation only and the subscription paid is for life. Most members now live south of the border.

The Caledonian Society of London had been founded in 1837, and before this time there had been only two societies in London besides the two national charities – the Highland Society of London and the short-lived Club of the True Highlanders. Neither of these two societies was considered suitable for the more Lowland and commercial city Scots since they did not meet 'the wants of the average Caledonian in London, the first being too restrictive, and neither being sufficiently representative'. In fact, Michie Forbes Gray, secretary of the Caledonian Society, speaking in 1854, rather more bluntly explained how the society 'came to the conclusion that something was wanting – a Society that might have similar objects to the two named, but "confined as much as possible to the class called middle;" to have membership open to all men from all parts of Scotland; to make it in short a really Scottish institution'.[1] In the 1840s the Caledonian Society survived debt, deficiency and competition when about twenty members out of the usual one hundred had been left, but these men held fast and its spirit was revived as the rival Scottish Society fell apart. In addition to clearing its debts, over £400 was disbursed between 1847 and 1853 to its charities.

The Caledonian Society had specific aims, and after early abandoning the cause of Scottish education in Scotland, its defined objectives were essentially 'to promote good fellowship and brotherhood, and to combine efforts for benevolent and national objects connected with Scotland, and also to preserve the picturesque garb of Old Gaul'. On joining the Caledonian Society of London, new members had to (and still do) swear allegiance to the two great Scottish charities that the society had long supported – the Royal Scottish Corporation and the Royal Caledonian Asylum for Scottish soldiers' orphans (today, the Royal Caledonian Schools Trust). These and many smaller charities 'benefited largely from the treasury of the Society', and the charities in turn gained many 'fresh subscribers' from its members and appeals.

In the early days of the Caledonian Society, a few Englishmen and Irishmen were allowed to join its ranks, but by 1890 only those of Scottish blood were permitted to do so. 'Thus it maintains in its integrity its national character, which is its finest mainstay and surest safeguard,' wrote David Hepburn. Even then, only one hundred, excluding office bearers, were allowed to join in total. The small membership meant that by the 1890s there was also a waiting list. The Victorian society, in addition, prided itself on being the first club (not just in

---

[1] It has also been suggested that the Scottish nobles and lairds of the Highland Society perhaps were actually none too keen on having dinner with their bankers.

London but in the whole country) to allow 'the good custom of inviting ladies to sit at table at public banquets'. Although the exact date of such an 'excellent innovation' was unknown to Hepburn, he did know that at the 1844 banquet at the London Tavern there had been 140 gentlemen and 72 ladies present. By the 1850s it was considered 'one of the most desirable Societies for Scotsmen in London' to join. By 1877, with men like Robert Hepburn and Dr Charles Hogg (and later David Hepburn), the Caledonian Society was providing most of the shrewd Victorian administrators of the Royal Scottish Corporation, and in 1890 the society was being described as the 'playground of the workers in the London-Scottish charities'. A later description of a 1905 gathering of 'exiled Scotsmen' was given by William Will, president of the society and chairman of the Corporation's committee of management; in 1924–25 he pictured them 'serious in their business and in the work of mercy which calls them together, enjoying a social hour in which they bring to the bustling city a breath of their native air, and recall the glorious story of their native land. The fog of London is trans-figured into the mist in the valleys, through which float scenes of Auld Lang Syne'.

The Corporation's St Andrew's Day festival dinners in the nineteenth century seem to have been especially fun with members of the Caledonian Society in attendance. In turn, the Royal Scottish Corporation governors also amused themselves with the society's own regular dinners and meetings – especially at the society's Burns Nights when many toasts were drunk, eminent guests attended and nostalgic national speeches or 'sentiments' were applauded. Like the Scots Corporation dinners, those of the Caledonian Society were also held at the Freemasons' Tavern. In the 1840s, 'The Scottish Hospital' was among the many toasts of the night which also included one for the Scotsmen's new home, being addressed to 'The Land we Live in'. Over a hundred years later, things had changed little and by 1960 Caledonian Society candidates for membership had to be 'Scots, males, prepared to contribute in cash and in kind, prepared to attend all meetings to the exclusion of all other social engagements; and must consequently live near enough to London Town to enable them to fulfil these requirements; and finally candidates must be what the Council would be prepared to describe as a credit to Scotland'. General membership was extended to life membership after twenty years' service, and since the average age was rather on the elderly side, vacancies occurred fairly frequently, ensuring fresh albeit older blood for the Corporation's management.

Freemasons also provided another network for professional Scots in London. A Scots Lodge was set up by a group of Caledonian Society members and rented space for ten guineas a year alongside the other Scottish societies at the Corporation. Vero Shaw sent a letter on 6 May 1889 from his office at the *Morning Advertiser* telling the Corporation of the idea for a new lodge of freemasons composed only of Scotsmen in London. The new lodge needed a meeting place before the Grand Lodge would grant its establishment and Shaw wrote about its anxiety to ensure that the new group reflect 'only credit upon our country'. They intended also only to elect members of 'fair fame and good position'. 'We shall,' Shaw wrote, 'exclude all those who are likely to cast discredit upon us.' The Corporation granted their request a year later.

Although some societies, like Glasgow University Women's Club, still meet at the Royal Scottish Corporation, a gentlemen's club in Belgravia's Halkin Street now mainly plays host to the capital's Scotsmen as the Corporation once did. The Caledonian Club, described as 'quite a stronghold of Scotsmen in London', has also become popular amongst City professionals and their sons. Such demand has encouraged modernisation, with around £2 million set aside for a revamp and extension of the club's premises. The institution had military beginnings, having been founded in 1891 by Neville Campbell and Marcus Tullibardine, both officers of the Highland Brigade. They wanted a place in town to meet at weekends when stationed in Aldershot and settled on a suitable house in St James's Square. The club was later bought by its members in 1917 and moved to Halkin Street in 1946. Today it employs 58 staff, mostly Scots, and hosts activities such as shooting, golf, Burns Nights and St Andrew's Day celebrations. As a non-profit-making organisation, the club is still owned by its 1,300 members, and revenue was £1.74 million in 2000. The club's secretary, Paul Varney, said that the members in 2002 'had an average age of 56, owned three racehorses between them, spanned business, sport and the arts and probably included several millionaires'. Members could make use of 31 bedrooms, a bar, a smoking room, a billiard room, a library and a 'ladies' sitting room' (if in the company of one), as well as a formal dining room. Varney thought 'there's a better feeling among business members ... and they are finding that the club is still able to offer values and traditions that seem to be eroded in the rest of society'. These include a ban on children under eight, mobile phones and women members. This last rule has begun to be relaxed slightly since the club's formation, and from the 1970s wives and daughters of members have been offered associate membership for a lesser fee. The separate entrance for these 'lady associates' has also been done away with, for reasons of club security and because of the expense of manning two front doors.[2]

---

[2] The Royal Scottish Corporation and the Caledonian Club have come together over a number of years on a charitable culinary matter. The Lord Forte Fund was created for the Corporation in 1996 with a donation of £20,000 from Lord Forte. This was to be awarded as educational bursaries and prizes 'to young Scottish people employed in the catering and hotel industry'. In the last few years it has mainly been used to provide a £1,500 grant to a deserving trainee Scots chef in the Caledonian Club's kitchens.

CHAPTER 30

Case Numbers, Types and Trends

A circular issued in March 1831 provided an update on the Corporation's activities and London's Scottish poor, stating that from 1825–29 'the society administered relief to no fewer than 14,242 cases of distress; – making on an average of these five years 2,848 Cases annually.' By 1830 the number had gone down to 2,454 a year, including 292 passages home, and 72 pensioners received annuities totalling £700 a year. In November 1832 the charity was reporting that it had 'examined & relieved upwards of 315 cases of distress in each month, besides pensions given to 70 infirm and aged persons, Natives of Scotland, and sea passages granted to 240'. This meant a total of 3,780 cases for the year; a cholera epidemic in London had no doubt increased the figure. Little is known about what happened between the mid-1830s and the 1870s, but the Highland potato famine of 1846–47 no doubt elicited some charity from the Corporation.[1]

The chairman of the St Andrew's Day festival in 1873, the Lord Mayor of the City of London, Sir Andrew Lusk, retold the story of the Royal Scottish Corporation's foundation and re-incorporation under George III and its success into the late Victorian period, adding that 'While people were disputing about the mode in which charitable societies should be administered their society did the work and set the example'. Lusk told his audience that the Corporation had that year examined many applications, and money had to be raised for 200 pensioners and 200 other cases. Among those who received such relief, he said, 'were many persons who had once occupied a good position. There were doctors of divinity, doctors of medicine, artists, men of science and of literature, and others'. The following year, the charity was firmly concentrating on pensions and in 1874 helped a total of 170 elderly individuals with allowances of £25, £15, £12 and £6. There was no breakdown of the numbers of cases for casual relief, but when the Corporation's minute books started again after the fire in

---

[1] Certainly its governors promoted items made in the Highlands and Islands when they attended the gatherings of the Caledonian Society of London. These came from the London Industrial Relief Depot at 126 Piccadilly, 'where a variety of hosiery, shirts, plaids, hand-wove cloth for kilts and trowsering, are exposed for sale'. Other groups of London Scots also gave money to the Highland cause, including the Government of India in 1837 (£105) and 1847 (£1,000).

1877, the 170 pensioners and the 384 petitioners on the books were also grouped by age:

1877–78

AGE OF PENSIONERS	AGE OF PETITIONERS
5 over 90	12 over 80
45 over 80	73 over 70
106 over 70	136 over 60
10 over 68	77 over 50
4 under 68 (paralysed and blind)	32 over 40
	54 under 40 (mostly widows and orphans)

At a 'Special Court' for the 'Election of Pensioners' on 24 April 1878 nine governors were appointed 'Scrutineers'. This time there were 24 vacancies to be filled, and Mary Farquharson topped the list of successful candidates with 5,598 members' votes. There were 31 unsuccessful candidates. Later court minutes show that many poor Scots tried more than once or twice to obtain a Corporation pension. On 30 April 1879 unsuccessful applications were received for the seventh time from William Dickson and Ann Huddleston; at the same court six people made their sixth application, one a fourth, one a fifth, four their third, two their second, and for nine people it was their first time. By the following April, Anne Huddleston at last received a £12 pension on her eighth application. Patience was obviously another old Scottish virtue that was eventually rewarded. Pension vacancies in April 1882 were as usual filled by the candidates with the highest number of votes; successful candidates for this election showed their number on the list and the number of votes polled – some governors appear to have had hundreds or thousands of votes which accounted for the high scores.[2] The unsuccessful candidates were also listed and a grant of money was occasionally allowed if they looked like being successful in the future.

In January 1882 the Corporation had decided that all applicants petitioning for interim relief were required to state the reasons for their making an application and provide a statement of their circumstances, and 'that a record of the same, with the amount granted, be entered in a book kept for the purpose and that the applicants be required to sign the entry'. Thereafter monthly relief was carefully recorded and also whether the pension was paid at home or at the hall and also the type (or amount) of the pension. Usually about eight or nine out of ten cases that were considered were eventually granted relief. By May 1882

---

[2] A letter from the Duke of Atholl in the committee minutes of 27 June 1883 reveals that he had been allotted 2,544 votes as manager of the Caledonian Ball. He was now abroad and so was unable to use them; he wanted to know if the votes were lost or could he carry them over?

there was also a sub-committee to revisit existing cases, and twenty were investigated; all except one were recommended for continuing relief. Women as widows still figured strongly as the key pensions group benefiting from the Corporation in this period (as was also common among the 'deserving poor' petitioners). When the pension applications for the £6 pension on 12 July 1882 had been examined, over 60 percent of cases were classed as widows. These women were also long-lived. When the death of £12 pensioner Jane Charteris was reported in 1883, she had reached the age of 102, and, elected in 1860, she had been a pensioner for 23 years.

An additional sub-committee was set up in early 1883 to visit each of the 363 pensioners in their own homes. In some instances relief was discontinued but in most cases the committee reported that 'it would be highly desirable that the pittance your Charity gives should be increased'. It also added, 'Further, from the fact of the distress already existing, your Committee anticipate considerable increase in the number of applicants for relief during the coming winter', and it told the charity's management that it failed to see a way of 'making any reduction in the expenditure but on the contrary'. Four of the fifteen cases revisited in February 1883 were reduced because the children had been elected to the Caledonian Asylum. In April fifteen cases were revisited and three cases received an extra 2s. Another case received £2 'as a Donation to enable one of the petitioners to set up in business'.

Sometimes pensions went astray in the post and on 8 August 1883 one monthly pension of 20s. for a Mrs Anderson was delivered to another Mrs Anderson living in the same street. The wrong, but equally in need, Mrs Anderson cashed the cheque. The postmaster managed to recover half of the money 'but said he feared he could not get more for some time, as the woman's husband is very poor'. The committee asked the postman to keep trying. A number of the saddest Corporation cases concerned pensioners struck off the list when they went into an asylum or 'the House'. On 12 March 1884 the visitor reported 'that Mary Paul is at present an inmate of Islington Workhouse Infirmary ... a letter from the Master of the Workhouse ... says she will most probably never come out'. Her name was removed from the pensions list and a vacancy was declared.

A less hopeless case concerned Corporation pensioner Robert Kennedy. On 10 May in 1884 Dr J. J. Pringle, one of the honorary surgeons, sent a letter explaining that he had seen Kennedy as an out-patient of Dr Finlay's at the Middlesex Hospital (while Finlay, another honorary surgeon, was away). He reported that 'A woman who stays with him and apparently looks after him asked me in regard to his being supplied with wine or some other form of stimulant out of the funds of the charity, and I think the case fully deserving of such assistance'. The Corporation granted 10 shillings a month for three months, a sum which was to be paid via Dr Finlay, 'if necessary'. On the other hand the committee refused to give £2 to Mrs A. Ford of Clapham who had got behind with her rent following the death of her eldest son, although no doubt there were circumstances that went unrecorded in the minutes (and debt cases were usually frowned on). A more deserving case was put forward for a Mrs Dalton of Stoke Newington by the Reverend Thain Davidson, one of the Corporation's honorary chaplains. Her husband had died about a fortnight previously, leaving her 'with two infants & utterly unprovided for', wrote Davidson:

> Her husband during his illness (consumption) received some help I think from the Corporation, but I am not so familiar with the rules as to know whether any relief can be given to the young and destitute widow. I have given her a trifle, but promised I would write to you on the matter, and I have promised to let her know. It is a case in which I take a special interest.

Mrs Dalton was granted eight shillings a month for her two children. By 9 July Dr Finlay was back in action and wrote to say that he had ordered 'an instrument' to be made for Jane Murdoch, a petitioner, the cost of which would be under 10 shillings but which would 'make all the difference to her between comfort and misery'. He hoped the committee would not grudge the amount. It did not.

Sometimes the Corporation allowed pensions to be continued outside the then 12–mile charitable boundary. One pensioner in September 1883 lived in an almshouse that was due to be pulled down and had had to move north of London, but the Corporation continued to pay her allowance. A friend of a pensioner called Marion Henderson told the Corporation governors in July 1884 how she 'had met with an accident in Eastbourne' and was unable to return to London but hoped the pension could still be paid, which it was for a year. Sometimes the Corporation paid money to landlords when pensioners died in their lodgings, either because the landlord had paid for the funeral or was owed rent. On 11 April 1885 one landlord asked for the 18 shillings rent outstanding that he was 'ill able to afford to lose'. Since the Corporation usually gave £1 to relatives on the death of a pensioner, it voted to use it this time to pay the deceased tenant's debt instead.

Early in the next decade, and during the last months of 1893, demands on the charity were being called 'exceptionally heavy' and the increase appeared to be coming especially from 'those advanced in years but yet able for work if it could be found'. By the end of the following year, unemployment was still increasing and the Corporation was bemoaning its lack of income once more and wishing that it could have done more to help. 'Owing to the great depression in trade, the demands on the funds of the Charity by able-bodied men out of employment have increased to a lamentable extent,' it noted. And in its mid-December report for the previous month it added that 'no fewer than 443 were relieved, while a larger number of known vagrants were turned away'. By the end of 1899 the Boer War had started to take its toll on the more casual cases when the Corporation saw 'the recall of many thousands of breadwinners to the colours'. It felt 'a duty' to contact 'various agencies in the hope that during the coming year every case of distress eligible for assistance from the corporation may receive full attention'. In November 1901 the charity was again keen to improve the welfare of the people it helped. Its annual investigation into the 'poorer and more aged among the recipients' showed 125 seriously needy individuals, and it increased the monthly allowance for all with 'one or two exceptions'. A list was also compiled of the 25 'oldest and most friendless among the present recipients who have outlived Governors likely to have supported their claims'. These included:

> Helen Buchanan, widow, 80; a native of Kyleston; in London 50 years.
> Elizabeth McDonell, widow, 82; a native of Belldrum; in London 56 years.
> Alexander McMillan, widower, 83; a native of Fort George; in London 40 years
> Isabella Mackintosh, widow, 80; a native of Glasgow; in London 51 years.

Widowed women were again in the majority, there being only four men on this list out of a total of 25 candidates.

Printed lists pasted into the minute books at the turn of the century reveal the past occupations and conditions of the Corporation's monthly applicants. In 1901 they were described variously as: 'Formerly in domestic service'; 'a clerk'; 'earns a trifle by needlework'; 'unable to work owing to age and bronchitis'; 'earns a little by knitting'; 'her husband has been in the asylum for ten years, she is dependent on help from her family and an allowance from the Scottish Hospital'. From 1903 applicants were described as: 'formerly an insurance agent'; 'formerly a nurse'; 'formerly foreman on railway'; 'formerly a caretaker'; 'a carpenter but unable to follow trade owing to accident to thigh two years ago'; 'earns a trifle as a washerwoman'. Often people were classed as unable to work owing to age and debility and, in accordance with one of the Corporation's pension conditions, most had been in London for over 20 years. Those of the Corporation's pensioners who were aged over 70 began to need help with their government paperwork from 1909 as a result of 'the new conditions' created by the Old Age Pensions Act passed that year. The Corporation's own pensions were suitably altered, it said, 'by withdrawal or curtailment according to individual needs'. In 1916 the Corporation complained that 'the new Regulations for the increase of Old Age Pensions have turned the whole matter again into the melting pot'.

The First World War had brought in more 'distressing appeals', and by the end of 1916 the Corporation felt able to enlarge the scale of allowances granted to war widows who had been left with young children. This was an improvement that had been needed for some time and was, the Corporation said, 'rendered urgent by the present high price of necessaries, and by more than one known case where the mother was found to be going short in order that the children might have more'. The harshest winter on record for 22 years in early 1917 had caused the elderly pensioners' death rate to rise exceptionally and the Corporation recorded that 49 individuals of an average age of '74¾' had died, many coming originally from all parts of Scotland, 'from the Orkney Islands to the extreme South'. By the end of 1918 the death rate had gone back to 'normal' with 29 deaths. Coal was given out to pensioners for a number of years from 1920 to help with the rise in the cost of fuel and to mark the services to the Corporation of the Prince of Wales. A few years later, in 1923, much larger numbers of poor Scots than expected began to clamour for the Corporation's relief because of post-war unemployment, causing 'a heavy and serious drain' on the charity's resources. The Corporation secretary, Thomas Montcrieff, then reported that he had himself in recent years witnessed homes 'in bitter winter weather' which had 'no food or firing or bedclothes, and with practically no stick of furniture left to pawn'. He had met yet another desperate young mother, 'with the barest remnants of clothing for herself', who had pawned the shawl in which her baby had been wrapped to buy bread for her other crying children.

The elderly Corporation pensioners – 'their well being is our constant care, their well being our pride' – continued to be long-lived well into the twentieth century. Figures for 1925–26 show 256 over 70 and 83 over 80 years of age. By 1929 there were 89 pensioners over 80 and 11 over 90. One 100-year-old widow from Leith was carefully watched that year until she died at 102. Montcrieff had remembered in December 1923 'at least four centenarians' in his time and a near fifth that year. One centenarian, William Haining, who had arrived in London at the age of fourteen, had been known as the 'Waterloo bairn' in his Scottish village and in all the surrounding countryside when he was born on the day 'Napoleon's portentous career was dashed into irretrievable ruin'. A couple of elderly pensioners thought they had been born Scottish nobles; one claimed the chieftainship of Clan Macnab and looked the part sufficiently to become an artist's model for Lord Leighton and other distinguished painters at the Royal Academy. Many pensioners, said Montcrieff, were also failed inventors of such things as 'collision mats for use at sea ... a solid cork tyre for use in the desert ... [and] an umbrella, the cover and ribs of which could be rolled up and put inside the stick'. One pensioner, still alive in 1923, thought he could 'revolutionise the shipping industry of the world by fixing the propellers at the bow instead of the stern', and also thought he had found a new way for aircraft to fly to New York in around ninety minutes. Although described as charmingly sweet and placid, during the First World War he had, Montcrieff recalled, 'directed his efforts to death-dealing explosives and propounded such schemes as would have annihilated the enemy at one fell swoop'. Although the Corporation's pensioners 'embraced all classes', according to Montcrieff most of the pensioners in the

1920s (and excluding the old soldiers of the Kinloch Bequest) had been domestic servants who had outlived their original employers.

By 1928 the Corporation was feeling administratively under pressure as never before as 'every care is taken to ensure that the applicants obtain benefits to which they are entitled under the Statutes'. At the same time, despite such seemingly wide-ranging state welfare, the Corporation could still report that 'Never in its long history has there been before it cases of poverty and distress so numerous and so clamant in their character'. Never before (in living memory) had the charity felt that it had been 'a greater blessing' for the less fortunate Scots. Unemployment, high prices and extreme shortages of even the most 'humble accommodation' had continued to pile on the pressure. In the earlier 1920s, and in 1923 alone, some 7,000 applicants for temporary relief had come to the attention of the Corporation. Many of them had been homeless, unemployed men and Montcrieff said that not one was turned away without something; money, though, was rarely given. By 1935 things had 'to some extent improved', but the Corporation still regarded unemployment as a 'serious' problem, and by now it was especially affecting 'the professional classes and those of middle age'. The charity noticed that those applying were of a different sort: 'applications for financial aid are being received in greater numbers from men and women whose knowledge, experience and length of service would, under more prosperous conditions, have entitled them to anticipate some reasonable measure of security in their employment'. Many more Scots had recently been arriving in London to look for work. This 'increased flux of our compatriots to the Metropolis' made considerable calls on the Corporation, and although 'the benevolence' of contributors enabled the charity to satisfy 'immediate requirements', it found it increasingly difficult to be more generous and 'treat those in distress as liberally as their unfortunate circumstances necessitate'. Until 1938, bed and meal tickets were the means used ('according to the class of the individual') to provide for people whom Montcrieff had previously described as 'tramping the country in search of work'.

After September 1939 the 416 pensioners could no longer gather monthly in the Corporation's hall but home visits were kept up. Assistance for further relief had begun after the outbreak of war but the Corporation's subscribers were also feeling the pinch and contributions had fallen off. A year later a lower number of 361 pensioners was recorded and the bombing of London at the end of 1940 had 'seriously affected' many. Only one pensioner had been killed 'but already the homes of 38 have been destroyed or damaged', and these people had been quickly aided by the charity, financially or otherwise. Those who had wished to leave London had 'been assisted to safer areas'. By 1941 a greater number of the pensioners, classed as more at risk, had been persuaded to leave the city, but 'many have firmly declined to leave their homes' and the Corporation praised the brave Scots for their 'courage' during 'their long and painful ordeal, greatly aggravated by advanced aged and infirmity'.

A new government 'Supplementary Pension' had been introduced in August 1940, and created more 'adjustment' work for the Corporation's secretary, but this ensured that the qualifying pensioners got the most out of the state's new benefit. Despite some pension reductions, the Corporation could report at the end of 1941 that 'the income from all sources, now enjoyed by these pensioners, is considerably higher than at the outbreak of the war'. They were also being visited regularly. The allowances of other beneficiaries, not qualified for Government aid, were increased so that 'they, too, are more comfortably placed,' the Corporation added. The numbers of these more casual applicants for relief had gone down since the outbreak of hostilities as employment in London had again risen and many Scots had been taken on for 'war work'. Nevertheless, some were still suffering and had lost just about everything they had in air raids. Although some state provision was available for such losses, the Corporation had declared in 1940 that 'there are many instances in which it has been necessary to augment the relief given by official sources'. By the end of the war times were still hard, especially for 'the elderly folk'. To commemorate the end of war in Europe another special pension was created – the 1945 Victory Pension – for which the names of two pensioners (one woman and one man) were 'nominated for all time'. Pensioners were also given 'a special cash gift', and on 13 June 1945 they enjoyed a celebration tea and a concert in the Corporation's hall.

Having seen a preliminary government white paper on the subject in 1944 (and not expecting much lessening in relief costs), at the beginning of October 1946 the Corporation observed the first stage of the National Insurance Act as increased Old Age Pensions came into operation. The act affected only those who had already been drawing government pensions of less than 26s. a week in the case of single people and less than 42s. a week in the case of married couples. The Corporation's pensioners who gained were few – amounting to 54, of whom 31 received an extra 2s. 6d. a week. By the middle of 1948 other legislation, 'which has for its object the provision of a comprehensive scheme of social security', meant that the charity had again to adjust the pension allowances of most of its 212 pensioners, but the new legislation also permitted the charity to put up its relief amount 'without relieving the State of any of its obligations'. The cost of living was still rising and the Corporation calculated by the end of the following year that it had supplemented the government's own 'modest' pensions by 40 percent, allowing the elderly pensioners an otherwise 'unattainable' standard of comfort.

The government's old age pensions had once more increased in 1951 by 4s. for single pensioners and 6s. 6d. for married couples. The charity considered this rise 'hardly sufficient to cover the cost of living', but at least it was good to talk and the Corporation assured its pensioners that 'they may, at all times, seek and receive advice and guidance on any question affecting their well-being'. But some, as always, were too reserved. In 1955 the government pensions went up again but still barely covered the cost of living, according to the charity. Pensioners especially needed clothing and new blankets and bedding in the winter months of 1956–57, and in the following year charities were again allowed to increase their own pensions without the state benefits of the beneficiaries being reduced. The number of 'other' applications to the Corporation, from existing pensioners and other Scots in London, had been gradually increasing from 1948 when 600 people applied for aid. Between 1955 and 1963 these applications had again reached further peaks of 600 in 1955 and 1959. From 1961–64 there was an average of just over 200 pensioners on the Corporation's books and the numbers receiving casual relief had gone down to 400. By 1966 pensioner numbers had gone down to 180 and their needs were considered to have been 'generally met'; over 500 general applicants, 'upon whom misfortune and distress had fallen,' were also relieved.

By 1971–72 pensioner numbers had increased to 220, but during that year only 150 'others' had been helped. In 1975 the Corporation doubled its pensions 'since the amount which can be disregarded by the DHSS [Department of Health and Social Security] has been increased'. During times of cutbacks in social services, as in 1977, the Corporation was heavily in demand from the Scots community and stepped in to provide cover, as did other charitable and voluntary agencies. The Corporation's visitors were regularly in touch that year with 394 individuals or families and gave more 'ad hoc' help to another 87; but, wrote the chairman in his annual report that year, the 'figures cannot even begin to convey the extent and variety of the need, in some cases quite desperate need, which the Visitors encounter each week'.

The *Glasgow Herald* of 6 September 1978 celebrated the birthday of 'one small Scotswoman' who had for some time been living in a Kilburn flat, 'increasingly harassed by other occupants', her food being stolen and her small vegetable plot uprooted. The newspaper reported that she then 'found herself in a split-new, two-room flat in a peaceful little enclave called St Ninians Court'. This Scotswoman was the first resident of the new sheltered housing scheme opened by the Corporation that year, and more charity pensioners soon moved in to occupy the other flats in Bawtry Road. Another new resident was a 79–year-old woman, originally from Ardrossan, who had recently been living in a Hammersmith basement flat. She previously had a tin bath which she had filled with hot water from boiling kettles and was, the *Herald* wrote, 'understandably entranced with her immaculate tiled bathroom, fitted with a floor-to-ceiling pole for support … and with levered taps'. It seemed to her, wrote the *Herald*, 'like the Ritz'.

Over 7,000 visits were made in 1983 to individuals and families, and 266 regular allowances were paid along with many welfare grants. A part-time youth worker had dealt with 284 young people and had held 565 interviews and 'counselling sessions'. And this was not to mention the help that continued to be doled out to casual callers at King Street. Many of the cases visited by the welfare visitors by 1985 were described as people trying to overcome their difficulties and live independent lives as far as they could. Around 310 pensioners were receiving pensions of £5 a week plus special summer and Christmas grants in 1988. Examples of relief for this year ranged from 'the provision of an electric wheelchair for a young person stricken with multiple sclerosis, to the purchase of a few items of essential winter clothing for an elderly single man living in a hostel'. At the end of 1990 there were 324 pensioners up to the age of 98. The sheltered housing for 76 pensioners meant that those living in the homes certainly felt a bond with fellow-occupiers and they enjoyed 'being with people with whom you share a nationality'. That year, the Corporation was, as always, aware that it might, one day, have to restrict its aid if resources were not increased. The problems facing the poorer Scots in London, and that the charity had to deal with, were still many – 'chronic illness, violence and disruption within the home, homelessness and inadequate accommodation as well as those of general deprivation'. One child and his mother in Luton became a special case in January 1991. The Corporation bought a car for the mother when her two-year-old son had to get to Great Ormond Street Hospital in London for dialysis while he awaited a kidney transplant. In September, when a donor kidney became available at one o'clock in the morning, 'the car was invaluable in getting Thomas to hospital in time'.

The total number of people receiving aid in 1995 had reached 1,000 individuals. Two trends emerged that year which had an impact on the charity's resources – the increasing numbers of frail elderly Scots who were remaining in their own, often inadequate, homes as a result of the 'Care in the Community' policy of local authorities and the growing number of referrals of single-parent families. The 152 single parents on the charity's books had a total of 343 children among them. Nearly all were responsible mothers with an average age of 35, being divorced, separated, widowed or simply abandoned; 'few if any of them are feckless young girls having children to get a council flat,' wrote H. Stewart Hunter, the Corporation's chairman. Some had experienced 'actual physical abuse from their partners' and were 'literally left holding the baby and largely dependent on the State for their living expenses'. The Corporation felt responsible for helping with these problems but at the same time considered them 'the subject of wider political argument because of the social and financial impact they are having'. There were 41 new cases of single parents in 1997, compared to 32 in 1996. The Corporation that year was also worried about the increasing age of its pensioners, especially the residents of its flats, 'none of which are equipped to offer nursing care'. Shortfalls in income for such care were recognised as an area of increasing need. By 1997–98 the first welfare 'co-ordinator' was appointed and a review of the charity's welfare was underway.

A 'strategic appraisal' by a working group of the trustees was also taking place by 1998, deliberating the Corporation's 'future direction'. An external study of the Corporation's work amongst Scots in London and their future needs was also planned. 'This will inevitably be influenced,' wrote chairman Bruce Cairns, 'by the Government's current programmes for the under 25s ("Welfare to Work") and for single parents ("New Deal for Lone Parents") which aim to make it possible for these groups to gain employment and so better their circumstances.' Further shifts and evolutions in state welfare underlay the charity's work in 2000, and an important aspect of the Corporation's work, as always, was to keep an eye on the trends that would most likely have an impact on the charity's activities. That year, Cairns wrote, they included 'the emergence of Primary Care Groups and Primary Care Trusts, the publication of national minimum standards for the care of older people, the changing pattern of arrangement for older people in care, and the setting up of the Supporting People initiative'. A summary of the Corporation's key activities for 1995–2002 includes the numbers of clients visited, corporation flats, pensioners and weekly pension amounts, and new cases approved and average grants handed out.[3] Other forms of help during this period included assistance with residential or nursing home fees and community care costs, the provision of television sets and help with licence fees for the housebound, clothes and necessary household items, help with winter heating costs, contributions towards mobility or disability aids, student training grants and casual assistance to street homeless. Even in 2002, cases for donations towards funeral expenses continued to be heard and Corporation grants awarded – for some these had meant sudden death or even murder and for others a more natural bereavement at a time of straitened circumstance.

One final Corporation activity for its pensioners deserves a special mention. James Kynneir had specified a St Andrew's Day dinner for the Corporation's pensioners in his will of 1681, and today the Royal Scottish Corporation prefers to entertain its London pensioners with a lunch on the second Wednesday of every month. This has been the practice since it was first introduced by Allan Freer in the early 1900s. During the 1920s and 1930s the fare was not as substantial as it is today and the pensioners received 'their usual soup and bread' (at a cost of £1 2s. a year) after having been paid their allowances. From 1980 the pensioners' lunch moved to the basement hall of Crown Court Church and a larger 'hot meal' was provided by the welfare visitors and volunteers. Today a

---

[3] See Appendix 4 for a table of services provided by the Corporation, 1995–2002.

some elderly pensioners and the Corporation honorary physicians and a few trustees additionally help serve the food and clear the paper plates. On the second Wednesday in December a Christmas lunch is provided after the carol service – a more recent tradition begun in 1994. Christmas crackers are on the table, raffle tickets are sold and the pensioners enjoy a 'turkey dinner', while sherry 'replaces the more usual cup of tea'.

CHAPTER 31

Costs of Welfare Relief

B y the 1830s the cost of sending poor Scots home was the smallest of the relief activities but provides the only figures that have survived from these years concerning the charity's spending. In November 1832 the 249 sea passages granted cost the London Corporation £1,800. On the other hand, the Edinburgh branch found that the numbers they had to look after, and send on to (often) Highland homes, were relatively few. By the end of 1833 they had relieved the 40 cases for just £9. 11s. Numbers decreased further the next year, and of the 28 cases for 1834, 12 had been paid for by William Cassells at a cost of £2. 10s. 9d, and the other 16 cases by David Taylor, the Leith agent, and a man named 'Wallace' at a combined cost of £3. 4s. 6d.

The next time records come round again in 1874, more information is available to show that the Corporation was spending £1,820 on pensions for a total of 170 individuals. Pensions were broken down into four groups – five pensioners received £25 each, another five got £15, while 110 received £12 and 50 had £6. A further £1,800 was spent on casual relief and passages home. The resumption of the books after the fire in November 1877 showed that charity payouts from 1876–77 until 1881–82 were fairly level in total but there was an increase in petitioner claims and passages home by the end of the period, while pensioner expenditure went down (especially in 1880–81).[1] Relief was up in 1883 compared with previous years and had especially increased since 1881. The Corporation had encroached on its capital to fund the expense of relief over the previous six years, having an average annual deficiency of £780 which it met with stock withdrawals. Even though James Fraser, the charity's auditor, was giving warning signs about the decreasing capital, the charity's court considered that the institution was 'never in a sounder condition generally than at present'. Since other costs had also been brought down as low as possible, the committee thought that any saving would have to come from reducing relief (in this it began agreeing with Fraser), thus 'reducing the pittances of your poorer Scottish Brethren, a course much to be deplored when one looks around and sees the amount of

---

[1] See Appendix 3 for a breakdown of relief costs, 1876–1882.

misery which exists and which increases every year'. The answer was that a large addition to the annual income was needed from donations, 'otherwise,' the committee wrote, 'the usefulness of the Charity must be considerably curtailed'.

Relief consequently came down at the end of 1884, but by St Andrew's Day 1886 it was up again on the previous year, totalling £3,911 – an amount following on the extra amounts paid out for 'unemployed fellow-countrymen' when in February and March the Corporation's 'Special Relief Committee' had twice had to 'relieve this exceptional class of distress', helping many, it reported, 'who do not usually come within the sphere of the charity's operations'.[2] By the end of 1888 the total relief bill was £4,125, and in 1889 claims on the charity's relief showed that they were becoming 'yearly more numerous and pressing'.

In May 1887 a proposal had been put forward to elect 50 Jubilee Pensioners to celebrate Queen Victoria's fifty years on the throne and her generosity as a subscriber of one hundred guineas annually throughout this time to the Corporation. The cost of the new pensions would be £2,000 and £1,760 had already been collected. Relief costs generally increased again by the end of 1893 and more Scots went home than usual. At the end of 1894 the charity reported a breakdown of the relief spent on adults (£1,964) and child (£456) petitioners for the first time as the old school fund interest was distributed, now that the government provided free education. The following year the allowance paid to widows for their children had gone down but was increased again by four percent the following year. The annual £12 pension, which was paid in monthly instalments of £1 a month, was also proving insufficient and the Corporation raised it to £13 a year. Two years later in 1897, the Corporation wished it could do more to help when it saw that it was still 'a hard struggle' for the petitioners 'to make ends meet on 10 or 15 shillings a month'. Queen Victoria's Diamond Jubilee that year, though, brought more good news for the elderly Scots when another round of pensions was created in celebration. Twenty-five new pensioners in March 1901 received the newly-created £13 pensions and were grouped together to form the Coronation Pensioners on the death of the queen and the accession of Edward VII. The new places were filled by the previous year's unsuccessful candidates. By 1901 the cost of pensioners' relief was £2,000, adult petitioners received £2,700 in total, children were granted £700, and £50 was spent on passages home.

In 1916 new 'Old Age Pensions' brought about some changes in the charity's calculation of pension amounts. Thomas Montcrieff, the charity's active secretary, made calculations for turning monthly pensions into weekly amounts, hoping to

2 A Royal Scottish Corporation deputation also met with the City of London's Mansion House Committee for the Relief of the Unemployed on 18 February 1886 but a donation was not forthcoming. A letter to all 'Scotchmen' was then sent to the *Times* appealing for subscriptions towards the 'many cases of exceptional and distressing destitution' that the Corporation had to deal with.

find a margin that could somewhat improve the allowances of the 'minorities under seventy'. He had long thought that 'the years in the sixties when earning powers diminish until seventy when national benefit becomes applicable are now the most serious time of all for the Corporation's beneficiaries and demand of us vigilant care that unnecessary hardship does not fall on the individual'. The governors agreed and new payments were made from January 1917.

Twenty years later, in 1937, pensions (except those held on special trusts or 'conditions') went up to £1 a week from 10s. a week. That year there were 423 pensioners on the charity's books – the 'highest in the corporation's long history' – and the Corporation regarded their allowance as still insufficient. And while it thought that 'industrial conditions' had 'improved', there was still much distress to be seen amongst the poorer London Scots. The Corporation knew that such increases would lead to more expense but expected extra revenue to come from a renewed appeal to supporters. By 1938, £190 was annually being spent on casual relief in the form of bed and food tickets given out to homeless callers at Fetter Lane. This, William Miller, the Corporation's secretary considered, was expensive and he had calculated that it comprised 2,000 nights' lodging at 10d. a night and 3,000 meals at 8d. a meal. Costs of such relief went down during the Second World War when many of the more casual relief applicants were employed in industry for the war effort, although some money was spent on helping the poorer London Scots come to terms with the loss of their homes in air raids, especially during 1940. Post-war, in 1955–56, the Corporation spent a total of £12,000 on welfare relief, supplementing the provisions of the new welfare state.

Twenty years later, and by the end of 1975, the Corporation had spent £36,000 over its budget in providing for over 400 'elderly and needy Scots in their own homes'. The increasing demand from young families was putting pressure on the charity. Capital released with the sale of Fetter Lane was not for spending either, having been put into a 'Property Fund' for planned social housing schemes. The subscriptions received that year, amounting to £4,000, were totally inadequate to cover such expenditure. The great cutbacks in spending by local authorities in 1977 meant consequently greater expenditure on welfare by the Corporation, which rose by £19,000 to over £63,000. By 1979–80 costs had risen to £152,000 for the now June to June accounting period and to £168,000 during 1980–81. The total cost of welfare activities in 1984 had risen to £193,300 and cash amounts of relief increased markedly in 1985, while by 1986 relief expenditure came to £269,000. The annual rise had been especially due to some extremely cold weather which had meant payouts of extra grants for fuel, although it probably also indicated that need was either increasing or had expanded to fit. New referrals increased expenditure for 1987 and 1988–89 when it reached £351,000 ('a new record'). The rise was also due to new government policies regarding welfare support as the new Department of Social Security (DSS) offices passed responsibility for such provision to charitable bodies wherever it could. Luckily the Corporation's accountants had been able to anticipate the increase, although not the income shortfall. The Corporation appealed to Scots in London to rally to the cause of their brethren in need, telling them, 'We never reject a case without full investigation and the cost of this alone is considerable'.

In 1993–94, the charity could claim to be spending £2,500 a day, 365 days a year, and that included £1,500 on charitable giving alone. In 1993 there had been a total of 146 cases, including 31 pensions, and the approved expenditure for new cases, excluding pensions, was £36,110. A summary of approved cases for 1993 was as follows:

> 27 welfare cases for pensioners (£8,482)
> 28 cases for 'Lone Parents' (£9,826)
> 60 cases for other non-pensioners (£17,804)
> 7 cases of assistance with nursing home fees
> 11 cases for holidays
> 7 cases for cookers
> 17 for washing machines
> 2 for fridges
> 16 for clothing

By the end of 1995 the total costs of welfare had almost doubled, having risen to £647,438; this was in itself a 14 percent increase on the previous year. A detailed breakdown of the estimated cost of each welfare item had been prepared in a 'Welfare Budget Report' in November 1997. Considering the report, John Brown, a trustee and a member of the welfare sub-committee, felt that over the previous five years the percentage of expenditure between the two categories – primary care, 'the relief of acute hardship and distress', and secondary care, 'quality of life improvement' – had got out of balance. He was keen to ensure that the balance between the two had not 'slipped too far' to the detriment of primary needs. He acknowledged that changes in 'Christmas Grants and Discretionary Payments' had somewhat 'reversed the drift towards the Secondary Category'. Brown suggested a balance of 79 percent for the primary category (approved cases, pensions, nursing home fees, discretionary payments, callers at King Street, training grants and Borderline) and 21 percent for the secondary category (summer grants, pensioners' lunches, televisions, holidays and their arrangement, caravan costs, outings, Christmas grants – apart from fuel and warm clothing, and other housing social events).

Relief of Scots in London by the Corporation has thus continued even though government benefits have long been available; and such welfare should not come to an end. In November 1987, Douglas Robertson, the charity's chairman, looked to the future and wrote: 'Despite the growth of the Welfare State and the formation of new charitable organisations the need for the Royal Scottish Corporation remains as great now as it did when our predecessors founded it all those centuries ago'.

CHAPTER 32

Referring and Managing Applications

A mong other conditions by 1868, applicants had to live within twelve miles of the Corporation's 'Hall' and also had to have lived for at least two years in London (both rules could be waived in special circumstances). Elderly pensioners had to have lived in London for twenty years and within twelve miles of the 'Hall'. Since the charter renewal of 1974, applicants have had to live within a thirty-five-mile radius of Charing Cross to be eligible for the Corporation's help.[1] Charing Cross was always a good place to start from, as Dr Johnson, a Corporation neighbour, had once said: 'Fleet-street has a very human appearance but I think the full tide of human existence is at Charing Cross'.

People have come to the Corporation in many different ways but the charity would never help just any Scot. 'Sturdy' beggars and vagrants were expressly forbidden aid as early as the Scottish Hospital's first charter in 1665. Careful vetting of applications had always been a tradition of the charity's administration and that of the Kinloch Bequest. The lengths that the Kinloch secretary had gone to during the 1820s to avoid being taken in by fraudsters has already been seen. Further away, those receiving sea passages home from the Corporation, and arriving in the port of Leith for a number of years from 1831–34, were authenticated by a certificate signed by the Corporation's London secretary. Lachlan Mackintosh, one of the governors, wrote to James Nairne, the man on the ground in Edinburgh, on 30 October 1830 letting him know that 'in order to guard against fraud, as well as to save unnecessary trouble to you or your Officer, every person to whom we might grant a Leith passage, should be the bearer of a letter from our Secretary to yours stating the result of any enquiries we might have instituted into his or her character, or circumstances'. This certificate not only proved their provenance but also announced their arrival to the charity's Leith agent.

It was not only the visitor and governors who found the relief application process tiring. Petitioners (as opposed to pensioners) had to have monthly signatures from a supporter, and the case of a Mrs Alexander Forbes of Pearson

---

[1] This had actually begun to be used a number of years earlier, though less formally.

Street, Clapham Junction was highlighted in September 1882. C. W. Marriston, a friend of hers, apologised for having to send in the latest form unsigned by Sir Henry Peck. 'Sir Henry' no longer wanted to be 'put to the trouble and inconvenience of signing this document month after month which in all probability is likely to extend for some considerable time,' wrote Marriston, 'and he felt it was imposing too much on the applicant to have to wear out their friends by these monthly applications and asked if something could not be done.' Marriston had received no reply from the Corporation, was despairing of ever getting Sir Henry to sign in future and of Mrs Forbes ever receiving any more charity. He suggested a quarterly or half-yearly signature and the Corporation eventually agreed to the latter.

Honorary physicians could also institute new ways of working during this period. One who did was Dr Finlay[2] who on 13 December 1882 wrote from Montague Street, Portman Square that it had occurred to him 'that applications of relief are often supported by allegations of bodily disease', and he suggested that he 'might do some useful work ... by furnishing the Committee with a Medical report on certain of these cases'. He was already seeing outpatients at the Middlesex Hospital every Monday and Thursday, and offered to see those of the charity's applicants who looked likely to need such a medical report. He thought it best that the applicants should bring one of his 'cards of admission' with them, provided by the visitor. The charity's secretary should send the doctor advance warning by postcard telling him who was coming 'for examination' and when. 'Assuming that the Applicant came as instructed', Finlay would then prepare a report 'as to his or her bodily condition' in time for the next committee meeting. If the applicants needed immediate hospital treatment rather than charitable relief, it would be very easy for him to refer them straightaway and get them admitted as 'in-patients in the Hospital'. The Corporation thought this a suitable plan and arrangements were made with Finlay to put it into practice the following January.

Pensioners were elected by Corporation voters (governors, other donors and executors of legacies) who had read a list of the cases. Many people were also personally referred by governors. In September 1882, Isabella Hepburn asked the Corporation for more help with the case of a Mrs Woods, who had suddenly had a great increase in expenses owing to sickness and death in her family. An amount of 20s. was awarded in addition to Mrs Woods's usual monthly allowance. On 12 March 1884 the petition of a Mrs Mackay was signed by Corporation governor and leading banker, Sir Nathaniel de Rothschild. At the beginning of January 1884 a sub-committee of nine governors had once again been appointed 'to investigate the List of monthly relief cases with a view to ascertain the

2 Finlay was to leave the Corporation nearly ten years later in 1891 to take up the chair of medicine at Aberdeen University.

propriety of continuing relief in each individual circumstance'. It reported back on 12 November 1885 that it had checked the books and had reviewed 363 cases and recommended that 284 be continued 'at the present scale'. It had decided that thirteen should be raised to pension level and that forty-four should be discontinued; thirteen should be decreased and four should be increased; and the five who had died could be struck off the list. At a meeting on 3 June 1885 petitioners had also been divided into four classes:

1. Those eligible for the £12 pension; 'to be visited once a year only'
2. 'Widows who receive for children also to be visited at least once in each year; the Visitor to report when each child reaches the age of 12 years – whether the mother remains unmarried and any other special circumstance.'
3. Those not 'in every way eligible under the Bye Laws' but who were in 'temporary difficulty, from ill health or want of employment.'
4. 'Those to whom donations are given.'

Nearly a year later in March 1886, when the beadle was told not to take down the names of any tramps, the Corporation revealed that this further class was no longer to be relieved 'for the future'.

At the end of the century, while dealing with additional numbers of cases as a result of the war in South Africa, governors of the Corporation were occasionally the victims of unscrupulous beggars trying to extract money with begging letters, and scrutineers were still appointed to investigate new cases and pensions applications. In 1911, 'impostors' were considered a big problem and the Corporation was warning its subscribers that as a result of 'An almost incredible number of cases of imposition passing daily under his observation, the Secretary ventures to urge on subscribers the advisability in general of their referring to the Corporation all cases of unknown applicants writing or calling on them for pecuniary assistance'. This was in the same year that the charity gave out lodging and food tickets to 2,000 casual callers. By 1912 the £25 pensioners were selected from 'a class of persons who have occupied a respectable social position', who could satisfy the committee that they had a guaranteed income of not less than £15, and not more than £30. They had to be at least 65 and had to have lived for twenty years within twelve miles of the 'Hall'. 'But in cases of complete physical or mental disability,' the charity stated, 'the Committee having regard to all the circumstances may accept candidates of not less than 55 years of age.' Printed lists of candidates since 1901 had shown an individual's proposer and seconder, together with their addresses. The Corporation's 'New Cases' books for the 1920s through to the 1960s similarly record names of the society, governor or other person recommending the applicant. The new cases of this early twentieth-century period now showed fewer widows and many more unemployed men applying to the charity. Those listed for March 1925 included the following:

NO.	M/F	AGE	BIRTHPLACE	GOVERNOR	GRANT	REMARKS
103	M	39	?	Secretary	–	False claim to birth in Scotland
104	M	36	Banff	ditto	22s. 6d.	Clothing for work [12s. 6d.] Donations for food [10s.]
108	M	43	Dundee	ditto	–	Wants better paid work and help for wife in confinement
110	M	57	Arbroath	ditto	3s.	Hostel. Robbed following voyage and arrival in London
111	M	64	Mortlach	Committee	£2	Kinloch allowance
112	F	67	Edinburgh	Rev. Archibald Fleming	£6 10s.	Provided by Sons of Clergy and Indigent Gentlewomen's Fund
117	M	77	Brechin	George C Robertson	£1 12s.	March allowance on leaving infirmary

Note: the names of the applicants have not been shown in this table but are in the case books.

Those not awarded anything in November 1926 were remarked on thus: 'Has some means. Annuity suggested for consideration of relatives'; 'Education asked for of boy in USA'; 'Employment wanted. Secretary to Companies'; 'Wanted promise before filling up form. Abusive and threatening'; 'Resident in Dover'; 'Ex-Scots Guardsman in need of work. Bank Messenger or such like'; 'Probably not a native of Scotland'; 'Wants Sanitary inspectorship'; 'Widow of a medical man but no Scottish connection'; 'A marine engineer in need but has not applied as asked'; 'Wants to work. Has been a traveller'; in the case of many, the remarks section simply noted, 'Case not proceeded with'. By December 1932 most of the successful cases were given donations for food and lodging, or passages home with money for provisions during the journey to places such as Dundee or Paisley. One woman (aged 46 and from Helmsdale) was given money by the Corporation for her 'services on premises', and other applicants were turned down: a man aged 22 from Dumfries had already been in prison for counterfeiting, another woman aged 46 from Aberdeen 'says husband has deserted'. The Corporation added the remark, 'Doubtful'. One man from Paisley aged 34 called in a drunken state and another, aged 56 and also from Paisley, 'left office and did not return'.

The 1930s depression saw even more unemployed Scotsmen claiming casual relief from the Corporation. Some were genuine cases, but by 1938 William

Miller, the Corporation's secretary, had done his sums and research carefully and felt that the charity was being taken for a ride by its casual callers, or 'scroungers' as he termed them. He had come to the conclusion that those who took advantage of the Corporation's bed and meal tickets had 'little to recommend them'. In fact, it was well known in both London and Scotland that the Corporation provided such aid to men who asked for it, and he thought that most of those picking up the tickets were 'well acquainted with the methods of living on charity, and few of them can be regarded as good Scots'. Not only had he found the relief to be expensive (£190 a year), but he had contacted the Church Army Authorities and the superintendent of the London County Council's Welfare Department. The 'Officer-in-Charge' of the Church Army Embankment Home had replied with what Miller called 'a somewhat unconventional letter:'

> I am convinced that if you can cut a lot of this out altogether it will be a saving on your funds, and stop some of the scrounging that is going on. As you will have noticed, men do not apply to you on Fridays, they draw the Dole or Relief, and for a couple of days have a good fling, then get one night off you, one off Welfare, one from the Churches, one from the Silver Lady, and call the rest of us mugs. Why not ease off. The Parson at St. Matthews in this street helped them all one time, 30 tickets a night; he was pestered so much he had to get the Police to clear them. He put a notice on his door 'No more tickets. Applicants for help must apply at the Welfare Office'. He lived happily ever after; no one calls now.

The LCC, in fact, felt that the Corporation was getting in the way of its own relief efforts and was encouraging the charity to stop handing out the tickets. Miller thought the council should be listened to because of its greater experience and for what he called its 'sources of information'. He also considered that its help was likely to produce better results and had himself recently interviewed 31 applicants for the Corporation's casual relief. He found that 21 of them were already known to the LCC and that in most cases the charity's help 'was encouraging the applicants in idleness and actually retarding the constructive measures the LCC had in view'. He knew that when the tickets were suddenly stopped (as he proposed), it would initially mean 'much unpleasantness' for the Corporation's staff, but after a short time, he thought, 'we should be comparatively free of trouble'. He considered a brief notice would suffice, announcing to callers 'the futility of making personal representation'. There were probably a few quarrels on the doorstep of Fetter Lane later that year but, as wars always brought jobs, the outbreak of the Second World War the next year soon meant fewer cases of casual relief for the charity, and especially by the end of 1943. Even so, the few applications that were received were carefully and 'sympathetically investigated, and, where genuine need existed, adequate help was given'.

Pensioners and others whom the corporation helped were also advertisements to others and helped spread the word. Ministers of the Scots churches in London at Crown Court in Covent Garden and St Columba's in Pont Street have also long actively led the way in referrals, and so too have their English counterparts in many London parishes. Scottish organisations in London and Scotland, hospitals, local authorities and other charitable bodies have also been, and are today, key agents in putting applicants forward. The welfare visitors also played a part in getting the local authorities in their area to act for those in need, sometimes coordinating several local agencies in a community and even reporting cases of local-authority neglect. By 1968 the charity was actively talking to other groups to 'make known our purpose' and to 'take a more positive part in integrating our effort with the many other bodies pursuing a similar course to our own'. A year later both the elderly pensioners and the Corporation were starting to feel the benefits of the Welfare State, 'but there is clearly a vast field in which charitable bodies like ourselves can function and it is our endeavour to be far seeing enough in this important aspect to appreciate our place'. The temporary help was, as always, important for many Scots, and a 'greater number now' were finding the Corporation 'on the recommendation of other Societies'. Although what the Welfare State meant was still a little hazy, it was becoming clearer the following year, and the Corporation now considered it essential to be known to all appropriate local authorities and 'to be of strength to meet any demand'. This was especially important by the early 1970s when many younger Scots 'descended upon London' who were 'totally unprepared in any way for independent life in the Metropolis'.

The new Social Security Act of 1986 and its 'Social Fund Provisions' became law from April 1988. 'Under the new legislation,' wrote the Corporation's chairman, Douglas Robertson, 'single lump-sum payments from Supplementary Benefit will be abolished and replaced by a cash-limited discretionary loan repayable from consecutive weekly benefits.' Other benefits were also due for a change in type and amount and the Corporation anticipated an increase in referrals from social workers. Applications started increasingly to come through the welfare visitors in London areas by 1991 and the Corporation, disliking the uncoordinated manner of such application, explicitly had to ask that 'new referrals ... should be made in writing to the Secretary, not to individual visitors'. Referrals and the number of charities keen to work alongside the Corporation 'whether as a primary agency or as a provider of assistance by way of secondary grants where the case details supplied meet our criteria' were increasing by the end of 1997.

Welfare is considered the 'raison d'être' of the Corporation, and the welfare sub-committee chairman, Stuart Steele, has been responsible for making sure the charity takes its responsibilities in this area very seriously. Its remit includes the broad application of the policy for effectively and economically improving the welfare of London Scots 'in need, hardship or distress'. A 'cases panel' is a function of this sub-committee and both meet every second Wednesday. The additional panel evolved with John Brown's and Dr Archie MacDonald's help during the 1990s and now includes a few members of the committee of management and Ruth Smith, the welfare manager. Its members discuss the cases brought to their attention by the welfare visitors who have interviewed the applicants in their own homes, and who have made assessments and written a report. All applicants are already on income support and usually have a need of essential household items; children's needs such as help with school clothing and shoes are also considered. The more expensive forms of relief (such as cars) that were offered in the past have been scaled down to allow for extra relief. Decisions on applicants are usually made at the regular monthly meeting, and recommendations on cases are made to the committee of management later that same day. Administration of the case begins the following morning. But 'if they really are in trouble and they knock at the door now, they'll be helped within five minutes, if there's a need for it until the next meeting'. They might then be voted a larger grant once their case has been properly reviewed. All cases, for the most part, according to Ruth Smith, 'appear to need items that we would assume that in modern society most people would be able to afford'. These are people, she says, 'largely living in poverty, mainly through no fault of their own; it's difficult for these people to come forward and ask for help'. She thinks that the charity still 'needs to make more effort to find these Scots in need across London, even though the local agencies are again aware of the existence of the Royal Scottish Corporation'.

The charity had contacted social services, NHS Trust hospitals and other agencies and fellow charities, numbering over 500 in all, during the second half of 2002 in a renewed referrals drive. After a lull in publicising its activities to referral agencies and other charities at the end of the 1990s, leaflets about the Corporation were sent to doctors' waiting rooms, primary care trusts, walk-in clinics, housing associations, the police, universities and colleges and other charities for distribution. Since people apply as a result of circumstance, this new drive will take time to develop in the long term, but there has been a marked rise in the rate of referrals in the short term.

Figure 25 Poor Londoners receive a Christmas gift of coal, c. 1840s; the Scots charity also provided coal for its poor from the seventeenth to the early twentieth centuries (*Guildhall Library, Corporation of London*)

Figure 26 'The Haunted Lady' or 'The Ghost in the Looking-Glass'. 'Madame la Modiste': "We would not have disappointed your Ladyship, at any sacrifice, and the robe is finished à merveille,"' *Punch*, 1863; many poor Scotswomen in Victorian London also tried to earn a living from sewing (*Guildhall Library, Corporation of London*)

Figure 27 Governors of the Scots Corporation meeting at Crane Court, c. 1860s (*Guildhall Library, Corporation of London*)

Figure 28 Firemen tried in vain to save the Crane Court premises and contents when the charity's Hall caught fire on 14 November 1877 (*Guildhall Library, Corporation of London*)

Figure 29 Joseph Lister, Lord Lister, an honorary surgeon of the Corporation from 1878–1912 (*Reproduced by kind permission of the President and Council of the Royal College of Surgeons of England*)

Figure 30 Scottish emigrants on board a train in Quebec, Canada, 1911; a number of Scots were also helped during the charity's own Canadian emigration project the same year *(Public Archives of Canada)*

Figure 31 Volunteer soldiers of the London Scottish Regiment at a railway station in France, 1914 *(London Scottish Regiment)*

Figure 32 The Corporation's Fetter Lane building after World War II fire damage restoration (*Royal Scottish Corporation*)

Figure 33 Douglas Robertson, c. 1964–65, when he was elected annual president of the Caledonian Society of London; already a Corporation supporter, he later became chairman of the charity's committee of management, 1977–89, and has been a vice-president since 1977 (*Royal Scottish Corporation*)

Figure 34 The coat of arms of the Royal Scottish Corporation, granted by the Lord Lyon King of Arms in 1979 (*Royal Scottish Corporation*)

Figure 35 Patron of the Royal Scottish Corporation since 1952, Her Majesty Queen Elizabeth II sits beside the Lord Mayor of the City of London at a banquet held at the Guildhall to mark her Golden Jubilee, 4 June 2002. Seated far left is Tony Blair, Britain's Scottish prime minister *(Corporation of London/Clive Totman)*

Figure 36 London Scottish hospitality: enjoying the charity's monthly Pensioners' Lunch at Crown Court Church of Scotland in March 2003 *(Royal Scottish Corporation/Charlotte Krag)*

Figure 37 The present offices of the charity at 37 King Street, Covent Garden in March 2003 (*Royal Scottish Corporation/Charlotte Krag*)

CHAPTER 33

Welfare Visiting

The work of visiting the elderly and disabled pensioners and other cases has been a unique service of the Royal Scottish Corporation for many centuries and has always been regarded as difficult, even 'onerous'. Initially, 'visiting' was undertaken on a voluntary basis by two of the court assistants. A collector (of subscriptions and donations) was in post by 1815 and a single, salaried official was some time later appointed who combined the functions as the Victorian 'Visitor and Collector'. Thomas Inglis is the first name recorded as being associated with this office, occupying the post for nineteen years until around the later 1870s.[1] Lockhead had been the visitor and collector at the time of the fire in November 1877. He resigned at the end of 1879, perhaps affected by the death in December of his fellow worker and charity tenant James Lennox, the Corporation's beadle. A new visitor and collector, Alexander Harvey, was appointed in December 1880. A few weeks after his appointment, Harvey professed himself, in a letter to the committee of management, 'anxious to do the duties of Collector and Visitor', but saying that 'he desired to have an honorary appointment such as Sub Treasurer or Assistant Secretary so as to give him the status of gentleman in connection with the Scottish Corporation in the West End Clubs and drawing rooms'. The Corporation's management 'unanimously' agreed that 'they had no power to entertain Mr Harvey's proposals and that they could only act in accordance with the By-laws which clearly defined his position and duties', and which he had 'unconditionally' agreed to. The committee allowed him to stay in post as long as he continued to perform his duties appropriately. It then received a further letter from Harvey on 30 April 1881. In this second letter he revealed what his thoughts had been when he had first applied for the job:

> I believed the work to be comparatively light, and I thought that by system and method I should have a fair share of leisure for myself. In this I have been disappointed. My whole time & energy has been absorbed by the duties of my post, and I have found myself obliged to give, not only my days, but my

---

[1] Inglis was still in post at the end of 1873. On 27 June 1888, John Bruce of Wadhurst left £1,000 to the Corporation; the legacy was brought about by Thomas Inglis, and he was made a life governor as a result.

evenings to the Service of the Corporation. I believe it to be impossible for anyone who has not actually done the work to have any adequate conception of the laborious nature of the appointment.

He had decided to resign and proposed to finish his duties on 8 June. He also stated that he had visited all the pensioners in their own homes 'without one exception'.

At their 8 June meeting, the governors reviewed the list of twelve men who had applied to take Harvey's place. The number was soon whittled down to three candidates and the position was finally awarded to James Clement. By December that year the new visitor was also feeling the strain. A letter from him left the members of the charity's committee of management wondering if they had misrepresented the office when interviewing candidates for the post. Clement told the governors that he had

> no idea of the excessive, and often disheartening nature of the duties; but being then full of health and energy, I thought that what others had done, I could do. After two years arduous work however, I find my health so much deteriorated that I think the interests and future prospects of myself and family will be best consulted by seeking an appointment connected with the profession for which I was trained, or work requiring less physical exertion than my present office.

He added he would leave in three months' time.

As the second visitor in three years prepared for departure, was the dual nature of the office proving too much for one individual? The charity was not going to take any chances of being misunderstood again and, at its next meeting on 9 January, passed some new resolutions on the clauses in the Corporation's by-laws concerning the post of the visitor and collector:

> 1. He shall perform all the duties required by the Bye Laws, and shall in addition work under the instructions of the secretary, and be guided by him
>   ...
> 2. He shall enter into the office Receipt book any monies paid to him at the Hall in the absence of the Secretary, and shall not claim poundage on same, unless it be allowed by the Committee.
> 3. All Letters and Circulars he may write on the business of the Corporation must be signed by the Secretary.

He should also keep a diary of his daily work, have no fixed business hours and 'shall assist at all times when the Secretary requires him'. He would be paid £75 a year as 'Visitor', and as 'Collector' should receive 'five percent on monies collected by him on the Secretary's instructions'. Free lodging would be provided in the hall, and lighting and fuel for his accommodation would also be free. Travel expenses would be paid when on 'visiting business', but 'not when collecting'. He would have to find the Corporation's usual security guarantee of £200 and there would be three months' notice on either side. If he disobeyed orders or neglected his duties, the secretary could suspend him until the next general court or meeting of the committee of management. These arrangements were then printed for the guidance of applicants for the new post, which had been advertised in the *Times*, the *Daily News* and the *Scotsman*.

By 13 February 1884 the Corporation had received 140 applications. It set up a sub-committee which drew up a short list of nine names. Eight came from Scotland and the ninth applicant was a Scot in America – A. B. Leckie of Peoria, Illinois. Their ages ranged from 23 (Alexander Buchan of Blackdog, Aberdeen) to 42 (James Donaldson of Edinburgh). All candidates were seen a week later at a special meeting, and, as usual, members of the committee of management voted for their favoured candidate. A. K. Sandison of Wick was chosen with a runaway lead and he then sent in his sureties from the secretary of the Bank of New South Wales in Old Broad Street and the agent of the Chartered Mercantile Bank of India and China in Calcutta. The resigning visitor and collector, Clement, was given a reference that he 'was honest, obliging, industrious and of good ability'. He had shown 'great energy and success' as Collector and was considered carefully accurate in his Visitor duties. Four years later, Sandison's successor Alexander Buchan (possibly the 23-year-old listed first among the 1884 candidates) was appointed visitor and collector in June 1888 and flourished in the post.

Miss E. C. Kerr was appointed the Corporation's first female visitor in 1915, and her 'sympathetic manner' and 'faithful and valuable services' were recorded when she also became the longest-serving visitor on her retirement in 1952 after 37 years in the post. She had helped to guide the Royal Scottish Corporation through the administratively gruelling days of the first old-age pensions and had also experienced the beginnings of the post-war welfare state. She appears to have instituted a programme of volunteers to help her in the visiting task during the First World War; although who these people precisely were is not recorded, but certainly some of them were governors and the chaplains as well as the honorary physicians and surgeons whom the pensioners knew had 'always been at their command in time of need'. In 1924 the pensioners were described as 'solely dependent on ministrations of active workers, who have for long rendered devoted service on behalf of the Charity, and whose regular visits are looked forward to with keen interest by the old people'. Such 'loving kindness', probably given by the remaining members of the Hepburn family and others, had meant, the Corporation reported, a 'brightening of the lives of our aged and friendless recipients'. Visits were also kept up as a matter of importance even during the Second World War when many of the pensioners refused to leave their homes for places of greater safety.

Miss Kerr was followed by another long-serving visitor, Mrs M. J. MacNaught, whose time with the Corporation, when she retired in 1985, had spanned 33 years of social change from 1952, and when, as Miss Alexander, she first had the 'onerous task' of making more frequent visits to the 230 pensioners. It proved hard work as usual, and in 1967 a second visitor was appointed, which meant that the charity could make more frequent and regular calls on the elderly pensioners. This 'personal attention and advice' was considered 'even greater value than the regular financial allowances provided'. As a consequence the number of pensioners increased, 'reversing a trend of recent years', and even more visitors were thought to be beneficial, permitting an increase in services to other Scots in need. By 1968, housing was starting to figure more seriously on the charity's agenda and so too the visitors' visits. The Corporation now considered such 'visiting' an area 'in which we can broaden our service', since some of the more elderly Scots were not so much in financial need as in want of a sympathetic ear. Another four visitors were appointed to cover a wider area but still within the remit of the charter (twelve miles from the hall). In the 1970s, the Corporation's welfare visitors kept diaries of their daily routine, the people they visited and for how long, together with money paid out and mileage travelled (as they do similarly, but more formally, today). One diary was compiled by Hilary Gibson, a welfare visitor for the south-east London area, from January to June 1972. It shows she travelled on average 30–50 miles, usually making six visits a day:[2]

> March 15
> 9am – In Penge. Bought kettle £5.95 for Mr__; Iron for Mr__ (paid £1 over amount rec'd).
> 10am – Visited Mrs__, Peckham. Left £5 of £25 grant. 1¼ hours.
> 11.45 – Visited Mrs__, Keetans Rd. (Collected letter re Clothing Grant fm. Mr Clack Educ. Welfare – Request for fare to Glasgow fm Mrs__). ¾ hour.
> 1.30pm – Visited Mrs__, Willowbrook Est. ¾ hour. 63p tinned meat.
> 2.15 – Visited Mrs__, Willowbrook. Left 1b Butter & Tea 48p. ½ hour.
> 3.15 – Visited Mr__, Old Kent Road. Left Iron. ½ hour.
> 4.30 – Called on Mrs__, Penge – took dog to vet at Norwood. 1½ hours.
> Home 6.15pm
> 30 [miles]
> Travel 2 hours.

In 1978 the Corporation was still much impressed by its welfare visitors, considering their work to be 'the most effective service being offered by the Corporation'. Consequently the number of visitors was again increased, this time from five to nine. At the end of 1978 Douglas Robertson, chairman since

---

[2] Thirty years later, a consultant's report of 2002 showed that visitors in that year had been making an average of eight visits a week at a unit cost of about £100.

1977, expected another increase in pensioners as the new visitors settled into their jobs. As part of the control on costs introduced in 1980, the number of visitors was reduced by one, from nine to eight. A part-time youth worker, introduced in 1978, was still among their number, and although the appointment of a second youth worker and a senior social worker continued to be postponed, visits were increased.

Nearly ten years later in 1987 the 'hand of friendship' of the welfare visitors was again highlighted as the key relief activity for that year. In 1988 the Corporation felt the role of the welfare visitor was going through a period of change and visitor education was needed. 'As welfare provision by the state changes ... Regular staff training is necessary to keep abreast of new legislation so that the Visitors can identify needs not covered by statutory benefits,' wrote Alan Robertson in his annual secretary's report for 1988. By 1989, after once again recruiting a ninth visitor, the charity planned to use three specifically for south London, where there was a growing workload beyond the capacity of the existing staff. Until then, one had looked after casual, usually homeless, callers at the King Street offices while the London Boroughs and other places within the 35-mile radius from Charing Cross were allocated among the remaining seven visitors. In 1991 another warden was appointed for the new flats at Rothesay Court, bringing the welfare section numbers to ten. Regular visits were still very much welcomed by the pensioners, enabling them to talk through problems or to get help with completing the complex paperwork now needed for claiming benefits. In 1993 the charity's chairman wrote that the then eleven visitors had been presented

> with a formidable array of problems, many apparently insoluble, and by helping to shoulder these burdens they give help and comfort which cannot be priced in cold financial terms. That is not to say that money does not play a large part in the Visitors' working day and the direct financial help that a Visitor is authorised to give often means the difference between going hungry and having some food for the weekend.

The work of the welfare visitors and wardens in 1995 was described as often 'unpleasant' and never 'a garden of roses'. But on a lighter note, the welfare visitors have also organised the pensioners' lunches, days out and holidays for families and groups. Burns suppers for the residents of the housing schemes and other social occasions were also arranged. Today's welfare manager, Ruth Smith, has said that a certain type of personality is needed to visit a caseload of around seventy new and existing 'clients' a month. Such work needs someone who has experience of working in social services or a similar charity, she says, and especially 'someone who is resilient, who is able to cope (in a way that's helpful to the client) with quite a lot of emotional material that's often presented to them'; in particular, someone 'who is able to make astute judgements about individuals and their circumstances'. The job, she has said, requires 'compassion and certainly, in many cases, a sense of perspective and a sense of humour' in order to deal with such 'a mix of people – some elderly, some with physical disabilities, some with perhaps mental health problems or a learning disability'. For many of the pensioners and welfare-grant beneficiaries in 2000, the welfare visitor, as described by one Corporation client that year, was 'my friend as well', or by others as 'brilliant', and also 'they've helped me so much'. Or just: 'I'm glad the social worker wrote the letter'.

CHAPTER 34

Homelessness

F or many years the Royal Scottish Corporation has also helped those who have been in London for only a few days or even hours. In the 1920s it saw homeless men arriving in rags and provided them with a suit of clothes from second-hand items donated by the charity's governors. The months of unemployment worsened and in the 1930s the Corporation gave out what it called 'bread and food tickets' that appeared to be as well known in 'the larger towns in Scotland' as they were in London. By 1938, William Miller, its secretary, calculated that the charity was annually giving away around 2,000 nights' lodging and 3,000 meals to these casual callers. Alcoholism, drugs and family breakdown are three of the wide variety of causes of homelessness amongst Scots in the capital today.

Those who do not want to return to Scotland, but who are classed as unemployed and homeless, are now looked after by the Corporation's partner, Borderline. This Church of Scotland charity looks after the housing and homelessness issues of city Scots, as well as their benefit and employment concerns. A Glasgow University study, commissioned by Borderline and published in September 2000, estimated that between ten and fourteen percent of London's homeless people were Scots or of Scots descent. It also found that most had come from 'economic blackspots' and had suffered a childhood of family disruption. The report was based on a (somewhat limited) study of 41 Scots aged between 17 and 59, and many of those interviewed had left home at 16, leaving school with few or no qualifications. The study found that older men were likely to have experienced homelessness in Scotland even before they came south. A significant number of women said mental health problems, violence and sexual abuse were among the main reasons why they had left Scotland. Most said they did not want to return home while others said they were ambivalent about remaining in the capital but were reluctant to go back because they felt ashamed of having 'failed' in London. The availability of cheap, rented accommodation was the most important factor in providing for these homeless Scots.

This was a similar conclusion of a homelessness study undertaken for London generally and published in 1971. In April 1969 the UK's Department of Health

and Social Security had invited John Greve, the Professor of Social Administration at Southampton University, to head an investigation into London homelessness. 'The study was to be mounted as a matter of urgency' and a research
team was immediately formed. The research took a year and a final report was
issued the following June.[1] Greve's study also foretold what the result of the
Glasgow University study and other future reports might be: 'Whatever their
characteristics, these reports will all have something in common – and this they
will share with past ones – their roots will be in continuing social problems of
which the lack of an adequate or secure dwelling is dominant and persuasive'.
That it should be affordable was also vital: 'the greatest need of the majority of
homeless ... is for housing of a reasonable standard, at rents they can afford, and
with security of tenure'.

In 1968 Inner London had six percent of the population of England and
Wales, but 37.5 percent of those people who were registered as homeless.
Homelessness in London was not new; people had always slept rough in parks,
in railway stations, on the Thames embankments and in extremely basic lodging
houses, if not the workhouse. George Orwell, in his *Down and Out in Paris and
London* published in 1933, and other authors since, have 'described the plight of
thousands'. From 1911 to 1914 the medical officer of the London County
Council (LCC) had made an annual census of the homeless in the whole
metropolitan county. After the First World War until 1949, the LCC's then
Welfare Department made a 'midnight count' of the homeless in central London
every year. Migration to London had resumed after the war and households had
split into more separate or singular groups. By 1951 around 3,500 homeless
people were living in the LCC's 'rest centres' and old Poor Law institutions.
New housing was nearing completion but had only temporary palliative effects.
The homeless 'count' was again carried out twice in November 1963 by the
Welfare Department with some volunteer helpers. The individual 'sleepers out'
numbered 129 and 120 on each count, and probably did not include all those
who could have been found.

Family homelessness had been increasing during the late 1950s according to
LCC reports of the early 1960s. The number of people squatting in unoccupied
buildings, which had increased after the Second World War because of bomb
damage and lack of time, money and resources to build new homes, now rose
again dramatically. Acts to protect against eviction in 1964 and the Rent Act in
1965 helped some cases and the LCC reports eventually led to even more reports.
The television showing of Ken Loach's film *Cathy Come Home* in December
that year focused the attention of both the media and the public on London's

---

[1] The report was revised, updated and published in 1971 as *Homelessness in London*. The book
records Irish immigrants as a body of the homeless but did not seem to regard the Scots as a big
enough group to mention.

homeless families as social workers began to solve the problem by taking children of homeless parents into care instead of providing them with suitable accommodation.[2] In 1966 and 1967 the Ministry of Health, alarmed by the increase of homeless people in local authorities' temporary housing, issued circulars aimed at improving services. These

> encouraged "early warning" systems designed to prevent eviction from private and council housing; urged that families should not be split up but kept together as a unit in temporary accommodation; proposed standards for the improvement of this accommodation; and also emphasised that local authorities should "give consideration to improving their preventative and rehabilitative services."

As usual, the circulars left out provision for the large numbers of single individuals on London's streets. 'Provision for the homeless,' Greve wrote, 'has concentrated overwhelmingly on providing shelter for people actually without a place to live; and then almost invariably for "families", thus excluding considerable numbers of homeless people without dependent children.' A 1965 survey had shown that there were then an estimated 11,000 single homeless people in London. Ninety percent of them were men living in hostels and lodging houses; 300 were sleeping rough. Mostly homeless due to family breakdown, many were also new arrivals in London.

Voluntary agencies helped the local authorities to provide homeless services, including 'advice, family casework, financial support, and housing in different forms'. Greve's research team talked to as many of these agencies as it could usefully find. They especially wanted to know 'the extent to which voluntary agencies were (as is widely believed and even intended) filling in the gaps between statutory services, and how far they were duplicating existing services leaving gaps to be filled'. The report showed that the voluntary agencies were usually doing the duplicating and, Greve pointed out, 'particularly in the crucial service of housing, where both statutory and voluntary agencies not infrequently pursue policies which withhold assistance from many whose needs are greatest'. By the end of September 1970 the number of homeless Londoners had increased by 25 percent since Greve's report had first been commissioned as 'urgent', eighteen months earlier. This meant that there were now 8,600 people living in temporary accommodation provided by the Inner London boroughs. Provision reflected need but it also showed a growing awareness on the part of the authorities which had fuelled the growth. The selection procedures of the agencies helping homeless people were also different – and so too was the success rate of applicants. Again, single men, in particular, found support the most difficult to obtain.

---

[2] The film had also immediately led to the establishment of Shelter, the homeless charity.

Although Greve did not talk to the Royal Scottish Corporation, the charity was being much influenced by the increasing numbers of homeless people needing help – if not by his report. Young, mostly single, Scots 'descending on London' were now approaching the charity in much greater numbers. By the end of 1972 the Corporation found that they were 'totally unprepared in any way for independent life in the Metropolis' and saw that there was 'an urgent need for temporary accommodation for these young people which organisations such as ours can provide'. The charity thought it had found a niche, and at the end of 1975 the Corporation had bought the hostel building it had been seeking for a number of years. After a period of repairs and renovations, it eventually opened on 20 September, at the end of the long hot summer of 1976, equipped to house 35 young Scotsmen. The Corporation hoped to provide them with some sort of short-stay 'haven' from the 'vicissitudes' of the great city. The charity also hoped that the hostel would provide them with 'a good start in a new life avoiding the pitfalls in which one meets so many of them'.

Two social workers had been appointed to the new hostel's staff during 1976 and the 'National Council of the YMCAs' was responsible for the hostel's administration on behalf of the Corporation. The greatest advocate of the new idea was in fact the Corporation's new secretary, a caring man called Ian Macleod, who had joined the charity in December 1976 after 27 years working for the YMCA. The Corporation's management therefore seemed well prepared. After its first year of operation the hostel received a 'substantial subsidy' from the Corporation's welfare funds. Hostel expenses for this first year were about £16,000 and social workers' salaries and expenses were nearly £6,000. The Corporation managed partly to offset these costs with hostel residents' payments of nearly £5,500. A 'qualified' social worker was also appointed warden of the hostel towards the end of 1978. The availability of places for young Scotsmen in the Corporation's new hostel had also been widely publicised amongst local social services and other organisations working in London's homeless sector and was by this year considered 'well-established in the minds of those working in the Referral Agencies'. A 'detached youth worker', based at King Street, was also appointed in 1978 to 'seek out' and offer help to 'rootless' young Scots 'in the West End'.

The main aim of the Corporation's hostel project, and the reason why the charity was prepared to devote such efforts and resources to the single men's homeless cause, was to prevent 'some of the youths who come from Scotland to the West End of London' falling into a 'sub-culture'. In addition to the roaming and station-based youth workers, advice and tea had begun to be provided to individual callers at the King Street offices. Proximity to such hardened cases meant that the Corporation was beginning to see at close hand the depths to which such young men 'adrift' could soon sink. Douglas Robertson, chairman of the committee of management, described this effort as 'a time consuming piece of work, requiring the qualities of patience, firmness and insight' on the part of the welfare visitor concerned. 'Despite all that we do,' he wrote, 'we are left with the knowledge that in so many cases there is no way of providing the real help that is needed.' The Corporation could not make a difference in some cases; the 'applicants' themselves would have to have 'a readiness and a determination to change their way of life … Too often this is lacking and all that can be done for them is to make provision for a meal and a bed'. These young Scots were certainly candidates for charitable aid. What they needed was help in finding accommodation and a job in the bewildering city. Few of them had behavioural problems (as most were unfairly thought to have); they were just neglected by local authority agencies who had not assumed responsibility for them.

Three years after it had opened, in June 1979, the Corporation's hostel was no longer working. 'It has not been well-used and has required to be subsidised to a much greater extent than was warranted by the numbers helped,' wrote Douglas Robertson at the end of that year. In fact it was improperly managed and the hostel was put 'in abeyance', literally overnight. Robertson added that 'the whole future of this part of our work' was under immediate review. In 1980–81 the hostel building was sold to a housing association that aimed similarly to help homeless youngsters, and a number of places in the new hostel were earmarked for the use of young Scots nominated by the Corporation. The charity had not been able to make the difference it had hoped for. Certainly there were warning signs at the end of 1978: 'In this area of work it is difficult to quantify success,' Robertson had written that year. But at the same time he had added that the Corporation had received some positive feedback: 'some of those who were helped in the hostel through their first difficult weeks are now well established in regular employment and good accommodation'. Recently Robertson remembered that the staff was not composed of the 'right sort of people', and in such a situation 'it doesn't take very much for things to go wrong'. The failure of the hostel experiment, like the Corporation's workhouse hospital over three hundred years earlier, showed that the charity was once again overwhelmed by numbers and also dissatisfied with its lack of success. It had been trying to do too much for too many with too few resources.

Despite unsatisfactory results, the Corporation was not to be dissuaded from continuing to help the homeless in other ways. By the end of his first year in 1979 its youth worker reported that he had dealt with 211 young people and had taken part in 809 meetings with them. Some had been found jobs and places to stay, while others had been persuaded to take the bus home. The Corporation felt that perhaps taking the time to listen to their stories was one way forward and another youth worker was recruited. This approach mirrored what the voluntary agencies interviewed by Greve's researchers in the earlier 1970s had also thought: that the staff of local authorities responsible for dealing with homeless people should 'develop a more pragmatic and realistic view of homelessness'. The agencies had also emphasised 'the need for advisory, conciliatory, and material assistance in order to prevent homelessness where possible'. The Corporation still sought to work closely with other organisations dealing with homelessness issues in a supplementary capacity, and was keen not to duplicate their work. By January 1982 a number of social work agencies known as 'the Scots group' had put together advice for young Scots planning to come to London for the first time. This was issued as part of an information pack from the Scottish Council for Single Homeless. The advice aimed to deter Scots from heading south unless they had already organised a proper job and somewhere to live. The leaflet told them that about £200 was the minimum amount required to get any young arrivals through their first days in London. Landlords would want two or four weeks' advance rent and many would expect a deposit of a further £200, and that without such a permanent address, a young person could not expect to find a steady job. Other homeless agencies and shelters like Alone in London and Centrepoint offered similar advice.

The Royal Scottish Corporation continued to provide homeless help via a grant to Borderline in the 1990s and set aside a £2-million fund to invest in housing and support for the homeless. In 2000 the Corporation suspended the service for casual homeless callers at its King Street office and these people were now advised to contact the charity's partner Borderline in order to receive more professional help. The tea and sympathy had been welcome, though, for a number of regulars with mental health problems and the occasional disorientated Scot, unused to London's thrills. One of these had been a young girl aged 17 who had left Stirling 'because her parents were always fighting and did not seem to care much for her'. She came to the Corporation from hospital, having collapsed after becoming dehydrated during a night's dancing on an ecstasy tablet.

The problem of homelessness in London is unlikely ever to disappear, and all that voluntary agencies can really do is to educate young Scots before they even come to London and provide support when they do. The *Aberdeen Press and Journal* declared in September 2000 that the agencies also needed to expand 'the breadth of counselling services … and the range of safety nets' to prevent the young arrivals 'falling into the clutches of heroin addiction and prostitution'. Such education, expansion and funding, the newspaper considered, was 'as much a responsibility of the Scottish Executive as it is of Westminster'. This emphasis on government responsibility (now available north and south of the border) mirrors the final sentence of John Greve's introduction to the 1971 study: 'the initiative on the scale required can be taken only by central government, the Greater London Council, and the London Boroughs'.

The head of Borderline, Elizabeth Fox, was interviewed by the *Sunday Herald* when the charity's homelessness report was published in September 2000. She said that on arrival young Scots would be unlikely to find any London government aid available for them because the capital's politicians 'were much more interested in helping the economically active, with low-cost accommodation and cheap mortgages on offer for teachers, nurses and junior doctors'. She especially highlighted the fact that London and the surrounding south-eastern region were 'almost a different country', and that 'Scots need to think of emigration, not migration'. London, Elizabeth Fox added, was 'an international city and, economically, going there is like moving abroad'. Those homeless young Scots who do survive and actually manage to take themselves off the streets have had to work 'enormously hard, doing two or three jobs'. Her final rhetorical question was not optimistic about the future of further arrivals: 'Why do people still come when they haven't a chance?'

CHAPTER 35

Going Home or Away

By the mid-nineteenth century, many more people were coming south to seek their fortunes and a number of them always wanted to go home again when things did not work out as they had hoped. Passages home were an easy and relatively cheap way to provide aid and prevent the English taxpayer complaining about poor, homeless Scots cluttering up London's streets. For those who knew about it, such help was available from the Royal Scottish Corporation. Word of mouth among the poor Scots community in London meant that many would have known where to find it. They would have been told that the Corporation provided poor Scots with passages back home to Scotland, if they were well enough to make the journey and did not want to, or could not, stay in London.

Sometimes the charity paid for new clothes for the journey as well as the passage and on 11 July 1883 loaned £3 for the outfits of Henry Smyth's two children 'who were going to their relatives in Aberdeen'. By June 1882 passages were being paid to the London & Edinburgh Shipping Company, the Aberdeen Shipping Company and the Dundee Shipping Company. But the railways were also being used to send the Scots home, and in February 1881 the secretary had paid £4 to a Mrs Noon and her daughter to cover their rail passages to Scotland, plus extra money for the journey. The Corporation's beadle was charged with accompanying them to the station and ensuring that the rail fare was bought. The Corporation started negotiations in February 1883 with the General Steam Navigation Company to try and get reduced fares for passages to Edinburgh over three to five years. In April the charity's secretary also tried a similar deal with the London & North Western Railway but the company replied that, having fully considered the matter, it could not see its way to 'granting reduced fares in favour of indigent Scotchmen returning to Scotland'. Nor could the steamer company.

The charity's applicants sometimes needed to travel further away than Scotland and received donations towards fares to Australia, Canada or America. On 10 May 1882 a Dr Ramsay asked for help with the expenses of a boy called William Graham to whom the Corporation had been paying relief for some years (probably as school fees). His guardians were preparing to take him with them when they emigrated, but they needed help with his fare. The 'Boy Graham' was brought before the governors who, after questioning him, granted him £6 towards his passage to the 'Colonies'; (which colony his guardians then took the boy to is not recorded). At the next examination of cases on 14 June, one of a mother wanting to join her daughter in America was examined. She was already a petitioner receiving 10 shillings a month and the committee agreed to give her £3 3s. towards her passage across the Atlantic. In March 1883 a grant of £2 was awarded to the two sons of a Mrs Fulton 'to assist them in paying for their outfit to Canada'. Margaret Martin had been receiving six shillings a month for her child when she decided to go to Australia in March 1885. She asked the Corporation to help with her fare and was granted a £1 donation. A project for Canadian emigration was also run by the Corporation in 1911.

By the 1920s people were still keen to emigrate, and the Corporation this time had what Thomas Montcrieff, the secretary, called 'a scheme for settling lads in Australia'. Two brothers were given help and a new suit of second-hand clothes. Since he thought clothes made the man, Montcrieff was pleased to see the boys looking more respectable:

> They arrived in Crane Court, unkempt and not over clean, with boots from which the soles had departed; with breeks with ventilation never intended by the tailor, and with their scanty under-raiment conspicuously displaying itself in the rear. Two hours later they had been bathed, their hair cut close, and equipped with boots, stockings, suitable clothing and travelling cases fitted with the requisites for their starting a new life. Indeed, such was the effect produced that the boys hesitated to return to their humble dwelling for the fear of being chaffed by their neighbours.

Another four boys sent to Australia and supported by Montcrieff in 1923 were aged between 15 and 16 years. They also had their passages to South Australia and two years' training paid for by the Balliol Boys Club. The Corporation gave one (born in Thurso) £4 and paid nothing to the others (all listed as having been born in London); one of these already had 20s. for his 'kit, with pocket money' and 60s. for 'landing money' from the Royal Caledonian Schools, and the others had their equivalent from the Orphan Working School.

Sometimes returning Scots only wanted a holiday, and in 1882 the Corporation contributed towards a Scottish break for one very deserving case. Alexander McKay, a 42–year-old inmate of St Pancras Workhouse, was paralysed and blind but had 'a great longing to revisit his Birthplace – Inverness', and he 'craved' the committee to grant him an allowance to help with his travel costs. His case was supported by governors David Laing and Robert Hepburn, and on 9 August the Corporation gave him £2 towards his passage to Scotland.

Over a hundred years later, the Corporation's caravan was especially suitable for family holidays and the charity's pensioners sometimes went on holiday as a group, providing themselves with 'ready-made company'. Two trips away were made in the summer of 1985 and in July 1986 a group of 28 pensioners and three of their welfare visitors were able to spend a week's holiday at Porthcawl in Wales, enjoying 'the sea breezes'. Thank-you letters showed the value of such a holiday 'in congenial company' for those mostly living alone, without a 'proper degree of companionship'.

CHAPTER 36

'The Edinburgh Branch of the Scottish Hospital'

A 'corresponding board' of the Royal Scottish Corporation may have existed in Edinburgh in 1794. If this was indeed a local office in the city, another Edinburgh branch was needed by 1830.[1] In June that year, William Scott, a London stockbroker, was staying with James Nairne, his brother-in-law in Edinburgh and a Writer to the Signet. On 22 June Scott had received a letter from Lachlan Mackintosh, a stockbroker in London and also a member of the committee of management of the Corporation. Mackintosh's letter to Scott explained that Robert Auld, the London-based secretary of the charity, had left some papers for him with his brother, who also lived in the city.[2] The brother, William Auld, soon visited Nairne and handed over the documents; both he and Nairne soon met again to discuss the subject close to Mackintosh's heart and also that of Robert Auld. Their idea had been to set up a branch of the Corporation or 'Scottish Hospital' in Edinburgh and they had so far only included Robert Johnston in their discussions. Johnston was already helping them with Kinloch Bequest business and so was familiar with the Corporation's main charitable work. Nairne had found Johnston 'not sanguine upon the success of the measure', recommending that he talk to the Reverend Dr William Manuel of Morningside 'who had long been one of the Chaplains of the London Institution'. Late in August, Nairne also met the Honourable William Fraser, the charity's London treasurer, at the 'Inverness-shire Election' and talked to him over several days on the subject.

Early in November Nairne received a letter from Mackintosh, dated 30 October, in which he apologised for the delay in writing due to the pressure of finding a new president for the Corporation. As Prince of Wales, the new King William IV had been the charity's active president for the past twenty years and his accession to the throne had left a large gap at the top; but, Mackintosh assured Nairne, 'things are now in a state that gives promise of success to the plan we meditate'. The fifth Duke of Gordon had saved the day and had

---

[1] The 1794 date is referred to in a chronology published in the 1874 account of the Corporation, which added the words 'Commission under seal granted to'.

[2] Auld had taken over from James Dobie and was secretary by September 1819.

consented to be nominated to the presidency at the next general court on St
Andrew's Day. Mackintosh had also been out raising money for the proposed
new branch and explained that the king had given an audience to Fraser, 'the able
and indefatigable Treasurer', and 'most graciously declared himself anxious for
the success of the proposed experiment in Edinburgh.' His Majesty generously
said he would himself subscribe if the project took off – in addition to his existing
subscription to the London-based institution.

Copies of the charters and recent by-laws of the Corporation were sent to
Nairne, and Mackintosh explained that

> a case has arisen, which though *literally* out of the Charter is yet strictly within
> the spirit of it. We are empowered to grant passages home to natives of
> Scotland who may be in such distress here as to preclude the possibility of
> their attaining this object at their own expense. But having done so for them,
> our authority is at an end; and on their arrival at the Port of destination, these
> unfortunate objects are landed penniless to find their way to their homes,
> frequently at a remote distance from the point of disembarkation.

Mackintosh and Auld had also considered appointing agents at all the Scottish
east-coast ports that received the charity's homebound poor, 'but this also is
beyond our powers'. For the previous seven years the number of poor sent to
Leith alone had been 'somewhat above' 215 a year on average. The total number
of passages for this period to all ports was 1,912, with Leith receiving 1,507.
Ports receiving the other 355 individuals included Berwick, Carron, Montrose,
Banff, Dundee, Aberdeen and Inverness.

Mackintosh appealed to Nairne's 'acknowledged zeal' and hoped he would be
able to promote such a worthy project and thought it would be relatively easy to
set up. He also thought that the clergy should be very much involved. Twenty
eminent men 'usually' living in Edinburgh were already subscribing to the
London charity, and could be called on to help. These included the city's top
judges and William Trotter, the late Lord Provost, as well as Robert Stevenson,
the lighthouse engineer, and the novelist Sir Walter Scott. In fact, the Corporation's treasurer, William Fraser, had already written to Scott, requesting his help
and cooperation. Unfortunately the novelist's support was unlikely to be forthcoming, since Scott was travelling abroad for his health.[3]

On 20 November, Nairne, Manuel, Auld and Johnston met together as
friends 'interested in the prosperity of the Scottish Hospital, a Corporation in
London', at Johnston's house in Edinburgh, 42 North Bridge Street. It was
decided that Nairne and Manuel should, using information from London,

---

[3] Scott in fact died in 1832. He had become seriously in debt several years earlier to the tune of
over £120,000, having entrusted his fortune to the unbusiness-like Ballantyne brothers. The
brothers became closely involved with the publishing house of Constable which, when it later
collapsed, took them and all Scott's money with it.

compile a statement about the plan for the branch which could be sent to those in Edinburgh likely to subscribe to such a venture. They sent a letter to London with the details of the initial meeting, outlining what they saw as their two main objectives. The first, they considered, was to raise money for the London Corporation and the second was to take care of the 'poor and destitute persons' arriving in Leith 'who often arrive here in such sickness or poverty or both, that they are unable to proceed without further aid to their ultimate destination'. They also hoped that they might even be able to appoint agents at the other ports to help in a similar fashion, but organised from Edinburgh, 'to be more widely useful', and hoped that there would be other things they could do at a later date. Finally, they 'beg that you will give us whatever hints may be thrown out by the Court or may suggest themselves to your own minds that may be of service to us in concocting our plan'. A letter of 8 December confirmed London's support and left all details of the plan's application to the Edinburgh group. Both the London secretary and treasurer would be happy to write any letters of support that were needed by the local branch.

Manuel sent a proposed list of officers, headed by the king as patron and the third Duke of Buccleuch as president, to Robert Auld in London on 20 December.[4] The vice-presidents proposed by Manuel were himself, Nairne, Johnston, William Auld and a number of the existing Edinburgh subscribers to the London charity. His major request, though, was for help from William Fraser or the Duke of Buccleuch, to get the king formally on board as patron. In a further letter (29 December) he wrote again to recheck details on the number of passages to Leith; to confirm that Edinburgh donors of ten guineas and one guinea would have the same rights as governors in London; and he also had a number of parish settlement questions, especially concerning a 'correct statement on what gives a Scotchman or Scotchwoman a parochial settlement in England?' He told London he just wanted to be sure of his facts.

Answers to Manuel's questions come in the New Year. On 15 January Robert Auld told him that although the Duke of Gordon had agreed to ask the king to be patron, he (the duke) thought 'it would be better not to break upon His Majesty's retirement at Brighton, but wait until he shall come to St James'. This would be about the middle of February 'so that the request for the Sovereign to condescend to allow himself to be named the Patron of the Edinburgh Branch of this ancient Charity must be deferred till then – unless either the Duke or Mr Fraser should think fit to pay a Visit to the Pavilion before that time'. Concerning other matters in his December letter, wrote Auld, Manuel's first statement concerning the passages was correct; the second statement on what the governors of the new branch could expect from the London society needed the approval of

---

[4] Henry, the third Duke of Buccleuch, was also a friend of Sir Walter Scott's, who said of the duke that 'his name was never mentioned without praise by the rich and benedictions by the poor'.

the general court, 'who, no doubt, will make the regulations upon a liberal principle'. Auld suggested that Manuel himself might even be able to advise them: 'You will in that be able to guide us, in some measure, from knowing what were the Privileges granted to London Subscribers to the Society for Propagating Christian Knowledge in the event of their having at any time been in Edinburgh at General Courts of that Society or in other respects'. As to Manuel's third query concerning English parish settlement, he explained:

> I have to state generally – that illegitimate Children have the settlement in the Parish where they are born; legitimate Children follow the settlement of the Father; a wife in all cases takes her husbands settlement, if he have one, – if not ... her own [parish] continues to her; servitude for a year by any unmarried person, not having a child, gives a settlement; apprenticeship under Indenture gives the same, if the Party has been 40 days in place. Rent of £10 per annum, (I rather think that, the amount of Rent has been by some late Act increased) in a separate or distinct dwelling gives a settlement but the tenement must have been held and the rent paid for a whole year. Paying rates on a Tenement above the rent of £10.10 per annum also entitles to a settlement. A Scotch-woman immediately on her marriage to an Englishman becomes entitled to his Parish.

Nairne was busy between December and February. He persuaded the Lord Chief Baron (Abercromby) to become one of three presidents and to preside at a preliminary meeting. Nairne and Manuel then issued their circular on 21 February to seventy interested parties requesting their attendance at a meeting in Edinburgh's Gibbs Hotel, Princes Street, on Friday 25 February at half-past three, 'preparatory to issuing a Prospectus of the proposed institution and holding a larger Meeting, for the purpose of founding it'. The usual difficulties of raising interest and money were further aggravated by the inclemency of the weather: 'But for an almost unprecedently sudden and severe Snow Storm which began only an hour and half before the Meeting, it would have been at least three times as numerous. Only one seventh of those summoned attended,' Nairne reported back to London the next day. Besides the Lord Chief Baron, Nairne, Manuel and Johnston, the others who had managed to brave the freezing Edinburgh streets were Vice-Admiral Sir David Milne, the Reverend Dr Gordon, William Paul, William Renny, John Gibson Junior (Buccleuch's agent) and the engineer, Robert Stevenson. Seven others from Edinburgh apologised for their absence; and not one of the 'Leith Gentlemen' had been able to make it at all because of the violence of the storm.

The group had agreed that Nairne and Manuel would put together a prospectus and call the 'foundation' meeting on 11 March. From his home in Picardy Place the same evening, Nairne also wrote to John Gibson asking him if the Duke of Buccleuch could be persuaded to become the senior president – since he was already one of the vice-presidents of the Corporation in London. 'None of us except Dr Manuel,' he wrote to Mackintosh the next day, 'are sanguine of success *upon a large scale*',

> ... and with the exception of him we were unanimous that it is wiser *at Present* to say nothing of sending monies to the Parent Institution. That at best must be a work of time, and bringing it forward at present would just have the effect of paralysing our efforts, because the Public would plainly hold us to be mere Agents of your Charity and as that virtue, cardinal as it is, proverbially begins at home, the more we make our Institution a *home* measure, the better chance have we of success.

But, he urged, 'Do let us have Royal authority for our Patron, *quam primum*'. He wrote that he himself would approach others in Edinburgh for two presidencies and a number of vice-presidencies, including 'my excellent friend the Lord Advocate, whose name I shall insert at my own hand, well knowing his generous nature'.

A circular was approved on 2 March at a meeting at 22 Albany Street which outlined the aims of the London charity, the number of cases relieved over the past five years in the English capital, and the number of individuals receiving passages home, especially via the port of Leith. It stressed that: 'Upon their arrival at Leith, the great majority of the objects of the Charity have long journies before them to their homes, and by their want of funds to undertake such journies, many of them become burdens upon the Inhabitants of Edinburgh and Leith'. The circular stated that the initial object was to take up 'the Cases of those forlorn individuals by extending to them the helping hand of Kindness and Charity, when the compassionate agency which have forwarded them thither has ceased to act'. The circular also expressed the hope that its 'affluent and charitable' readers would 'not only support the financial part of the Measure, but honour the Meeting on 11th inst.' with their presence at the Gibbs Royal Saloon at 3pm, 'for the purpose of founding the Institution'.

Royal patronage was also assured when Nairne received a letter from Mackintosh on 28 February. The king had held an audience with the Duke of Gordon, the Corporation's new London president, and the duke had immediately and briefly reported back: 'When I mentioned to the King that there was a Branch of the Scottish Hospital to be established at Edinburgh, His Majesty was graciously pleased to say that he would be the Patron'. Nairne hurried to put a notice in the leading Edinburgh newspapers over the next ten days, advertising the setting up of the branch as a truly patriotic act, 'the objects of which are of the most benevolent Kind *and are purely Scottish* ... We hope the Meeting shall be numerously attended, and that the Charity may be extensively useful'. William Blackwood ('in the chair') and Robert Cockburn now joined the existing committee of management to help prepare for the great day. The rules and regulations were further altered and the meeting agreed to appoint three medical officers in Edinburgh, and two or three in Leith.

Forty-five men attended the meeting on 11 March – and this time there was no snowstorm to excuse non-attendance. Other excuses, though, were received. Buccleuch sent a letter of support from Bowhill apologising for his absence but was unable to attend 'as I leave Scotland on the 14th and have a great deal to do, both here and at Langholm ...' In his stead, the Lord Chief Baron took the chair. William Allan, the Lord Provost, also apologised for his absence owing to city business but supported the organisation fully: 'I think it will be useful in this City, and the Provost should be connected with all charitable Institutions that and so [*sic*].' Sir John Sinclair apologised and signed up as an ordinary member for a guinea a year and Sir William Macleod of Bannatyne pleaded 'as a complaint the natural consequence of advancing years' for his absence. William Braidwood, manager of the Sea Insurance Company of Scotland, was among those who did manage to attend.

The rules and regulations for the 'Edinburgh Branch of the Scottish Hospital' were agreed with the object of giving relief to any sick and destitute persons that the London charity might send to Scottish ports, especially to Leith. Its organisation and officer election were much the same as in London. The new directors and medical officers wasted no time in setting up their operations and met for the first time on 15 March. It was agreed that they should have an officer or an agent at Leith, 'in order to save the Directors, both in Leith and Edinburgh, the annoyance of being intruded upon at unreasonable hours', and a meeting in Leith town hall was organised to appoint one. The Leith meeting got underway on 31 March with Robert Stevenson recommending 'Mr David Taylor, Light House Store Keeper in Leith' as 'a person highly fitted for the situation of Agent or Officer'; another man was also named and the Leith directors agreed to enquire 'into the respective merits of these individuals and of others who may be recommended to them'. Five more Leith directors were added and a sub-treasurer (and director) appointed who would have ready money or 'such funds as should be found requisite for the regular relief of the Patients to save the Leith Agency the frequent trouble and inconvenience of sending to Edinburgh for the necessary supplies'. Walter Cassells, agent for the Leith branch of the National Bank, took up this post. On 14 May Captain Taylor was given the position of the Leith agent for which he was to receive 'reasonable remuneration for his services'.

By the time the next meeting at Leith came round on 29 July, 'persons from the Scottish Hospital in London were now arriving by the Leith Smacks, with printed certificates signed by Mr Auld, Secretary, & soliciting relief'. The Leith Board could now act. Cassells was given the necessary funds and he, Taylor and one of the Leith directors (by monthly rotation) formed a 'Committee of Relief'.

By 22 March 1831, Nairne had been able to send £125-worth of subscription money to the Edinburgh branch's treasurers, Messrs Ramsays, Bonars and Co. He expected more money to come in as a result of a subscription book being taken round at this time and had calculated about £10–12 'for printing costs owed to my brother and me'. Advertisements were also to be placed in Edinburgh's *Courant*, *Scotsman* and *General Advertiser*. Eight months later, on 23 November 1832, the branch accounts were £177 in and out, including £3 interest on the subscriptions received. The meeting that audited the accounts at Nairne's house also voted to send £40 or £50 back to London the next St Andrew's Day, 'taking into view the vast numbers that are receiving monthly relief from the parent society, & the difficulties under which the Directors labour to raise the necessary supplies'.

It seems that only about a fifth to a quarter of those arriving in Leith sent by the Corporation from London actually used the forwarding relief offered by the Leith men by 1832. It was probable that not all those whose passages had been paid by London actually received certificates entitling them to further relief on arrival, either because they actually came from the Leith and Edinburgh area, or were not considered deserving enough:

> From the small number of persons to whom you have given letters, with a view to receive relief from us, our operations here, as a Branch of the Scottish Hospital, have as yet been very limited. We have however relieved all the Cases you have recommended to us, forwarding some individuals to very remote distances, who, upon their landing at Leith, owing to illness, or destitution, or both, were utterly unable to proceed farther, & who, but for our assistance, must have become burdens upon the Community, & remained still deprived of the anticipated comfort & relief from Friends, which they sought by returning to their Native Land. We have given lodgings, temporary support, medical aid, & the means of reaching their ultimate destinations to others, who, upon careful investigation, seemed to be entitled to our sympathy, many of whom have expressed much gratitude.

In a report back to London, Cassells included the following note he had written on 14 November:

> … on looking over the vouchers, I find that we have paid for lodgings in Leith, Conveyance to their houses, & a small supply on the way, to thirty-five individuals, who have consequently been no burden on the community; and all of them expressed much gratitude for the assistance afforded them. I have taken care to procure a conveyance wherever it was in my power, & particularly by the Boats on the Union Canal, when they were going west, & we have studied to give sums in proportion to the distance the parties had to go.

The branch committee thought that Captain David Taylor had been most useful and voted that he should continue his services, again agreeing that he should be paid. Other costs were postages, messages, stationery and advertisements. Funds stood at £164. In November 1833 the Edinburgh branch was hardly spendthrift; its costs were only £18, which sum included the relief for 40 cases. By 1 December 1834 the branch was again reporting that the number relieved 'had been very limited' and had apparently gone down even further, partly because Cassells had gone to Manchester and had not yet been replaced, but partly because the London institution had granted fewer passages to Leith than usual: 'the number having been only 170 whereas on former years their average number was 258'. The meeting recorded £152 paid in and paid out and raised the question of Taylor's remuneration. Cassels, 'through whose hands it should come', had 'either forgot or delayed to make it'. And 'Of course Captain Taylor had hitherto got nothing'.

What happened to the Edinburgh branch office after this time is not known, nor is it known whether Captain Taylor ever was paid for his services. The minute book abruptly ends at the bottom of the page in mid-sentence as if the writer (the Reverend Dr Manuel of Morningside?) was suddenly interrupted, called for dinner or otherwise paused for a break as he turned the page. Whatever it was, the writer did not take up his pen again.[5]

An interesting final note to this Leith story occurred twenty years later in 1852. By August that year, more immigrant poor were cluttering up London's streets and the justices of the peace of Middlesex ordered 'the removal of Scotch, Irish and other paupers', and asked the Poor Law Board if they would 'consider the same'. Under current legislation, magistrates had the power to see that 'all natives of Scotland, as to be removed, shall be conveyed from the Port of London by steamboat under cover to the several ports of Scotland … to which a steamboat shall run, or from London by railway to Liverpool and thence by steamboat to the port which shall be nearest their plan of destination'. Whether the Royal Scottish Corporation's Edinburgh branch directors arranged for these boats to be met is unknown. Certainly by 1874 the charity would have liked the Edinburgh branch to still have been active, recording that it was 'much to be regretted that this Branch Society no longer exists'. The number of passages home, though, had gone down significantly by this time.

---

[5] One group in Edinburgh who did not receive any aid from the branch or the London office of the Corporation was a number of English poor who wanted help with passages back to London. At a meeting of the Edinburgh branch in October 1831, a 'subject of considerable importance' was submitted to the committee by a Dr Russell, the minister of the English Church in Leith. He had been receiving their many petitions and had sometimes paid their passages out of his own pocket. The Corporation liked Russell's proposal, but they felt unable to approve it for constitutional reasons, 'benevolent and important as it was'. Much discussion and voting would be needed in London to change the rules and, besides, the funds of the Edinburgh branch had been donated for the specific purpose of helping Scots returning from London and should not be used otherwise.

CHAPTER 37

Fire and Rebuilding

The men who managed the Royal Scottish Corporation in its early Victorian heyday had taken over from those who had led it out of its late eighteenth-century doldrums and into the good times of the early nineteenth century. Some of them, like Sir John Heron Maxwell, were also to experience the charity's worst of times, and one in particular which was to 'cast a gloom over all London Scotsmen'.

On the night of 14–15 November 1877 disaster struck the Corporation's main building at No. 9 Crane Court. 'About half past eleven the keeper of the hall was alarmed by a smell of burning wood, and on going downstairs from his room, he found that fire had broken out in the western corner of the main hall, and that it had obtained a firm hold'. The fire spread quickly, 'the whole of the inside walls and passages of the buildings being of panelled wood'. Outside, Constable Hayes, one of the members of the city police, saw smoke coming from the lower part of the building and together with Sergeant James Lennox, the Corporation's beadle and 'keeper of the hall', raised the alarm. 'The fire-engines and fire-escapes from different stations of the Metropolitan Fire Brigade arrived on the scene with all haste.' The occupants of the hall, two men (Lennox and Lockhead, a visitor), two women and two children safely made their escape. Firemen and police also quickly raised the alarm amongst the surrounding tenements 'occupied by persons of the poorer class … these all, and wives and children had to remove all their goods from their dwellings for protection from the fire'. By 'midnight there were four or five steam fire-engines playing upon the burning building', and more engines arrived later, until 'a dozen or so steam and manual engines were engaged in pouring water on the blazing pile'. But nothing could be done, and 'in a short time the old hospital was in a ruin'.

Macrae Moir, the secretary, later told a governors' enquiry his story: 'At half past one, I was roused from my bed by a cabman who informed me that our Hall was in flames. I arrived at the scene shortly before two oclock, when I was horrified to find that the roof of the building had fallen in, and that nothing remained save the burning embers and the bare walls'. Lockhead and Lennox had been 'on the spot from the commencement and had with difficulty escaped with the other inmates in their night dresses'. Lockhead, the visitor, also recalled his night of activity for the governors:

> While sitting in my Kitchen on the second floor … about eleven oclock or half past, and my wife undressing in the bedroom she called to me that she smelt something burning, I laughed at her and she got to bed. Afterwards I smelt something burning and before I had time to examine saw the smoke coming through the floor. Immediately I called to my wife to wake up our children. I immediately ran upstairs to rouse Mr Lennox and his sister. By the time I got down stairs and got my children in my arms, we had to make our way through the smoke and fire which were issuing from the Hall, and heard the glass falling into the Court … I left my wife and children on a doorstep in Crane Court and ran for the fire engine to Farringdon Street …

James Lennox, the beadle, wrote the next day that he 'slept in the attic bedroom' and, having been roused by the visitor, he had seen the other man's rooms full of smoke. Knowing that Lockhead's kitchen fire was immediately above the hall fireplace, he checked the hall and found it ablaze. He too raised the alarm, and by the time the police and fire brigade arrived 'the flames were issuing from all the Hall windows'.

Lennox had also spread the flames himself by opening the door to the hall, he later remembered, recalling his earlier movements for the Corporation's committee of management. He also told them of his movements earlier that evening:

> It was my duty to lock up the premises. I was in my Office from 8. to 10. on Wednesday along with my son checking the relief books, and noting the pensioners who had not been paid. I then went to the Kitchen and had my supper. There was a fire then at the east end of the Kitchen, and that evening about 20 minutes past ten I posted two letters. My son had left. Up to that time I had not smelt any fire – or anything burning. Nobody could have got into the house. On my return I fastened the back door, and put out the gas in the passage. It was not customary to put gas off at the main.

He had seen no fire in his 'little room' at the front, although there had been one there during the day until about seven in the evening. He had watched his sister put out the gaslight in the secretary's room and had seen a gaslight on the staircase. He had not had to light any fires for meetings that day and the chimneys had been swept in the spring and few fires lit since and, although he had smelt gas a few months earlier and had called in the plumber to check it out, they had found no leak.[1] Lennox had checked the office at the time of the outbreak of the fire and recalled that he 'might have saved some books, but there was no fire there – and it did not occur to me to take books. I considered it was my duty to inform the Police and the public'. He told the committee that he had

---

[1] Fires had been lit for a meeting of the Caledonian Asylum Committee on the Monday at around 5–6pm and for the Council of the Medical Officers of Health on the Tuesday at 4pm.

not been able 'to save any of my own things', and that he had lost all his property – 'including my watch'.

Earlier in the day, at about five o'clock, a chimney fire had been reported to the Constable John Wilson, the city policeman on duty, by a Mr Levy, the keeper of the shop at the entrance to Crane Court. Wilson had looked up and had indeed seen three sparks coming out of the chimneys. He saw them again with Lennox but the beadle told him that the chimney belonged to someone else. Wilson had then checked this house ('It was a woman I saw') but found no fire in her grate. He had continued to check further but had seen no more sparks or flames. Professor Donaldson, the honorary architect, concluded that a timber had probably smouldered for some time near the chimney opening of Lockhead's kitchen and, since it ran along the length of the floor, had spread the fire quickly once it had caught alight. Gas explosions would have increased the damage further. The house had been built by Nicholas Barbon after the Great Fire around 1670, and a 'great quantity of timber' had been used in its central construction, floors and wainscoting. All this was now old and 'in a very dried and decayed condition' and so liable to be consumed rapidly by flames.

The Corporation's governors together with their treasurer Sir John Heron Maxwell, Macrae Moir the secretary, William Webster the solicitor, and Lennox, solemnly 'proceeded to the ruins of their Hall', and an 'Extraordinary Meeting' was hastily arranged to take place the following evening in the chapel in Fleur-de-lis Court, which, although damaged in parts by both fire and water, had fortunately escaped much of the devastation and was described as 'a capital room to meet in'. The committee of management had to announce 'the total destruction of their ancient Hall and all its valuable contents', but thankfully 'it will be some consolation to the Governors to learn that the destruction of so many memorials of the past has been unaccompanied by loss of life or limb, and owing to the efforts of the Fire Brigade … neighbouring premises were but slightly injured'. The firefighters had been led by Captain Shaw, the Superintendent of the Metropolitan Fire Brigade, and his curt official report was read out at the meeting and printed in the next day's papers. The two daughters of Robert Hepburn, chairman of the committee of management, more sentimentally, 'graphically and poetically portrayed' the scene. Isabella Hepburn painted the blackened building and her sister, Jessie Hepburn Starey, wrote some sad accompanying verses:

> The cruel flames' relentless breath had blighted as it burned,
> And left but smouldering ruins, over which we vainly mourned …

Nevertheless, she concluded her poem on a more positive note:

> Yet let us gather up to-day our still remaining force,
> And hand-in-hand, and heart-to-heart, shape out some future course

> Whereby the grand old work may soon, by God's own help, be done,
> And relics lost be soon forgot – in newer trophies won!

A committee was set up to work out how to carry on administering the business of the Corporation and also to investigate the fire. One of their number was the surveyor, Professor Donaldson, who with a practical presence of mind 'immediately inspected the premises and contacted the Sun Fire Office' which had insured the furniture and pictures. The committee decided that it would need to make only a slight alteration to the Corporation's chapel to make it fit for future meetings, while the anniversary festival dinner had already been planned to take place at the Freemasons' Tavern. Pensioners would be able to come to the chapel premises to be paid, but the monthly investigation of new cases would have to be temporarily suspended. Luckily for them, the Kinloch Bequest pensioners had been given their money a few days before the fire.

The Royal Scottish Corporation's history to date had been wiped out in one night. Archives, paintings, the seventeenth-century seal and no doubt many other artefacts were also destroyed in the fire. The Caledonian Society and other societies and clubs who used the Corporation's buildings also lost all their records and other artefacts. A fire insurance claim of nearly £4,000 was to be the only compensation for such a terrible loss. The *Daily Telegraph* published a report on the lost paintings, which it called 'really priceless art treasures',

> foremost among which is the sumptuous portrait of Mary Queen of Scots, by Zucchero – restored a few years since, under the advice of Mr E. M. Ward R.A., by the late Mr Merritt – one of the finest among the few undoubtedly genuine effigies of "Marie R", that were extant. This portrait was presented to the Corporation so long ago as 1753, by Mr James Douglas. It represented the hapless Queen at full length, in a long sable robe, and standing on a Persian carpet; the last being an accessory, which, for the sake of its richness of colour, was always a favourite with the painters of the Venetian school.[2]

Other paintings lost in the fire were portraits of the charity's two noble seventeenth-century benefactors: 'Sir Godfrey Kneller's half-length of the Duke of Bedford, in the robes of the Garter', and 'Sir Peter Lely's portrait of the Duke of Lauderdale, a wonderful specimen of facial modelling, of which happily, there is a replica at Ham House'. A further lost picture was a 'striking portrait of William

---

[2] The press report continued: 'The learned pictorial archaeologist, Mr George Scharf, has, in communication with a contemporary, given an exhaustive account of the burnt picture. Mr Scharf, however, does not distinctly assert that the portrait is by Zucchero. He merely points out that it corresponds with the well-known likenesses at Hardwick Hall and at Hatfield, which are known to have been painted by Oudry, at Sheffield in 1578. Whether Oudry was only the copyist of Zucchero is uncertain. Other repetitions of this type of portraits of Mary are to be found, so Mr Scharf tells us, at Cobham Hall, the seat of Lord Darnley; at the mansion of the Brocas family in Hampshire; and modified into a half-length by Beaurepaire, in the National Portrait Gallery'.

IV' by Sir David Wilkie. The *Telegraph* concluded that the loss of the hall was even sadder because it was also the past home of the Royal Society and 'their hall in Crane Court' had 'structurally undergone very little alteration since the days when Sir Isaac Newton occupied the presidential chair'. It concluded that destruction of the building and its contents was 'nothing less than a public calamity'.

Yet 'The Scottish Corporation has risen from its ashes', reported the *London Scottish Journal* on 8 December: 'Whether the Corporation is "Phoenix-like" or not, matters little: the St Andrew's meeting was a brilliant success. For a time it seemed as if London Scots were paralysed by the calamity in Crane Court … but Mr Macrae Moir and his committee came to the rescue. Consequently the Scotch poor are being attended to'. The St Andrew's Day festival was the 'largest on record', but so much more had still to be done. 'In fact much pecuniary help will be needed ere the Scottish Hospital is thoroughly on its legs again.' Donations were forthcoming from philanthropic Victorian Scots and their English supporters, and the next steps in its long history were hesitantly taken.

On 23 February the following year, Professor Donaldson made his report to the rebuilding committee and recommended that 'under existing circumstances the interests of the Corporation will be best advanced by rebuilding the Hall and Offices on the present site'. He thought this could be done to such an extent that they could also accommodate all the Scottish societies in one place. His rebuilding plan covered the Hall and offices on the old site, together with the reconstruction of the old tenements, nos 14, 15, 16 and 16a Fleur de Lis Court, which were now in a dilapidated state. The same accommodation could be provided – entrance hall, staircase, clerk's office, and secretary's office on the ground or entrance floor. 'On the one pair are the Hall and Committee Room, the communication between the main building and the Chapel being maintained. I propose the basement and the two-pair floor for the subordinate officers accommodation'; and no storey on a third or attic floor, 'being quite superfluous. In the old building they had ceased to be necessary, after the Secretary had discontinued residence in Crane Court several years ago, in consequence of the incompatibility of the locality for such an use'.

He would save them money: 'The Hall and other rooms occupy much the same accommodation … but I have ventured to alter somewhat the disposition of the Hall in order to give it a few more feet in width and a better proportion than the old one and all the floors will be higher than the previous ones – that of the Hall fifteen or eighteen feet instead of ten or eleven – to give good light and air'. He proposed that the tenements should be rebuilt as a warehouse, 'adapted for the neighbourhood', that could be 'rented for a higher price than any other class of building in the area'. He also planned to remove a partition 'so the length can extend under the Chapel for more storage'. The costs of rebuilding were outlined as 'main building £4,000; Warehouse £1,800; repair adjoining premises

£200; professional charges £500'. The insurance pay-out would amount to £3,000, rental of the new warehouse would raise '£100 capitalised at 6 percent would realize £1,600', and excess expenditure was estimated at £1,900.

Donaldson further acknowledged that a change of site had 'occasionally been mentioned'. He discussed the nature of the area and 'this end of Fleet Street' which once

> was the resort of literary men – such as Dr Johnson, Goldsmith and Smollett, and other distinguished writers of the day – who with their associates and friends frequented the taverns and held their social meetings there. But the professional men, and especially the literary circles, have migrated generally more westwards; the latter especially have formed themselves into clubs towards Pall Mall. This has arisen because trade and manufacture have gradually taken possession of this quarter, especially the printers, whose business, requiring steampresses & chimney shafts, has produced immense volumes of smoke & dirt, and has rendered the neighbourhood quite unfit for habitation. Thus the prestige of the locality has passed away.

The Corporation's offices were 'of an extensive character' and 'lay in the thick of a cluster of buildings between Crane-Court and a small narrow thoroughfare called Fleur-de-lis-Court which has an outlet to Fetter-Lane'. The surveyor's report outlined the inconvenience of such a location: 'The situation of the old Hall takes it from the public eye, being at the end of a narrow court of considerable length, which causes the access to the building to be inconvenient and it is uncovered and not approachable by a carriage. The access from Fetter Lane is equally objectionable, though shorter but through narrow passages & between a low class of buildings'. If the Hall were to move further westwards, its front could be 'upon a public thoroughfare, & of a Scottish style of simple character, it would more notice, & become more generally known than at present, & perhaps more widely enlist public & especially Scotch sympathy in its national & benevolent purposes'.

The Crane Court rebuilding proposal was eventually accepted, a building committee was established and work began in earnest at its first meeting on 3 July. Rebuilding plans were presented at the annual 30 November court and showed how the

> New Chapel and Waiting Hall will be in the lowest storey, with its entrance for pensioners from Fleur de Lis Court ... Connected with this will be the necessary accommodation for male and female pensioners, coal cellarage, heating apparatus and smaller pay and relief room, where the old and infirm pensioners will receive their pensions or other assistance, without the necessity when relieved of going up or down stairs, and with immediate exit to Fleur de Lis Court ... The principal entrance will be from Crane Court, with an ample staircase and vestibule leading to the Corporation Hall ...

The clerk's office would be on one side with the committee room on the other, and both would have communication with the Hall. Residences for two officers (the beadle and the visitor) were planned for the 'uppermost or second floor, each with sitting room, kitchen and two bedrooms', sharing a 'water closet, coal closet and scullery'.

But the committee of management was still unhappy and its members could not 'conceal from themselves the fact of the losses to the Corporation in consequence of the late disastrous fire, the depressed state of Trade and the exceptional claims on public benevolence'. Its accounts showed a decrease on nearly 'every head of income' compared with previous years. The good news was that the Prince of Wales had been re-elected president, the Earl of Rosebery and the Marquess of Bute were elected vice-presidents, replacing by rotation the Dukes of Argyll and Abercorn. One disastrous outcome of the fire could be put right and the 'Seal Committee' reported that the Corporation should make a new seal based on the old form. Accordingly, Professor Donaldson and a 'Mr Wyon', seal engraver to Queen Victoria, went to the Bank of England in December 1878. They were shown stock sale documents that had the old seal attached and 'Mr Wyon made drawings from the old impressions with the various details, as far as the defaced state of the surface allowed'. Wyon then went to the British Museum and consulted other documents and 'had been enabled to make an accurate and authentic restoration of the Seal to twice the size of the original'.[3]

A contract with a builder was made, donations were collected from wealthy and philanthropic Victorian Scots over the next two years, and a new castellated building, 'more appropriate to a Scottish moor' than to the 'somewhat dingy passage' of Crane Court, was built on the site. The final building report was presented to the Corporation's court on 21 July 1880. There was a deficit of £2,009 from other sources after insurance and still a need for furnishings and fittings. Donaldson's final report showed how the new premises had been built where the old hall and four blocks of tenements had previously stood. The 'block' of the old chapel had also been left to be leased out as necessary. The hall itself, wrote Donaldson, faced north:

> It is well lighted with a central bay window and two large windows on the north side. At the east end of the Hall is the fire place, with a handsome white marble Chimney piece, resembling that at Craigiear Castle, Scotland (illustrated by Billings in his Baronial Buildings) with granite columns on each side

[3] The documents consulted by Wyon at the bank no longer survive, but those from the British Museum are the eighteenth-century accounts of the Scots Corporation, now available at the British Library. The new seal is actually quite different from the original seventeenth-century seal found on James Kynneir's silver cup. The eighteenth-century printed accounts of the charity are different again; perhaps the seal had already been remade once or twice even before the post-fire reproduction. The depiction of Charity herself is different in all three versions and a red lion rampant replaced the cross of St Andrew in the shield of the Victorian remake.

and surmounted by a large Coat of the Royal Arms, as at Craigiear, here heraldically emblazoned. It is of stone and was saved from the unhappy conflagration of 1877, and consequently is a precious relic of the past.

Other royal shields were to be placed above the arms and Donaldson proposed 29 other panels around the room depicting shields of the Scottish nobility or clan chiefs: 'so natural a series would keep alive the traditional spirit of feudal brotherhood, a leading and attractive feature of the Scottish character'. These displays would serve to replace the paintings destroyed by fire. The committee room and secretary's office as well as nine other rooms for the visitor and the beadle were also ready. Overall, Donaldson had, according to the building committee, 'sought to infuse into the building as much as possible of the national sentiment. He has therefore largely adopted in the ornamental details the Lion Rampant, the Thistle and similar emblems; and in the architectural arrangement of the high pitched roof and small turrets to the front, and such-like features of Scottish architecture'. The building committee added that they had 'proceeded with the greatest economy in the erection of the new building, consistent with its purpose and as a representative establishment.'

The opening ceremony for the new building was presided over by the Duke of Argyll on 21 July 1880, and on 6 October the first quarterly court was held in the new hall. At the 30 November court meeting, the governors had high hopes for that evening's festival as a money-raising exercise to complete the project. The Corporation was already grateful for a number of gifts – General George Campbell had given chandeliers, James Shand had given 'Hydrant apparatus for protection against fire', and Alexander Duncan was thanked 'for a chair made from portions of oak taken from the ruins of the old Hall which the committee hope will long remain an interesting relic of former days'.

CHAPTER 38

Crane Court and Fetter Lane Management

The surrounding buildings still owned by the Corporation were made habitable and rented out. One tenant refused to pay up in the early 1880s and a 'Mr Hofman of Leicester Square' was finally called in to extract the money. By August 1881 Mackay, the new beadle who had replaced Lennox, was also cleaning the Corporation's offices and carrying out basic administrative duties – the 'Office Boy' and 'Charwoman' having been dispensed with. These two were given one week's notice, while the beadle gained an extra five shillings a week in addition to his usual pay. On 8 March 1882 the Corporation's committee voted to provide the beadle with a uniform instead of the £7 for clothing that had usually been given him. The long-serving secretary, Macrae Moir, had died on 12 July 1881, having worked faithfully for the Corporation for twenty years. The appointment of a new secretary was discussed at length and the by-laws brought out, re-read and the secretary's duties noted – especially the combined position of being both Corporation and Kinloch secretary at an annual salary of £250.

The charity's by-laws were only occasionally revised (a new set had come out in 1862 after the fraud case), and at the end of June 1882 a by-law revision committee led by James Laurie reported back to the general quarterly court held on that day. The 'main alteration' was, 'as to the mode of appointing the Secretary which we all think ought to be vested in a joint Committee', of the Corporation and that of the Kinloch Bequest. Such a larger body should mean that the governors would more easily find the best candidate. Under existing rules they would have had to hold three special courts besides other meetings, while this method relieved 'the Candidates from the trouble and expense of canvassing the large body of Governors at an expense and risk which might probably prevent properly qualified persons from putting themselves forward'. But the court could still fix the annual salary of the candidate and had the right to refuse to agree the appointment. Other bye-law alterations made for easier working practices and a number of changes were just catching up with current practices. Applications were invited for the post of secretary, and by 23 November these had been narrowed to three candidates; George Henderson won the ballot.

On 1 January 1883 there had been another scare and another fire for the London fire brigade, but this time at Messrs Bradley & Co nearby in Fleur-de-lis Court. Like the old Corporation hall, the building was burnt out and its roof had collapsed. Mackay, the beadle, told the secretary that he had made sure his family and that of Clement, the Visitor, were safe, he had put all the books and documents in a fireproof safe and had called Captain Shaw of the fire brigade who had already arrived and was attending to the fire. No fire had been found at the Corporation hall but, Shaw had told Mackay, if the alarm had been raised only a quarter of an hour later 'our Hall could not possibly have been saved!' As with the earlier fire, the origin of this one was unknown but fingers were pointed at the steam which had been spewing out of Bradley's new boiler and which the Corporation had previously asked the company to fix.

On 9 July 1884 the committee decided that the *Times* 'must be one of the two Morning London Daily Papers' in which the advertisement, calling each quarterly court, had to appear. Honorary officials were still being elected and re-elected at the annual November courts. By the end of 1888 these were three chaplains, four physicians and four surgeons, with an architect, an auditor and the solicitor. The president, treasurer, vice-presidents and the various commit-tees were also re-elected. So were the two 'keepers of the keys' (in addition to the treasurer who had the third one). As a result of the fraud discovered in 1861–62, the seal was always attached to a power of attorney for the sale of stock or some other official document in the presence of two witnesses 'not being members of the Corporation'; this was signed by the chairman and counter-signed by the secretary. The seal box, an iron chest with three keys, had been ordered for purchase in November 1885.

By the autumn of 1890 Henderson, the secretary, was becoming overwhelmed by his paperwork and he died in post the following year. Alexander Buchan, the then visitor and collector, replaced him. The end of the century saw plans again being drawn up for a redesigned building but their implementation was constantly put off, although surrounding property was gradually sold. The First World War came and went, during which the hour of the meetings was changed to earlier in the afternoon – 'In view of the darkness of the streets and the difficulties in travelling … 2.30 for inspection and 3.15 for general court meetings'. The reconstruction work for Fetter Lane eventually got the go-ahead in 1926 and the Corporation's staff moved out to 96 Farringdon Street, being kindly put up by the Waverley Book Company. The Reverend Joseph Moffett, the honorary chaplain, had also arranged for the pensioners' monthly services to take place in Crown Court Church. In the desire to save as much money as possible for a new building, little or no money had been spent on the cramped old offices. The staff had been hampered in their work with 'bad lighting, bad heating and other inconveniences', but had never apparently grumbled to the governors.

The new premises, now arranged to face Fetter Lane, were finally opened on 7 June 1927. The senior Corporation chaplain blessed the building and also gave comfort to the less deserving: 'Here may the lonely find friends, the weak find strength, the hungry find food, the sorrowful be comforted and the heavy-laden enter into Thy peace O God. And if there be wayward ones may they too be met by that Charity that hopeth all things, endureth all things and never faileth'. The Earl of Rosebery, president, was not able to attend but wrote to say that he thought the new building was an important step for the Corporation. The Duke of Atholl regretfully telegraphed his absence, adding, 'Good luck, Atholl'. Viscount Finlay, the treasurer, attended the gathering while passing through London on his way from Scotland to Holland. He told the assembled 'Scotsmen and Scotswomen in London' and other guests that it was 'indeed a very great thing that this Corporation was so early founded, and that it has been able to discharge such beneficial offices for Scots in London. (Cheers).' He told them that the national charity was 'a great centre for Scottish feeling' in the city and it would be a 'grave blank' if it were to disappear, creating as it did 'a sense of kinship and of mutual attachment amongst all classes'. Colonel Sir John Young followed him, saying that the Corporation had for 'too long had its head up what we in Scotland call a close, but here you call a Court' and telling the assembly that he was now pleased 'that we have … put such a good face to the open street'.

The Hewitt Trust was thanked for having given £3,000 towards the £28,000 cost. The property committee, led by George Paton, which had already raised much of it, was thanked, though more funds were also appealed for to completely wipe out the debt. Thanks were also due to Thomas Montcrieff, the charity's secretary. The building had really been 'a child of his – nurtured through good report and through evil report, through good times and through bad times'. It was also through Montcrieff's initiative that the Corporation had become the central meeting place of all Scottish associations, and his wishes had come true when the new building filled up at the end of 1927 with the 'numerous London Scottish charities'. Paton and Montcrieff both died in 1933, the same year that the Archbishop of Canterbury (Cosmo Lang), Lord Glendyne and Lord Macmillan were elected vice-presidents of the Corporation.

Thomas Collett, the secretary who replaced Montcrieff, was not a successful choice, though he had good Greenock credentials. A report by Price Waterhouse & Company on 12 June 1934, after their auditing of the charity's books, had found serious errors in his administration. An extraordinary court was called that October and the Reverend Dr Archibald Fleming opened the meeting, referring to the seriousness of the matter. 'Never before in his long connection with the Corporation had they had to deal with one so sad,' he told the assembled governors. Price Waterhouse and the Corporation's solicitor had found that Collett was 'not a fit and proper person to be a servant of the Royal Scottish

Corporation'. The facts were 'so damning' that the secretary, unable properly to explain himself, was dismissed from service. William Miller of Hatch End was a much wiser secretarial appointment and he took up his new post in 1935, having given a fidelity bond of £1,000.

The Second World War brought many concerns for Scots' homes lost in air raids, but in 1940 the committee still found time to congratulate Vice-Admiral Sir Andrew Cunningham 'on the daring and brilliant actions of the Royal Navy and Fleet Air Arm in the Mediterranean against the Powers of Aggression and in the cause of the liberation of small nations, and to wish him and those under his command God-speed and continued success in our fight against tyranny'. They also sent birthday wishes to Winston Churchill 'in our great struggle'. On the night of 10 May 1941 the Corporation suffered a direct hit and the charity's premises were once again on fire. The roof and upper rooms were completely destroyed. Only temporary repairs could be made until the end of the war but nearly all costs of the repair work were covered by London's War Damage Commission. Flying bombs on 19 July and 13 August 1944 brought more, though not serious, damage to the Fetter Lane building. At the end of 1947 the City of London tried to compulsorily purchase the Corporation's buildings; the charity strongly objected and was eventually excluded from the order. By 1949 the Corporation had received the licence they needed to make the final repairs to the war-damaged areas and restoration was in progress. At the end of 1956 the Fetter Lane and Fleur-de-lis court buildings were valued at over £51,000.

As they had been in the 1930s, in 1958 Caledonian and Corporation Scots were again worrying about a decline in the Scottish character. W. E. Swinton, in March 1958, thought that there was now

> a lack of the national vitality, that creativeness, that not so long ago was characteristic of the blue bonnets as well as the blue jerseys. Part of this is the last of self-sacrifice, that is now in scarce supply in all these islands. Nearly everyone has a right to go, for example, to the University these days and the Carnegie Trust and the Welfare State have sapped much of the strength of will of parents as well as sons. "Who wants to be strong all the time?" someone will ask, and with reason, but in the days of our youth we were proud (that sin again!) of our accomplishments in a competitive world. Now we need neither be proud nor grateful.

Even so, Swinton next acknowledged that he was addressing countrymen 'so distinguished, so influential and so determined'. These successful Caledonian Society members still provided the essential manpower of the Royal Scottish Corporation, which was perhaps far more important than the money the society gave to the charity.

One long-lived Corporation chairman, Caledonian president and also its historian had been William Will. Born in Huntly, Aberdeenshire, he had died on

4 February 1958 aged 91. Will had come to London as news editor of the *St James's Gazette* and became a director of Allied Newspapers from 1924 to 1935. During the Second World War he had been appointed chairman of the Newspaper and Periodical Emergency Council and did 'valuable liaison work between the Government and the Newspaper industry'. He received a CBE for his war work in 1945. He had been a subscribing member of the Corporation since 1918, a life managing governor in 1924 and was made a vice-president in 1933. He was ever 'jealous of its high reputation and conscious of its noble purpose' and had used his 'abilities, talents and influence' to further the charity's aims. Especially, his fellow Scots wrote, he showed 'wise counsel in its administration and his sympathetic concern for those compelled to seek its aid'.

Twelve years later, it had taken Will's successors some time at the beginning of the 1970s to decide what to do with their Fetter Lane building. 'The question of the advantageous sale of the freehold' had 'exercised the minds of the Committee of Management for some considerable time'. In July 1972 it finally came to a decision and the premises were offered for sale by public tender. Chairman J. Murray Napier was keen to accept the first offer of £650,000 but Douglas Robertson, a fellow trustee and an experienced property man, knew that the building was worth much more. Eventually the highest offer of £2,850,000 was accepted and the sale was completed in 1973. A significant amount of capital could now be released to fund new charitable projects. The committee wondered how best to use it: 'particularly do our minds turn to acquiring suitable accommodation for both the young and the old'.

CHAPTER 39

New Corporation Property and King Street Management

The Corporation's committee of management reported in 1973: 'We have been offered freehold property of a size in keeping with our needs and of a quality to fit in with the character of the Charity'. The Corporation came back to the area where they had first held property as a result of the generosity of the Duke of Bedford in the 1660s, when it moved to its present offices at 37 King Street, Covent Garden in 1974. These premises had originally been built in 1773–74 for John Lane, a lawyer and vestry clerk, who had been active in a number of charitable causes and the establishment of the local parish work-house in Covent Garden. The house's subsequent owners included various clubs, and its most recent occupiers had been a theatrical costumier and a number of theatre agents. Major reconstruction took place up to the end of 1974 but charity staff sturdily carried on with their duties despite the inconvenience. An honoured visitor, Queen Elizabeth the Queen Mother, was able to open the building on 30 January 1975. Nearly ten years later, by 1984, the building was proving inadequate to cope with the charity's administration and another bout of refurbishment was organised. Nevertheless, the charity's trustees signalled 'the privilege of occupying a building of special architectural interest' which 'carries with it the responsibility of a high standard of maintenance'.

King Street management and the charity's other property plans had been placed under the stewardship of Douglas Robertson who succeeded J. Murray Napier as the Corporation's chairman from 1977 to 1989 (also a vice-president from 1977 to the present) and it was to take him some time to acquire suitable premises for the charity's pensioners. The Presbyterian Housing Society offered the Corporation nine flats that it was planning to build on a site recently acquired in East Dulwich; it also proposed to build the Corporation twenty more. Unfortunately this deal fell through the next year and the Corporation looked elsewhere. Another site in North London with the potential to build eighteen flats and renovate twelve others was also under negotiation. This housing plan would contribute towards providing the charity's many elderly Scots, 'now living in very uncomfortable and disagreeable circumstances', with 'more comfortable dwellings'. The charity had only just got to the point of exchanging contracts by the end of 1975 and was also looking at another site to provide twenty more flats in south London. Property purchase was 'a tortuous and slow process'.

The year 1976, however, was a good one for such projects. The Corporation had completed the purchase of the north London site on 10 May, and later in the summer it had opened its homeless hostel in Bina Gardens near Gloucester Road. The freehold premises at Bawtry Road in Whetstone now provided it with twelve existing flats, eight of which needed to be repaired and four more of which needed to be rebuilt; a further sixteen were now also to be built on the site and planning consent had been given by the local council. The twenty-eight Whetstone flats were ready in 1978 and were 'the most notable feature of the work' of the Corporation that year. Already occupied or allocated, the flats were in 'surroundings of grassed areas, planted with flowering shrubs and trees'. The self-contained flats provided the much-prized quality of 'independence', and by 1980 the Whetstone flats were proving insufficient to meet demands for better housing, and a new development scheme was authorised. Land was bought in 1982 to create the Kinnear Court flats in Wimbledon (named after the charity's first master). Here, out of the Corporation's own funds and other special gifts, the Corporation built sixteen self-contained flats for elderly and disabled Scots which were completed in 1984.

By 1986 housing was again on the agenda. The Corporation was offered the chance to buy a home for the elderly in Putney owned by St Columba's, the Pont Street Scots church. Among other reservations, Douglas Robertson could see that the building required considerable expenditure to make it suitable. As a commercial property it might have been viable but as a place of charitable housing it was seriously inappropriate. The Corporation's trustees were split on the issue and Douglas Robertson's building expertise won through when, as chairman, he made his casting vote against the project. A sum of £500,000 was earmarked for another housing project in 1991, this time in south-east London at Grove Park, Lewisham. Once this had been bought – and including King Street and the other housing stock – the Corporation would have nearly £1.5 million in property assets. The Rothesay Court purpose-built flats were felt to be an especially good buy: 'we could certainly not have built that sort of accom-modation ourselves for anything like the money we paid for it'. The Rothesay Court flats were officially opened by Princess Alexandra on 19 March 1991, and the charity reported that the princess 'met and spoke to each and every one in a most delightful and informal way, which gave so much pleasure'. The Corpora-tion properties were valued in June 2000 at a total of just over £9 million compared to £3.4 million in July 1999 (their 'net book value' was £8.5 compared to £2.9 million in June 1999). This valuation had included the King Street build-ing, valued at £1.9 million.

On 4 October 1973 the Charity Commissioners for England and Wales, according to the Charities Act of 1960, sections 15 and 18, had made a new charitable 'Scheme' relating to the Royal Scottish Corporation (now charity number: 207326). This could not come into operation until the Corporation's charters of 1665, 1676 and 1775 had been amended. An 'Amendment' was duly made on 25 January 1974 in the presence of 'the Queen's Most Excellent Majesty' and the new charter was granted. The Corporation today operates in accordance with this and its other royal charters and subsequent by-laws. Specific investment powers were set out in a supplementary royal charter granted to the charity in 1984. The Corporation had also gained a new visual identity in addition to its seal when a Scottish 'Grant of Arms' was made by the (Scottish) Lord Lyon King of Arms on 5 April 1979.

Computerisation began in 1989 and the Corporation's pensions were now handled 'on the machine', while, the charity proudly boasted that 'the whole expenditure on welfare can be analysed and monitored'. The new computer was also being used to develop a mailing list 'to keep track of our many supporters.' A newsletter, entitled 'The Scots Box', was introduced for the first time in 1993. By 1995 the Corporation was feeling it necessary to consider itself 'in the light of up to date requirements under the Charities Act' and to keep 'an ever watchful eye' on performance. Over ten years later, in the year 2000, the Corporation's administrative team was restructured after the retirement of its secretary, Alan Reid. A new secretary, Valerie Tufnell, was appointed from the charity sector and a finance manager and a professional accountant were also hired. A new post of 'business administration manager' was created to help launch a website and provide Internet access and e-mail, together with the collection of online donations through the Charities Aid Foundation. All these were, wrote Bruce Cairns, the Corporation's chairman, 'the essential tools of a modern charity'.

CHAPTER 40

Income and Expenditure, Funds and Investments

The property dealings and financial investments of the 1970s and 1980s have been managed with careful stewardship. But in the mid-nineteenth century the Royal Scottish Corporation experienced a financial jolt when a deep enquiry into its affairs uncovered a series of fraudulent dealings by the Corporation's secretary. This brought about a firm change in financial accounting practice after 1862. The charity's official was only caught out when a number of small errors showed up in his accounts at the annual court of November 1861.[1] These were evident in an abstract the secretary had made from his financial accounts and on his resignation the Corporation's ledgers and journals were then looked at in greater detail and the 'defalcations' were found to be extensive. Initially he had taken only small amounts, perhaps as a temporary expedient, but since 1855 his fraud had got larger and more ambitious. By November 1861, the committee set up to investigate the crime discovered that a total of £3,119 8s. 3d. was missing. This amount included money from the Kinloch Bequest, which he had also raided, selling some of its stock without authority to pay back the money he had stolen from the Corporation. Worse was to be found.

The secretary had first begun stealing the Corporation's income tax repayments, pocketing £575 between 1848 and November 1861. Most of the money he had taken came from selling large amounts of stock without proper authority, or rather, without any proper control by the Corporation's managing governors. The Corporation's management had made no check on his dealings, nor did they ask him for any account of the stock sales. He had sold £550-worth of 3 percent stock, and a further £400-worth of new 3 percents from the Kinloch Bequest had also been sold to cover his tracks; more Kinloch stock was also missing. The total amount of stock from both sources sold amounted to over £1,500. The committee of management had left eleven sales of stock unquestioned. Cheques for relief amounts above what was required had also been signed by different governors at different times and the difference pocketed by the secretary. He had also received legacies and donations which he had then paid into his own private

---

[1] This secretary was never named. By conjecture it was possibly the Major Adair and Corporation secretary who addressed the Caledonian Society in the 1840s.

bank account. These included £400 paid in several instalments by the Duke of Sutherland.

The committee investigating the fraud, under the chairmanship of Sir George Clerk, included the Duke of Buccleuch, the Duke of Argyll, the Marquis of Breadalbane, the Marquis of Abercorn, the Bishop of London (Archibald Campbell Tait), Lord Elcho, Sir Arthur Kinnaird, Sir John Heron Maxwell and William Maul Webster (solicitor). These men were amazed that such a gross fraud had escaped the notice of the Corporation's committee of management. An auditor was appointed and strict procedures for firmer financial management on a monthly basis were instituted forthwith. A final report on 26 March 1862 recommended that from now on the charity's books were to be 'reconstructed' and then regularly examined. The committee of management 'should be regularly made aware of the state of the funds' and a financial sub-committee of seven members should be formed to meet once a month. Cheques should be signed by two governors and a quarterly account should be examined by an auditor. 'Great caution should be taken in granting powers for sale of stock', and powers should only be granted by the general courts unless recommended by the committee of management in a written proposal. Similar investigations were ordered into the Kinloch Bequest. The fraud committee finally recommended that a more convenient bank closer to the Corporation than the Bank of England should also be found.

By the time extant accounts start again ten years later – in a single report of the society for 1873–74 and a resumption of record-keeping after the destructive effects of the 1877 fire – the recorded amount invested in 3 percent annuities stood at £36,223 for 1873–74 (excluding the stock of the Kinloch Bequest). On 30 November 1877, despite the devastating fire, the Corporation was still able to check its bank accounts. The balance on the Union Bank account was £951 with a deposit of £1,000 (from James Graham's legacy). There was an amount of £35,073 in 3 percent 'Reduced Annuities' and £7,229 in 'Consolidated 3 percents' standing to its credit at the Bank of England. These figures excluded the stock of the Kinloch Bequest which had been 'invested in the New £3 percent Annuities and of which £42,364.17.6 remained'.[2]

By the end of 1883 the charity's income totalled £4,611. Annual subscriptions were down but donations and life subscriptions were up; no legacies had been received. On 26 November the committee received a letter from James Fraser, the Corporation's auditor. He had previously told the committee several times about his worries concerning the 'continual shortcoming of the Income to meet expenditure'. He eventually decided to put it in writing:

---

[2] More detailed income and expenditure accounts just before and for several years after the fire give an idea of the various sources of income and items of expenditure. The financial year ran from 20 November to 20 November and accounts can be seen in Appendix 3.

The Matter cannot be more forcibly brought before you than by the base statement that in 1877 your investments in the Funds amounted to £42,302 whereas today they are only £36,163 ... a decrease in six years of £6,138. At this rate the entire invested funds of the Corporation will disappear in the lifetime of a single generation; for it is to be observed that the deficiency will be forever at an increasing ratio, in as much as for every £1,000 of Stock sold out, a permanent reduction of income of £30 per annum takes place.

What, Fraser thought, made things worse was that during the previous six years legacies ('a very uncertain source of income') amounting to over £4,300 had been used up as well as over £6,000 of the money from stock sold plus 'what may be considered the ordinary and normal income of the Corporation'. A legacy, although welcome income, also meant a loss of a subscriber to the charity. He suggested adding legacies to investments. He did not feel it was his place to set the policy, if the charity wanted to use the capital sold to make up for deficiencies in income and use it to cover relief expenses, but, he felt, 'I am not sure if it is quite creditable to use the accumulated funds which have come down to us from the past to relieve the distress of the present – better to provide it from the income of the investments of such funds'. He felt that these funds should be kept 'whole' to hand on 'unimpaired' to those who came after. He could see it was a difficult decision – 'whether to cut off a large proportion of your relief and put a stop to the selling out of Stock, or to continue your present expenditure and supply your deficiencies as has been the practise for a good many years by the sale of Stock?' The best solution, he considered, would be to increase the donations and subscriptions 'by say £1,200 per annum, but how is this to be done?' He thought it hard to reduce the miscellaneous expenses below £1,000 or £1,100 – and saw the reduction in relief as the easiest way out. But since this was the 'special object of charity', he understood it was a difficult thing to do. Finally, the only solution he could advise, if 'the present relief scale' had to be continued, was that the charity's income should always exceed the relief by £5,000 a year.

On 13 February the chastened finance committee examined the Corporation's ledgers and journals and found that the system of bookkeeping was inadequate and recommended that it should be referred to an auditor for comment and report. All forms of subscription increased by the end of 1884 and legacies totalled £1,035. Relief and miscellaneous expenses had come down and the following year showed an even better return, there being a £100 surplus before legacies were taken into account. It was the first time for several years that the committee of management were able to invest the legacy money left to the charity, and £2,800 of stock was bought which it was hoped would 'partly make up losses from fire'. With an increase in donations, the charity hoped that 'in time' it would 'reinstate the funded Capital of the Corporation as it stood ten years ago'.

At the outbreak of the First World War the Corporation's investment account stood at £105,000, with £97,000 in its main investment account and £8,000 invested in a building fund. The investments of the main account in 1913–14 at 23 November were detailed as follows:

£ AMOUNT	STOCK TYPE
41,000	2½% Consolidated Stock
2,000	3½% Straits Settlements Stock
6,500	3% India Stock
6,500	2½% India Stock
2,200	2½% London County Consolidated Stock
2,500	3½% London County Consolidated Stock
3,000	3% Metropolitan Water Board Stock
6,500	2½% Midland Railway Guaranteed Stock
6,500	3% Debenture Stock L & NW Railway
1,000	3% Edinburgh Corporation Stock
1,000	3% Glasgow Corporation Stock
7,000	3½% Dominion of Canada Stock
5,000	4% Dominion of Canada Stock
3,000	3½% New South Wales Stock
1,000	3½% Madras and Southern Mahratta Railway Capital Stock (3½% interest guaranteed by the Government of India)
1,300	4% Great Eastern Railway Debenture Stock
1,200	4% New Zealand Government Inscribed Stock
97,000	Total

By the end of 1916 the Corporation's books showed a reduced total of around £92,000 and money was moved in and out of different war loan stocks. The charity was urged by its stockbrokers, Hedderwick and Storey, to take money out of the 5 percent War Loan in March 1917 and re-invest it in the 2½ percent Consols. By 1920–21 the charity was well up financially with a total of £207,000 invested (not including the building fund). Over twenty years later and by the end of another world war, the Corporation had increased its investments by £90,000 to over £297,000. Most was tied up in 3 percent government savings bonds (£92,000), a 3½ percent Conversion Loan (£70,000), 3 percent Local Loans (£30,000) and a 4 percent Consolidated Loan (£11,000). London Passenger Transport Board stock had attracted £10,000, while the rest of the investments were made in city or county corporation stock (Birmingham, Bristol, Dundee, Manchester, Plymouth, Stirling and London). The railways – the Great Western, the Great Eastern and the London Midland and Scottish – had attracted some of the charity's funds; the Metropolitan Water Board still figured vaguely, and the

British Empire was represented in Sudanese and Southern Rhodesian stock. Finally, there was 'Guaranteed "A" Mortgage Debenture Stock' of Bowater's Newfoundland Pulp & Paper Mills Ltd and a tiny amount of Looksan Tea Co. Ltd £1 shares. Dividends and interests were £10,316 (gross). Legacies amounted to £2,232. The book value of investments by 1955–56 totalled nearly £306,000.

Later twentieth-century investment decisions benefited from the 'prudence' of auditors and trustee advisers, notably Sir William Slimmings who wisely helped the Corporation to invest after its great property deal of 1973. The year before, the Corporation had still seen a deficit of nearly £2,000 in the income and expenditure balance, but the committee was looking forward to the following year when the 'pending release' of capital from the freehold sale of the Corporation's Fetter Lane premises could be enjoyed. The 1975 complaints of welfare expenditure increase continued, and 1976 still saw a 'wide gap' between subscriptions received (£4,351) and the amount of welfare relief expended (£44,120). This relief cost rose to £63,000 in 1977, and the funds to support such a rise of £19,000 on the previous year were considered sufficient to cover the expenditure, but the charity still needed to ask for additional monetary support from its benefactors to keep boosting the reserve. 'Our earnest hope,' said Douglas Robertson, 'is that the annual contributions from subscribers will increase to match the cost of our relief work.' The investments of the Corporation (excluding the Kinloch Bequest and the St Andrew's Scottish Soldiers' Fund) were listed under a number of different funds. By 1978 these funds totalled over £4.6 million and were divided up between the 'General Fund' (£151,000), the 'Special Fund' (£4.5 million) – 'the surplus on sale of Fetter Lane property' – and the 'Common Good Fund' (over £16,000); this last contained the proceeds of the 1977 sale of paintings bequeathed to the Corporation during the nineteenth century and which were used for the further development of the King Street offices.

During 1980, in common with other charities and voluntary organisations in London, the Corporation's financial health was affected by high inflation and continuing local authority cutbacks. The Corporation's committee of management began to concentrate on better financial organisation to support more relief expenditure rather than looking to expand into new projects. 'The substantial rise in costs because of the high rate of inflation has made it necessary to reassess the programme of capital developments and to keep current commitments within reasonable bounds,' wrote secretary Alan Robertson in November that year. A decrease in inflation was expected by the end of 1981 but the Corporation could still not afford to be deflected from its course of keen financial management. Although it wanted its pensions, grants and more casual relief to be 'as generous as possible', demands were still increasing and some income had to be put aside for the capital funds 'to preserve, as far as possible, the value of these Funds'. The 'day-to-day work' of the Corporation in 1981 was absorbing income from around £3 million of the invested capital. As well as the £168,000 for welfare needs and £80,000 spent on administration and King Street, the Corporation made £5,000 donations to both the Royal Caledonian Schools and the housing association that had taken over the Bina Gardens hostel. In 1981 the special and general invested funds were brought together and a new 'Special Range Fund' was created to cover the Corporation's fixed assets.

In 1984, on the motion of Alan Robertson and Sir William Slimmings, it was resolved to ask the Privy Council to grant a supplementary charter to make provision for, firstly, the Corporation to have wider powers of investment than was permitted under the Trustee Investment Act 1961 and, secondly, for its general court to have power to amend or add to the charter where it concerned such investment powers. By 1989 the 'investment position' was healthy, or rather as healthy 'as the current climate will allow'. Fortunately the charity's capital of over £13 million could now support the 'present welfare and administrative commitments' but future changes meant external help would be needed as plans were worked through. But by 1991 both 'financial and political uncertainties' were on the horizon and had, wrote the Corporation's chairman, H. R. Stewart Hunter, 'made us pause to reflect on our position … and take stock for the future'. Income had fallen after the sale of investments in order to purchase Rothesay Court in April 1990, and expenditure had risen £179,453 in the following twelve months. Although investments were still providing 'by far the greater part of the income', the Corporation thought that 'it would be unrealistic to anticipate an overall increase in yield from these sources'. Expenditure would have to be controlled: 'Welfare is the very heart of the Corporation and it is only by prudent financial care that it can be kept in a healthy financial condition'.

By the end of 1995 the Corporation's net assets reached nearly £20 million. Income was £1.1 million and showed a rise of over £66,000 compared to the previous year's accounts. Interest from the investment portfolio increased, as did rents from the sheltered and other housing properties. But covenants and donations were down nearly £24,000. Expenditure increased to £960,793, including an increase of over £80,000 for welfare payments. The excess of income over expenditure was £176,263. Over £26,000 was paid out on maintaining and repairing the Corporation's King Street offices as well as the pensioners' residential accommodation. Rents were still down in 1996 accompanied by higher costs of maintenance, but legacies had gone up by over £31,000 and the charity's net assets were now just over the £20-million mark, 'indicating that the Corporation is able to maintain its current welfare support and consider plans for additional projects to meet future welfare needs,' wrote its new chairman, Commander Bruce Cairns. Financial improvements (new accounting procedures, policies and plans), which had to be in place by July 1996, were also made in line with the

Charities Act of 1993 and the associated 'Statement of Recommended Practice'.

Administrative costs for 1996–97 had been held down to 10 per cent of the charity's total expenditure of £1.1 million with only 1 percent spent on marketing, PR and fundraising. Income had reached £1.3 million, with 82 percent coming from investments, 16 percent from housing rents and 2 percent from donations, covenants and legacies. By the end of 1998 the Corporation was still awaiting the government's promised White Paper on charities, which had been due to be published in the spring. The 1998 budget had included a 'heavy imposition on charities through the tapering to extinction over 5 years of the recovery of tax credits associated with UK dividends'. The charity thought it would see its investment income reduced by £50,000 a year by 2001 and by £150,000 by 2005. This was indeed a worrying trend, especially when the Corporation's income was 'critically' dependent on its portfolio, and the start of new projects, like assistance towards the 'New Deal for Lone Parents', would have to be deferred once income surpluses were no longer to be expected. Cairns recorded that the Corporation was already lobbying the government on the issue, asserting its view 'that, if charities are to continue to provide an effective complement to State welfare provision, commensurate compensation needs to be made for the tax relief withdrawn'. This 'tapering of tax relief' had begun to take effect by the end of the following year. The promised 1988 government White Paper on charities never came to anything, but a further Treasury 'consultation paper' was published in March 1999. There appeared to be no hoped-for compensation for charities on the gradual loss of their tax-free status.

The 'prudent management' of the finance committee and its broker's advice during the millennium year of 2000 (and its monthly meetings) meant that the Corporation weathered the stock market storms and the charity's investments had been 'sheltered from the general market volatility generated by the boom in the new technologies sector'. The Corporation's property, and especially dividends from stock investments, had been its main sources of income since its regeneration at the end of the eighteenth century. The realisation of its property capital after 1973 and sound investment under Douglas Robertson's chairmanship, combined with Sir William Slimmings's financial expertise, brought the charity to new financial heights. External factors in the property and financial markets beyond its control have brought the Corporation the best and, more recently since 2000, the worst of times. At its highest, the Corporation's total fund balance was worth just over £33 million. By November 2002 the total value of the Corporation's portfolio had dropped to £31.3 million. Dividend income and interest had increased by 12.3 per cent compared to 2001.

CHAPTER 41

Appeals and Gifts

Throughout its long history the Royal Scottish Corporation has relied on royal and other generous benefactors, especially in the three hundred years before the greater investments in property and the stock market were made in the 1970s.

Some benefactors gave one-off donations and the top five giving this form of gift from 1815–69 were:

YEAR	BENEFACTORS OF OVER £200, 1815–1869	AMOUNT
1819	Queen Adelaide (wife of William IV)	£1,246
1869	Arthur Anderson	£1,000 (legacy)
1820	James Kinloch	£360
1832	HRH the Duchess of Kent	£350
1817	British Prisoners in France Relief Fund	£300

Lesser donors of single amounts of over £100 included Leopold, King of the Belgians (£166 in 1817) and Viscountess Keith (£160 in 1848). Sir Robert Peel MP gave £52 10s. in 1822, and other contributors of over £50 during these years included Prince Albert, the Duke of Roxburghe, the Marquess of Bute, the Marquess of Breadalbane, the earls of Moray and Wemyss, Mrs Catherine Blackhurst, Sir David Baxter and William Drysdale.

Contributors of annual donations of over £200 by 1874 can be listed in order of amount as follows:

YEAR	SUBSCRIBERS OF £200 AND UPWARD, 1818–1874	AMOUNT
1837–73	Her Majesty the Queen	£3,570
1864–74	Robert Hannay	£652 10s
1836–70	The Duke of Roxburghe	£652
1866–73	Peter Reid	£600
1829–73	The Duke of Buccleuch and Queensberry	£369 10s

1848–73	Caledonian Society of London	£367 10s
1818–65	The Duke of Montrose	£308 15s
1833–73	Highland Society of London	£304
1844–73	Messrs Coutts and Co.	£262 10s
1832–70	Thomas Murray	£231 10s
1823–73	Benjamin Bond Cabbell	£231
1869–70	The Marquess of Bute	£220
1844–66	Messrs. Drummond and Co.	£210
1864–73	John Young	£207 18s
1871	Sir Richard Wallace, Bart.	£200

Among other subscribers of £100 over these years were the Prince of Wales who as president gave £126 from 1863–69, the Corporation of London which gave £100 in 1865, and the lord mayor, Alderman Sir Andrew Lusk MP, who gave £121 between 1855 and 1873. The Norwich Society of Universal Goodwill (originally another Scots' charitable society established in 1775) gave £167 in 1826. Significant contributors of over £50 and under £100 were the dukes of Sutherland and Abercorn; the earls of Home, Leven and Melville, Selkirk, Dalhousie, and Rosebery; MPs Lord Elcho and Robert Jardine, philanthropist Baroness Burdett Coutts and steamship owner William Mackinnon.

The Royal Scottish Corporation was especially keen to try and meet relief expenses with this money rather than eat into any of the capital it had managed to save. For the period 1877–1882 relief averaged around £4,000 a year, and subscriptions and donations were well down at just £2,664.[1] Publicity was always needed to accompany the fundraising appeals and anniversary dinners which lifted income. The appeals for donations to the new building fund after the fire of 1877 increased printing, postage and advertising costs slightly but brought in greater subscriptions than usual. Monthly income from wellwishers and bene-factors in 1883 and 1884 totalled between £100 and £400 a month according to the collector's reports. Scots abroad continued to play a part and in May 1884 a donation was received from the Port Elizabeth Scottish Association in South Africa. An £800 donation from Canada received at that year's festival dinner also appears to have been regarded as a great coup. By the end of 1886 some mem-bers were beginning to think that advertising should be increased again to help raise funds, one especially wishing that the charity could be 'more widely known'.

Towards the end of the century the Corporation continually reminded its governors to remember 'the pressing need' and again to harness the 'liberality of their friends'. For 1890–91 subscriptions and donations came to £1,989, and there

---

[1] A breakdown can be seen at Appendix 3.

were lots of legacies, bringing in another £2,264. Executors were also heartily thanked, and if there was any surplus it was invested whenever possible. By November 1894 the Corporation found it had to appeal once again: 'If each of our Subscribers would kindly set himself the task of obtaining during the year one new subscriber of a Guinea to the Charity (surely not a very difficult task!) its income would soon be doubled'. It may have worked on Mrs Christina Mackay of Hammersmith (or her executors), for she left the charity the whole of her estate, totalling £3,700, in 1896. By 1899 the benefactors were heartily thanked for their support of Scots so 'that it may continue', but at the end of 1901 the Corporation was mourning many of its longest-serving members and was starting to write about the 'death roll'. The most notable was Queen Victoria who had died at the beginning of the year after 63 years as patron and one of the charity's greatest benefactors. Robert Hepburn, its vice-president with 60 years of service, also died that year and the charity reported the deaths of 59 other members and supporters. In the years that followed, many other similar roll calls were printed as the Corporation lost the support of stalwart members who would be hard to replace in a modern age.

By 1909 annual subscriptions were £1,876 and donations were £3,250. The £25 pensions in 1912 also included money for the 'Lawrie' pensions which were created in honour of James Lawrie, an active governor, who had left two-thirds of the residue of his estate to the Corporation (over £10,000). The death of Allan Freer on 16 September 1915 had once again brought sadness for the governors on the 'intimate' loss of a great friend in the London Scottish network as well as a 'steadfast comrade and ardent fellow-worker' since 1873. They remembered 'his numberless deeds of kindness, his manifold activities for the good of others, his constant courtesy and geniality'. It was on Freer's suggestion that pensioners were provided with 'tea and soup with bread' at their monthly service; his wife was 'an ardent worker in helping, with other ladies, to dispense the much-appreciated repast'. Freer was an elder of St Columba's and had been president of the Caledonian Society in 1909–10. His early business training had been under his father at the Royal Bank of Scotland in Melrose and he had come to London and gained a partnership in a firm of East India merchants, eventually running the business himself and travelling to Java and India. Freer left the residue of his estate to the Corporation, subject to two life rents, and the income from these was specifically 'recommended for the aid of subscribers who in later years have become reduced through ill-health or business reverses'. More pensions were created in 1917 when Captain Jatham Paton VC, MC of the 4th Grenadier Guards and one of the very youngest of the governors, died. He was the only son of George Paton, a life managing governor and a president of the Caledonian Society. Paton wished to remember his son's 'all too short life and the splendid end granted to him' and gave two £18 pensions in his name.

During the Second World War, subscriptions had begun to be made 'under covenant', and a special appeal by the treasurer during 1942–44 to sign covenants had added £380 to the charity's revenues. By 1953 and 1954 the Caledonian Ball proceeds were bringing in around £500 and the Scottish Clans Association, a regular American donor, gave £257; the two Scots churches and 44 Scottish clubs in and around London also made annual donations. Over ten years later, similar subscriptions and donations for 1965–66 amounted to £5,571 in total. Of this, £800 came from the Ball, £1,302 came from the Caledonian Society of London and its members, and £200 came again from the Scottish Clans Association. The remaining amount came from Crown Court and St Columba's churches and from 45 Scottish clubs and societies. The following year's donations were again similar except that the charity also received £200 from the Festival of Scotland in London which continued for a number of subsequent years. In addition, in 1967–68 another American donation of £175 was received from the St Andrew's Society of the State of New York.

By the end of 1978 the annual subscriptions and donations amounted to only £4,500 but the Corporation continued to chase the support of London Scots, believing that 'the service to young and old which we offer is something with which the whole Scottish community in London can be proud to be associated, and that it deserves the generous support of Scots and Scottish societies'. The year 1983 was a good year, and income from subscriptions and donations increased to nearly £12,000 compared to around £7,000 or less for the previous three years. Good years for legacies, though, as always, also meant a loss of key subscribers. An amount of around £118,000 was received in legacies in 1992 (topping a previous high figure of £70,000 in 1991). This legacy money, although credited as income, was still only to be used to 'augment the portfolio' or as special expenditure, in other words, that of 'an extraordinary or capital nature'. A more immediately welcome and edible gift to the charity was provided by United Biscuits in December 1996 when the company donated 'family selection tins' of McVitie's biscuits. These were delivered by the welfare visitors to 300 Corporation 'families'. In previous years, as McVitie's, the company had also given the Corporation £1,000 up to 1933, and a pension had also been created in its name.[2]

Aside from investments and rental income, external sources accounted for only 4 percent of the charity's income in 1998. Gift Aid had been introduced in 1993–94 as tax relief on single cash gifts for UK residents and added a third to the value of any gift. It fully replaced the Deed of Covenant relief in the year 2000 as a result of that year's government budget, and the £250 net minimum tax relief on Gift Aid donations was also removed. The Corporation took advantage

---

[2] Such pensions created by the Corporation in the name of the honoured supporters or more substantial donors, including McVitie's, have been recorded for posterity and are inscribed on a wooden panel in the King Street court room.

of these charges as well as a government legacy campaign. Legacies were actively sought and publicity, in the form of a video and desk calendar, was mailed to solicitors' firms throughout the UK in the hope that they might influence their clients. The total amount for legacies, covenants and donations by the end of 2002 reached just over £29,000. All subscriptions and donations to the Corporation had always gone directly towards charitable projects. The royal charters have been essential to the charity's survival, but many annual or one-off donations and bequests to the Corporation have provided it with much-needed impetus, enabling the charity to continue to provide immediate and pensionable relief.

CHAPTER 42

Royal Patronage

William, Duke of Clarence, had been an active charity president from 1808–30, had chaired numerous festivals and as King William IV had continued to support the charity for a further seven years as its patron. The Corporation continued its royal tradition when it presented an address to Victoria, its new queen and patron, on 10 July 1837. On 17 June 1887, a Jubilee address was sent, lavishly illuminated:

> Your Royal patronage and sympathy have been freely extended, not only to Art, Science, Literature as well as the Commercial and Industrial pursuits of the Nation, but also especially to the Claims of Charity in every form – We acknowledge with gratitude and pride that Your Majesty's patronage of this Charity during the past fifty years has been of inestimable value, and that Your Majesty has contributed more to the funds of the Corporation than any other benefactor in its long history of upwards Two Centuries.

The governors had also written to Edward VII, as Prince of Wales, every time he was re-elected president. The prince acknowledged these Corporation letters through his private secretary, Francis Knollys, who wrote in 1878 that 'the Prince is very sensible of the compliment that has been paid to him'. On 30 January 1901 a special court of all the governors chaired by the treasurer, Lord Rosebery, was held to mourn the death of the queen and at the same time to celebrate the accession of Edward VII, who had now been the charity's president for over thirty years. The meeting began with a prayer by the Archdeacon of London, one of the Corporation's honorary chaplains. Rosebery addressed the gathering in solemn terms: 'We mourn the death of our Patroness, and we congratulate our President, and no event could possibly touch the Royal Scottish Corporation more closely'. But he also celebrated Queen Victoria's role as a ruler of Empire and highlighted the world's latest technical innovation as the news of the queen's death went 'with the rapidity of the electric telegraph to every race and every quarter of the globe'.

Queen Victoria had given the charity a hundred guineas a year for the previous sixty-three years, donating a total amount of £6,615 – more than any other subscribing member. The Corporation created a new class of Coronation

Pensioners to celebrate her son's accession, and more of the same class were created when Edward VII died in 1910. At the special court held on the king's death, Rosebery and the Archdeacon of London again mourned their royal benefactor. Rosebery, who had known him well, said, 'When it behoved him to be a King he was a King, but all the time he was one with a man's heart, a man's nature, and more than a man's compassion for those who were less well placed than himself. He loved peace and he loved the poor'. On 20 January 1936 the Corporation yet again conveyed its sympathy to the royal family on the death of its patron. This time it was George V, whose 'unfailing practical concern which he displayed in its welfare' they remembered. The charity also sent good wishes to the new king, Edward VIII, and thanked him for the 'close personal interest' he had shown when, as Prince of Wales, he had been its president.

Having sent these messages, the Corporation's committee of management was in for a shock on 1 April that was not a fool's joke. For the first time the charity found that it was not quite the 'Privileged Body' it thought it was in being allowed to present its addresses of condolence and congratulation to its royal benefactors, and in this case to Queen Mary and Edward VIII. The Secretary of State for Scotland explained the situation to the Corporation's governors. He told them:

(1) that it was His Majesty's wish that the number of Addresses presented should be curtailed, as far as possible, and confined to Privileged Bodies
(2) that the list of such bodies was a short one of ancient date
(3) that the Royal Scottish Corporation did not appear in that list, to which, for a long time no additions appear to have been made
(4) that admission to that list seems to have been on no more fixed principle than of ancient precedence
(5) that while on the accession of the last two monarchs King Edward VII and King George V the Corporation's Addresses were presented to the Sovereigns in person, these precedents were not considered adequate, and were probably admitted on some personal grounds, possibly that of the close personal connection of its Treasurer of the Corporation, the late Earl of Rosebery (who appears to have headed the deputation) with the Royal Family
(6) that in view of the above, the Address was handed to the Secretary of State for Scotland, who, in turn, would hand it to the Home Secretary for its early submission to his Majesty's notice.

The Corporation was not to be easily put off such communication and in 1947 sent King George VI (now its patron and one who claimed descent from Robert the Bruce) a 'humble address' to Princess Elizabeth on the occasion of her marriage to Lieutenant Philip Mountbatten. The princess, as Queen Elizabeth

II, has now been the Corporation's patron for 51 years, since her accession to the throne in 1952. With the Duke of Edinburgh, she attended a reception of the charity in 1981. Her mother, Queen Elizabeth the Queen Mother, had honoured the Corporation by opening its new King Street building in 1975, when she declared, 'The value of any charity is not only the degree to which it meets the demands of those in need, but rather the quality of love engendered in meeting that need'.

CHAPTER 43

Great Corporation Scots

The Scot has played a splendid part in the past, on every shore, in every type of human activity. He is badly needed today. Let us hope that like Stevenson's lighthouse, Scottish character may be preserved 'immovable, immortal, eminent'.

Sir John Reith, Chairman of the BBC, speaking at the Caledonian Society of London on 11 December 1930

'Let us imagine ourselves married and fairly settled in life, and seated in our easy chair, cigar in mouth ...', wrote David Hepburn in 1890, as he no doubt himself sat back, like his pictured readers, and reminisced about the men associated with the Caledonian Society of London during the year 1867. As well as a 'playground', this society had then regarded itself as 'the worthy henchman to the Scottish Corporation and the Caledonian Asylum' and Hepburn well knew most of the men associated with these two institutions, and some he knew better than others.

Hepburn's father, Robert, had been the name most associated with the Royal Scottish Corporation for almost seventy years. Having started out as a supporter in 1832, Robert Hepburn sat on the committee of management, the committee of the Kinloch Bequest and also that of the 'School Money Fund', and for the last twelve years of his life he had supported the charity as a vice-president – 'an honour granted to very few commoners'. In addition, he had been a founding member (and 'father') of the Caledonian Society and was its president in 1848–55 and 1865–66, when he had also initiated the establishment of the London Scottish Regiment. In addition, he had 'worked hard in the management of the Royal Caledonian Schools'. It was through the two great charity institutions, he was remembered as saying to his fellow-dinner guests at an 1857 society dinner and ball, that 'they had raised a standard in London around which men with honest hearts might rally,' and he had declared that, as a charitable body, they had 'not been unmindful of the claims of the orphan and fatherless, or neglectful of the tottering steps of age and infirmity.'

Hepburn was a Scot of the pioneering sort and had been one of the original surgeons and the first lecturer in mechanical dentistry at the Dental Hospital of

London. There being few opportunities at home, he had decided to come to London in 1831 at the age of 17 after some basic training in Edinburgh, and his recollections show his steadfastness of purpose, eagerness for education and an early example of his charitable nature:

> Starting from Leith in a small smack, I narrowly escaped drowning, as the vessel was wrecked off the Farne Islands; but after three weeks I completed my journey, having spent most of my small stock of money on the sailors of our ill-fated little vessel ... After sixteen weeks attempting to procure employment, trying everybody and going everywhere, I heard from a man in Brighton that a situation was vacant. I walked to Brighton to be curtly greeted at this man's door by the announcement that "he had changed his mind and did not need anybody." My Highland blood was up, but I restrained myself, and without a word started on my homeward walk. When I arrived at London Bridge I fainted from sheer exhaustion. I had given up all hopes of doing anything when I was sent for by Mr W— of Leicester Square, to assist him, but when I began to do so I found myself ignorant of any real practical knowledge ... I worked for several months successively from seven in the morning till ten at night, daily labouring to gain the necessary experience in the mechanical branch of my profession. In so doing I at last became so successful and rapid in my work that I found I could start upon independent ground.

The Hepburn family, like several other families of London Scots, was to have a long Corporation and Caledonian Society tradition. Born in 1851, David Hepburn was president of the society three times in 1889, 1890 and again in 1905–6. He was also chairman of the Corporation's committee of management during this period. Hepburn was a dental surgeon, a dominant leader and 'a Scot of Scots'. Surgeon-General W. G. Don[1] said of the junior Hepburn when he died in 1907: 'Never have I known a more complete man, mentally, morally, physically; a cultured gentleman of fine presence and charming manners; a scholar, antiquary, artist, and traveller'.

Two of the few women to be recognised by the Royal Scottish Corporation (besides its two long-serving royal patrons) were David Hepburn's sisters. In August 1882 Isabella Hepburn and 'the ladies who assisted her' were thanked for 'their kindness in coming to distribute Flowers among the Pensioners and Petitioners on last relief day'. Isabella Hepburn was made a life governor with the privileges of a donor of fifty guineas on 1 April 1891, an honour that was to be 'properly emblazoned on Vellum'. Her sister, Jessie Hepburn Starey, was the last survivor of the Hepburn family when she died in 1922. For forty years she had been 'an unwearied and enthusiastic worker' amongst the charity's 'aged beneficiaries'. She had regularly attended the pensioners' monthly services, and

---

[1] Don was an honorary Corporation surgeon and an enthusiastic singer of songs 'in his own able, cheery way'.

had founded the Hepburn Starey Blind Aid Society 'to whose welfare she had devoted her life'. The Corporation had lost, it said, 'the last of a family whose enthusiasm for the cause of the Scottish Poor in this metropolis was at once an example to their fellow-countrymen and an inspiration'.

The Hepburn sisters shine quite strongly at intervals, but, until the employment of the twentieth-century welfare staff, other women glimmer only occasionally through the Corporation's predominantly masculine history. As patronesses, women danced at fundraising balls or patiently sat in the gallery of the Freemasons' Tavern on St Andrew's Day, watching the great charity festival dinners and accepting toasts to 'the Ladies'. More sadly, they left legacies when they died, and as wives or daughters of Corporation committee of management members, acknowledged letters of condolence on the deaths of their husbands or fathers. 'I received your most kind letters … in the midst of my deep grief', wrote Mrs Helen Clark, the death of whose beloved husband, 'ever deeply interested' in the affairs of the Corporation, had left her in 'utter prostration'. Happier women sang to raise money for the Corporation. Madame Albani Gye, in June 1894, received the privileges of a donor of one hundred guineas, for 'the kindly and spontaneous way in which she gratuitously exercised her great and rare gift as a vocalist' at a fundraising concert.

One eminent surgeon who no longer appeared at committee meetings by 1898 and who seemingly had no wife to console was Dr Charles Hogg. He had long been Robert Hepburn's fellow-surgeon on the committee of management. Like Hepburn, he had sat on and chaired most of the Corporation's committees, probably since the 1850s until around 1886. He had also risen through the ranks of the Caledonian Society, becoming a councillor in 1863, vice-president in 1866, the society's president in 1869 and its honorary secretary in 1879 during a period of deep crisis; but when he had joined its ranks (and would then have sworn to help the Royal Scottish Corporation and the Caledonian Asylum), nobody knew – 'it was so long ago'. He had received his 'medical qualifications' in 1835 and was nearly 80 in 1890 when David Hepburn could write of him that 'The Doctor ever was, and is, a true Scotsman to the backbone, and his well-known presence was rarely to be missed from any gathering in London held for the furtherance of national objects'. Quite the most colourful anecdote of all the Caledonian chronicles is the one of Hogg being urgently called away from a 'great Caledonian Reunion':

> the Doctor was, as usual, arrayed in all the splendour of his Highland dress, when an urgent messenger arrived, requesting his immediate attendance at the bedside of a female sufferer. The Doctor, ever ready to start at duty's call, arose, and apologizing to the assembled Caledonians, obtained the loan of the largest greatcoat that was at command, and so completely enveloped himself that even his buckles might have escaped the notice of the keenest observer.

Thus attired, he presented himself in his patient's room. The case seemed a critical one, and the Doctor, absorbed in his attentions, inadvertently allowed the head of his dirk to protrude between the buttons of his ample overcoat. This at once caught the eye of the sufferer, and that curiosity which characterizes the fair sex being awakened, she begged the Doctor to reveal what was hidden from her view. Unable to resist this appeal which, from the apparent gravity of the case, he feared might even be her last, and hardly daring to think what the result might be, he threw off the borrowed garment. The effect was magical. The lady was so charmed, especially with the red waistcoat, that from that moment her malady took a favourable turn, and the doctor had the satisfaction, at the end of an hour, of returning to receive the congratulations of his brother Caledonians on his remarkably successful treatment of a most critical case.

Another honorary surgeon who supported the Corporation from November 1877 with Robert Hepburn and Charles Hogg was Professor, later Lord, Joseph Lister, the founder of antiseptic surgery. Lord Lister's death and loss to the Corporation in 1912 was rightly mourned.

One active medical benefactor was Dr Daniel Forbes who, as a supporter of the Royal Scottish Corporation and Royal Caledonian Schools, 'always loyally united both charities in any reference to them, and his connection with them'. He was a governor of the Corporation for thirty-three years, and an honorary surgeon for fifteen years. One governor remembered that 'the two charities were his first thought in the morning and the last thought at night. Half in humour half in earnest he said that when he died he expected that their names would be graven on his heart'. Forbes had also belonged to the Caledonian and Highland Societies of London, the Scottish lodge of freemasons, and the London Caithness Society. 'He was a typical and enthusiastic Mason, the brotherly and charitable spirit of the Craft appealed to every fibre of his fine, open, manly soul, and the dignity, solemnity, and religious principles of the Order found in him an appreciative supporter'. His 'unfailing kindness, hearty greeting, and cheery smile' should be highlighted when compared to what the society's chronicler writing in 1903 called 'these days of much partisanship and bitter party feeling'. Another supportive honorary surgeon still talked of today was W. Alexander Law, also known as 'Scottie' – 'a man of great renown in medical circles'. 'We need people like Scottie to join us,' the Corporation mourned when he died in 1989.

Sir John Heron Maxwell, who died in 1885, had experienced the fraud case investigation of 1861–62, and was a long-standing treasurer and then chairman of the Corporation's court at the time of the 1877 fire and during the period of rebuilding and regeneration. Another long-serving chairman of committees, especially those of the Kinloch Bequest, was J. Chisholm Gooden – known always as 'The Chisholm'. He had tried to stand down from the Kinloch chair at the St Andrew's Day court in 1889, 'owing to advancing age and infirmities', but the Corporation refused to accept that he would at last leave and begged him to stay on, preferring even an absent chairman when he was one so good; the charity told him he would only have to come in if he felt well enough.

In 1896 Sir Donald Currie was a vice-president of the Corporation, and much sadness was felt by the charity in June that year at the loss, with few survivors, of the *Drummond Castle*, one of the steamers of his Union Company, whose ships plied between England and South Africa. The Corporation highlighted what it called the 'first accident of a Castle Line steamer' and expressed its 'deep sympathy' for the 'friends and relations of those who unfortunately lost their lives' in the 'sudden and appalling disaster'. Currie himself was not famous for his benevolence until his last years when he gave away thousands of pounds to many worthy causes, especially those connected with 'true religion, medicine and the best in education'. Rather he was regarded by contemporaries as a Scot of the more dour type; Cecil Rhodes had called him the 'Scotch Fox', and *Vanity Fair* in 1884 described him as 'very Scotch, and well aware of the value of money'. Currie, born in 1825, was the youngest of three barber's sons from Greenock. He had spent his childhood in Belfast and came back to Greenock to work at the age of fourteen. In 1844, seeing little opportunity in Scotland, he left for Liverpool and the Cunard Company, striking out on his own in 1862. His self-interested business style amazed even his contemporaries and his 'enterprise was conducted above all as an aid to his pursuit of personal security, independence, wealth and status. Beyond self and family there were few loyalties'. Currie's success 'is a small but perfect example of the initiative and expansiveness characteristic of mid-nineteenth century Scotland'. Once in England, Currie and other Scots like him before and since derived their own independence from working the Scottish system of 'contacts and capital'. The Royal Scottish Corporation must have had a rare honour when Currie later agreed to become its vice-president and donated over £1,400 in 1909.

In 1929 the death of the fifth Earl of Rosebery, president since 1901, hit the Corporation hard, coming as it did with the deaths of its treasurer and two of its vice-presidents. Rosebery, 'a great fellow-countryman' and Corporation governor since 1868, had been made treasurer in 1885 and then president on the accession of Edward VII. On 1 December 1947 at a general court held at 4pm the sixth Earl of Rosebery was elected president of the Corporation. William Will, the court's chairman, expressed the great debt the charity owed to the Roseberys. The sixth earl's father, 'of revered memory', had been 'a great Scot and Imperial statesman' and a 'silver-tongued orator of Victoria and Gladstone' as well as a great Corporation supporter. 'Scotsmen all over the world were unfeignedly glad,' said William Will, 'when Mr. Churchill selected Lord Rosebery to be his Secretary of State for Scotland, following in his father's footsteps as 'a mouthpiece of patriotic Scotland'.

Lord Balfour of Burleigh, another big supporter of the Corporation, 'although a vigorous member of the House of Lords and chairman of one of the largest banks in the country', seconded the earl's presidential nomination – pleased that they were both serving the Corporation as their fathers had done before them. Rosebery in reply said that 'notwithstanding the improvement in social services, the Corporation would still find a wide field for its important activities'. Balfour's father had died in 1921, a trusted leader of the Church of Scotland for 'over half a century', who had also been a Royal Scottish Corporation governor since 1877, before succeeding the fifth Earl of Rosebery as the charity's treasurer in 1903. The Corporation had benefited from his 'influence, sagacity and wise counsel'; and his presidency at three St Andrew's Day festival dinners in 1895, 1905 and 1906. Through his son, the Corporation had, by 1925–26, been able to attract 'the best men in the country' for the charity's 'high offices'. Balfour had been 'actively concerned' with the Corporation since 1908 and had been treasurer for twenty-five years since 1942. His son took up the post of treasurer the following year – at which appointment Lord Alness, then a Corporation vice-president as well as Secretary of State for Scotland, said, 'no better appointment could be made'. Viscount Finlay had been made a Corporation governor in 1869, and had become treasurer in 1921 on the death of Lord Balfour of Burleigh. In 1929 the Corporation missed 'a wise counsellor, an honoured friend and colleague, as modest and sweet in disposition as he was distinguished and independent of character'.

The eighth Duke of Atholl was the Corporation's treasurer for thirteen years from 1929. As well as raising £28,000 from Caledonian Balls, he had also led the charity's 1927 festival appeal which had only once been exceeded before his death. On 1 April 1941 the Corporation held a special meeting to remember the duke and created a Corporation pension in his memory, 'for all time'. The meeting's chairman, William Will, said that Atholl had 'led a well-ordered, active, almost tumultuous life, ever fighting in some cause, as befitted the descendent of a House, many of whose Members fought for and with Prince Charlie, and who at all times were ready to draw the sword and strike a blow for Scotland'. His army services were well known and 'part of the military history of Great Britain', and Will reminded his audience that the duke had raised the Scottish Horse for Lord Kitchener during the Boer War. Will also remembered Atholl's service to his own country's parliament: 'his work as his Majesty's Lord High Commissioner to the General Assembly of the Church of Scotland (1918–20); his interest in Scottish arts and sports; and, privately and through the Highland Society of London, his encouragement of Piping and Highland Dancing, Lowland and Celtic music and the preservation of the Gaelic tongue'. William Will especially recognised the duke's leading role in raising the Scottish National War Memorial in Edinburgh, with the support of Lord Alness.

In 1989 Douglas Robertson stepped down after twelve years as chairman. He had become a vice-president of the Corporation and chairman of the committee of management in 1977. Experienced in managing his family's building firm, Robertson was instrumental in pushing for a higher price for Fetter Lane and for ensuring the right properties and sites were bought for pensioner accommodation. He calls his late committee colleague, Sir William Slimmings, the financial brains behind the 1970s investments. Like many senior Corporation officials before him, Robertson was also (and is still) a member of the Caledonian Society of London, having been elected in 1948 and becoming annual president for 1964–65. Of its new president, the Caledonian Society wrote that he was 'wise in judgement, generous in spirit and zealous in his love of Scotland'. In 1993 Robertson received an OBE from the Queen for his dedicated work amongst Scots in need; it was 'an award well earned' and one in which the Corporation's management said 'we all take great pride'. A key London Scot whom Robertson persuaded to help was fellow Clan Donnachaidh member John Robertson Brown. Brown, a Hampstead-born pensions specialist from the insurance industry, had joined the Corporation in December 1975 and became a vice-president in 1995. He has spent much of his time on the welfare side of the Corporation and oversaw the opening of the Bawtry Road flats in 1978. Robertson (aged 92) and Brown (aged 86) continue to sit on the committee of management as the most senior members (in age) of the Corporation; both are full of vision about how the charity should continue to help needy Scots and how such charitable giving should be managed. The Corporation could not today carry out the activities it does or the new strategy it is now implementing without having first had Robertson's past management and vision.

Many other men and women have given the Royal Scottish Corporation their unfailing support over four centuries. On the subject of such charitable London Scots, perhaps one last mention should be reserved for an unnamed governor who himself had been saved from utter destitution by the charity. He had 'actually been taken from the gutter to where he had been reduced by dire poverty to carrying a sandwich board for the meagre remuneration of a shilling a day'. A donation from the Corporation allowed him to set up as 'a hawker', selling his wares on the streets. Before he died in 1923, 'he had so succeeded that he had established a factory where he employed a large number of workers'.

Twenty-First Century Challenges

Should auld acquaintance be forgot
And never brought to mind? ...
We'll take a cup of kindness yet
For the sake of auld lang syne ...
And there's a hand, my trusty fiere!
And gie's a hand o'thine!

Robert Burns, Auld Lang Syne, *1796*

The history of the Royal Scottish Corporation has been much influenced by the history of the generations of Scots who for centuries have made their homes and money in London since the early days of James I's reign in 1603. Such a history has also reflected how a number of these Scots additionally took advantage of British colonial expansion, heading both east and west, even in its earliest years – and how they influenced it greatly. The management of the Corporation's charity caseload has in its turn mirrored the history of the development of London's parish relief, private philanthropy and state social welfare for four centuries. Creating the niche where the charity can continue to flourish will be crucial to the Corporation's future survival.

Poverty is always relative to the age in which people live, and the passing of centuries has not brought a lessening of hardship for the capital's poor Scottish community. Modern social problems, such as drug and alcohol addiction and the breakdown of family life, have exacerbated the comparative poverty and hardship experienced by those Scots living in London on income support during the last twenty or thirty years. The homeless rootlessness of unemployed men and the single-parent families needing urgent and sometimes specific help have also not gone away. Although the nineteenth and twentieth centuries saw great strides in the public and private care of London's sick, orphaned and elderly poor, state support may never be able to keep up with all of Greater London's needs; indeed social workers and the educational system have badly failed a number of children. Nevertheless, at no time in the past has there been such support for the less well-off or for those who have wanted to find their own way in life.

The fact that the Royal Scottish Corporation has survived for so long shows that it has been, despite a few temporary lapses, a well-managed and successful charity, and, by responding well to change, it has been innovative if perhaps not unique in its activities. Such an achievement must be celebrated. The charity was in the right place at the right time and did what needed to be done – sometimes the Corporation moved before other similar institutions, and at other times it followed the philanthropic trend. Most of the time it chose suitable men to administer its business and to lead it out of difficulty. Even in an age without social welfare, the Corporation had tried to do something that was not provided by others, something that would provide poorer Scots with a way out of a situation and not keep them in an underclass. Careful investment of money from subscriptions, donations and bequests since the late seventeenth century, and property and stock dealing since the early eighteenth century, have also meant that the Corporation has been able to keep up its near 400-year tradition of charitable giving.

In 2002 the charity provided help for nearly 1,300 Scots in London, ranging from student grants to pensions for the elderly and disabled. The charity spent some £1.3 million on relief, including weekly allowances for 269 pensioners, and owned 78 sheltered flats in three parts of London. It also provided various other welfare services and grants for a large number of Scots on low incomes. Going forward, it will continue to consider helping anyone who is in need and who was born in Scotland, has a parent born in Scotland, or is the widow or widower of a spouse born in Scotland. Although the charter limitation means that help can only be given to first- or second-generation Scots, such relief means that these people become 'less of a burden' on the London taxpayer in general. The Corporation will have to remain pro-active and anticipate the needs of the Scottish community in the city. The government is again changing its social welfare programmes and the charity, as it has always tried to do, must keep up. It will have to become well aware of where social welfare gaps might appear in the future, complementing, without subsidising, the state's benefits. Whether such things still need to be done is a matter for debate in some quarters, and the Corporation has consequently begun to readjust and prepare itself to meet the needs of the 118,000 people registered as having been born in Scotland in 2001 and their families (estimated to total a population of around 380,000).

In July 2001 the charity had commissioned a report from a consultant called Bob Eggington. He carried out seventeen interviews with trustees, senior staff and welfare visitors, as well as charity outsiders. Eggington described the Corporation as a 'conservatively-trusteed charity' in which change 'was approached slowly and cautiously' and the finances 'subject to very careful stewardship'. He considered this for the most part admirable and proper, and he praised its financial state, but, Eggington added, the great interest in operational detail and 'the innate caution of the organisation and the system of Governance sometimes act as a brake on beneficial change, as well as deterring rashness and imprudence'. This had also been the conclusion of the Corporation's own Strategic Working Group which had already produced a report addressing a number of issues, including a younger and less male management. Eggington encouraged the charity's committee of management to take up the working group's report and act on it:

> It would change the age profile and ... the gender profile of the Committee, without losing valuable experience and expertise. It would reduce the number of committee and sub-committee meetings, which is currently very high. It would clarify lines of authority and delegate most of the work of running the charity to the professional staff. It should lessen the likelihood of adversarial positions becoming entrenched in the future.

The members of the committee of management were now encouraged to focus on strategic issues affecting the charity and leave the day-to-day running of the Corporation to salaried staff. A strong chairman and experienced chief executive would be needed to carry through the changes.

'The Corporation and our committed team of experienced people have a long-standing reputation of helping in a huge number of difficult situations ... we plan to modernise our charity and expand the range and extent of our support,' said Wylie White in the charity's press release when he became the new chairman of the Corporation on 10 April 2002. Born in Scotland, White was formerly a senior executive with Legal and General Assurance in London and had been a Corporation trustee for five years before his appointment. He will drive the Corporation in partnership with an equally new chief executive, Willie Docherty, who became the charity's first chief executive, with genuine delegated authority, on 13 May 2002. Originally born in Rutherglen, but latterly from East Kilbride, Docherty had previously worked for a number of charities in London and Scotland and was most recently chief executive of Action Acton, a partnership responsible for regenerating Acton, in west London. Docherty has also been head of the Wester Hailes Partnership in Edinburgh, and his experience in developing and implementing strategies for the regeneration of poor communities, addressing their housing, unemployment and health concerns and turning round failing institutions should provide the Corporation with a beneficial instrument of change. Updating the Corporation – its administration and welfare activities as well as its buildings – is the key challenge facing Whyte and Docherty. They will have to apply their skills at times with diplomacy and tact, listening to the experiences of an older generation of Corporation Scots in order to achieve their future aims. Docherty is in turn helped in his efforts by a team of twelve staff – including experienced professionals, Ruth Smith, the welfare manager, Alison MacRury Gandhi, the housing manager and Patricia Marshall, the finance manager. Two other full-time and four part-time staff help to keep the Corporation's administration and King Street premises running. Four client support officers and two wardens care for the charity's pensioners and other 'clients' and also assess the new cases.

In 2003 Her Majesty the Queen is patron of the Royal Scottish Corporation and Sir Thomas Macpherson of Biallid was appointed its new president in February 2003, bringing to the charity his considerable business experience and City skills. Macpherson and the treasurer, Lord Balfour of Burleigh, are joined by six vice-presidents and three levels of governors – annual governors, life governors and life managing governors. Fifteen of the life managing governors are (along with the Corporation's chairman, vice-presidents, two honorary chaplains, three physicians and four surgeons) members of the charity's committee of management. This governing body of trustees meets on the second Wednesday of every month (the same day as the pensioners' church service and lunch) and goes through the welfare cases and the business of the Corporation. A 'Court' has met quarterly and managed the Royal Scottish Corporation since its first charter of 1665. Members of the committee of management are elected for a three-year period by the 'Annual Court' according to 'their suitability to promote the aims of the Corporation and their willingness to take an active part in its management'. A number of sub-committees, each with its own chairman, report to the committee of management and cover the areas of finance, welfare and public relations. And, with a frequency unusual for a charity, the finance sub-committee meets monthly every second Monday and checks its investment position with external advisers. Among the Corporation's advisers are the auditor, honorary solicitor, its bank and an investment management company.

In preparing for its twenty-first century future, the Royal Scottish Corporation has formulated a new way forward. Willie Docherty has been actively comparing the Corporation's experiences and discussing issues and best practice with other similar charities. The charity's new strategy for 2003–2005 is in the process of being implemented and the Royal Scottish Corporation envisages a community of 'Scots in London providing and benefiting from mutual support'. It has a restated aim to 'offer a helping hand to reduce or remove need, hardship or distress, in a manner that empowers our clients to help themselves'. By 2006 the charity plans to be a more modern and better-known institution, and to have increased its beneficial impact on the poorer Scots community. Work in refurbishing the King Street Headquarters has been undertaken and concentrated on reorganising the basement areas and the court room on the ground floor. In addition, renovations have been carried out according to the building's listed heritage status, preserving the especially 'fine staircase with round-headed semi-circular niches and outswept crinoline banisters'.

Even though its funding will be more diversified, the Corporation plans to continue to preserve its inherited capital by providing greater value for money.

Its efforts will be focused on low-income individuals in three groups: older people and people with disabilities, people of working age, and students. These 'clients' are now offered access to a help line called 'Scotsline'; an assessment of their present and future needs and training; help with finding appropriate existing services outside the Corporation; and access to social, leisure and cultural events. A team of five or six welfare staff support these focused activities as well as organising and managing a volunteer programme. These volunteers will visit the charity's most vulnerable and isolated pensioners, in particular helping to combat what the charity calls, 'social isolation'.

Maintaining a sense of independence has been a special concern of the charity. The overcrowded workhouse hospital had closed at the end of the seventeenth century precisely because it took away such 'Scottish' independence. The Elizabethan Poor Law of 1601 that forced London Scots to set up their box club a few years later had in fact aimed to encourage such self-help. By 1861–2 journalist Henry Mayhew's social commentary (unusually compared with the evangelistic philanthropists of the time) had advocated a similar approach:

> There is but one way of benefiting the poor, viz. by developing their powers of self-reliance, and certainly not in treating them like children … Let the rich become the advisers and assistants of the poor, giving them the benefit of their superior education and means – but leaving the people to act for themselves – and they will do great good …

Twenty-first century London Scots must now learn from an early age to be more responsible for their own lives and for the lives of others who cannot, because of infancy, age or disability, help themselves. To this end, the Corporation's support group is planning to introduce 'personal development plans' for the charity's working-age clients.

The stock market crashes of the past few years, and more recently the war in Iraq, have made for uncertain times; nevertheless dividends from investments have continued to contribute to the charity's income. The funds of the Corporation are permanent endowment. The income from these funds also pays for the day-to-day work of the Corporation's charity and building administration. Careful observation and understanding by new trustees of their responsibilities under the rules of the Charity Commission of England and Wales are crucial to preserve the inherited capital, as is the guardianship of the tenets of the Royal Scottish Corporation's charters. These key disciplines and their application by caring men of vision, all strongly motivated by welfare needs and many with keen financial brains and a sound knowledge of past experience, have been the charity's past salvation at other key moments of change. The same, although perhaps with an increased female element, is very likely to be the secret of future success if it is to survive the bad times and take advantage of any future city booms. There have always been enough concerned Scots in London with the patience and energy to take an interest during difficult times in the charity's past. Those with the time and experience to make a difference will no doubt be found again. The Corporation is optimistic that they will come forward to help.

The Royal Scottish Corporation is not a fashionable charity and has certainly 'kept its light under a bushel for many, many years', as one of its trustees has said. Certainly there is now 'a need for us to show our head above the parapet a bit more than we have in the past,' thinks another. 'We've been around for nearly four hundred years. And ask people, say, "What's the Royal Scottish Corporation?" They say, "The Royal Scottish what?"' Furthermore, the Corporation has yet to cut its teeth on serious publicity and fundraising. Patricia Parsons, a trustee and the deputy mayor of Richmond, has encouraged the charity to set up a group of 'friends' to encourage Scots in London and elsewhere to subscribe to its worthy cause, as well as to volunteer to visit its pensioners. Such a new kind of rallying point for Scots generally, from all walks of life – in London, Scotland and abroad – must be provided if the charity is to raise the necessary 10 percent of income it needs from sources other than investment and housing by 2005.

The Royal Scottish Corporation is a charity, as the fifth Earl of Rosebery and a past president wrote in 1927, 'which for history and antiquity is not easily equalled'. It is also the oldest Scottish charity outside Scotland and was once described as 'a small seed planted in an alien soil'. Since then it has grown steadily and proved the point that for four-hundred years rich and poor Scots have never been far apart.

Perhaps the simplest and most effective final plea on behalf of such an original and lasting cause is for all its supporters, in London, Scotland and elsewhere, to drink from Burns's 'cup of kindness' and to 'Down with the dust'. Remembering all the while that wealth was made

> Nor for to hide it in a hedge,
> Nor for a train attendant,
> But for the glorious privilege
> Of being independent.

Appendices

Key Dates for the Royal Scottish Corporation, 1603–2003

1603	Union of the crowns; James VI of Scotland became James I of 'Great Britain'; many Scots followed the king and his court south to London
1613	Earliest date for Scots Box mutual-aid society operations; Scots in London not entitled to local parish relief if they fell ill or died, or were orphaned, disabled, or elderly
1638	Twenty members of the society met in Lamb's Conduit; 'Allowed 20s. for Funerals of those dying of the Plague, 30s. for others'
1651	War in Scotland; Scots in London ordered to have a licence to stay or to leave Oliver Cromwell's Commonwealth
1656–57	Scots box club members met at the King's Head tavern in Covent Garden
1664	Weaver merchant James Kynneir survived serious illness, gave a substantial sum to the Scots Box and persuaded its members to incorporate their society by royal charter
1665 11 Apr	Petition of 19 Scotsmen to set up a workhouse for 'poor Scots artificers' sent to Charles II
1665 30 June	Royal letters patent for establishment of 'The Scottish Hospital of the Foundation of Charles the Second' with the help of the Earl of Lauderdale; Kynnier became first master; monies received at first meeting totalled £116
1665 July	Great Plague took hold; over 300 Scots buried 'with as much decency as the publick Calamity would permit'
1666	Meeting held at the Cock & Pie Tavern, Covent Garden; the Duke of Bedford gave property for the charity's hospital in White Hart Yard, Covent Garden sometime between 1665 and 1666; the Great Fire began to rage in the City of London on 2 September
c. 1669-70	Land leased in Blackfriars from widow, Katherine Austen; foundations laid for new hospital
1673	Scottish Hospital opened
1676 18 Nov	Second royal charter granted; James Kynneir again elected master

1680	Scottish Hospital and Corporation had 338 subscribing members
1684	Scots Charitable Society of Boston (USA), originally founded around 1657, looked to the example of the Corporation for its reorganisation
1686	Donation of £200 received from Royal Burghs of Scotland
1695-96	Banker and Corporation governor James Chiesly carried papers of William Paterson's colonising Darien scheme to Edinburgh; other Corporation governors also supported the project and Paterson (also the founder of the Bank of England) later contributed to the charity
1698	'Scots Foot-Guards' donated £202
1707	Union of English and Scottish parliaments – more Scots came south to London and were now able to join the East India Company's army, navy and administration; the Corporation closed its hospital and workhouse around this time
1715, 1719, 1745	Jacobite rebellions culminated in the Battle of Culloden in 1746; the wearing of highland dress by Scots banned from 1747 until 1782
1775	Third Corporation charter, granted by George III, introduced a presidential system; Charles, Duke of Queensberry, began a noble tradition when he became first president
1781 Nov	James Graham, Marquis, and later third Duke, of Montrose, elected president
1782	Buildings in Blackfriars sold to the City of London for £1,050; premises bought in Crane Court, former home of the Royal Society, for £1,000
1785	Under the influence of Montrose and others, 4,648 Bombay rupees were sent back to the Corporation as the first of many donations from India
1809	£1,000 received from Bengal via Lord Minto, Governor-General of India
1810	Appeal for a charity school fund, signed by many Scots nobles and East India Company directors
1811	William, Duke of Clarence, became president; the City of London gave £200
1818	Kinloch Bequest established for poor and disabled Scots soldiers and sailors, wounded in the service of their country; William Kinloch, a Calcutta merchant, had died on his way back from India in 1812 and left the charity the residue of his estate for such a purpose
1830	Edinburgh branch office organised; Leith agent appointed in

	1831 on the recommendation of Robert Stevenson; William IV became patron of the Corporation and its Edinburgh branch on his accession
1862	Serious case of fraud found and secretary dismissed; new financial rules instituted
1863	Viscount Palmerston presided over St Andrew's Day festival – £1,200 raised
1877 Nov	Crane Court building burnt down; many valuable paintings and archives lost
1878–1880	Premises rebuilt in a baronial style
1901	Queen Victoria died having given one hundred guineas annually for 63 years; Edward VII, a past president, became patron; long-serving past chairman Robert Hepburn died – also a founder of the Caledonian Society of London and the London Scottish Regiment
1914–18	The Corporation's managers ran the Federated Council of Scottish Associations; its activities included sending 'comforts' to Scottish frontline troops and prisoners-of-war
1928	Author J. M. Barrie presided over the St Andrew's Day festival
1973	Corporation's premises sold; capital invested and housing schemes began under the chairmanship of Douglas Robertson, aided by financial adviser, Sir William Slimmings
1974	New royal charter granted by HM Queen Elizabeth II
1975	Queen Elizabeth the Queen Mother opened the new charity headquarters at 37 King Street, Covent Garden
1978	First sheltered-housing scheme of 28 flats set up for elderly and disabled Scots at Bawtry Road in Whetstone, north London
1984	Second block of 16 flats (not requiring a warden) completed at Kinnear Court in Wimbledon, south-west London
1990	Custom-built block of 35 sheltered flats bought at Rothesay Court in Grove Park, south-east London
2002	New chairman and chief executive appointed (Wylie White and Willie Docherty); a three-year plan of reform to focus and modernise the charity established; the Corporation owned 78 flats and provided pensions for 268 elderly or disabled pensioners; £1.3 million spent helping 1,200 people in total during the year
2003 May	Sir Thomas Macpherson elected president on the retirement of the Earl of Rosebery; King Street headquarters refurbished.

Masters, Presidents and Treasurers of the Royal Scottish Corporation, 1665–2003

MASTERS AND TREASURERS, 1665–1730

Compiled from accounts of the 'Scots Corporation' for 1714 and 1730

MASTERS		TREASURERS
1665	Mr. James Kinnier, first Master	Mr. Andrew Caldwall, first Treasurer
1666	John Allan, Esq.	Mr Robert Rayning
1667	David Jollive, Esq.	Mr Andrew M'Dowgall
1668	Mr. John Ewan, Merchant	Mr James Seewright
1669	Mr. James Donaldson	Mr Robert Paterson
1670	Mr. Alexander Blair	Mr John Alexander (merchant taylor)
1671	Mr. James Blacklaw	Mr John Rayning
1672/3	The Hall built	
1672	Mr. Andrew Caldwall (sometimes Caldwell)	Mr Andrew Hodges
1673	Mr Robert Rayning	Mr William Watts
1674	Sir Andrew M'Dowgall	Mr James Foulis
1675	Mr John Alexander	Mr James Bruce
1676	Mr James Kinnier	Mr Dowgall Campbell
1677	Mr John Rayning (or 'Renney' according to 1677 account)	Mr Dowgall Campbell
1677/8	William Watts, Esq.	Mr William Parks
1678	Mr Andrew Hodges	Mr William Parks
1679	Mr James Foulis (or 'Fowles' according to will of James Kynneir)	Mr John Murray
1680	Mr James Bruce	Mr Francis Grierson
1681	Mr William Parks	Mr William Bizet
1682	Sir Andrew Forrester	Mr John Hay
1683	Mr Edward Callender	Mr Alexander Man
1684	Mr John Hay	Mr Alexander Culbertson
1685	Mr Alexander Man, Gent.	Mr James Cuningham
1686	Richard, Lord Maitland	Mr James Trumble

1687	Henry, Earl of Stirling	Mr Alexander Lorimer
1688	Mr James Cunningham	Mr Alexander Goodalle
1689	Mr Francis Grierson	Mr Archibald Wilson
1690	Sir David Nairn	Mr Andrew Cooke
1691	Mr James Trumble	Mr William Bain
1692	Mr Alexander Lorimer	Mr John Young
1693	Sir James Gray	Mr William Graham
1694	Robert Graham	Mr William Sinclair
1695	Mr William Graham	Mr Walter Stewart
1696	Mr Walter Stewart	Mr William Murray
1697	Mr Archibald Wilson	Mr Thomas Frazer
1698	Mr William Sinclair	Mr William Elliot
1699	Capt William Ker	Mr James Campbell
1700	Mr William Elliot	Mr Herbert Williamson
1701	Mr Thomas Frazer	Mr Robert Petre
1702	Dr James Wellwood	Mr John Chalmers
1703	Mr Thomas Coutts	Mr Thomas M'culloch
1704	Mr Robert Petre	Mr John M'culloch
1705	Mr James Campbell	Mr David Campbell
1706	Sir James Wishart	Mr John Campbell
1707	Col. Robert Stewart	Mr John Spence
1708	David Campbell, Esq.	Mr Alexander Stratton
1709	Capt John Man	Mr John Graham
1710	Mr Robert Hogg	Mr Thomas Hall
1711	John Montgomery Esq.	Mr James Douglas
1712	Mr John M'culloch	Mr Will. Elliot, Woollen-draper
1713	Mr Alexander Stratton	Mr William Bouden
1714	Mr James Douglas	Mr Alexander Hamilton
1715	Mr Thomas Hall	Mr Andrew Makane
1716	Mr William Elliot (Jan)	Mr Robert Todd
1717	Mr Alexander Hamilton	Mr George Middleton
1718	William Mitchell Esq.	Mr Patrick Cuthbertson
1719	Mr Andrew Makain	Mr James Laggan
1720	Mr Alexander Stephenson	Mr Gilbert Gordon
1721	The Hon. Brigadier Robert Hunter Esq.	Mr Adam Hogg
1722	Mr Andrew Drummond	Mr Alexander Thomson
1723	Capt. Thomas Agnew	Mr Thomas Twaddell
1724	John Drummond Esq.	Mr Alexander Jollie
1725	Mr George Middleton	Mr Adam Richardson
1726	Mr Adam Hogg	Mr James Campbell

1727	Robert Ferguson Esq.	Mr John Waldenshaw
1728	Mr James Cockburne	Mr James Hay
1729	Mr Alexander Jollie	Mr John Patterson
1730	Mr James Campbell	Mr David Cooper

MASTERS, 1731–1769

Taken from a table on the wall in the Court Room of the Royal Scottish Corporation, 37 King Street

1731	James Hay
1732	William Hamilton
1733	John Paterson
1734	John Wilkinshaw
1735	Alexander Hamilton
1736	John Wilson
1737	Claud Johnson
1738	Henry Douglas
1739	Robert Oliphant
1740	James Hume
1741	James Gordon
1742	William Hay
1743	James Gordon
1744	Alexander Grant
1745	Adam Anderson
1746	William Mather
1747	Alexander Mackrabie
1748	George Mercer
1749	Robert Ogilvie
1750	John Thomson, Senr.
1751	William Richardson
1752	Thomas Williamson
1753	William Bouden
1754	John Paterson
1755	William Crammond
1756	James Edington
1757	George Campbell
1758	—
1759	Sir Alexander Grant, Bt.
1760	Sir James Cockburn, Bt.
1761	Alexander Small
1762	William Strahan

1763	Andrew Rickard
1764	Richard Oswald
1765	James Campbell
1766	William Innes
1767–74	(left blank)

PRESIDENTS, 1775–2003

Taken from a table on the wall in the Court Room of the Royal Scottish Corporation, 37 King Street; a manuscript book in the RSC Archive listing presidents, vice-presidents and treasurers, 1877–1976; and annual reports, 1976–2003

1775	The Duke of Queensberry & Dover
1778	The Duke of Buccleuch
1780	The Earl of Findlater
1782	The Duke of Montrose
1811	HRH The Duke of Clarence
1830	The Duke of Gordon
1837	The Duke of Sutherland
1845	The Duke of Richmond
1847	The Duke of Montrose
1861	The Duke of Sutherland
1863	The Duke of Montrose
1865	The Duke of Roxburghe
1869–1902	HRH The Prince of Wales
1903–29	The Earl of Rosebery
1929–34	(no president)
1934–36	HRH The Prince of Wales
1936–47	(no president)
1947–2003	The Earl of Rosebery
2003	Sir Thomas Macpherson

TREASURERS, 1877–2003

Taken from a manuscript book in the RSC Archive listing presidents, vice-presidents and treasurers 1877–1976; and annual reports, 1976–2003

1877–85	Sir John Heron Maxwell
1885–1903	The Earl of Rosebery
1903–21	Lord Balfour of Burleigh
1921–29	Viscount Finlay
1929–42	The Duke of Atholl
1942–	Lord Balfour of Burleigh

Details of Income and Expenditure for the Royal Scottish Corporation, 1876–1882

The detailed income and expenditure accounts, just before and for several years after the fire in November 1877, give an idea of the charity's various sources of income and items of expenditure. The financial year ran from 20 November to 20 November and the accounts are shown in the following two tables.

The first table for income generally ran as follows:

£s	1876–77	1877–78	1878–79	1879–80	1880–81	1881–82
In						
Balances	859	950	500	1660	878	1006
Subscriptions	1344	1457	1071	1186	1125	2917
Donations	1427	1046	821	1652	1750	193
Property Rents (and from 1881 'Pensioner's Hall' hire)	404	260	107	140	256	549
Stock Dividends	1375	1248	1165	1148	1096	1175
Legacies	1699	0	1894	1000	38	1400
Total income excl. extras from capital, building fund, insurance payout, cash withdrawn from deposit, bank loan or balances	6249	4020	5058	5126	4265	6234
Total plus extras and bank balances	9029	10775	11026	10087	8254	7249

'Subscriptions, Donations and Legacies' can be further broken down as follows:

£s	1876–77	1877–78	1878–79	1879–80	1880–81	1881–82
Total Subscriptions	1344	1457	1071	1186	1125	2917
Life Subscriptions	231	506	152	34	278	1517
Annual Subscriptions	1113	949	918	841	847	1400
Total Donations	1427	1046	821	1652	1750	193
General	1310	911	618	1465	1652	0?
Caledonian Ball (half proceeds)	116	134	202	187	96	193
Legacies	1699	0	1894	1000	38	1400

The expenditure table ran as follows:

£s	1876–77	1877–78	1878–79	1879–80	1880–81	1881–82
Out						
Relief	4069	4323	4051	3993	3892	4108
Lost in the fire	55					
Misc. expenses (fuel, lighting, postage, printing advertising etc)	665	828	578	684	800	748
Salaries	532	527	489	499	460	498
Repairs to property	367	321	105		519	
Furniture for temporary offices		28				
Festival expenses	221	309	140	203	230	185
School Fund payments	145	171	169	171	101	86
Bank interest	24				16	
Total expenditure less extras	6078	6507	5532	5550	6018	5810
New safe and fittings						38
Temporary loan paid off	1000		1000			
Cash put on deposit	1000	3768	304			
Expenditure on rebuilding account			2531	3660	1230	
Bank balances	951	453	1570	779	1006	1402
In sec's hand		47	91	99		
Total plus extras	9029	10775	11028	10088	8254	7250

Costs of relief for these years can be seen in the following table:

RELIEF 1877–1882	1876–77	1877–78	1878–79	1879–80	1880–81	1881–82
Pensions	1756	1746	1701	1663	1586	1603
Petitioners	2266	2525	2311	2296	2264	2441
Passages to Scotland	46	50	38	33	43	63
Total Relief	4069	4323	4051	3993	3892	4108

An Overview of Charitable Services provided by the Royal Scottish Corporation, 1995–2002

ACTIVITY	1995–96	1996–97	1997–98	1998–99	1999–2000	2000–01	2001–02
Number of client households visited/ small grants expended			1000 (£68,000)	1000 (£60,000)	1200 (£55,000)	1000 (£60,000)	£26,800
Number of flats in Corporation housing	79	79	79	78	78	78	78
Number of elderly and disabled pensioners	324	330	300	291	282	280	269
Amount of pensioners' weekly allowance		£7.62	£8.73	£8.84	£9.50	£9.95	£10.11
New cases (substantial) for welfare and training grants approved	155	171	190	168	155	141	221[a]
Average grants for new cases	£434	£478	£403	£515	£590	£543	£315
Summer and winter grants (approx. number of households)	Yes	Yes	700 (£39,000)	700 (£38,000)	500 (£54,500)	500 (£42,700)	£47,300
Holidays or days out, including use of caravan	Yes	Yes	Yes (£49,000)	Yes (£45,500)	Yes (£55,800)	Yes (£42,800)	Yes (£35,900)

[a] This figure reflects an increase in referrals from other agencies during the second half of 2002.

The Scots' Charitable Society of Boston, Massachusetts

By William Budde, MS, FSA Scot.

'May this Society Subsist so Long as Charity Shall be a Virtue'

On 6 January 1657 twenty-eight 'Scottish men' signed the 'Laws Rules and Orders of the Poor Boxes Society' in Boston, New England and formed the Scots' Charitable Society. The founders stated that '… our benevolence is for the releefe of our selves being Scottishmen or for any of the Scottish nation whome we may see cause to helpe.'[1] Almost 350 years later this dedication to benevolent acts continues to guide the work of the Scots' Charitable Society of Boston.

In 1841, when its members marched in the Boston funeral procession in honour of President Harrison, the society was recognised as the oldest charitable society in the United States. Among the Boston organisations that marched, only the Ancient and Honorable Artillery Company, founded in 1638, was older. The next oldest Boston society was the Irish Charitable Society which was founded in 1737.[2] Today the Boston society remains the country's oldest charitable organisation.

FOUNDATION

It is likely that the society was founded in part to assist a specific group of destitute Scots – those captured by Oliver Cromwell at the Battle of Dunbar in 1650 and also those captured exactly one year later at the Battle of Worcester. Prisoners from both battles were sold as indentured servants to the London Company of Undertakers, a venture capital group in the city that had invested in the first successful iron works in the American colonies. Bound to these iron works at Lynn (now Saugus), in Massachusetts, most of the indentured Scots were required to complete seven years of labour for the company (a usual term

---

[1] Laws, Rules and Orders (1657) in *The Constitution and By-Laws of the Scots' Charitable Society of Boston, (Instituted 1657) with a list of members and officers, and many interesting extracts from the original records of the society,* Cambridge, MA, 1878, p. 25. Revisions made 1684 and 1770.

[2] Marshal's Notice: 'Funeral Ceremonies in Honor of President Harrison', *Daily Evening Transcript,* Boston, MA, April 19, 1841, vol. XII, no. 3292.

for such indentures). It seems that these began to expire between 1655 and 1657 when the Scots' Charitable Society was formed.[3]

While the needs of the indentured Scots may have been a factor in the founding of the New England society, it was modelled on a similar organisation in London, England. This earlier organisation was the Scottish Hospital of the Foundation of King Charles II, also known as the Royal Scottish Corporation. Like the New England society, the London charity was founded to aid Scotsmen and Scotswomen who found themselves in need while in the English capital. The New England society recognized this historic tie in several ways, including references found in revisions of their 'Rules and Orders'. Both groups used what was referred to as a 'Scots Box' to hold the monies that they had collected. The Scots Box in London was in operation at least by 1613, while the Boston box society is first referenced in 1657. The initial reference to the London box in the Boston society's records appeared in its 'Rules and Orders' of 1684 which alluded to earlier charitable societies of Scots as 'good workes of this kind ... in their severall societies, and also of our Countriemen at home & abroad in many parts of the world'.

The 1770 revision of the 'Rules and Orders' is more specific in recognition of the Boston society's relationship to the London charity. These stated that the Boston Scots were 'particularly encouraged by the success of a Scot's Society in London of the same nature, established by Charter of King Charles 2^d,' and followed its 'laudable Example'. The rules also stated that contributions from natives of any nation were welcome, 'noting that some persons of other Nations having generously contributed to the Scot's charity in London'.

EARLY CRISES

The Scots' Charitable Society faced two serious threats during its history. The earliest challenge nearly killed off the fledgling society which seemed to have run short of members and money by 1665. In 1770 it was recorded in the order book that the society floundered due to 'the Smallness of their Number, Lowness of their Stock, & Mismanagement of some Private trustees', and the society seems to have been dormant from 1665 until 1684 when a new set of Rules and Orders were written. Only four of the original 27 founders returned with the reorganisation of 1684 – Alexander Simsom, James Webster, William Gibson and James Ingles.[4] The membership crisis is seen in the clearest light when the list of new members from 1657 to 1665 is compared with a similar list from 1684 to 1693. In the first eight years only 34 new members were admitted,

---

[3] Hartley, E. N., *Ironworks on the Saugus*, University of Oklahoma Press, 1957.

[4] Scots' Charitable Society, Microfilm Roll No. 79-1, reel I, vol. 1: Minutes, rules, receipts, quarterly payments of the Society, 1657–1739; name index; on deposit at the New England Historic Genealogical Society, Boston, Massachusetts.

while 154 were admitted in the eight years between 1684 and 1692. Accounting and management practices were also addressed in the 1684 reorganisation. The treasurer was now obliged to invest the excess box monies in order to generate income from interest. Later, in the 1770 orders, the treasurer was also required to be bonded 'with sufficient Sureties in double Value of the Stock'.

The second serious challenge occurred during the Revolutionary War (the American War of Independence). After surviving the first crisis, which could be described as an organisational hiatus, the society faced a serious political issue. Membership was becoming deeply divided along party lines. Following the Boston Tea Party of 16 December 1773, minutes for a meeting held on 10 May the following year showed that members were aware of an uncertain future in Boston. At this meeting the membership voted to call in the outstanding money bonds issued by the society, and ten months later the society entrusted all of the 'Books, Bonds, Obligations, & Notes' and cash in hand to Andrew Cunningham, one of the joint treasurers. [5]

When the British evacuated Boston following the American siege in March 1776, the Loyalist members of the society took the books, bonds and records with them. This started a struggle for the assets that was not resolved until 1803, when the society passed a resolution thanking 'the Secretary for procuring the Books and Papers of the Society'. [6]

It appears that the delay in the return of the books was due to the unresolved problem about distribution of the society's assets. The Loyalist treasurer, Andrew Cunningham, proposed the dissolution of the Scots' Charitable Society. In a letter dated 1783 he insisted on an equal distribution of the assets to all members. [7] Cunningham also pointed out in another letter the following year that the majority of members had left Boston when the British evacuated the city: 'Therefore give me leave to inform you, that at the Evacuation of Boston by the British Troops, The Scotch Society's Books & Securities (but no cash) were legally in my hand, as an officer, & almost the whole of the members then quited the Town ordered me to take them'. At that point (1782) there may have been as few as twelve members of the society left in Boston. [7]

The return of the records and bonds was not resolved until the intervention of a Dr Danforth, a personal friend of Cunningham's. Correspondence between Cunningham and other members of the society remaining in Boston seems to be incomplete. However, one of the remaining letters offers an interesting insight into attitudes towards the Scots in Boston, or at least to Cunningham's own

[5] Minutes, 10 May 1774 and 29 March 1775, *Constitution and By-Laws*, 1878, p. 47.

[6] Meeting of 2 August 1803, *Constitution and By-Laws*, 1878, p. 47.

[7] Archibald Cunningham letters dated New York, 16 July 1783 and Shelburne (Nova Scotia), 23 July 1784, *Robert May Collection, 1771–1929*, Boston, MA, Massachusetts Historical Society Manuscript Collection.

perception of such attitudes. In a letter to John Scollay dated 14 August 1786, Cunningham comments on the application for incorporation filed with the Commonwealth of Massachusetts. He notes the historical mistrust towards the Scots and states that this is the reason for the limits in funds and membership imposed by the Commonwealth:[8]

> The authority that has given you Powers, are fearful of your acquiring too large a Fund, as they have confind the Society to the Annuall income of Two hundred pounds.~ but what appears more stricking to me their having a jealous eye, over you, is in restricting the number of members to one hundred, This is a convincing proof of [their] fears of the Scotch nation, and allows me to say, that [this is the] very reason that the Scotch Charitable Society could never obtain an act to Incorporate them before.

RULES AND ORDERS

The early Scots' Charitable Society was governed by various revisions of its Rules and Orders. When the society was reorganised in 1684 the Rules and Orders were specifically revised to address the earlier mismanagement. The rules included the following:

- Two locks now protected the box holding the society's assets. The two keys each held by a separate member of the society.
- Monies for charitable purposes could only be disbursed with the consent of five members and once a ledger entry had recorded the transaction.
- Ledger entries had to include the name of the borrower, amount and date.
- Any loan over ten shillings required a bond to ensure repayment.
- Only the truly needy were to receive aid.
- Society funds were to be invested with interest; the interest to be used to support its charitable works.
- Members of the society were not to benefit from the aid unless they had contributed, the exception being 'strangers of our natione that is cast in by a shipwreck or otherwayes'.

These were updated from time to time for clarification. In 1770 the purpose of the society was clearly identified as 'the Relief of the poor aged or infirm, helpless widows and orphans, indigent, Sick, the distress'd shipwreck'd, & to pay the charges of those who are desirous but not able to Transport themselves to their native Country'. The Rules and Orders, now referred to as the 'Constitution and By-laws', were last revised in 1992.[9]

---

[8] Letter from Cunningham to John Scollay dated Shelburne (Nova Scotia), August 14, 1786, *Robert May Collection.*

[9] *Constitution and By-Laws of the Scots' Charitable Society of Boston as of October 23, 1992.*

MEMBERSHIP AND EARLY MEETING PLACES

Membership of the society, which stood at 155 in March 2003, has always been open to native Scots or those descending from a Scottish ancestor. Other than Scottish heritage the only other serious requirement, stipulated since 1684, ensured that 'no profane or dissleut person, or openly scandalous shall have any part or portione herein, or be a member of the Society'. There seem to have been two reasons for including this rule – the first was the early mismanagement of the Poor Box funds, and the second seems to have been the English, and later Scottish, practice of using forced indentures or banishment to the colonies as an alternative punishment for convicted criminals. New England was spared the worst excesses of this practice for a number of reasons, but the southern plantations complained bitterly about the practice of sending felons across the ocean. For example, in 1670 Virginia made it clear that they did not want any more prisoners, especially dangerous felons, and forbade 'any person trading hither to bring in and land any gaol birds or others who, for notorious offenses, have deserved to dye in England'.[10]

Admission to the society was, and still is, by invitation. The general procedure, established by 1684, requires potential members to be invited to learn of the 'designe of our charity'. If the society felt the individual was qualified to become a member, he was invited to join by the presentation of one of the 'keyes … that theirby he may be encouraged to concur with you in this charitable work'. The procedure was refined by 1770 when potential members had to apply to the managers at their meeting and recommendations were made to the general membership at its next quarterly meeting.

Early meeting places included some of the most notable taverns and coffee houses of Old Boston – the Green Dragon, the Exchange Coffee House, and the Bakers' Arms. The Bakers' Arms was located on Union Street as early as 1665 and was one of the first homes to the Scots' Charitable Society. The Green Dragon Tavern became the new meeting place for the society about 1690. This tavern, also located on Union Street in Boston, was 'probably the counterpart of the Green Dragon in Bishopgate Street, London'. It appears that several society members were active innkeepers in early Boston. These include William Browne of the Castle Tavern about 1674; both John Borland of the Star Tavern at the corner of Hanover and Union Streets and possibly Duncan McFarland of the Cromwell's Head Tavern on School Street in 1692 (Borland was also a supporter of the Scots Corporation in London sometime after 1714); and William Douglass and his sister, Catherine Kerr (whose husband John was a society

---

[10] Peter Wilson Coldham, *Bonded Passengers to America, Volume I: History of Transportation 1615–1775, A Study from Original and Hitherto Unused Sources of Some Human and Some Inhuman Aspects of Transportation and Sale of English Convicts*, Baltimore, MD, 1983.

member) of the Green Dragon, by about 1771. When John Kerr died, his widow then sold the tavern to the St. Andrew's Lodge of Freemasons in 1771. Members of the lodge were active participants in the Boston Tea Party protest against the Stamp Act.[11] Given the strong loyalist feelings of many Scots' Charitable Society members and the strong feelings of the St. Andrews' Lodge membership for independence, the atmosphere at the Green Dragon must have been tense at times.

CHARITABLE AID

Since the founding of the society in 1657 the types of charity provided have changed little. Aid to the sick and indigent, assistance with transportation home, burials and housing have been its cornerstones. The newest form of aid has been the granting of scholarships for undergraduate college education. However, not all aid was available in the society's earliest days. From the first meeting, aid to the poor was the stated goal of the society. This was clarified in 1684 when it was agreed in the Rules and Orders that monies collected for the box and the aid of the poor were not to be spent for any other purpose than to increase the charity of the society. Members were 'to spend nothing out of the sd box lest it be reputed sacriledge'. The only monies to be used for charitable purposes in 1770 were limited to the interest earned on the society's investments. Monies for the fund were collected through quarterly membership dues and donations solicited from residents and travellers.

The early assistance focused on monetary support. As time passed and experience grew, the society began to expand the type of assistance. One of the first recorded statements of this expansion reported the inclusion of sickness and burial assistance in 1685. Three years later the membership approved the purchase of a 'morcloath' for the good of the company. Use of the mort cloth for funerals was to be free for those in need.[12] Undoubtedly burial and mort cloth benefits were necessitated by the epidemics that ebbed and flowed through the early colony. Boston was spared the outbreak of bubonic plague that struck London in 1665, but measles and smallpox were two recurrent epidemics (measles in 1657 and 1687 and smallpox in 1648–49 and 1677–78).[13] It appears that the early society assisted with burials of Scottish descendants at various

---

[11] On the night of the Tea Party, the scheduled St. Andrew's Lodge meeting was 'adjourned for lack of attendance ... public matters being of greater importance'. See Samuel Adams Drake, *Old Boston Taverns and Tavern Clubs*, Boston, MA, 1917, p. 90.

[12] Minutes, 9 June, 1685 and 12 Nov, 1688, *Constitution and By-Laws*.

[13] Sept–Oct, 1997, Newsletter – Genealogical Society of Santa Cruz County; the original sources are listed as: *Ancestors West*, SSBCGS, Vol 20, No 1, Fall 1993, South Bend (IN) Area Genealogical Society; and John Duffy, *Epidemics in Colonial America,* Louisiana State University Press, 1953 on the web at *http://www.geocities.com/Heartland/Acres/7241*. See also *Encyclopedia of Plague and Pestilence*, George C. Kohn, editor, Facts On File, 1995 at *http://www.rootsweb.com/~wijuneau/Epidemics.htm*.

cemeteries in the Boston area. Between 1831 and 1847 the society purchased a burial plot in Mount Auburn Cemetery in Cambridge, Massachusetts. The cemetery opened in 1831 as the first garden cemetery in America.[14] The Scots' Charitable Society lot consists of 1,819 square feet surrounded by a cast-iron fence, erected in 1847, with a statue of St. Andrew. In 1890 the Mount Auburn lot was filled with a total of 216 internments. The society then purchased a new lot in Mount Hope Cemetery.

In 1872 the Scots' Charitable Society purchased what was known as the Scots' Temporary Home at 77 Camden Street, Boston. This building apparently replaced an earlier one located at 73 Concord Street. The home was discontinued in 1892 for several reasons, which, according to the society, included a lack of need and changes in the United States immigration laws.[15]

Today the society is focused on providing academic scholarships and limited financial support for individuals and families in need. It also sponsors an annual Scottish culture event in the form of a yearly St. Andrew's Dinner held in November and open to the public.

---

[14] Mount Auburn Cemetery, December 20, 2002 on the *Let's Go Boston* web site at www.letsgo.com/BOS/04-sights-678.

[15] *Constitution and By-Laws,* 1896, p. 156–59.

Notes on Sources

ABBREVIATIONS

Explanations of abbreviations in the text footnotes, chapter reference notes and the bibliography are as follows:

A. Porter – Andrew Porter, *Victorian Shipping, Business and Imperial Policy*
BL – British Library, London
Cameron – George G. Cameron, *The Scots Kirk*
Chronicles (vol) – *The Chronicles of the Caledonian Society* (nine volumes)
Clark – Peter Clark, *A History of British Clubs and Societies*
Colley – Linda Colley, *Britons*
Coward – Barry Coward, *The Stuart Age*
CSPD – *Calendar of State Papers Domestic* (especially those of James I, edited by M. A. E. Green and R. Lemon)
Devine – Tom Devine, *The Scottish Nation*
DNB – *Dictionary of National Biography*
EIC – East India Company
Greve – John Greve, *Homelessness in London*
Guildhall – Department of Manuscripts, Guildhall Library, London
IOR – India Office Records, Oriental and India Office Collections, British Library, London
McMenemey – W. H. McMenemey, 'The Hospital Movement of the Eighteenth Century and its Development', in F. N. L. Poynter, ed., *The Evolution of Hospitals in Britain*
Magnusson – Magnus Magnusson, *Scotland*
Mayhew – Henry Mayhew, *London Labour and the London Poor*
M. D. George – M. Dorothy George, *London Life in the Eighteenth Century*
Merchants' Directory – *A Collection of Names of Merchants living in and about the City of London*
Mills and Oliver – Peter Mills and John Oliver, *Survey of Building Sites in the City of London after the Great Fire of 1666*
NA – National Archives, London (formerly the Public Record Office)
NEHGS – New England Historic Genealogical Society, Boston, USA
NLS – National Library of Scotland, Edinburgh
OIOC – Oriental and India Office Collections, British Library, London

R. Porter – Roy Porter, *A Social History of London*

RSC Archive – Royal Scottish Corporation Archive, King Street, London

Sahibs – Hilton Brown, *The Sahibs: The Life and Ways of the British in India as Recorded by Themselves*

Scots Corporation (date) – an early account of 'The Scottish Hospital of the Foundation of Charles II', periodically printed 1667–1815; also for 1874–75 and 1910–11 (see Select Bibliography for a list)

Smith – David L. Smith, *A History of the Modern British Isles*

Source Book – P. Meadows, *A Source Book of London History*

SP – State Papers

Steel – Tom Steel, *Scotland's Story*

Stow – John Stow, *A Survey of London*

URCHS – United Reformed Church History Society, Cambridge

Waddington – Keir Waddington, *Charity and the London Hospitals*

War Diary – George Macaulay, *War Diary of a London Scot*

Weavers – Alfred Plummer, *The London Weavers' Company, 1600–1970*

Wellcome – Wellcome Library for the History and Understanding of Medicine, London

CHAPTER REFERENCES

The notes below provide a general guide to the source material for each chapter, and further references can also be found within the book's text. Although they are not intended to be an exhaustive set of academic references, I hope they will be useful enough to those interested in looking deeper into the history of the Corporation or Scots in London. A select bibliography of primary and secondary sources cited in the text and notes has also been provided; suggestions for further reading have also been included.

As a brief overview, a number of works are worth highlighting for having been particularly helpful in the writing of this charity history, both specifically and generally. Information from general histories of Stuart, Georgian, Victorian and twentieth-century Britain have provided historical context and background, especially the revised edition of Barry Coward's *The Stuart Age*, together with David L Smith's *A History of the Modern British Isles, 1603–1707* and *British History, 1815–1906* by Norman McCord. London histories have, of course, been especially useful. Roy Porter's *A Social History of London* has been much used. Jerry White's *London in the Twentieth Century* also provided later background and Ben Weinreb's and Christopher Hibbert's *London Encyclopaedia* gave more exact detail on city places. Tom Devine's *The Scottish Nation, 1700–2000* and *Scotland's Story* by Tom Steel have been particularly helpful in providing a Scots dimension. M. Dorothy George's study is invaluable on the harshness of life in eighteenth-century London. Samuel Pepys's *Diary* and James Boswell's *Life of Johnson* give contemporary views of the city society of the seventeenth and eighteenth centuries in which the Scots found themselves; Christopher Hibbert's *George III* is also a readable royal view of the late eighteenth and early nineteenth centuries. Material for the general history of London's hospitals was found in F. N. L. Poynter, ed., *The Evolution of Hospitals in Britain*, particularly the chapter by W. H. McMenemey, 'The Hospital Movement of the Eighteenth Century and its Development'. Also useful for background to earlier hospitals and philanthropy is a study of later Victorian developments by Dr Keir Waddington, *Charity and the London Hospitals*. Jonathan Rose's *The Intellectual Life of the British Working Classes* includes a number of interesting examples of mutual improvement amongst literary working (and weaving) Scots in the twentieth century. A serious survey of homelessness in the late twentieth century, with a useful historical introduction, is provided by John Greve's *Homelessness in London*, published in 1971. For today's charity and voluntary-sector management, the website of the Charity Commissioners, that of the Directory for Social Change, and a published guide entitled *Managing without Profit* by Mike Hudson, provide essential information and further reading.

More specifically, Peter Clark's *British Clubs and Societies, 1580–1800* was a most useful starting point for a study of the Royal Scottish Corporation's history and provides many comparisons with other similar institutions of the time. Very useful too was George G. Cameron's *The Scots Kirk in London*, and this book gives an overview of a Scottish religious community in the city whose story in many ways parallels that of the charity; it additionally has a chapter focusing on the Scots Box and Corporation. A particularly enlightening source for the charity's management and activities, as well as the business and social side of Scots life in London from 1837 to 1967, is the series of nine volumes entitled *The Chronicles of the Caledonian Society of London*.

Above all, the original petition, warrant and charter of 1665 of the Scottish Hospital of the Foundation of Charles II and the subsequent petitions and charters for 1676 and 1775 in the National Archives have provided the earliest original source material. Records in the archive of the Royal Scottish Corporation (mainly since 1877) have added much new detail for the study of the charity's nineteenth- and twentieth-century activities, administration, cases and donors. All older records were lost in the fire of November 1877 but valuable, albeit sporadic, contemporary annual reports published by the Corporation from 1677 to 1911 survive in the British Library and a number of other UK and US library collections (a list of these early accounts can be seen in the Select Bibliography below).

INTRODUCTION. Information about the Royal Scottish Corporation in the twenty-first century can be found on its website at *www.royalscottishcorporation.org.uk* and also in its latest annual report. Alien surveys and occupations of city Scots in the 1560s come from an edited version of the returns preserved in the National Archives in London, published in R. E. G. Kirk and E. F. Kirk's *Returns of Aliens Dwelling in the City and Suburbs of London from the Reign of Henry VIII to that of James I*; the number of Flemings in London is given in *Scots Corporation*, 1794, referring to a government survey of 1567. R. Porter's Scotland Yard footnote reference can be found in his *Social History of London*.

CHAPTER 1. The references to pilgrim badges can be found in B. Spencer, *London's Medieval Pilgrim Badges*. I am grateful to Robert Baldwin for this reference, for the William Dunbar poetic connections and also for the information about the Scottish sailors with secret Thames knowledge. I am also grateful to him for emphasising the charitable pressure in the late years of Henry VIII's reign. The Stow reference comes from his *Survey of London*, a contemporary view of the city. Background and further references for Thames trading, the city's size and population and early 'community government' come from R. Porter; he also writes that there was 'a remarkable social cohesion', providing for 'broad-based prosperity'. More information on livery companies ('the civic cement') was also provided by R. Porter and Weavers.

CHAPTER 2. Information for this chapter is based especially on Coward and Smith, together with Steel. The footnote reference showing Scottish ships' cargoes for 27 March (first and third) and 28 July (second) in 1619 comes from the Exchequer King's Remembrancer Port Books, Bundle 22, No. 9, the Customer's Book, extracted and transcribed in an appendix to Astrid Friis, *Alderman Cockayne's Project and the Cloth Trade*. Information on London immigrants and crowds can be found in R. Porter and Stow.

CHAPTER 3. Coward, Smith and Steel again provided useful background for James I and his court; so too Magnusson. The Bedford family tree can be seen in Gladys Scott Thomson's *The Russells in Bloomsbury*, and the first account of the duke donating property to the charity can be found in *Scots Corporation*, 1738. The reference to James I writing to Cecil about patronage is a quote from G. P. V. Akrigg, ed., *Letters of King James*, quoted by Coward; Smith gives some idea of the numbers of recipients. Many cases of Scots patronage can be seen listed in the *CSPD* for James I from 1603 to 1605. Information on William Alexander comes from his entry in the *DNB*, from Thomas H. MacGrail's *Sir William Alexander, first Earl of Stirling: a biographical study* and from T. Crowther Gordon's chapter on him in *Four Notable Scots*; Alexander can also be found amongst the list of Stuart secretaries of state compiled by Smith. For the Shakespearean footnote references see E. K. Chambers, *The Elizabethan Stage* and also *An index of characters in English Printed Drama to the Restoration* by Berger and Bradford. Futher information on William Alexander, and references to Sir Robert Aiton, William Murray and other 'poets of Scoto-Britaine' in London and their output, can be found in Helena Mennie Shire's interesting *Song, Dance and Poetry at the Court of Scotland under James VI*. Henry, Earl of Stirling, appears in the list of masters of the Corporation (see Appendix 2) and Sir John Aiton's name occurs in the earliest list of benefactors from 1665, for which see *Scots Corporation*, 1714.

CHAPTER 4. George Heriot's story can be read in the *Merchants' Directory*, in *Chronicles*, Vol. 3, and in Steel and Magnusson. Further information will be found in Bruce Lenman's article, 'Jacobean Goldsmiths – Jewellers as Credit Creators: the Cases of James Mossman, James Cockie and George Heriot', in *Scottish Historical Review*, 74(2). Examples of David Ramsay's clocks are on display at the Clockmakers' Company museum at the entrance to the Guildhall Library (with a small amount of biographical information) and also at the British Museum's clock gallery. Further detail for this chapter comes from Coward and Smith.

CHAPTER 5. Background for Charles I and the Civil War/Commonwealth period comes from Smith and Steel. I am grateful to Professor Allan Macinnes and Dr Keith Surridge for additional comments on the Covenanting Movement and explaining this generally complicated period. The order for the exile of Scots from Commonwealth London in 1650 can be found in *Thomason Tracts*: 158, E.1061/13. The source for the prisoners marching through London after the Battle of Worcester is *Thomason Tracts*: 98, E.641 (14). The New England information comes from Bill Budde's history of the Scots' Charitable Society of Boston; for an overview and references, see Appendix 5. Further useful background concerning the city lives of Scots during the Civil War period can be found in Dagmar Freist's 1997 study, *Governed by Opinion: Politics, Religion and the Dynamics of Communication in Stuart London, 1637–1645*: 'In 1639 a hectic enquiry was launched by the Privy Council concerning the whereabouts of Scots in London and 'disorderly gatherings' which were liable to breed seditious talks. The justices of the peace duly returned notes listing the various dwellings of Scots, among other places at Blackfriars, Lombard Street, Rood Lane and Mill Dock'. The NA references for these lists are: SP 16/418. 85 (1639); SP 16/420. 154–54i (1639); and SP 16/421.26 (1639). In addition the lord mayor of the City of London and the justices for Middlesex were ordered to suppress certain victualling houses after the councillors had provided them with information, for example, for the Scottish Arms at Millbank (see SP 16/418.37, SP 16/418.99, SP 16/418.42 and SP 16/418.55); see also Peter Clark's *The English Alehouse*.

CHAPTER 6. References to medieval hospitals and their administration come from *Memoranda, References, and Documents relating to the Royal Hospitals of the City of London* and McMemeney. Information on the poor relief acts comes also from McMemeney and Coward. R. Porter and Coward provide information on London's population and the city's poverty during this period; the 1609 quote from Robert Gray is from Coward. The letter from Sir William Waad to Robert Cecil and the plague proclamation can be found listed in *CSPD*, James I for 10 and 17 September 1603. Other information on the 1603/4 plague can be found in *Source Book*, which quotes the plague order from 1593 (probably still standing ten years later), found in Lansdowne MSS, Malone Society, *Collections*, I, ii, xix.

CHAPTER 7. The apprehension of idle Scots in 1615 is detailed in two letters, both dated 11 April, found listed in Rogers, ed., *The Earl of Stirling's Register of Royal Letters*. The Weavers' Company poor box is referenced in Guildhall, Weavers MS 4646 f. 290; and a picture of the box in 1666 can be seen amongst the plates of *Weavers*. See Bill Budde's historical overview at Appendix 5 for the box used by the Boston society. References for the Scots Box can be found inside the box itself (at the charity's King Street offices) and in the 1923 court minutes in the RSC Archive. I am grateful to Norman Macleod, a past welfare visitor of the Corporation, for the thought of the symbolism and lasting intention of the box.

CHAPTER 8. R. Porter and Coward provide background for this chapter. The earliest historical account of the Scots Box turning into the Corporation is dated 1677 and is printed in *An Answer to Letters written by Scotish Gentlemen in His Majesties Dominions beyond the Seas*. The Scots Artificers' petition of 11 April 1665 and accompanying comments by the Attorney General can be found at NA SP 29/117, the royal warrant of 31 May is at NA SP 44/22 and the letters patent of 30 June are at NA C66/3076/24663. I am grateful to Robert Baldwin for further explaining the issue for Scots of taking the oaths of Allegiance and Supremacy and its relevance in the charter. Details of the life of John Maitland, Earl of Lauderdale, can be found in his entry in the *DNB*. The waiving of fees for the second charter was mentioned by William Maitland in his *History of London*. The Duke of Bedford's property gift has already been cited. The charity's Covent Garden tavern meetings are referenced in the chronology compiled for *Scots Corporation*,1874

CHAPTER 9. The references for the Scots petition, the letters patent and James Kynneir have already been mentioned in the notes on the previous chapter. The earliest list of charity benefactors, showing the names of Kynneir and his wife, and the amounts they gave, can be found in *Scots Corporation*, 1714. The list of masters at Appendix 2 shows Kynneir's dates of office. His will of 1681 can be found at the Family Records Centre in London. Background on the Weavers Company and its administration can be found in *Weavers*, plus also the reference to 'Kynneir's Gift'. Kynneir's name is listed several times in the records of the company at Guildhall, Weavers – especially MS 04710 (a 1679 indenture for the gift of 'James Kennier'), and more on the gift and his executors' payment at MS 4646, f.113, 118, 125, 254b-255 (here Kynneir also called 'Kymier'); MS 4657A/1 under 'Denton' and MS 4660 ('James Kenier'). The Weavers' silver cup can be seen as one of the plates in *Weavers*. James Kynneir's silver cup and later cover can be seen at King Street. Extracts from Robert Kirk's account of his visit to London in 1689 are published in Cameron, quoting from the original journal in Edinburgh University Library at MS La.III.545. The *London Encyclopaedia* is helpful for finding places that might have been Miles Lane, so too *The A-Z of Restoration London* (ed. by Hyde, Fisher and Cline).

CHAPTER 10. The story of the hospital during the plague and fire is taken from the first account of the charity, *Scots Corporation*, 1677. Quotes from the Reverend T. Vincent's plague book can be found in *Source Book*. W. G. Bell's *The Great Plague* is also useful for background. Information on Bunhill Fields can be found in *London Encyclopaedia* and by visiting the Finsbury site. Samuel Pepys records the busy city in his diary on 5 January 1666 and his eye-witness fire accounts on 26 and 28 September 1666. R. Porter gives useful background; so too does Mills and Oliver.

CHAPTER 11. The Corporation story of its rebuilding after the fire is continued in *Scots Corporation*, 1677; also the granting of its second charter towards the end of the chapter. Further information on Katherine Austen comes from her memoranda at the BL's Department of Manuscripts in Add. 4454; her Christ's Hospital will request can be found at Guildhall MS 12894 – 19 September 1683, the £40 payable every 20 years on lease granted by her to the Scots Corporation now to be paid to Christ's Hospital, 'the money to be devoted to the setting up in trade of eight young men who have served their apprenticeships well'. The Nova Scotia baronies sold are mentioned in the chronology of the *Scots Corporation*, 1874 and by Cameron, but no further reference has been found. The layout of the foundations for the Corporation can be discovered in Mills and Oliver – Vol. 3 records the entry on 30 July for 'Newen', Vol. 5 the Fitch reference and Vol. 1 the 1673 reference. A 'Mr Calwell, Colemans Alley' is also listed in the *Merchants' Directory* and is possibly Andrew Caldwell, the first signature on the Scottish Hospital petition. Caldwell was treasurer of the new Scottish Hospital and Corporation in 1665 and became master in 1672 (see also Appendix 2). John Ewing, one of the first eight governors of 1665, is mentioned in the same merchants' list as contactable (with Benjamin Norington) 'at the Angell and Crown in Lumbard str.' The second petition and letters patent or charter can be seen at NA SP 44/46 and C 66/3181/24663. Kynneir's will has been referenced above. The names of Kynneir and James Foulis appear as London merchants in the listings of the National Archives of Scotland's *Register of Deeds* from 1661–1685, and Foulis is described in some of these as a 'merchant taylor'. This is confirmed by the list of freemen of the Merchant Taylors' Company (Guildhall MS 324) where a 'James Fowlis' was admitted by redemption and granted freedom on 21 August 1667 and livery on 9 February 1682. He was removed from the livery by order of James II in October 1687. The Drummond reference to Foulis's character can be found in the Stowe Collection at the Huntington Library, California, ST 58/ Vol 1, Incoming Brydges correspondence, 1700–1707: Amsterdam, 30 March 1707, Drummond to James Brydges; (I am grateful to Dr Andrew Mackillop for this reference). Mourning rings from 1658 to 1732, like those prescribed by Kynneir in his will, can be seen at the British Museum – hoops of enamelled gold depict skeletons and *momento mori* symbols derived from Bills of Mortality; inside the ring was engraved the name, age and date of death of the person remembered. Information and quotes on the early eighteenth-century hospitals in London can be found in Waddington. An account of the French Protestant hospital was printed in 1741 as *Ordres et Reglement pour la Corporation des Gouverneur et Directeurs de l'Hôpital pour les Pauvres François Protestants, et leurs Descendants residents dans la Grande Bretagne*. The comparison comes from Waddington, who also quotes Lindsay Granshaw, 'The rise of the modern hospital in Britain', in Andrew Wear, ed., *Medicine in Society: Historical Essays*.

CHAPTER 12. Background on Scotland, emigration and union comes from Devine. The Darien story is told by Devine and can also be read about in more detail in John Prebble's *Darien Disaster*. Additional background on the 1707 union is from Smith. Colley also has useful views on Scots emigration. Scottish traditions and their invention can be found in Hugh Trevor-Roper's chapter, 'The invention of tradition: The highland tradition in Scotland', in E. J. Hobsbawm and T. O. Ranger, eds, *The Invention of Tradition*. Sir John Clerk of Penicuik's Saxon-speaking Scots are mentioned by Devine. R. Porter provides London background, and for its imports and exports he quotes from Colquhoun's *Treatise on the Commerce and Police of the River Thames*. *Source Book* provides the quote on the South Sea Company's collapse. Macky's daily rituals and coffee-house information are also from R. Porter. The transcription of an interview with Hazel Forsyth of the Museum of London (for the Corporation's video in 2000) provided further detail about the 'dish', as well as Scots coffee and chocolate houses. Boswell's quote is from his *London Journal*. The account of the mail delivery is from *Source Book*, quoting Delauney's *Present State of London*; further London background, citizens and the customs official quote are again from R. Porter. M. D. George provided other useful background, especially information on the better-educated boys, more immigrant workers (quoting Burrington, a contemporary writer) and Dr Bland's Scottish patients.

CHAPTER 13. Devine provides Scottish background for this chapter. *Source Book* has Penicuik's and the Duke of Queensberry's arrival in London. See also Trevelyan's *Select Documents for Queen Anne's Reign*. See Boswell's *Life of Johnson* for 'the noblest prospect' (6 July 1763) and his first meeting with Johnson in London (16 May 1763). His explanation of Johnson's prejudice is found in his *Journal of a Tour to the Hebrides*, edited by Peter Levi. The footnote reference for George Macaulay's French views can be found in *War Diary*, 17 January 1797. See also Christopher Hibbert's *George III* and Colley for more background on London's 'Scotophobia' during this period.

CHAPTER 14. Livery company information and background on London's poor come from R. Porter. Further information on poverty and the references to friendly societies come from M. D. George. Clark provides further information on free-masons and clubs and societies generally. Dr Cheyne's donation is recorded in *Scots Corporation*, 1730. *War Diary* (25 May 1798) provides information about city foot-pads. The sorting of sick poor, workhouses, hospitals, illness in poverty and Scots doctors is well covered by McMenemy, and he also provides Johnson's comment on hospitals, quoting from *The Idler*, no. 4, 6 May 1758. The Corporation's fundraising events are listed in the chronology in *Scots Corporation*, 1874. As for footnote references, the 'imposters' are mentioned in the annual account of the Corporation for 1910/11 (at NLS; see list of these accounts in the Select Bibliography below); the 'scroungers' are referred to in a loose note in the minutes of the committee of management for 30 June, 1938 (RSC Archive).

CHAPTER 15. An apothecary is first noted in *Scots Corporation*, 1730 (several more apothecaries and many other medical men occur in later lists). Curing J. Garland is mentioned in the charity chronology of *Scots Corporation*, 1874 and these accounts, plus that for 1738, provide further information about the closure of the Scots workhouse and its earlier, and later, administration. The Association Oath Roll for the charity can still be seen at NA C/213/169/103415. Extracts from Robert Kirk's diary are again quoted by Cameron. Charity case numbers can be found listed in a detailed table in *Scots Corporation*, 1815. The archive of Coutts Bank in London still has the Corporation's bank accounts for 1755–56 and later accounts for 1802–04. The petition for the 1775 charter can be found at NA PC 1/3074, while the charter at C66/3757 was recorded by the NA as missing when last asked for. (Printed leaflets produced after the 1974 charter show a summary of the 1775 act and are available from the Corporation on request.) A further account of the Scots Corporation in 1779 is attached to Henry Hunter's printed sermon, found at BL. 4457.aaa.52. The Wellcome papers on the Scottish Hospital for 1781–1799 (MS 6825/1 & 2) provide the financial detail of the charity's assets. References to James Dobie's festival dinners can be found in *Scots Corporation*, 1807 and 1815.

CHAPTER 16. Further ways of raising money for the charity are recorded in the chronology of *Scots Corporation*, 1874. Donors are recorded in all these Scots Corporation accounts (see the list below). Robert Kirk is quoted by Cameron. The last subscribing member is noted in the chronology of *Scots Corporation*, 1874. Hunter's sermon has been referenced above. Information for the life of James Graham, third Duke of Montrose, comes from his *DNB* entry. Donations up to 1815 were printed in *Scots Corporation*, 1815.

CHAPTER 17. Background for the Scottish kirk comes from Devine, and also from Olive Checkland's *Philanthropy in Victorian Scotland*. The strict Scots stories are told by Macnee in *Chronicles*, Vol. 1. Help for the Kinloch Bequest from the English clergy in 1830 is described in a letter preserved at Wellcome MS 6825/3b. Information for Gilbert Burnet comes from his *DNB* entry, the *Scots Corporation*, 1714 and 1874; his *History of his Own Time*, Vol. VI is the source for the quote.

CHAPTER 18. References in this chapter come especially from Cameron, quoting other useful sources on the history of Presbyterians in London (especially Walter Wilson, *History of Dissenting Churches and Meeting Houses in London, Westminster and Southwark*) and the records of the Scots Churches held at the United Reformed Church Society in Cambridge (with many now at the London Metropolitan Archive). Donor lists from these records can be usefully compared with those of the *Scots Corporation*, 1714 and 1730. I am grateful to Tracey Earl, Archivist at Coutts Bank, for the information on Thomas Coutts. Further references to Henry Hunter come from his *DNB* entry, and the *Gentleman's Magazine* (Vol. lxxii, pt. ii); his sermon to the Corporation has already been cited. The Reverend Dr Manuel probably owned and wrote up the minute book of the Edinburgh branch of the Scottish Hospital (and Corporation) in 1830–34 and his earlier sermon is noted in the chronology of *Scots Corporation*, 1874. References to Cumming's educational classes come from K. Macleod Black's *The Scots Churches in England*, and are quoted in the guide to Crown Court Church by Louise Luke. Sermons of the Corporation are listed in the account of the charity for 1910/11. Further information on later ministers comes from the minutes of the Corporation's committee of management in the RSC Archive and the guide to Crown Court. The Reverend Stanley Hood's memories can be found in the video transcript of an interview held in 2000 and include the fact that the church used the Corporation's hall.

CHAPTER 19. The Caledonian Society's help for schools is recorded in Chronicles (Vol. 1), so too that of the Royal Highland School Society. Robert Kirk is quoted by Cameron. Edward Drummond's printed sermon on the poor can be found at BL

4175.b.105(2) and in the NLS. *Scots Corporation*, 1805 provides information on the 1801 idea for schools. The 1810 school appeal signed by the EIC directors is preserved in the RSC Archive. Directories for East India/Bengal, in the reading room of the Oriental and India Office Collections of the BL, provide information on William Kinloch and Fairlie, Gilmore and Co. (see references for Chapters 22 and 23 below for more details). Similar Madras directories show the local charities in that city. Forbes's donation is recorded in the chronology of *Scots Corporation*, 1874. I am grateful to Allan Macinnes for the footnote information on the West Indies money sent back for the academy movement in Scotland. Information on the school fund comes from the court minutes of 30 November 1878 in the RSC Archive. References to Bowers can similarly be found in the committee of management minutes, so too the list of mothers. The later training of children in 1911 and the Canadian emigration project are described in the 1910–11 annual account of the charity and in the dinner speech for 1911, also published in the same volume. The encouragement of widows is shown in the minutes of the committee of management, RSC Archive. Information about Donald Currie comes from A. Porter, who quotes the *Jubilee Memorial of Canning Street Presbyterian Church Liverpool (1846–1896)*. The Hood and Cruickshank interviews for the charity video in 2000 give their thoughts about the characteristics of Scots. The introduction to Greve provides the *savoir faire* quote. Alan Robertson's annual report for 1989 recorded the charity's educational help for that year. A history of the Caledonian Asylum and its directors for 1815 can be found in the same BL tracts series as *Scots Corporation*, 1815. A 1996 publication by the Trust (*Life and Times at the Caley*) provides a recent overview and reproduces many photographs. Information about John Galt came from *Chronicles*, Vol. 2, and James Thomson's life story is told in a biography by Tom Leonard, *Places of the Mind: The Life and Work of James Thomson ('BV')* – also reviewed in the *Financial Times* of 20 February 1993; other information on Thomson and his famous poem was taken from *The Penguin Book of Victorian Verse*, edited by Daniel Karlin. Corporation and Caledonian Asylum references are from the Corporation's court minutes of 4 October 1878 and later annual reports of the Corporation for the years mentioned (all in the RSC Archive).

CHAPTER 20. Scots in Europe are mentioned in general by Devine and their names specifically show up as donors in *Scots Corporation*, 1714 and 1730, including those from the West Indies. Background on fighting Scots also comes from Devine and I am grateful to Dr Andrew Mackillop for confirming further information about the numbers of Scots in the British Army during this period. Nova Scotia baronetcies are mentioned by Cameron, and other Canadian emigration detail can be found in the 1910–11 account of the charity. Boston information comes from Bill Budde's research written up in Appendix 5, information on William Trent was found in Charles P. Keith's *Chronicles of Pennsylvania*, and his name was listed in the records of the Scots Charitable Society, Vols 1–6, Index T, microfilm roll 79–1, held at the library of the New England Historic Genealogical Society, Boston. Other background on the Scots diaspora can be found throughout the nine volumes of the *Chronicles*, including the stories of Australian Scots (Vol. 4). The brief lives of some EIC recruits and the money they sent back are currently being researched by Santhi Hejeebu of Iowa University and I am grateful to her for this detail.

CHAPTER 21. More information on Scots in India can be found in Devine and Colley. The records of the Company of Scotland Trading to Africa and the Indies have been preserved in the archives of the Royal Bank of Scotland, and early printed information will be found in the BL and the NLS. Two publications by G. P. Insh provide more detail on the company and its founders (who included a few Corporation Scots). The life of the adventurer Hamilton is recorded in his *DNB* entry (which also quotes the *Gentleman's Magazine* death notice), and the donor Hamilton can be seen listed in *Scots Corporation*, 1714, 1730 and Appendix 2. Further information on the Scots writers in Bengal has been provided by Andrew Mackillop, and he has found an Alexander Hamilton at IOR B/58: Court Book for 10 June 1724; in this Hamilton revealed that by staying to defend the EIC's Gambroon factory in Persia he had lost out on selling his commodities at Surat. For information on nabobs I am grateful for the views of Tillman Nechtman of the University of Southern California. The survivor's story comes from an extract in *Sahibs*. For much biographical detail on East India Company directors (and the Scots amongst them), see a bound but unpublished Edinburgh PhD of 1977 by James Parker entitled 'The directors of the East India Company, 1754–1790,' available in the reading room of the OIOC (at OIR354.5P). Also for an unpublished typescript history of Scots in India, see the papers of Francis Mudie in the OIOC at MSS EUR F164/62; Mudie also produced a useful card index to the Scots he found (F164/61). The story of several Scots and Mountstuart Elphinstone reading in bed can be found in Mudie's typescript. Devine writes of the power of Clan Campbell in India, and more can be discovered about the family in Major Sir Duncan Campbell's *Record of the Clan Campbell in the HEIC, 1600–1858*. Hastings's donation is recorded in a list of benefactors, *Scots Corporation*, 1815. *The Cornchest for Scotland* remembers Sir Walter Scott's quote, and another exhibition guide by Colin Cavers, *Relations – Scotland & India*, provides additional information, including references to Alexander Duff, taken from A. A. Millar, *Alexander Duff of India*. The stories of the St Andrew's Day dinner in Calcutta (from the *Calcutta Gazette* of 3 December 1812) and the baby's funeral carriage have been taken from extracts in *Sahibs*.

CHAPTERS 22 and 23. Information on the Kinloch Bequest comes from records of this additional charity, also kept in the RSC Archive – especially the minute books, which also provide details of late nineteenth-century cases. A section on Kinloch in the 1864 Corporation bye-laws provides an overview of the bequest; high-level reports and financial accounts are covered in the court minutes and annual reports of the Corporation itself. Further information on William Kinloch and his employers was found amongst the 'List of European Inhabitants in Bengal' in the *East India Register and Directory*, 1803–12 (available in the reading room of the OIOC); these show that he was a merchant by 1811 and assistant to Fairlie Gilmore and Co. up to 1809–10; Kinloch's departure from India aboard the *Lady Lushington* is revealed in the *Original Calcutta Annual Directory and Calendar* for 1813. Further details on this ship and her crew for the season 1812–13 can be seen in Charles Hardy's *Register of Ships of the HEIC, 1760–1833;* this book also gives an idea of the length of voyages. The ship's log of the *Lady Lushington*, at IOR L/MAR/B/221, provides the details of the voyage and William Kinloch's death on board. Kinloch's will was found in the IOR – Bengal Wills, 1813, L/AG/34/29/25, and an inventory of his estate in 1814, Vol. 1, L/AG/34/27/49. Further information on military doctors and military and naval hospitals can be found in *The Evolution of Hospitals in Britain*, edited by F. N. L. Poynter. The *Madras Almanac* in the OIOC reading room shows hospitals and asylums in that city. A Major William Kinloch of the 1st Battalion, 57th Regiment was doing Calcutta duty in 1814 (according to the Calcutta directory cited above). The letter of William Fraser, chairman of the Kinloch committee, can be found at Wellcome MS 6825/3a and provides much detail of the bequest's administration. References to Robert Auld, Robert Johnson and the footnote about Manuel's stamps are also to be found in the minute book of the 'Edinburgh Branch' in the RSC Archive. I am grateful to trustee John Brown for more recent information on the Kinloch Bequest.

CHAPTER 24. Military donations to the Corporation show up in various lists of bene-factors, especially in *Scots Corporation*, 1714. Clyde is remembered by the old Highland soldier in Mayhew and by the Caledonian Society in their *Chronicles*, Vol. 2. The death of Lord Wantage was remembered in the court minutes, RSC Archive. The St Andrew's Day dinner of 1873 is reported in *Scots Corporation*, 1874 and the letter about the Ashanti War can be found in the Duke of Portland's papers, Nottingham-shire Archives, DD 4P/62/108/60. Boer War demands and the death of the Earl of Airlie can be found in the court and committee of management minutes, RSC Archive. The activities of the Federated Council of Scottish Associations can be found detailed in Chronicles, Vol. 2. A small body of records of the St Andrew's Scottish Soldiers Club is among the Corporation's records in the RSC Archive. Detail on the London Scottish Regiment comes from its website (www.london scottishregt.com" *www.londonscottishregt.com*) and from *Chronicles*. Douglas Robertson gave me his views on the charity's relationship with the regiment and John Clemence kindly provided me with more military detail and added further information on the relationship between the regiment and the Corporation.

CHAPTER 25. Devine provided this chapter's Scottish background; other sources include A. Porter, also quoting Thomas Chalmers, *The Application of Christianity to the Commercial and Ordinary Affairs of Life*. Mayhew's social survey of London's poor provides the Highlander quote, while R. Porter gives the numbers of Londoners, and the Sydney Webb and 'contemporary writer' (C. F. G. Masterman) quotes. The Edinburgh minute book is in the RSC Archive. The greater London numbers come from Greve.

CHAPTER 26. Figures for capital donations come from *Leigh's New Picture of London*, published in 1819: 'the several livery companies of the city of London distribute above 75,000*l.* annually in charities: and there is a multitude of institutions, of a less prominent nature than the foregoing, which render the total of charitable donations immense. The sums annually expended in the metropolis for charitable purposes, independently of the private relief given to individuals, have been estimated at 850,000*l.*' Other background for this chapter comes especially from R. Porter and Mayhew. Further information on the 'benevolent economy' comes from Waddington. McCord also provides additional detail. The hospital report referenced is the 'First Report of the Select Committee of the House of Lords on Metropolitan Hospitals', *Parliamentary Papers* 1890, xvi, 3–4.

CHAPTER 27. R. Porter describes the lives of London's citizens, and Hepburn's account of incoming Scots is from *Chronicles*, Vol. 1. Mayhew provides further information on the daily lives of a few poorer Scots. J. M. Barrie's *What Every Woman Knows*, Act 2 gives his quote. J. Seton Ritchie's comment is recorded by Hepburn in *Chronicles*, Vol. 1. For early twentieth-century numbers of Scots in London, see White's study of the city and government census detail more recently released for 1991 and 2001 at *www.statistics. gov.uk*. Dr Forbes's Scotswoman story is retold in *Chronicles*, Vol. 2 so too the 'Imprived Englishman' quip. Reith's views and Turnbull's footnote request were reported in *Chronicles*, Vol. 3, and Boyne's parliamentary record in *Chronicles*, Vol. 8. Businessman Don Cruickshank and Corporation trustee Jimmy Brown were interviewed for the charity's promotional video in 2000. I am grateful to Spencer Neil, publisher of the *New Statesman*, for permission to publish this extract from Doug Cameron's article.

CHAPTER 28. The 1831 St Andrew's Day dinner ticket's contents were recorded in the Edinburgh minute book in the RSC Archive, so too the deliberations about hosting a dinner in the Scottish city. Also in the RSC Archive is the 1820 letter from the Duke of Clarence (presented by governor John Douglas in 1927). Details of later nineteenth-century festival dinners come from the chronology and 1873–74 dinner reports in *Scots Corporation*, 1874. Details of guests can be found in the minutes of the committee of management for 11 November 1885, and other details in various further minutes of the committee. J. M. Barrie's attendance at the Corporation's dinner in 1928 was reported and pictured by the *Glasgow Herald* on 1 December. Annual reports record the congratulations and donations read out at later festival dinners, including pictures of the float. Files exist in the RSC Archive covering the arrangements for these dinners for most years (except during the war) from 1938 onwards. The Scottish concerts are remembered in Chronicles, Vol. 1, and early balls are recorded in the chronology of *Scots Corporation*, 1874 and by David Hepburn in *Chronicles*, Vol. 2. Later balls and the help of the Duke of Atholl and Simon Campbell Orde are remembered in committee minutes and annual reports in the RSC Archive. So too are the Mansion House dinners, which also generated special files.

CHAPTER 29. The late nineteenth-century minutes of the committee of management in the RSC Archive provide rental detail for the hall, and ledgers record its later hirings. Post-war dances are fondly remembered by Jimmy Macintosh, a Corporation pensioner, and dancing classes were recalled in the c. 1999 newsletter of the

Scottish Country Dance Society. A number of files of other Scottish associations in London are held in the RSC Archive and were compiled by Norman Macleod, a past welfare visitor at the Corporation. I am grateful to Douglas Robertson and John Brown for information on the Harrow Caledonians and the Clan Donnachaidh. The Highland Society's history by Alistair Campbell provides an interesting account of the activities of this institution. I am grateful to Jimmy Brown, Corporation trustee and Highland Society member, for further detail, especially concerning the society's more recent charity activities. M. F. Gray's Caledonian history and other early information were recorded by David Hepburn in *Chronicles*, Vol. 1. William Will remembered them again in *Chronicles*, Vol. 3. The request to host the Scots Lodge was recorded in the minutes of the committee of management in 1889–90. I am grateful to Ian Menzies, the chairman of the Caledonian Club, and to club member and Corporation trustee Jimmy Brown, for information on the Caledonian Club. Paul Varney was interviewed by Vanessa Masterson of *Business am* on 15 July 2002, and further detail about the club can be found in its newsletter and on its website at *www.caledonian-club.org.uk*. The Corporation's annual report for 1995–96 records the footnote details of Lord Forte's bequest, and the PR Committee of the charity has provided a more recent update.

CHAPTER 30. The circular of 1831 is quoted in the Edinburgh branch minute book in the RSC Archive. *Chronicles*, Vol. 2 records the Caledonian Society's promotion of the Highlands and Islands during the 1840s famine. For the East India Company's concern for Scots, see OIOC IOR H/740, 'Donations granted by the EIC Company Court of Directors and Secretary of State for India, 1792–1859'. The 1873 dinner is in the *Scots Corporation*, 1874 and the table of pensioners' ages was recorded in the court minutes of 30 November 1878, now in the RSC Archive; so too are further cases, all quoted from the minutes of the committee of management. Thomas Montcrieff's recollections from the 1920s are published in *Chronicles*, Vol. 3; so too his memories of charity centenarians and the provision of relief for 7,000 unemployed men. Further cases and state benefit developments for the rest of the chapter are recorded in the Corporation's court minutes and later annual reports.

CHAPTER 31. The minutes of the Edinburgh branch record the 1832–33 cost figures. Most of the information for this chapter has been taken from the financial accounts in the court minutes and later annual reports in the RSC Archive. The daily spend calculation comes from the charity's newsletter for Spring 1994. I am grateful to trustee John Brown for providing me with a copy of his note to the chairman of the committee of management and the welfare sub-committee, dated 9 January 1998.

CHAPTER 32. The original 12 miles from the 'Scots' Hall' was extended to a 35-mile radius, probably during the later 1960s, although not formally recorded until the 1974 charter. Dr Johnson's Charing Cross statement was recorded by Boswell in his *Life of Johnson* for 2 April 1775. Kinloch Bequest administration is recorded in the letters of 1830 at Wellcome MS 6825/3a and b and the Edinburgh Branch minute book states that Scots returning home were given certificates by the London charity.

The Corporation's minutes of the committee of management, case books and annual reports all periodically record how other cases were referred, accepted and managed. I am grateful for further information on the welfare sub-committee and cases panel from trustee John Brown and welfare manager Ruth Smith (whose thoughts are also recorded in a transcription of her interview for the promotional video, made in 2000).

CHAPTER 33. Most of this chapter comes from the court minutes, the committee of management minutes and later annual reports of the charity; the promotional video and interviews with Ruth Smith and the charity's pensioners, during several pensioners' lunches, were also very useful. The 1972 diary of Hilary Gibson is also in the RSC Archive.

CHAPTER 34. William Miller's note on 'Casual Relief' is a loose paper in the committee of management minutes for 30 June 1938. Much of the rest of this chapter comes from later Corporation annual reports and the book on homelessness by Greve.

CHAPTER 35. Railways and steamer companies are mentioned in the committee of management minutes for 14 February, 11 April and 7 July 1883. Montcrieff's boys dressed for Australia are mentioned by him in his reminiscences published in *Chronicles*, Vol 2. Australia cases show up in the charity's new cases book for March 1923, cases numbered 46–49. The pensioners' holiday is reported in the annual report for that year.

CHAPTER 36. The source for this chapter is the minute book of 'The Edinburgh Branch of the Scottish Hospital of London', now in the RSC Archive but which had probably belonged to the Reverend Dr William Manuel of Morningside (and his name is written on the book's paper cover). The book had been written up after the formation of the branch's management committee and (as was recorded) was first shown at a committee meeting in Edinburgh on 30 November 1832. The details of Scots being sent home in the 1850s were reported in NA HO 45/4060. The footnote on the dates of Robert Auld's secretaryship is based on a letter from him in 1819 to Nicholas Carlisle, secretary of the Charity Commissioners, at NA CHAR 2/162. The papers of Robert Stevenson at the National Library of Scotland may throw more light on his charity involvement; certainly according to Bella Bathurst, in her book, *The Lighthouse Stevensons*, he would have understood the plight of poor Scots, being 'terrified of being unable to provide for himself and family, haunted by the remembrance of poverty and sliding back down the social ladder to oblivion'.

CHAPTER 37. The quote about the post-fire 'gloom' comes from *Chronicles*, Vol 1. The newspapers of the day reported the story and the *Illustrated London News* pictured it. Much of the rest of this chapter comes from the court and committee of management minutes of the time. The builder's contract still exists in the RSC Archives. W. G. Bell in his book, *Unknown London*, calls Crane Court 'a dingy passage', and adds a picture (not reproduced here) to show how dingy it looked.

CHAPTERS 38, 39, 40. The sources for these three chapters are the by-laws of 1863 and 1883, the committee minutes, court minutes and annual reports of the Corporation. Interviews with Douglas Robertson and John Brown have provided further detail. The 1862 fraud case was investigated and conclusions were written up in the *Report of the Select Committee of General Enquiry into the Affairs of the Scottish Hospital, appointed 29 January 1862*; this printed account is now available at NLS: 6.1502(27) (a charity secretary called Major Adair was recorded as speaking to the Caledonian Society during the 1840s in *Chronicles*, Vol. 1).

CHAPTER 41. Late nineteenth-century donors are recorded in the list of benefactors in *Scots Corporation*, 1874. The 1910–11 account of the Corporation also provides a full list of early twentieth-century benefactors. The court and committee minutes record pensions created and legacies bequeathed. Later donations were reported in the charity's annual reports. A wooden panel listing pensions can also be seen in the annexe to the 'Court Room' at the Corporation's King Street offices.

CHAPTER 42. The Corporation's illuminated addresses to Queen Victoria still survive at the National Archives, London. Other royal references are from *Scots Corporation*, 1815 and 1874. The court and committee minutes record other royal correspondence. The Queen Mother's words in 1975 are quoted by Cameron.

CHAPTER 43. David Hepburn's reminiscences are written up in *Chronicles*, Vol. 1; so too is his father's account of his arrival in London. The death of his sister is recorded in the committee minutes of 6 September 1922. The names of patronesses are found in all accounts of the charity, starting with *Scots Corporation*, 1714. The minutes of the committee of management record grieving widows' letters. Dr Charles Hogg's story is reported in *Chronicles*, Vol. 1; so too that of Dr Forbes. Sir Donald Currie's life has been studied by A. Porter and his legacy is recorded in the 1911 list of benefactors. Later Scots are remembered by the charity in the minutes of the committee of management that record their deaths or by William Will in his addresses to the Caledonian Society, reported in *Chronicles*, Vols 3–9. Douglas Robertson and John Brown were also kind enough to tell me how they came to take an interest in the charity. The unknown governor who died in 1923 was remembered in *Chronicles*, Vol. 3.

EPILOGUE. I am grateful to Wylie White, Willie Docherty and the charity's committee of management for allowing me access to the reports of the charity's new strategy. I am also grateful to Douglas Robertson and John Brown for further comments, as well as to the strategy's consultants, Keith Smith and Nigel Goldie of the Compass Partnership. John Brown also provided me with a copy of the Eggington Report from his own papers. The description of the King Street staircase is taken from *Scottish Field*, April 1977. The final poetic reference is from Robert Burns's 'Auld Lang Syne', quoted in the account of the 1873 festival dinner in *Scots Corporation*, 1874.

Select Bibliography

PRIMARY SOURCES

The Royal Scottish Corporation Archive (RSC Archive)

The archive of the Royal Scottish Corporation dates mainly from 1877 onwards, with very few earlier records. It is currently held at the Corporation's King Street offices (with a small number of items at the charity's bank). Arrangements are currently being made to place the archive on permanent loan at the Department of Manuscripts of the Guildhall Library, Corporation of London. A survey was undertaken in October 2002 by Gavin Henderson of the British Records Association and Justine Taylor; this survey listing is available from the Corporation on request.

Aside from the new strategy papers of 2002–2003, the principal records in the RSC Archive used for this history can be outlined as follows:

School appeal letter, 3 April 1810
Letter from William, Duke of Clarence, 1820
'Edinburgh Branch of the Scottish Hospital,' minute book, 1830–34
Court minutes, 1877–2002
Committee of management minutes (including sub-committee minutes), 1877–2002
List of presidents and honorary officials, 1877–1976 (also list of masters and presidents since 1665 on wooden panel in the 'Court Room' at King Street)
Summary of charter of re-incorporation and bye-laws, 1864, 1883, 1974
Royal charter, 1974
Annual reports, c. 1950s-2002
New cases books, 1922–1974
Financial and stock investment ledgers and papers, 1877–2002
Festival dinner files, speeches and donations, 1906–98
Caledonian Ball correspondence, 1950–69
Subscriber and donor lists, legacies and bequests, other papers, c. 1903–1986 (see also pensions listed on wooden panel in the 'Court Room' annex)
Deeds relating to Crane Court/Fetter Lane (mainly employment, property and building contracts), 18th, 19th and early 20th centuries
Property, building and insurance files, c. 1930s-80s
Welfare visitor files and diary, 1970s-80s

Miscellaneous administrative correspondence, mainly 20th century

Promotional video made in 2000, with copy of footage transcripts (from Story Shop)

Records of the Kinloch Bequest – minutes 1877–2002, applications for allowances 1950s-60s, 1913 scheme amendments, financial ledgers, annual reports and correspondence

Records of the St Andrew's Scottish Soldiers' Club, 1915–2002

Various correspondence files, historical accounts and brochures of a number of London Scottish associations, including the Caledonian Society of London, the London Caithness and London Perthshire Associations, and the Saltire Society, c. 1960s-1990s.

Other archive collections researched

UK

Bank of England Archives, London

(Royal Scottish Corporation bank accounts found to be no longer surviving after a search by the bank's archivist)

Various papers *re* William Paterson and the establishment of the Bank of England (on display in the Bank's museum)

British Library, London – Department of Manuscripts

Katherine Austen Collecteana: essays, meditations, memoranda, etc., in prose and verse by Katherine Austen, 'Book M', 1664–1668, Add. 4454

Papers of Sir Julius Caesar – 'Memorial of William Bruce, LL.D., to the Duke of Lenox, touching the hospitals for Scottishmen in Germany', 2 October 1603, Add. 12503

British Library, London – Oriental and India Office Collections (for Scots in the EIC (East India Company)

India Office Records: indexes to Bengal wills (Kinloch:1813 – L/AG/34/29/25); inventories of deceased estates (Kinloch:1814 vol. 1 – L/AG/34/27/49); ship's log for the *Lady Lushington* at L/MAR/B/221; Military Department, Madras – L/MIL/17/3; H/740 for EIC 1840 famine donations.

European Manuscripts: for papers of various EIC directors, especially David Scott's patronage book and letter book at MSS EUR D1087 (more papers of Scott are in IOR H728); papers of Francis Mudie (Indian Civil Service), MSS EUR F164/ 61 (index cards) and 62 ('Scots in India' draft); Minto papers, MSS EUR D1105 and D1226 (with information on a Madras army mutiny, 1809–10)

Corporation of London, Guildhall Library, Department of Manuscripts

Extract from will of widow Katherine Austen, 19 September 1683: £40 rent paid by the Corporation every 20 years to go to Christ's Hospital – MS 12894. Weavers' Company records: especially freedom registers, 1600–47 – MS 4656/ 1; alphabetical lists of freemen (and apprentices), 1661–94, A-K and L-Z – MS 4657A/1 and 2; apprentice binding books, 1655 – MS 4657B; alphabetical lists of apprentices, 1665–70 – MS 4660; court minutes, 1610–1765 – MS 4655/1–16; account and memorandum book, 1489–1741 – MS 4646 (B2) (ff. 251–25 'schedule of deeds and other papers relating to charity estates in

Shoreditch and Holborn,' and 244B and 255A has an indenture between the Weavers Company and James Kynneir for a gift, plus accounts of gift payments in 1679/80 and executor's final payment in 1684/85; also general Weavers' poor box payments); trust estate and property ledger – MS 4648 D concerning almshouses in Shoreditch etc, 1817–27; register of receipts and disbursements, 1670–83; Renter Bailiff's accounts of receipts and payments at meetings of court, Vol. 1 A 1672–73 – MS 4649 B; book of printed forms and subscribers to rebuilding hall after fire, 1669–70 – MS 4658; Kynneir's gift can also seen in the indenture of 24 November 1679 at MS 04710. Merchant Taylors' Company records: List of freemen, MS324.

Corporation of London, Record Office
City Lands Committee Box 5, no.18: leases and other deeds relating to property of the Scottish Hospital in Blackfriars, 1773, 1782, 1786 and 1788; see also Box 22, no. 22 for lease, 1774
Plan and elevation of the Scots Hall, Blackfriars, c.1780s?
City freedom records, 1495–1649, 1668–9 and admission papers 1681–1940

Coutts Bank, London – Archives
Bank accounts for the Scottish Hospital, 1755–56 and 1802–04

Edinburgh University Library, Department of Manuscripts
Robert Kirk, minister of Aberfoyle: description of his London visit during the printing of the Gaelic bible, 1689 – MS La.III.545

Family Records Centre, London
Will of James Kynneir, 1681/1683

National Archives, London
Scots artificers' petition, 11 April 1665, and comments – SP 29/117
Royal warrant to issue Scottish Hospital letters patent, 31 May 1665 – SP 44/22
Scottish Hospital petition for second charter, 1676 – SP 44/46
Scottish Hospital petition for third charter, 1775 – PC 1/3074
Letters Patent (charters) – C66/3076/24663 (1665), C 66/3181/24663 (1676), C66/3757 (1775) (?missing)
Association Oath Roll for Scottish Hospital, 1696 – C/213/169/103415
Orphan case of Sarah McGhie v William Fynmore – TS 11/385
Charity Commissioners – Char 3/12, /38 and /57; Char 2/162 (1819 charity commission enquiry into Scottish Hospital)
Hearth tax return for St Anne's parish, Blackfriars (missing)
Listings of dwelling places of Scots in 1639 – SP 16/418.85, SP 16/420.154–54i, SP 16/421.26; Scottish taverns in 1639 – SP 16/418.37, SP 16/418.99, SP 16/418.42 and SP 16/418.55
Poor law board: sending Scots and Irish home, 1852 – HO/45/4060
Verse, 'To a' the fowk in London town', a tailor's advertisement in Scots dialect (*J Conn's address to the public*, London 1790) – PC 1/3127

National Archives of Scotland, Edinburgh (formerly Scottish Record Office)
Deeds 1661–1685 of James Kinneir and James Foulis

National Library of Scotland, Edinburgh
Papers of the Highland Society of London – Acc. 10615; no. 87, letters to A. C.

Read, includes Royal Scottish Corporation papers, 1933–51
Papers of the Scots Club, London (for Scottish-born journalists), 1911–1961 – Acc. 9943
Nottinghamshire County Record Office, Nottingham
Duke of Portland archive – DD 4P/62/109/60
School of Oriental and African Studies, University of London
Papers of Sir William MacKinnon
Scottish Record Office – see National Archives of Scotland
Wellcome Library for the History and Understanding of Medicine, London
Scottish Hospital papers: 'progressive state of funds', 1781–1799 – MS 6825/1–2; Kinloch Bequest letters, 2 and 8 March 1830 – MS 6825/3a and b

USA

Huntington Library, California
Stowe Collection ST 58/vol 1
Massachusetts Historical Society, Boston, Mass.
Robert May Collection, 1771–1929
New England Historic Genealogical Society, Boston, Mass.
Records of the Scots' Charitable Society of Boston; also microfilm roll 79–1

More research in the above and other archive collections remains to be done, including the private papers of the charity's more important benefactors.

A Note on the Records of the Scots Churches in London and the United Reformed Church History Society

George Cameron used the archives of the United Reformed Church Society's records for his book *The Scots Kirk in London* but much of the material has now been relocated. I am grateful to Margaret Thompson, Administrator at the URCHS, for the following information and references:

The accession numbers for the congregational records now at the London Metropolitan Archives were separated into 'London North' and 'London South'.

The 'London North,' churches were:
Islington (Chadwell St/River Terrace/Colebrooke Row) LMA/4369
London Wall, LMA/4356 (Baptismal Register, 1822–1836 only)
Marylebone, LMA/4365 (includes Swallow Street from 1734)
Regent Square, LMA/4358 (includes Cross Street, Hatton Garden Register 1826; the paucity of Regent Square's records results from damage to the building by a V2 bomb in 1945)
Shakespeare's Walk, LMA/4347 (Baptismal Register, 1820–23 only)
Oxenden, LMA/4323 (may not be relevant as it was a Secession Church but there is material from 1786)

The 'London South' churches included:
Lambeth Verulam LMA/4399 (Baptismal Register only, 1831–35)
Woolwich LMA/4385 (Baptismal Register only, 1822–26)

More Woolwich records were deposited by the continuing URC congregation with the local archive centre for Woolwich. Baptismal Registers from Crown Court (1831–35), Swallow Street (1821–37) and Wells Street (1753–1875) are at the City of Westminster Archives (Accession no 2210). The one for St Andrew's, Vincent Street is at the Bancroft Library in Tower Hamlets. The records for Founders Hall were sent to the Guildhall Library c. 1948. St Columba's church in Pont Street was destroyed in the Blitz and rebuilt.

The URCHS has retained the manuscript volumes of the Scots Presbytery in London from 1772 to 1843, and these can be consulted any weekday except Wednesday. Alternatively, names can be sent for checking against attendance. Other material at the URCHS now consists mainly of cuttings from various nineteenth-century Presbyterian periodicals.

SECONDARY SOURCES

Printed accounts of the Scottish Hospital and Corporation, 1677–1911

Various early histories and administrative overviews of the Corporation for periodic dates – from 1677 until 1815, and for 1874–75 and 1910–11 – exist in a number of research libraries. Most have been consulted for this history, notably those available in the Bodleian Library in Oxford, the National Library of Scotland in Edinburgh, and the British Library and the Guildhall Library in London. The following is a list of all the accounts I have found to date. The list includes the main UK sources for these accounts; other source references, marked '°', can be found via the *English Short-Title Catalogue* of early printed books, 1700–1801, available on CD-Rom or online via major research libraries. (Copies of a few of these early accounts were also listed in 1995 as being in the RSC Archive but were not found during the current archive survey.)

An answer to several letters written by Scotish Gentlemen in His Majesties Dominions beyond the Seas, to the Master and Governors of the Scots Corporation and Hospital in London, giving a true account of the erection of the said company, and its progress from the year 1664, to this present 1677, London 1677 (Source – NLS: multiple holdings) (This is an account written from experience ('we…'), possibly by James Kynneir after the granting of the second charter in 1676. It was printed when John Renney was master)

An answer to several letters written by Scots gentlemen in His Majesty's dominions beyond the seas, to the master and governors of the Scots Corporation and Hospital in London, giving a true account of the erection of the said company, and its progress from the year 1664, to this present 1710, London reprinted 1710 (Source – Columbia University, Teachers' College: K362.942.L85) (Not seen for this history; probably reprint of the 1677 overview, and likely to be a third-person account)

The original design, progress, and present state of the Scots Corporation at London, of the foundation of K. Charles II. To which is added, a list of the masters and treasurers,…, London 1714 (Sources – BL: 1391.b.59; NLS: 1.55 (3); Bodleian: Pamph. 322 (21); ° in North America; microfilm) (Has earliest list of benefactors)

The original design, progress, and present state of the Scots Corporation at London, of the foundation of K. Charles II. To which is added, a list of the masters and treasurers, as also of the benefactors, London 1718 (Sources – NLS: 1.573 (7); ° in North America)

The original design, progress, and present state of the Scots Corporation at London, of the foundation of K. Charles II. To which is added, a list of the masters and treasurers,..., London 1730 (Sources – NLS: ABS.3.85.54; Guildhall Library: A3.2.no. 64)

A summary of the rise, constitution and present state of the charitable foundation of King Charles the Second, commonly called The Scots Corporation in London, London 1738 (Sources: Bodleian: G.Pamph. 1809(7); NLS: APS.4.92.7; ° in North America)

A summary of the rise, constitution and present state of the charitable foundation of King Charles the Second, commonly called The Scots Corporation in London, London 1756 (Sources – Bodleian: 117(22); ° other British Isles, 'unverified'; microfilm)

A summary of the rise, constitution and present state of the charitable foundation of King Charles the Second, commonly called The Scots Corporation in London, London 1761 (Sources – BL: 8282.dd.32; Guildhall Library: Pam 5645; ° microfilm)

A summary of the rise, constitution and present state of the charitable foundation of King Charles the Second, commonly called The Scots Corporation in London, London 1766 (Sources – BL: 8282.dd.29 (missing pp. 9–10); ° in North America)

A short account of the institution, progress and present state of the Scottish Corporation in London, of the foundation of King Charles II. anno 1665. Re-incorporated by King George III. Anno 1775. With the by-laws,...and an alphabetical list of the benefactors taken from the registers,..., London 1777 (Source – BL: 1502/328(30))

An account of the institution, progress and present state of the Scottish Corporation in London, of the foundation of King Charles II. anno 1665 and 1676... With an alphabetical list of governors taken from the registers, London 1783 (Sources – BL: 1502/328(6); ° in North America)

Scottish hospital, Crane-Court, Fleet-Street, published by order. Anno Domini MDCCLXXXVI. A list of the officers and governors of the Scottish Corporation of the foundation of King Charles the Second, Anno 1665 and 1676. Re-incorporated Anno MDCCLXXV..., London 1786 (Sources – Bodleian: Gough Lond. 42(14) and Gough Lond. 266(9a))

Scottish hospital and Corporation in London, of the foundation of King Charles the Second, Anno Dom. 1665 and 1676. Re-incorporated by King George the Third, Anno 1775.... The Scottish hospital is a charitable institution for the relief of industrious and deserving poor persons,...in and about the cities of London and Westminster, born in Scotland, or of Scots parents,...; docket title: '1792. A brief account of the institution and nature of the Scottish hospital, of the government thereof, and the number of poor persons relieved for one year, from St Andrew's day, 1791 to St Andrew's day, 1792', London 1792 (Source – Bodleian: Gough Lond. 42(15))

Concise view of the Scottish Corporation in London, London 1794(?) (Source – Bodleian: Gough Lond. 42(5)) (This account includes a picturesque history of Anglo-Scottish relations for the first time)

Concise view of the Scottish Corporation in London, London 1796 (Sources – BL: 816.k.5.(12); ° in North America)

In pursuance of a resolution of a late General Quarterly Court of the presidents, vice-presidents, treasurer, and governors, of the Scottish Hospital and Corporation, at which was taken into consideration the great loss annually sustained by the institution, from the various avocations, and other unavoidable causes which occurred, to prevent the noblemen and gentlemen connected by birth, property, or other ties with North-Britain…from associating with their fellow countrymen, at the Spring meetings of the Society; and referred it to a committee of Governors then appointed to deliberate and determine on the best method of making this misfortune to the charity known to such Noblemen and Gentlemen, and to devise a remedy for the same…, London 1797 (Source – Bodleian: Gough Lond. 272(20)12)

Scottish hospital and Corporation in London, of the foundation of King Charles the Second, anno Dom. 1665 and 1666 (sic). *Re-incorporated by King George the Third, anno 1775, …The Scottish hospital is a charitable institution for industrious and deserving poor persons,…in and about the cities of London and Westminster, born in Scotland, or of Scots parents,…*; docket title: '…and the number of poor persons relieved from St Andrew's day 1796, to St Andrew's Day 1797', London 1797 (Source – Bodleian: Gough Lond. 53(73))

An account of the institution, progress and present state of the Scottish Corporation in London, of the foundation of King Charles the Second,…and established at the hospital in Crane Court, Fleet-Steet. To which is affixed, a list of officers, governors, and patronesses. London 1797 (Source – NLS: 3.2834(7))

An account of the institution, progress and present state of the Scottish Corporation in London, of the foundation of King Charles the Second, … and established at the hospital in Crane Court, Fleet-Steet. To which is affixed, a list of officers, governors, and patronesses, London 1799 (Source – Library & Information Services, Department of Health, London) (Not seen for this history)

An account of the institution, progress and present state of the Scottish Corporation in London … To which is affixed a list of the officers and governors …, London 1801–12, 1815 (Sources – BL: 1806, 1807, 1809, 1812, 1815 – 8275.bb.8 (6) and 8275.d.3 (1); NLS: 1801 – multiple holdings, 1803 – 3.322, 1807 – Jac.iv.7/2.1 (8), 1808 – 6.769 (1), 1812 – 3.2838 (10))

An Account of the Scottish Corporation, with List of Benefactors and Patronesses, London 1874 and 1875 (Source – BL: 8275.aaa.17 (1))

List of Governors of The Royal Scottish Corporation 1910 and 1911, with a Brief History of the Corporation, London 1911 (Source – NLS: multiple holdings)

OTHER SECONDARY SOURCES

A Collection of the Names of the Merchants Living in and about the City of London, London 1677

A letter from a Scots factor at London, to a merchant in Edinburgh, concerning the proceeding of the House of Commons, to prevent the importation of wines and other goods from Scotland (17 April 1707), London 1707

A perfect list of the several persons residenters in Scotland who have subscribed as adventurers in the joynt-stock of the Company of Scotland Trading to Africa and the Indies: together with the respective sums which they have severally subscribed..., Edinburgh 1696, reprinted 1827

Ackroyd, Peter, *London: The Biography*, London 2001

Airy, Osmund, ed., *The Lauderdale Papers*, Westminster 1884

Akrigg, G. P. V., ed., *Letters of King James VI and I*, Berkeley and London 1984

Alexander, William, *An Encouragement to Colonies*, London 1624

Alison, William Pulteney, *Illustrations of the practical operation of the Scottish System of Management of the Poor* (from the *Quarterly Journal of the Statistical Society of London*), London 1840

Alvey, Norman, *From Chantry To Oxfam: A short history of Charities and Charity Legislation*, London 1996

An Account of Charity Schools lately erected in England, Wales and Ireland, London 1709

'An Act to Prohibit all Commerce & Traffique between England and Scotland, And Enjoyning the departure of Scots out of this Commonwealth', 2 August 1650, London 1650 (*Thomason Tracts*: 158, E.1061/13)

'Another Victory in Lancashire against the Scots ... and an account of the Scots prisoners which marched through the city on Saturday last', 12 September 1651, *Thomason Tracts*: E: 641/14

Anderson, Michael, *Approaches to the History of the Western Family, 1500–1914*, London 1992

Anglo-Scottish Year Book, London 1874

Bannister, Saxe, *The Writings of William Paterson*, London 1859

Barry, Jonathan and Jones, Colin, eds, *Medicine and Charity before the Welfare State*, London 1991

Bathurst, Bella, *The Lighthouse Stevensons*, London 1999

Beer, E. S. de, ed., *The Diary of John Evelyn*, Oxford 1955

Bell, W. G., *The Great Plague in London in 1665*, London 1951

——, *Unknown London*, London 1926

Berg, Jonas, and Lagercrantz, Bo, *Scots in Sweden*, Stockholm 1962

Berger, Thomas L. and Bradford, William C., *An Index of Characters in English Printed Drama to the Restoration*, Colorado 1975, 1998

Better, John, *The Story of the Irish Society*, London 1913

Booth, Charles, *Life and Labour of the People of London (1891–1902)*, London 1903

Boswell, James, *Boswell's London Journal*, ed. Frederick A. Pottle, London 1950

——, *Life of Johnson*, ed. Mowbray Morris, London 1903

Bradley, S. and Pevsner, N., eds, *London 1: The City of London*, London 1997

Brenner, Robert, *Merchants and Revolution: Commercial Change, Political Conflict and London Overseas Merchants, 1550–1653*, Princeton and Cambridge 1993

Brett, Edwina, *A Kind of Gentle Painting* (catalogue of an exhibition of Elizabethan court artists Nicholas Hilliard and Isaac Oliver), Edinburgh 1974

Brown, Hilton, *The Sahibs: The Life and Ways of the British in India as Recorded by Themselves*, London 1948

Brown, I. G., 'A new Scotch novel called Waverley: an appreciation from Madras', *Bibliothek*, xxii, 1998

Brown, K. M., *Kingdom or Province? Scotland and the Regal Union, 1603–1715*, London 1992

Bryant, G. J., *Scots in India in the eighteenth century*, London 1986

Burnet, Gilbert, *A History of his Own Time*, Oxford 1823

Burnet, Margaret Kennedy, Lady, *Letters from the Lady Margaret Kennedy to John, Duke of Lauderdale*, Edinburgh 1828

Cage, R. A., ed., *The Scots Abroad*, London 1985

Cain, Alex M., *The Cornchest for Scotland: Scots in India* (National Library of Scotland exhibition catalogue), Edinburgh 1986

Cameron, George G., *The Scots Kirk in London*, Oxford 1979

Campbell, Alastair, of Airds, Yr., *The Highland Society of London, 1778–1978*, London 1983

Campbell, Major Sir Duncan, *Record of the Clan Campbell in the HEIC, 1600–1858*, London 1925

Carlson, Stephen P., *The Scots at Hammersmith*, Saugus, Mass. 1979

Carlyle, Thomas, *Selected Writings*, ed. Alan Shelston, London 1986

Cavers, Colin, *Relations – Scotland & India* (Scottish Indian Arts Forum & Collins Gallery), Glasgow 1998

Chalmers, Thomas, *The Application of Christianity to the Commercial and Ordinary Affairs of Life*, Glasgow 1820

Chambers, E. K., *The Elizabethan Stage*, Oxford 1923

Charities: a framework for the future (Home Office), London 1989

Champion, J. A. I., ed., *Epidemic Disease in London*, London 1993

——, *London's Dreaded Visitation: the Social Geography of the Great Plague in 1665*, London 1995

Checkland, Olive, *Philanthropy in Victorian Scotland: Social Welfare and the Voluntary Principle*, Edinburgh 1980

Cheney, George, *The English Malady*, London 1733

Clark, Gregory, *The Charity Commission as a source in English economic history*, University of California (*www.econ.ucdavis.edu/faculty/gclark/papers/reh.pdf*) c. 1997

Cathy Come Home, film by Ken Loach, 1965

Clark, Peter, *British Clubs and Societies, 1580–1800: The Origins of an Associational World*, Oxford 2001

——, *The English Alehouse: a social history 1200–1830*, London 1983

Clout, H., ed., *The Times London History Atlas*, London 1991

Cobbett, William, *Rural Rides*, ed. George Woodcock, London 1987

Coldham, Peter Wilson, *Bonded Passengers to America, Volume 1: History of Transportation 1615–1775, A Study from Original and Hitherto Unused Sources of Some Human and Some Inhuman Aspects of Transportation and Sale of English Convicts*, Baltimore, MD, 1983

Colley, Linda, *Britons: Forging the Nation, 1707–1837*, London 1996

——, *Captives: Britain, Empire and the World, 1600–1850*, London 2002

Consitt, F., *The London Weavers Company*, Oxford 1933

Constitutions of Free and Accepted Masons ('first compiled by J. Anderson. A new edition, enlarged and brought down to 1784 … by J. Noorthouck'), London, 1784

Coward, Barry, *The Stuart Age: A History of England, 1603–1714*, London 1980, 1994

Creaton, Heather, *Bibliography of Printed Works on London History*, London 1994

Crofton, Eileen, *The Women of Royaumont: A Scottish Women's Hospital on the Western Front*, East Linton 1997

Crookshank, William, *The sin and danger of abusing eminent deliverances considered. In the substance of two sermons preach'd to the Scots Church in Swallow-street, Westminster, on the ninth of October, being the Thanksgiving day, for extinguishing the late unnatural rebellion. To which is added, an appendix, containing the sufferings of the Presbyterians in Scotland, from the Restoration to the Revolution*, London 1746

Dale, T. C., *The inhabitants of London in 1638*, London 1931

Davies, Godfrey, *The Early Stuarts, 1603–1660*, Oxford, 1949

——, and Keeler, Mary F., eds, *Bibliography of British History: Stuart Period, 1603–1714*, London 1970

Defoe, Daniel, *A Journal of the Plague Year*, ed. Paula R. Backsheider, New York 1992

——, *A Tour thro' the whole Island of Great Britaine*, London 1724

——, *Caledonia: a poem in honor of Scotland and the Scots Nation*, London 1707

Devine, T. M., *The Scottish Nation, 1700–2000*, London 1999

Dictionary of National Biography

Dobson, David, *Directory of Scottish Settlers in North America, 1625–1825*, Baltimore 1984–1993

——, *Directory of Scots banished to the American Plantations, 1650–1775*, Baltimore, 1984

Douglas's Peerage of Scotland, London and Edinburgh 1813

Drake, Samuel Adams, *Old Boston Taverns and Tavern Clubs*, Boston 1917

Drummond, George Hay, *On religious indifference. A sermon preached at the church of St Mary, Woolnoth, London April 22 1795; before the correspondent board in London of the Society in Scotland … for propagating Christian knowledge in the highlands and islands* ('And to be had at Scots-Hall and of the secretary'), London 1795

Drummond, Edward Auriol Hay, *On the religious education of the poor; a sermon preached at the Church of St Botolph, Bishopsgate, London, May 25th, 1800, before the Correspondent Board of the Society in Scotland ... for Propagating Christian Knowledge in the Highlands and Islands* ('And to be had at Scots-Hall and of the Secretary, Hoxton'), London 1800 (BL: 4175.b.105(2) and NLS: 1957.21(16))

Duncan, D., ed., *History of the Union of Scotland and England by Sir John Clerk of Penicuik*, Edinburgh 1993

Ellis, Hubert Dynes, *A Short Description of the Ancient Silver Plate of the Merchant Taylors' Company*, London 1892

Elmes, James, *A Topographical Dictionary of London*, London 1831

Erickson, Charlotte, *Invisible Immigrants: the adaptation of English and Scottish immigrants in nineteenth-century America*, Leicester 1972

Extracts from the accounts of the revels at court, in the reigns of Queen Elizabeth and King James I, London 1842

Farrington, Anthony, *Trading Places: the East India Company and Asia, 1600–1834*, London 1999, 2002

Fedosov, Dmitry, *The Caledonian Connection: Scotland-Russia ties*, Aberdeen 1996

Ferguson, W, *Scotland's Relations with England: A Survey to 1707*, Edinburgh 1977

Finlay, Richard J., 'The Burns Cult and Scottish Identity in the Nineteenth and Twentieth Centuries', in Simpson, Kenneth, ed., *Love and Liberty*, East Linton 1997

Fielding, Henry, *A Proposal for Making an Effectual Provision for the Poor*, London 1753

Freist, Dagmar, *Governed by Opinion: Politics, Religion and the Dynamics of Commonwealth Stuart London, 1637–1645*, New York 1997

Friis, Astrid, *Alderman Cockayne's Project and the Cloth Trade*, London 1917

Fry, Michael, *The Scottish Empire*, East Linton and Edinburgh 2002

Gadd, Ian, and Wallis, Patrick, eds, *Guilds, Society and Economy in London, 1450–1800*, London 2002

Garside, Patricia, 'London and the Home Counties', in F. M. L. Thompson, ed., *The Cambridge Social History of Britain, 1750–1950*, London 1990

Gauci, Paolo, *The Politics of Trade: the Overseas Merchants in State and Society, 1660–1720*, Oxford 2001

George, M. Dorothy, *London Life in the Eighteenth Century*, London, 1924, revised 1964

Gordon, T. Crowther, *Four Notable Scots*, Stirling 1960

Granshaw, Lindsay, 'The rise of the modern hospital in Britain', in Andrew Wear, ed., *Medicine in Society: Historical Essays*, Cambridge 1994

Gray, M., *Scots on the Move*, Dundee 1990

Green, M. A. E. and Lemon, R., eds, *Calendar of State Papers Domestic, Edward VI, Mary, Elizabeth and James I*, London 1856–1872

——, Daniell F. H. B., Bickley F., eds, *Calendar of State Papers Domestic, Charles II*, London 1860–1947

Greve, John, Page, Dilys and Greve, Stella, *Homelessness in London*, Edinburgh and London 1971

Hake, A. E., *Suffering London*, London 1892–3

Hamilton, Alexander, *A New Account of the East Indies: Being the Observations and Remarks of Capt. Alexander Hamilton who spent his time there from the Year 1688 to 1723*, Edinburgh 1728

Hardy, Charles, *Register of Ships of the HEIC, 1760–1833*, London 1835

Harris, Amelia I., and Clausen, Rosemary, *Social welfare for the elderly: A study in thirteen local authority areas in England, Wales and Scotland* (an enquiry carried out on behalf of the National Corporation for the Care of Old People and the Scottish Home and Health Department), London 1968

Hibbert, Christopher, *George III: A Personal History*, London 1999

Hills, John, ed., *The State of Welfare: the Welfare State in Britain since 1974*, Oxford 1990

Hobsbawm, E., 'Friendly Societies,' *Amateur Historian* iii (1956–8)

Hollen, Lynn, *The Solidarities of Strangers: the English Poor Laws and the People, 1700–1948*, Cambridge and New York, 1998

Hollingshead, J., *Ragged London*, London 1861

Hope, S. G., *Reflections of the London, Midland & Scottish Railway ...*, London 1980

Hope, Valerie, *The Worshipful Company of Weavers of the City of London*, London 1994

Hospital for French Protestants: Charter and Bylaws, London 1892

Howel, James, *Londinopolis*, London 1657

Houston, R. A. and Knox, W. W. J., *The New Penguin History of Scotland: From the Earliest Times to the Present Day*, London 2002

Hudson, Derek, and Luckhurst, Kenneth W., *The Royal Society of Arts, 1754–1954*, London 1954

Hudson, Mike, *Managing without Profit: The Art of Managing Third-Sector Organisations*, London 1999

Hume, David and Smollet, Tobias, *The History of England*, London 1825

Hunter, Henry, *A Sermon on the Duty of Compassion towards Poor Brethren preached before the Scots Corporation ...*, London 1779 (BL: 4475.aaa.52)

——, *A sermon preached Feb. 3, 1793, at the Scots Church, London Wall, on occasion of the trial, condemnation, and execution of Louis XVI ...*, London 1793

——, *A Brief History of the Society in Scotland for propagating Christian Knowledge*, London 1795

Hyde, Ralph; Fisher, John, and Cline, Roger, eds, *The A to Z of Restoration London*, London 1992 (a reduced facsimile of Ogilby and Morgan's map of 1676)

Imray, Jean, *The Charity of Richard Whittington: a history of the trust administered by the Mercer's Company, 1424–1966*, London 1968

Index to Register of Deeds, Scottish Record Office, Edinburgh 1931, Vols 1661–1685

Insh, G. P., *The Company of Scotland Trading to Africa and the Indies*, London 1932

——, 'The founders of the Company of Scotland', *Scottish Historical Review*, Vol. xxv, 1928

Johnston, T., *Our Scots Noble Families*, 1909

Jordan, W. K., *Philanthropy in England, 1480–1660*, London 1959

Keay, John, *The Honourable Company: A History of the English East India Company*, London 1993

Keith, Charles P., *Chronicles of Pennsylvania, 1688–1748*, Philadelphia 1917

Kidd, Alan, *State, Society and the Poor in Nineteenth-Century England*, Basingstoke and New York, 1999

Kirk, R. E. G. and E. F., eds, *Returns of Aliens Dwelling in the City and Suburbs of London from the Reign of Henry VIII to that of James I*, London 1900, 1902, 1907

Lach, Donald F. and Kley, Edwin J. van, *Asia in the Making of Europe*, Chicago and London (9 vols), 1965–93

Lane John, *Masonic Records 1717–1886, comprising a list of all the Lodges at home and abroad of the four Grand Lodges and United Grand Lodges of England …*, London 1886

Laing, David, ed., *Letters and Journals of Robert Baillie*, Edinburgh 1841

——, ed., *Royal Letters, Charters and Tracts relating to the Colonization of New Scotland and the institution of the order of Knight Baronets of Nova Scotia, 1621–1638*, Edinburgh 1867

Leigh's New Picture of London, London 1819

Lenman, Bruce, 'Jacobean Goldsmith – Jewellers as Credit Creators: the Cases of James Mossman, James Cockie and George Heriot', *Scottish Historical Review*, 74(2), 1995

——, 'The Scottish Linschoten: Alexander Hamilton and the Development of Scottish Knowledge of Eastern Waters to 1727', *South Asia Library Group*, 42, 1995

Leonard, Tom, *Places of the Mind: The Life and Work of James Thomson ('BV')*, London 1993

Letter from a Scots Factor at London, London 1707

Levi, Peter, ed., Samuel Johnson and James Boswell, *A Journey to the Western Isles* and *The Journal of a Tour to the Hebrides*, London 1987

Life and Times at the Caley: A specially written illustrated account of 180 years of the Royal Caledonian Schools, London 1996

Lillywhite, Bryant, *London Signs*, London 1972

List of the Patrons of the Anniversary of the Charity-Schools, London 1805

London Scotsman ('weekly journal of Anglo-Scottish news'), London 1867–1871

London Scottish Journal, 1876–78

Luke, Louise, ed., *A Guide to Crown Court Church of Scotland*, London 1999

MacAulay, George Mackenzie, *The War Diary of a London Scot, 1796–97*, ed. W. C. Mackenzie, Paisley 1916

Macaulay, Thomas Babington, *The History of England* (originally published 1841–1868), ed. Hugh Trevor Roper, London 1968

MacCarthy, Fiona, *Byron: Life and Legend*, London 2002

MacGrail, Thomas H., *Sir William Alexander, first Earl of Stirling: a biographical study*, Edinburgh 1940

Macinnes, Allan I., *Clanship, Commerce and the House of Stuart, 1603–1788*, East Linton 1996

——, *Scottish Power Centres from the Early Middle Ages to the Present Day*, Glasgow 1998

——, *Charles I and the making of the Covenanting Movement, 1625–1641*, Edinburgh 1991

Mackie, J D, *A History of Scotland*, second edition with Bruce Lenman and Geoffrey Parker, London 1978

Macky, John, *A Journey through England. In familiar letters from a gentleman here, to his friend*, London 1714

Macleod Black, K., *The Scots Churches in England*, Edinburgh and London 1906

McCord, Norman, *British History, 1815–1906*, Oxford 1991

McCrae, Alister, *Scots in Burma: Golden Times in a Golden Land*, Edinburgh c. 1990

McMenemey, W. H., 'The Hospital Movement of the Eighteenth Century and its Development', in F. N. L. Poynter, ed., *The Evolution of Hospitals in Britain*, London 1964

Magnusson, Magnus, *Scotland: The Story of a Nation*, London 2001

Maitland, William, *History and Survey of London from its Foundation to the Present Time*, London 1739 and 1756

Maré, Eric de, *Victorian London Revealed: Gustave Doré's Metropolis*, London 2001

Marmoy, Charles F. A., 'The Pest House, 1681–1717: predecessor of the French Hospital,' in *Huguenot Society of London Proceedings*, 25, London 1992

Marshall, H., *Twilight London*, Plymouth 1971

Marshall, Peter J., *East India Fortunes: The British in Bengal in the Eighteenth Century*, Oxford 1976

Mayhew, Henry, *London Labour and the London Poor*, ed. Victor Neuberg, London 1985

Meadows, P., *A Source Book of London History from the Earliest Times to 1800*, London 1914

Memoranda, References, and Documents relating to the Royal Hospitals of the City of London, London 1863

Millar, A. A., *Alexander Duff of India*, Edinburgh 1992

Mills, Peter, and Oliver, John, *Survey of Building sites in the City of London after the Great Fire of 1666*, London 1962–67

Milne, G., *The Great Fire of London*, London 1986

Minto, Sir Gilbert Elliot, *Life and Letters of Sir Gilbert Elliot, first Earl Minto from 1701–1806*, ed. the Countess of Minto, London 1874

Mitchell, Charles, and Moody, Susan R, *Foundations of Charity*, Oxford 2000

Mitchell, David, ed., *Goldsmiths, Silversmiths and Bankers: Innovation and the Transfer of Skill, 1550–1750*, Stroud 1995

Morgan, Kenneth O., *The People's Peace: British History, 1945–90*, Oxford 1992

——, ed., *The Oxford History of Britain*, Oxford 1988

Mowat, Sue, *The Port of Leith, its History and its People*, Edinburgh, n.d.

Navarro, Antonio de, *The Scottish Women's Hospital at the French Abbey of Royaumont*, London 1917

Ogborn, Miles, *Spaces of Modernity: London's Geographies, 1680–1780*, London and New York 1998

Ordres et Reglement pour la Corporation des Gouverneur et Directeurs de l'Hôpital pour les Pauvres François Protestants, et leurs Descendants residents dans la Grande Bretagne, London 1741

Owen, David E., *English Philanthropy, 1660–1980*, Cambridge, Mass. 1964

Pepys, Samuel, *The Shorter Pepys*, ed. Robert Latham, London 1993

——, *The Diary of Samuel Pepys Esquire*, ed. Lord Braybook, London 1902

Picard, Liza, *Restoration London*, London, 1997

——, *Dr Johnson's London*, London 2001

Plummer, Alfred, *The London Weavers' Company, 1600–1970*, London 1972

Pocock, Tom, *Sailor King: The Life of King William IV*, London 1991

Pooley, Colin G., *Local Authority Housing*, London 1996

Powell, James, *Whitefriars Glass*, London 1995

Powell, William S., *John Pory, 1572–1636: The Life and Letters of a Man of Many Parts*, North Carolina 1977

Porter, Andrew, *Victorian Shipping, Business and Imperial Policy: Donald Currie, the Castle Line and Southern Africa*, Woodbridge and New York 1986

Porter, Roy, *London: A Social History*, London 1994

——, *Enlightenment: Britain and the Creation of the Modern World*, London 2000

Porter, S., ed., *London and the Civil War*, London 1996

Poynter, F. N. L., ed., *The Evolution of Hospitals in Britain*, London 1964

Prebble, John, *The Darien Disaster*, London 1968, 2002

——, *The Highland Clearances*, London 1969

Price, F. G. Hilton, *A handbook of London Bankers: with some account of their predecessors the early goldsmiths … (1677–1876)*, London 1890–91

Prochaska, Frank, *Royal Bounty: The Making of a Welfare Monarchy*, New Haven and London 1995

——, *The Voluntary Impulse*, London 1988

Records of the Commissioners for Inquiring into Charities, 1817–1850, London (?) 1954

Report of the Select Committee of General Enquiry into the Affairs of the Scottish Hospital, appointed 29 January 1862, London 1862 (NLS: 6.1502(27))

Roberts, Lewes, *The Marchants Map of Commerce*, London 1638, Amsterdam 1974

Robson, John Osborn, *London Scots of the Napoleonic Era: the Highland Armed Association or Royal Highland Volunteers and the Loyal North Britons*, London 1970

Rogers, Rev. Charles, ed., *The Earl of Stirling's Register of Royal Letters relative to the Affairs of Scotland and Nova Scotia from 1615 to 1635*, Edinburgh 1884

Rose, Jonathan, *The Intellectual Life of the British Working Classes*, New Haven 2002

Royal Scottish Hospital. 269th (270th) Annual Festival … 1933 (1934), etc. (Menus; with newspaper cuttings containing summaries of the speeches), London, 1933 (BL)

Rudé, George, *Hanoverian London*, London 1971

Schuchard, Marsha Keith, *Restoring the Temple of Vision: Cabalistic Freemasonry and Stuart Culture*, Leiden 2002

Scots' Charitable Society of Boston: The constitution and by-laws of the … Society … with a list of members and officers and … extracts from the original records, etc, Boston, Mass. 1896 (NLS R.232.h)

Scots' Charitable Society of Boston: The constitution and by-laws of the … Society … with a list of members and officers and … extracts from the original records, etc, Cambridge, Mass., 1878

Scots' Charitable Society of Boston: Constitution and By-laws … as of 23 October 1992, Boston, Mass., 1992

Scott-Moncrieff, R, *Household Book of Lady Grisell Baillie 1692–1733*, Edinburgh 1911

Scott Thomson, Gladys, *The Russells in Bloomsbury 1669–1771*, London

——, *Life in a Noble Household, 1641–1700* (an account of the household of William Russell, 1st Duke of Bedford), London 1950

The Scottish Magazine and London Scottish Journal, Vol 1 no. 1, London 1878

Sennett, Richard, *Respect: The formation of Character in an Age of Inequality*, London 2003

Sheppard, F., *London: A Social History*, Oxford 1998

Shire, Helena Mennie, *Song, Dance and Poetry of the Court of Scotland under King James VI*, Cambridge 1969

Sinclair, Sir John, *An Account of the Highland Society of London, from its establishment in May 1778, to the commencement of the year 1813* (with a list of members), London 1813

Smith, David L., *A History of the Modern British Isles, 1603–1707: The Double Crown*, Oxford 1998

Smith, John, *Handbook and Directory of Old Scottish Clockmakers, 1453–1850*, Wakefield 1975

Smithies, Michael, *Alexander Hamilton: A Scottish Sea Captain, 1689–1723*, Thailand 1997

Smollett, Tobias, *The Expedition of Humphry Clinker*, London 1771

Smout, T. C., *A Century of the Scottish People, 1830–1950*, London 1986

——, *A History of the Scottish People, 1560–1830*, London 1969

Smuts, R. Malcolm, *Court Culture and the origins of a royalist tradition in early Stuart England*, Philadelphia 1999

Stow, John, *A Survey of London*, London 1598

Spence, Craig, *London in the 1690s: a Social Atlas*, London 2000

Spencer, B., *London's Medieval Pilgrim Badges*, London, 1986

Steel, Tom, *Scotland's Story: A New Perspective*, London 1984

Stephens, W. B., *Sources for English Local History: Studies in the Uses of Historical Evidence*, Cambridge 1981

Stevenson, David, *The First Freemasons: Scotland's Early Lodges and their Members*, Aberdeen 1988

The British Coffee House (a satire on Scots), London 1764

The Caledonian Phalanx: Scots in Russia, Edinburgh 1987 (NLS exhibition)

The Chronicles of the Caledonian Society of London (9 vols), London 1838–1967

The Grey Brigade and others. London Scottish. Civil Service. Kensingtons. Queen's

Westminsters (A camp journal) nos 1–32. March–December 1915

The little London directory of 1677: the oldest printed list of the merchants and bankers of London, London 1863

The Metropolitan Charities: Being an account of the Charitable, Benevolent and Religious Societies, London 1844

The Oxford Shakespeare: Henry V, Oxford 1982

The parochial charities of Westminster, Westminster 1890

The Penguin Book of Victorian Verse, ed. Daniel Karlin, London 1997

The Royal Charter of confirmation granted by his most excellent Majesty King James II to the Trinity House of Deptford Strond, London 1763

'The Scots Scouts Discoveries: by their London intelligencer, London 1642 (*Thomason Tracts* 27; E:153(22))

The Society of Writers to His Majesty's Signet, Edinburgh 1936

Thomas, Keith, *Religion and the Decline of Magic*, London 1971

Tomalin, Claire, *Samuel Pepys*, London 2002

Trevelyan, G. M., ed., *Select Documents for Queen Anne's Reign Down to the Union with Scotland, 1702–1707*, Cambridge 1929

Trevor-Roper, Hugh, 'The invention of tradition: The highland tradition in Scotland', in E. J. Hobsbawm and T. O. Ranger, eds, *The Invention of Tradition*, Oxford 1983

Van Vree, Wilbert, *Meetings, Manners and Civilization: the Development of Modern Meeting Behaviour*, London and New York 1999

Waddington, Keir, *Charity and the London Hospitals, 1850–1898*, Woodbridge 2000

Waller, Maureen, *1700: Scenes from London Life*, London 2000

Waugh, Alexander, *Messiah, the sun of righteousness: a sermon, preached at the Scots Church, London Wall, May 26th, 1799, before the Correspondent Board in London of the Society in Scotland for Propagating Christian Knowledge in the Highlands and Islands* ('And to be had at Scots-Hall, Crane-Court, Fleet-Street; and of the Secretary, Hoxton), London 1800 (BL: 4175.b.105(1) and NLS: 6.863(32))

Weinreb, Ben and Hibbert, Christopher, eds, *The London Encyclopaedia*, London 1983

White, Jerry, *London in the Twentieth Century: A City and its People*, London 2002

Whittet, Thomas Douglas, *The Apothecaries in the Great Plague of London, 1665* (Society of Apothecaries' Sydenham Lecture, 1965), Ewell, Surrey 1970

Willson, D. H., ed., *Parliamentary Diary of Robert Bowyer, 1606–07*, London 1931

Wills, Rebecca, *The Jacobites and Russia, 1715–1750*, East Linton 2002

Wilson, Adrian, 'Politics of medical improvement in early Hanoverian London', in Andrew Cunningham and Roger French, eds, *The Medical Enlightenment of the Eighteenth Century*, Cambridge 1990

Wilson, Walter, *History and Antiques of Dissenting Churches and Meeting Houses in London, Westminster and Southwark*, London 1808–14

Wells, Stanley and Taylor, Gary, eds, *The Oxford Shakespeare: The Complete Works*, Oxford 1998

Wormald, Jenny, 'James VI and I: two kings or one?', in *History*, LXIII, 1983

Young Scots in London (Scots Group), London 1976

Ziegler, Philip, *William IV*, London 1971

——, *London at War*, London 1995, 2002

Zettersten, Louis, *City Street Names, the Origin of the Names of the Streets, Lanes, Alleys and Courts of the City of London*, London 1917

UK theses

'The directors of the East India Company 1754–1790' – James Gordon Parker, Edinburgh PhD 1977 (to be found in the BL at OIR354.5P.OIOC)

The following look useful but time pressure meant they were not used for this history:

'The impact on England of James VI and I' – Diana R. Newton, Liverpool PhD 1996

'Friendly societies before 1834: an examination of their role, aims and activities' – Richard C. Lister, Leeds MA 1997

'Poor relief in Scotland before 1845, with particular reference to the contributions made by the Church of Scotland' – Yeon-Su Oh, Aberdeen PhD 1995

'The new poor law, 1834–75, with special reference to the City of London' – Andrea I. Tanner, London PhD 1995

A selection of websites:

Online guides to national research institutions, archive catalogues and online publications have been very useful for such broad research. The Archives to Archives website run by the National Archives provided initial starting points for research (*www.a2a. pro.gov.uk*), so too the National Register of Archives of the Historical Manuscripts Commission (*www.hmc.gov.uk/nra*), the National Archives (*www.pro.gov.uk*), British Library (*www.bl.uk*), the National Library of Scotland (*www.nls.uk*), the Bodleian Library (*www.bodley. ox.ac.uk*), the Guildhall Library, Corporation of London (*www.cityoflondon. gov.uk*), the Guildhall Library Print Room's 'Collage' database of prints, drawings and maps (*www.collage.cityoflondon.gov.uk*) and the Institute of Historical Research (*www.ihr.sas.ac.uk*).

Other websites used for more up-to-date information have included: *www. homelesspages.org.uk*; *www.cabinet-office.gov.uk*, *www.charity-commission. gov.uk*, the Charities Aid Foundation (*www.cafonline.org*), the Directory of Social Change (*www.dsc.org.uk*), London Health Observatory (*www.lho.org.uk*), *www.institutefor philanthropy. org.uk*, *www.statistics.gov.uk/census2001*, *www. londonscottishregt. org.uk*, *www.pensions policyinstitute.org.uk*, *www.shelter. org.uk*, *www.scotsman.com* and *www.theherald.co.uk*, also the Centre for Sheltered Housing Studies (*www.cshs. co.uk*).

The website of the NEHGS is *www.newenglandancestors.org*. Additional websites for many St Andrew's and other Scottish societies exist around the world for those who want to look further into the social activities of the emigrant Scot.

Index

The abbreviation RSC stands for Royal Scottish Corporation. A page number suffixed *n* indicates a reference to a footnote on the page specified.

Contact, Scotsline and how you can help

If you need help
Or if you know someone who could benefit from the Royal Scottish Corporation, please call Scotsline, our freephone help line, on 0800 652 2989 for immediate, informed and sympathetic guidance.

If you would like to help
Whether you have money, time or expertise to give, or whether you would like to organise a social event or raise funds, or perhaps volunteer to visit people in their own homes – please look at our website at *www.royalscottishcorporation.org.uk* or telephone us on 020 7240 3718.

In an average year the Royal Scottish Corporation spends more than £1 million in meeting its remit which includes assisting those on low incomes, but it can only alleviate a small part of the distress and hardship experienced by London Scots and is always grateful for additional funds.

Donate online via PayPal: One of the easiest ways to donate to the work of the Corporation is via our website using PayPal.

Donate via Gift Aid: Since 6 April 2000 charities have been able to reclaim tax relief on donations made by UK taxpayers. This means that gifts to charities like the Royal Scottish Corporation are now worth 28% more than before, and a donation of £15 is now worth £19.23. In order for us to be able to reclaim the tax, the donor must be paying as much in income tax or capital gains tax each year as the Corporation reclaims on the donations. Please contact us for a Gift Aid form.

Donate via cheque: If you do not pay tax in the UK or use the Internet, then you might like to send us a donation by cheque, sending it to the Royal Scottish Corporation, 37 King Street, Covent Garden, London WC2E 8JS.

Donate via a legacy: Legacies, no matter how modest, are an important part of our funding.

- By donating £10 you can become an Annual Governor – *An Annual Governor holds office for one year from the date a donation is given*

- A donation of £100 will qualify you for Life Governor status – *A Life Governor holds office for life without eligibility to join the Committee of Management*

- With a donation of £500 you can become a Life Managing Governor of the Royal Scottish Corporation – *A Life Managing Governor holds office for life and is eligible for appointment as a member of the Committee of Management.*

The Royal Scottish Corporation
A helping hand for Scots in London

37 King Street
Covent Garden
London WC2E 8JS

Tel: 020 7240 3718
Scotsline: 0800 652 2989
Fax: 020 7497 0184

Email: *enquiry@royalscottishcorporation.org.uk*
Web: *www.royalscottishcorporation.org.uk*

Registered Charity No: 207326